MAN'S IMPRINT FROM THE PAST

Readings in the Methods of Archaeology

MAN'S IMPRINT FROM THE PAST

Readings in the Methods of Archaeology

Selected by

JAMES DEETZ

Brown University

 LITTLE, BROWN AND COMPANY *Boston*

LIBRARY OF CONGRESS CATALOG CARD NO. 72-147161

SECOND PRINTING

Published simultaneously in Canada
by Little, Brown & Company (Canada) Limited

PRINTED IN THE UNITED STATES OF AMERICA

To
J. O. BREW
and
HARRY HORNBLOWER

CONTENTS

ix

MAN'S IMPRINT FROM THE PAST

Readings in the Methods of Archaeology

I
INTRODUCTION

1   Must Archaeologists Dig?

The definitive statement on archaeological method and theory has yet to be written. Until it has been, one must look at numerous articles scattered in journals and books to find the thinking that forms the basis of archaeological analysis. Although the literature of archaeology is vast, only a small fraction of it deals explicitly with theoretical issues. This volume represents an attempt to assemble some fundamental theoretical and methodological papers to give the reader an understanding of recent developments in archaeological method and theory. All the articles have appeared elsewhere, except for this Introduction which is a personal view of archaeology today, and of its possible future directions. Conspicuous by their absence are the kinds of articles often found in collected readings in archaeology. None is basically descriptive, the type that reports various discoveries and the circumstances under which they were found. Nor is any article devoted primarily to the significance of this or that archaeological site or assemblage. Both kinds of articles have their proper and important place in the literature. But a third, far less common type of writing — represented in the pages that follow — shows how the archaeologist manages to use the description of his site and its contents in order to understand their significance to man's culture in the past.

This volume will be most useful when combined with any of the introductory texts on archaeology. Many selections complement the approach used in my *Invitation to Archaeology*,[1] but other texts are equally suitable. Since the basics of archaeology are not discussed here, some introductory reading may be necessary for the beginning student. To have included the fundamentals in this collection would have produced a book either twice as long, or half as useful.

Archaeology is considered here as a part of cultural anthropology; hence, archaeologists are anthropologists who use a certain class of data to understand mankind. Their material, the remains of past cultures, is usually buried, so that digging is regarded as one of the primary activities of an archaeologist. True, excavation is central to a certain phase of archaeological

[1] James Deetz, *Invitation to Archaeology* (New York: Doubleday, 1968).

2

work, but most of the archaeologist's time is spent working with his material after its removal from the earth. If, after sampling several articles, the reader gains understandings that go beyond the end of the spade, then he may appreciate that archaeologists are more than anthropologists who have "more gray matter under their nails than between their ears."

The basis of archaeological theory must include the observation, measurement, and explanation of man's imprint upon his world. The works of man, from earliest times to the present, involve changing the environment in an orderly manner, and it is the order in this change that the archaeologist attempts to explain. A California Indian, for example, in making a shell bead was altering a portion of his physical world in a manner determined by his culture. The shape, size, and material of this bead owe something to ideas its creator learned from his fellows. Later, when the bead passed from use into a trash heap, it carried with it imprinted intelligence, to be read by the archaeologist hundreds of years later. The same is true of all of man's creations; all represent alterations of the world, and these alterations — from the smallest to the largest — inherently carry information about the lifeways of their makers. Another ordered accumulation of portions of the physical world, contrasting dramatically with the size of a shell bead having a quarter-inch diameter, is Manhattan Island's complex agglomeration of buildings, cemeteries, subways, streets, and bridges, which also have been assembled according to the imperatives of society.

The *sine qua non* of archaeology is a concern for the relationships between man's visible and measurable modification of his environment and his invisible and less easily measured social and ideological life. Both are regular, patterned, and interrelated. For example, broken fragments of pottery may yield information about family structure, although the family in question has long since vanished from the earth, as careful analysis of the remains of meals consumed centuries ago may reveal that the families were nomads. In a more specific example, absence of kivas — underground ceremonial chambers — in a New Mexican pueblo occupied by Indians after a massive church was constructed nearby testifies to the religious conversion of Indians now reposing in the mission cemetery. No one has ever excavated a religious belief or a society's idea of the proper place to set up house after marriage, but man's expression of his religious ideals or social concepts often affects his physical world. Intelligent and imaginative reading of this imprint of past actions is the essence of archaeology.

As a part of cultural anthropology, archaeology is legitimately a social science. Unlike other aspects of anthropology, however, archaeology frequently is supported by other disciplines. Physicists provide dates through radiocarbon measurements; botanists identify the remains of plants; palynologists provide pollen analyses that yield insights concerning man's environment; zoologists help determine what kinds of animals were hunted and domesticated; chemists perform soil analyses that aid in stratigraphic interpretation; geologists provide dates for early man. The list is long and impressive, but these dimensions of archaeology are ancillary. The best support of this kind will be to little avail if archaeologists do not consistently approach their material with sophisticated and logical anthropological theory. Yet I feel that archaeologists have still to use their data to the fullest. This failure, if such exists, may well be due to a less-than-clear understanding of what the archaeologist's intellectual realm should be.

Archaeology, by its formal etymology, is the study of the old; and the old, more often than not, is buried. As a result, archaeologists have traditionally been concerned with the subterranean world. Like Lewis Carroll's Alice, they are confronted with a curious underground world, and attempt to understand and explain it. It is quite possible that by returning to the surface and having a good look around, they may discover new ways to understand their underground world, so that the return trip, whether down the rabbit hole or into a five-foot-square excavation unit, will be more productive. The proper concern of the archaeologist is the totality of material culture, whether old or new, buried or superficial. Recently, there has been frequent mention of "above-ground" archaeology, as if this special qualification were necessary to make the study legitimate. The distinction is spurious to me, since identical operations can be, and often are, applied to material both above and below the surface. It may be something of an overstatement, but the surface of the earth acts as a barrier, forcing archaeologists to deal with less than a complete and legitimate universe of inquiry. I cannot distinguish any genuine difference between the questions and methods an archaeologist uses when excavating a site, level by level, to learn about the sequence of occupations, and those a restoration architect employs while dissecting a building, layer by layer, to determine its sequence of construction. One difference may exist, but it is one of degree; the architect will probably meet with greater success because his building is more complete and better preserved than the archaeologist's site. Similarly, Henry Glassie's excellent work,[2] which deals with the cultural context of contemporary data, is as much an archaeological treatise as is any report on excavations in early Paleolithic sites. (Paleolithic archaeology relies heavily on such natural scientific fields as paleontology and geomorphology for its explanations, rather than on social sciences.) Glassie's study contains important thinking about man's cultural imprint on his world, and the behavioral reasons for differences in the data. The archaeologist's reluctance to come out of the earth and consider the whole of material culture has probably had some unfortunate effects on the development of archaeological method and theory.

---

[2] Henry Glassie, *Pattern in the Material Folk Culture of the Eastern United States* (Philadelphia: University of Pennsylvania Press, 1968).

One of my most vivid childhood memories involves the dilemma described in a book by William Holland, a lepidopterist. The sex of an obscure species of Skipper butterfly cannot be determined by the standard criteria of size, color, and markings. The only way that the lepidopterist can discover its sex is to dissect the insect, but once this is done he no longer has a proper specimen for his collection. It is the same with archaeological sites. Once the excavation has been completed, nothing is left to posterity except the report prepared on the findings. Yet one of the most basic requirements for rigorous scientific inquiry is that of the repeatability of the experiment. When excavation is the sole means of observing archaeological data, any possibility of an independent worker repeating the process and getting (more or less) identical results is lost. True, various analytical exercises on the excavated material can be redone, but this is a poor substitute for initial observation of the total pattern of the residue of past behavior.

In spite of the nonrepeatability of archaeological fieldwork, much archaeological method and all excavation techniques have been devised using uncontrolled data. The major reason for lack of control is that the earth literally obstructs the archaeologist. It can only be cut and removed one way, and anyone who has done fieldwork is painfully aware that there is no single, right way to conduct excavations; depending on how they are done, different results may be obtained. Emphasis on deep vertical trenching will certainly cause loss of some details of patterning horizontally distributed in the site. On the other hand, save for the smallest of sites, complete horizontal excavation entails prohibitive expenditures of time and money. Even if such complete excavating were possible, it still does not guarantee the complete clarity of excavated detail, and does nothing to solve the other problem of self-destruction shared by all sites. I find it difficult to accept uncritically a body of theory developed under such circumstances. I do not mean that sites should not be dug, but rather that the theoretical underpinning of archaeological research should rely on data other than those obtained exclusively by excavation.

Through a consideration of how material culture manifests itself in the above-ground world, what its behavioral implications are, and how it can be made to yield information about the culture of its makers, it is likely that methods devised in an above-ground context could be very useful when applied to excavated materials. Such above-ground studies can be performed effectively by using either historical or ethnographic controls. An example of such an approach can be found in recent studies of gravestone designs of eighteenth-century New England. The basic assumptions of these studies are discussed in article No. 13. Colonial gravestones are material objects, fashioned by man in response to conditions imposed by his culture; their designs exhibit order and regularity in time and space, bearing witness to the order of the society which generated them. There is a common, but largely untested, assumption of certain types of archaeological inference which states that shared styles and types of artifacts indicate social interaction, and to test this assumption, maps were prepared to display the distribution of gravestones made by individual carvers in southeastern Massachusetts and adjacent Rhode Island. The resultant patterns of distribution were quite irregular in shape, showing their response to different restraints and incentives imposed by the society. For example, the distribution along known eighteenth-century roadways was expectably elongated in a direction parallel to the road. Identical types of maps were prepared to exhibit last-name distributions in the same area, using surnames taken from the same stones. Since shared surnames in eighteenth-century New England almost always indicate kin relationship, last-name maps provided a good measure of social connections between communities. The results were striking. Both surname and gravestone-style distribution were virtually identical, lending strong support to the proposition that product distribution in the form of stones, idea distribution in the form of the designs, and the distribution of related individuals followed the same irregular pattern of dispersal. This experiment is eminently repeatable, and enjoys powerful support from historical data. An assumption of coincidence between material objects and related people can then be made with greater confidence than is possible in situations where such rigorous controls are lacking.

A second problem produced by strictly underground archaeology is the lack of insight to the cultural context of the artifact. If materials have never been viewed while in use, and are seen in contexts which they never occupied — where they were left, either through design or accident — then it is difficult to imagine them functioning as essential equipment in the daily routine of life. This again may be an overstatement, but it is possible that in the total absence of people, artifacts are endowed with an existence of their own, totally apart from their creators and users. In certain studies on the relationships between various prehistoric cultures, as evidenced by similarities in the material inventories, an inappropriate genetic tone appears from time to time: this type of pottery is clearly descended from that type, or a particular projectile point represents a form of hybridization between two others. It takes little of this kind of analysis to raise the grotesque image of artifacts producing offspring without benefit of human agency. Furthermore, if work is restricted to formal inventories of the contents of sites, it is far easier to seek relationships among such inventories, while scant attention is paid to the relationships of artifacts within a single assemblage. Relationships between artifacts of similar type from two or more different sites are far more obvious than the internal relationships established by their makers and users between formally dissimilar artifacts from a single site — projectile points and shaft smoothers, for example. To follow the path of least resistance, it is only natural to explain the reasons for broad similarities between black or white painted pottery from a dozen sites in Northern Arizona rather than to inquire into the relationships between the pottery and architectural units, stone tools, or bone implements in a single site. The latter approach has been taken from time to time (see the work of William Longacre and James Hill), but not to the extent it should be, and will have to be in order to understand man in prehistory through archaeological data.

If archaeologists were to include material culture in all of its contexts in their purview, at the very least they would be more sensitive to the linkages that occur between different objects, and the relationships that are formed by their makers and users. But as long as the archaeologist's interest and energy are restricted to broken and buried artifacts, such insights will be difficult indeed to achieve.

The third result of treating only excavated material has been the isolation of classificatory schemes as they are developed by archaeologists on the one hand, and their ethnological colleagues on the other. It seems fair to say that most archaeologists think of themselves not as working with culture, but with its products. This is as it should be, as long as the archaeologist does not feel at the same time that the ethnologist who works with living peoples studies culture that is somehow more "real" than the archaeologist's data. Much has been said about material culture not being culture, but its product. Glassie states this succinctly: "Culture is intellectual, rational and abstract; it cannot be material, but material can be cultural and 'material culture' embraces those segments of human learning which provide a person with plans, methods and reasons for producing things which can be seen and touched."[3] It may well be that the visibility and tangibility of material culture has made it seem more different from culture than it truly is. There seems to be a genuine homologous relationship between artifacts and language; both are products of the intellectual dimension of culture, and both represent measurable and observable manifestations of shared thoughts and ideas. But, for that matter, so are the practices of living with one's wife's family after marriage, or of organizing all the young men of the same age in a society into a single social unit. Yet the latter two products of culture, termed by the ethnologist as "matrilocality" and "age-grading," respectively, are considered by many anthropologists to be more culturally real than physical objects.

Virtually all archaeological explanation is given in the categories of the ethnologist: pottery design clusters imply postnuptial residence; differences in burial furnishing indicate class differences; and artifact distributions within an excavated structure give clues to the rule of descent followed by the makers of those artifacts. It would seem, however, that there is no particular sanctity to be ascribed to ethnological categories; they are simply

[3] Glassie, *op. cit.*, p. 2.

classificatory devices that work for the ethnologist in carrying out his job. Why should the archaeologist adjust his material categories to conform to other categories which are just as arbitrary and abstract as his own? Both sets of categories are visible manifestations of the same range of behavior, which is conditioned in turn by the shared ideas of any given society. The archaeologist's problem is that he is working with an incomplete equation as long as he restricts himself and his interests to buried evidence. Probably a set of categories, when expanded to include material culture in a living context, could be established which would have more relevance to excavated materials. The basic requirement of such categories, it seems to me, would be the inclusion of both material and nonmaterial criteria for its definition. For example, why not define an institutional category to be known as "post-mortem residence" and include that set of rules governing the physical placement of the deceased members of a society in burial sets, dictated by social convention? There are many other ways to classify observed patterns of behavior, and it would indeed be odd if those useful to the ethnologist who is interested in kinship were the same as, or even similar to, those most helpful to the archaeologist to whom the use of space in the interior of dwellings is important.

The foregoing discussion has interesting implications for the use of analogy in archaeology. Lewis Binford and Robert Ascher present two viewpoints on ethnographic analogy in articles No. 16 and No. 17. In one way or another, both implicitly assume that archaeological analogies are in part established in traditional ethnological categories. I agree with Binford that there almost certainly were social customs in the past for which no modern equivalents exist, and that restriction to the modern range of variation could severely limit our ability to explain data. But I suspect that the analogy to seek is not between material complexes in the past and those in the present — nor between social complexes with their material corre-lates in the present and material complexes in the past — but between a set of newly defined categories that maximize the understanding of material culture's relationships to its producing society and the vestiges of these same categories in archaeological data. For example, how much could be said about a human activity like tool manufacture by studying its spatial manifestations in a living context? How much isolation is discernible in the debris left from woodworking or stone-flaking, and what techniques can be devised to locate and identify this activity (once it is known it occurred). Repeated studies of this type, done cross-culturally, should provide some idea of how regular and predictable such behavioral and material correla-tions are. Then, and only then can this approach be extended to include a search for analogies in the excavated evidence. The same approach, applied to all aspects of related social and technological activities, will ultimately permit descriptions of whole cultures in social-technical categories. The archaeologist's equation would then be more complete; he would be solving for only one missing quantity, without referring to, or relying on, descriptive categories that lack a material dimension and are useful only to the ethnologist.

Must archaeologists dig? The answer is clearly yes, with important qualifications. They must dig, but must also become more conversant with other kinds of research, so that results reflect and incorporate this knowledge to achieve the most meaningful explanations. Furthermore, it is possible to "do archaeology" without ever touching a spade, if any of the foregoing makes sense. The excavations should perhaps be viewed more as necessary evils than as indispensable searches for truth. In either case, they must be carried out. At a time when graduate programs are striving to make their requirements more efficient, it is probably unpopular to suggest that graduate students include ethnographic fieldwork as a part of their degree program. Yet such a procedure would enhance the ability of the next generation of archaeologists to study material culture in a more imaginative manner, and would ensure that some aspect of the relationship between society and its materials be investigated. Thus, when the archaeologist first encounters material culture in the ground, at least he will have seen and studied it while it was functioning in a living context.

The growing interest in historical archaeology among anthropologists in the past decade also promises to broaden the archaeologist's view of his discipline (see selection No. 13, "Late Man in North America"). In some ways historical archaeology provides a link between past societies and those functioning today, because the results of archaeological investigations of historical materials can be checked for accuracy against the written record. Appropriate adjustments can then be made in the archaeological explanations of the data and their rationale. At the same time, the application of archaeological methods to historical data promises to supplement the historical record considerably.

As more archaeologists turn their attention to data that enjoy this type of control, it is certain that archaeological theory will benefit. My hope is that in the years ahead there will be a greater concern for increasing the rigor and precision of theoretical tools through developing new realms of inquiry. This does not imply that past efforts have been lacking in methodological and theoretical rigor. On the contrary, results have often been gratifying. Even a cursory reading of the contents of this book will make this convincingly clear.

II
ARCHAEOLOGY
AND
ARCHAEOLOGISTS

JOHN HOWLAND ROWE

*Most college freshmen have had little contact with
anthropology, of which archaeology is a part. They discover
that unlike physics, history, or biology, archaeology is a new
field of inquiry, and many develop strong interest in the
subject and wonder what it takes to become a professional
archaeologist. John Rowe provides an excellent overview of
the training required and of career opportunities in the field;
his essay also is a useful introduction to archaeology for the
nonprofessionally minded. Rowe's training in classical
archaeology eminently qualifies him to discuss the discipline
as a part of either classics or anthropology. The archaeologist
develops many-faceted skills and interests during his training;
it is this diversity of subject matter in archaeology that
fascinates many people and guarantees that its study will
never become dull.*

2   Archaeology as a Career

Archaeology is the study of man's past in the broadest sense,
and it is the archaeologist's aim to reconstruct as much of that past as
possible. For this purpose he uses the evidence of written history, the
material remains of human activities that have survived destruction, and any
inferences that can legitimately be made from the study of languages and of
later or present-day human cultures. Archaeologists devote the major part of
their attention to recovering and interpreting the material remains of
human activities because these remains can give them much valuable

Reprinted, with the editorial changes noted, from "Archaeology as a Career" by John
Howland Rowe, *Archaeology*, Vol. 7, No. 4, pp. 229–236, copyright, 1954, Archaeolog-
ical Institute of America, by permission of the author and the Editor of *Archaeology*.
A revised version of this paper appeared in *Archaeology*, 1961 (14:1):45–55. Reprints,
with the bibliography revised to 1967, are available from the Archaeological Institute of
America, 260 West Broadway, New York, N. Y. 10013.

information about the daily life and interests of the people they are studying. Indeed, in dealing with periods and places in which written records were not abundant, there is usually no other evidence available for a reconstruction of cultural history.

As we have noted, archaeologists use any historical evidence which is available and combine it with what they can learn from material remains. Archaeologists who plan to work in areas with a long historical record usually find it desirable to learn the historian's techniques and to acquire an intimate familiarity with the historical literature on the region to be studied. This procedure involves learning the languages and writing systems in which the historical source materials for the area are written, so that the archaeologist will not have to depend on other people's interpretations of these materials in his work. Archaeologists have a somewhat different viewpoint from that of most professional historians, however; they are more interested in the interrelationships of the written record with the material remains and in reconstructing daily life and customary behavior. They have more in common with cultural and institutional historians than with students of political or diplomatic history.

Archaeology shares its interest in the material remains of human activities with the field of art history, and it is very desirable for people working in each of these fields to be acquainted with the methods and point of view of the other. The two fields are not identical, however, but differ in their subject matter and research methods. In subject matter, art history restricts itself to works of art, while archaeology is concerned also with common objects of everyday use. When an archaeologist is trying to reconstruct the life and customs of some earlier period, a broken cooking pot may give him invaluable evidence and prove as interesting in its own way as a statue or a bronze vase. In research methods art historians concentrate on studying the style of objects and do most of their work with specimens in museums and private collections, except when they are studying architecture. Archaeologists study individual objects also, but they are equally interested in the relationship of one object to another in the ground and hence do a good part of their research in the field, making excavations in which they can observe this type of relationship. It is important evidence for dating and for inferring the use of the objects.

The distinction between archaeology and art history is perhaps least clear in the field of classical archaeology where traditionally the same people have done both types of research. This situation is not surprising, for in the classical field archaeology grew out of people's admiration for Greek art.

In a general classification of research fields archaeology is logically a branch of anthropology, the latter being the discipline concerned most broadly with the study of people and their behavior. In American universities archaeology is often taught as part of anthropology, and archaeological collections in general museums are under the care of an anthropology department or division. This connection is a thoroughly satisfactory one from the point of view of the archaeologists concerned, since they find the broad comparative viewpoint of anthropology stimulating and helpful. Indeed, in that part of its work which is concerned with reconstructing ancient life and customs, archaeology is wholly dependent on general anthropological theory and the results of anthropological studies of the life of living peoples.

There are a number of special areas, however, the archaeology of which is usually not taught in an anthropology department. These are Greece and Rome, the Near East (including Egypt), and sometimes China. The areas named have abundant historical and literary records in languages rarely studied except by specialists. Special departments are usually devoted to them at the larger universities under the names of Classics, Near Eastern Languages, and Oriental Languages or somewhat similar titles. Because it is important for archaeologists to have a solid grounding in the ancient languages of the areas where they intend to work, it is convenient to have the archaeology of these areas taught in direct association with the languages. In some universities, courses in classical archaeology are also given in the art department because of the close traditional relationship between classical archaeology and art history.

Archaeology is a field of pure research, like astronomy or history. It is not economically profitable to anyone, nor are its results normally useful to business and industry. Consequently, there are no jobs for archaeologists in the sense that there are jobs for accountants or even for research chemists and engineers. Furthermore, it is difficult to raise funds to finance research projects in archaeology, even on a small scale, because the subject has little or nothing to offer to business, to national defense, or even to public entertainment. It is an unlikely field in which to look for solutions to modern social problems and hence has no appeal for reformers.

It is important to emphasize the economic difficulties of archaeology as a career because they are not always obvious to people whose imagination is fired by reading of archaeological discoveries or by visiting museums and ancient ruins. Employment opportunities for people trained as professional archaeologists are few and the salaries are comparatively low. At the same time it is a field that requires thorough training and usually a Ph.D. degree (i.e., three to five years of graduate work after the normal four years of college). No one should plan to make a career of archaeology unless he is so deeply interested in it that he is not really concerned about how much he is going to earn.

The best positions open to archaeologists are those as college teachers or museum curators, and these jobs are strictly limited in number. Not all colleges and universities teach archaeology, and relatively few museums can afford to have research men on their staff. In these jobs, of course, the archaeologist is expected to devote a substantial part of his time to teaching or to the care and exhibition of collections, and his research has to be carried on more or less in his spare time, evenings, weekends, and in vacations. Archaeologists do not work bankers' hours.

An archaeologist's chances of getting an appointment in college teaching or in museum work are much improved if he has broad training in something besides archaeology. If the kind of archaeology he is interested in is usually taught in an anthropology department, he should be prepared to teach general anthropology or to handle a variety of anthropological collections. A classical archaeologist should be prepared to teach ancient civilization and Greek or Latin literature, and so on, for the other special areas. It is not difficult to get this sort of broad training in a program of archaeological study, since few universities give so many archaeology courses that narrow specialization is possible.

Some archaeologists have been hired in recent years to teach anthropology or classics in junior colleges, but there are no such opportunities in secondary schools. Consequently, the M.A. degree, which primarily qualifies the holder to teach at the secondary school level, is of no direct value in archaeology.

The federal and state governments support a certain amount of archaeological research in fulfillment of their responsibility for the preservation of antiquities, the care of historical monuments, and the maintenance of archaeological sites as places of public interest in state or national parks. A considerable number of archaeologists work for the National Park Service, for example. Since 1946 some federal and state funds have been available for the emergency excavation of sites to be flooded by new dam construction, and qualified archaeologists have been hired to direct this work under the River Basin Surveys program of the Smithsonian Institution. All such work for United States government agencies, of course, involves the study of sites in the United States and its territories.

Much archaeology in the United States and Europe is done by amateurs working under the auspices of state and local archaeological societies or in collaboration with a museum. They are usually business or professional people who have learned archaeological methods by reading and experience and who devote their spare time to research without pay. These amateurs must be sharply distinguished from the more numerous plunderers or pot hunters who loot archaeological sites in order to sell the specimens found or out of idle curiosity. The plunderers are a public menace and their activities destroy archaeological evidence which can never be replaced. The genuine amateur archaeologists, on the other hand, have made many valuable contributions to our knowledge of European and North American archaeology.

American archaeologists whose field of interest lies outside the United States depend on research grants made by foundations or on the generosity of private benefactors for funds to pay the expenses of their fieldwork. The money is usually raised in the name of the university or museum for which the archaeologist works, and he applies for a leave of absence for the time he will be in the field. Occasionally an American archaeologist will enter the service of a university or museum in the country where his research interests lie in order to have more frequent opportunities for doing fieldwork. Such service is a valuable experience, but it is likely to be difficult to arrange, since in most other countries there are even fewer positions for trained archaeologists than in the United States, with no lack of local candidates for the positions.

Because most jobs in archaeology involve either university teaching or museum work, a prospective archaeologist should have the temperamental qualifications for one or the other of these types of work and should plan his studies with the kind of position he wants in mind. A general requirement for research in any field is intellectual curiosity, an interest in asking questions and looking for answers to them. This curiosity should be combined with impartiality and suspicion of conclusions presented without fair discussion of the evidence. Archaeological fieldwork demands some special qualifications. An archaeologist should be able to stand a considerable amount of physical discomfort without its interfering with his work or making him excessively irritable; he should be a methodical and systematic worker; and he needs some degree of manual dexterity. Above all, he should have patience. Most of the time an archaeological excavation is dull routine, and the work goes very slowly. Some spectacular discoveries may be made, of course, but they are likely to be a lot less frequent than the disappointments.

Training for a career in archaeology involves years of study, and the earlier the student can make up his mind the better. Much can be done even in high school to plan a program which will make later study more effective. A student should make an opportunity to talk over his interests and problems with a professional archaeologist as soon as he is reasonably sure that his interest is serious. It is worth a trip to the nearest university or large museum in order to do this.

In high school a program should be laid out that will provide training in background subjects. In the first place, it is important for every archaeologist to write well and easily, since a large part of his research time is actually spent in writing up notes on what he is finding and in preparing reports for publication. Next, foreign languages will be necessary. Most American universities require graduate students to pass reading examinations in French and German, and these languages are of especial importance to archaeologists, since there is a large and excellent archaeological literature in each of them. If the student hopes to do fieldwork in some area outside the United States, other languages will also be necessary. Some of them can be taken in high school: Latin, for example, for prospective classical archaeologists, or Spanish for those interested in Central or South America. Geometry and trigonometry are valuable for map-making, which is an important activity in every excavation. In his spare time the student should pick up some camping experience, do some reading on the area he is interested in, and study the collections at any archaeological museum that is available to him.

On admission to college the student should consult the adviser for the anthropology department (or the department handling the area of his interest) at the earliest opportunity, even though the regulations may not require it. Most colleges require students to devote a year or two to general studies before they are formally enrolled in a major subject, and careful planning of the program during this period will give the student a better basis for later work. The prospective archaeologist should continue his program of language study and take some elementary science courses (chemistry, geology, and paleontology are especially useful). Courses in history and in the history of art are also to be recommended. Care should be taken to fulfill the prerequisites for more advanced courses which the student wants to take later. For example, a course in elementary Hebrew may be a prerequisite to Assyrian and Sumerian, languages which are needed by archaeologists working in the Mesopotamian field.

Sometime during his preparation the student should get some instruction in typing, photography, freehand and mechanical drawing, and simple surveying. These are all skills which are needed in archaeological fieldwork in making the record of what is found. An archaeologist does not need all the skill of a professional surveyor or draftsman but he should be able to make a competent map or measured drawing.

An archaeologist gets his specialized training in his last two years of college work and in graduate school. Except for languages the whole program of specialized training can, indeed, be put off until graduate school without much loss of time. Hence the prospective archaeologist can get a satisfactory undergraduate education at almost any college with high academic standards. He should, if possible, major in the subject field in which he expects to do graduate work. If, however, the college he is attending has no department in his immediate field of interest (anthropology or oriental languages, for example), a major in some related field such as history, art, or geography would be the best second choice. Whatever his major subject, the student should make every effort to maintain a high academic standing so as to qualify for admission to graduate school.

The choice of a graduate school is very important, and the student should discuss the problem with an archaeologist in his own field of interest sometime in his senior year. It is worth traveling to the nearest large university in order to do this, but if such a trip is impossible the inquiry can be made by correspondence. The problem is that for any given archaeological field there are only a small number of universities giving first-class training at any one time. No university can afford to maintain specialists in all phases of archaeology, and each one usually plans to cover only a few of the various fields. The choice of fields covered at any given school will vary from time to time also as older faculty members retire and are replaced with young men whose interests are different, or as a faculty member moves to a different university to accept a job at a higher rank. It is important for the student to get up to date information about the siuation in this field of interest. A student interested in going into museum work should choose a university that gives courses in museum methods, or one located near a large museum where such courses are offered.

The actual techniques of archaeological excavation and recording can be learned only by field experience, and there are several ways a student can get experience in excavation. One is through organized summer field schools. A number of American universities, particularly in the Mississippi Valley and the West, offer summer session courses in which the students take part in the actual excavation of a local site. The usual fees are charged and the students pay their own living expenses. These summer courses are usually open to both undergraduates and graduate students. For students specializing in classical or Near Eastern archaeology the best opportunities for learning field method are provided by the schools of archaeology affiliated with the Archaeological Institute of America. There are three of these which have teaching programs: the American School of Classical Studies at Athens, the School of Classical Studies in the American Academy in Rome, and the American Schools of Oriental Research, with branches in Jerusalem and Baghdad. These schools admit graduate students for a year or more of study and provide opportunities to take part in organized excavations in their respective areas. In each of these schools some fellowships are available for outstanding students. Further details about their programs can be found in ... Kenyon ... [1953].

Other opportunities for field experience are offered by the weekend excavations carried out in many parts of the United States by the state and local archaeological societies. These programs of weekend excavation depend on volunteer labor, and anyone with a serious interest in the work is usually welcome. Whether the student is interested in local archaeological problems or not, work of this kind is very valuable experience.

To keep in touch with new developments in archaeology it is important to subscribe to and read one or more archaeological journals. Three of general interest are given in the reading list below. Membership in archaeological societies which meet near the student's place of residence is also a stimulating experience and provides opportunities to meet people whose advice will be helpful. The Archaeological Institute of America has forty branches in American cities and university communities which hold periodic meetings to hear lectures on archaeological subjects, and most of the state archaeological societies have similar programs.

In conclusion, some comments on choosing an archaeological field may be added. Specialization in archaeology is necessarily by area, as in the humanities, rather than by subject matter, as in the natural sciences. Archaeologists become experts in the cultural history of a particular part of the world and do their fieldwork in the area they are trained to know best. Occasionally an archaeologist changes fields, but most people become so interested in the research problems of the field in which they were first trained that they stay in it. In some area fields a further specialization by subject matter is possible; in classical archaeology, for example, there are specialists in inscriptions, in coins, in pottery, and in architecture as well as people with a general interest in the whole field.

Because the program of training for each area is different, it is important for the student to choose an area of specialization early and stick to it. For most students the choice of an area is not a serious problem because they become interested in archaeology through reading or studying about some particular area. For the few who start with a general interest, the choice may be difficult but it need not be a matter of serious concern. There are important archaeological problems in every part of the world and not enough people working at them. Even in fields where a vast amount of work has already been done the progress of discovery brings new problems to light, and earlier conclusions need constant revision. As archaeologists devise more refined research methods, too, old problems can be reopened. The problems vary in different areas, but they are all interesting.

READING LIST

There is a lot of popular literature on archaeology, but much of it is inaccurate and sensational. Book and magazine articles which give the reader the impression that archaeological fieldwork is a glorified search for buried treasure are especially pernicious since their effect is to encourage disturbance and looting of archaeological sites by idle curiosity seekers. Some sound works

of a nontechnical nature are included in the following reading
list, along with reference and other material helpful to the beginner.

1. Journals
Archaeology

>An illustrated quarterly specializing in popular but
responsible articles on the archaeology of all parts of
the world, published by the Archaeological Institute of
America at Andover Hall, Cambridge, Mass. . . .

Antiquity

>A quarterly journal dealing with archaeology in general
but with some emphasis on Old World prehistory.
Published by H. W. Edwards, Ashmore Green, New-
bury, Berks., England. . . .

American Antiquity

>A quarterly journal covering the field of New World
archaeology, published by the Society for American
Archaeology. Its business office varies and the address
should be secured from a recent issue in the nearest
library. . . .

2. Books and Articles
Barzun, Jacques

>1945   *Teacher in America*. Boston: Little, Brown and Co.
(Discussion of some of the problems of college and
university teaching which gives a good idea of what a
career in this type of teaching involves.)

Braidwood, Linda

>1953   *Digging Beyond the Tigris*. New York: Henry Schu-
man. (Life and work on an archaeological expedition
in the Near East.)

Careers in Museum Work

>1950   Careers Research Monographs, Research no. 91. 2nd.
ed. Chicago: Institute for Research. (Advice to students considering a museum vocation.)

Daniel, Glyn E.

>1950   *A Hundred Years of Archaeology*. London: Gerald
Duckworth & Co. (A history of Old World archaeology, with emphasis on European prehistory.)

Heizer, Robert Fleming

>1950   *Manual of Archaeological Field Methods*. 2nd ed. Palo
Alto, Calif.: National Press. (Includes a detailed
bibliography of archaeological methods.)

Kenyon, Kathleen M.

>1953   *Beginning in Archaeology*. Rev. ed.; with sections on

American archaeology by Saul S. Weinberg and Gladys D. Weinberg. London: Phoenix House Ltd.; New York: Frederick A. Praeger, Inc.

Matheson, Sylvia
　1950　"Teach Me How to Dig." *The Geographical Magazine* 22 (January 1950):378–86. (An account of experiences at a field school of archaeological method.)

Petrie, William Matthews Flinders
　1904　*Methods and Aims in Archaeology*. London: Macmillan and Co. (A classic work, still worth reading for its statements of the point of view and responsibilities of archaeologists.)

Thomas, William L., Jr., and Anna M. Pikelis, eds.
　1953　*International Directory of Anthropological Institutions*. New York: Wenner-Gren Foundation for Anthropological Research, Inc. (Lists universities, museums, societies, and other institutions all over the world which cultivate the field of archaeology. A good source of information about existing jobs, courses, collections, and sources of advice.)

Wheeler, Sir Mortimer
　1954　*Archaeology from the Earth*. Oxford: Clarendon Press.

Wissler, Clark
　1946　*The Archaeologist at Work; How Science Deciphers Man's Past*. New York: American Museum of Natural History, Science Guide No. 116. (Reprinted from *Natural History*, vol. 51, no. 3 [1943].)

Woolley, Charles Leonard
　1937　*Digging Up the Past*. Harmondsworth, Eng., and Baltimore: Pelican Books, A4.

ALBERT C. SPAULDING

Excavation, the work for which archaeologists are best known,
is only the first step in the long and complex task
that leads ultimately to the explanation of man's life in the
past. Excavation is the archaeologist's method of observing
his data; his observation is followed by systematic
organization of the data. Once the ordering and classifying of
the information have been accomplished, any pattern and
regularity reflected in the classification can be subjected to
behavioral interpretation, at which time archaeology
introduces more general anthropological analysis. For
example, a site on the banks of a river in Nebraska might
provide us with a picture of the remains of a dozen houses,
composed of their floors, the patterns of post holes remaining
from the superstructures, and the artifacts found within them.
If the excavating was done properly, we should have a
reasonably clear picture of the relationships among all the
materials uncovered. Later conclusions must ultimately rest
on how well we controlled our earth removal and recorded
locations of all objects and features we encountered. Before
these raw data can be used to advance our knowledge and
understanding of man and his culture, they must be
integrated into a larger universe of archaeological data.
   The next step after cleaning and cataloging the
archaeological assemblage — all the artifacts and related
materials from the site, such as animal bones, charcoal,
etc. — is classifying and ordering the collection to compare it
with other, similarly ordered lots. Albert Spaulding's article
relates to this point in archaeological research. He speaks of
the three dimensions of archaeology — space, time, and
form — and, indeed, archaeological integration takes place
along these dimensions. Once these have been adequately
controlled, the archaeologist can proceed to explain the
regularities he sees in his data.

3 The Dimensions of Archaeology

This paper is an attempt to describe clearly the fundamental operations of archaeology on its empirical data. Behavioral inferences may creep in, but they will be evidence of weak-mindedness. The goal is most definitely not a lecture on how archaeology ought to be done; it is rather a description of what is done when exposition is incisive, economical, and convincing.... A great gain would result if my purpose could be realized fully: questions of fact would be sharply separated from questions of theory, thus pointing accurately to those topics on which factual data are needed and providing a guide for research along the most effective lines. Since all the matters discussed here are essentially common knowledge, I have not provided any references.

METHOD OF ANALYSIS

I assume that on an elementary level we cannot improve on the concepts that are successful in other branches of science, especially in the physical sciences, which enjoy a long tradition of enviable precision and clarity, at least when viewed from the outside. These sciences can be thought of as studying the interrelationships of the dimensions appropriate to their specified subject matter. The subject of mechanics, for example, is physical objects, and the dimensions in terms of which the objects are considered are length, mass, and time. Classical mechanics can be defined economically as the study of the interrelationships of length, mass, and time exhibited by physical objects. Thermodynamics, on the other hand, can be considered a more complicated science because it deals with temperature in addition to the three dimensions of mechanics. A dimension can be thought of as an aspect or property of the subject matter which requires its own special measuring device. There are invariable rules for operating with dimensions (the examples given are not logically independent), of which we can mention:

1. The units of discrete dimensions do not possess additive properties. Any formulation of the type $L + T = x$ or $L = T$ (feet plus minutes equals x, or feet equals minutes) or "the artifact is older than it is heavy" is meaningless.

2. Ratios of discrete dimensions, usually called rates, are meaningful, familiar examples being miles per hour or pounds per cubic foot.

3. Concepts involving more than one application of the measuring instrument can be meaningful. Thus area is length squared, and volume is length cubed.

4. Dimensional equations must be homogeneous, that is, the same dimensions must appear on both sides of the equation. However, dimensionless numbers may be introduced into such equations.

SUBJECT MATTER AND DIMENSIONS OF ARCHAEOLOGY

It seems quite clear that the subject matter of archaeology is artifacts, using this term in its broadest sense as any material expression of human cultural activity and adding the qualification that I am concerned here with prehistoric artifacts. Although deciding whether or not a particular object is an artifact may be difficult, I will treat the artifact as given in this discussion for reasons of economy. The dimensions of artifacts which will be considered here are form (in the sense of any physico-chemical property of the artifact), temporal locus (meaning the dating of prehistoric events as inferred from artifacts, specifically the time of manufacture, period of use, and time of deposition of an artifact or a class of artifacts), and spatial locus (the position of the artifact in the three dimensional world). There is, I believe, general agreement that archaeologists are always concerned with these properties of artifacts, and there is an implication that archaeology can be defined minimally as the study of the interrelationships of form, temporal locus, and spatial locus exhibited by artifacts. In other words, archaeologists are always concerned with these interrelationships, whatever broader interests they may have, and these interrelationships are the special business of archaeology.

All of the rules for operation with dimensions apply to form, time, and space, and certain theoretical formulations can be dismissed at once on this basis. A statement of the type "the focus concept contains more of form than is does of time (or space)" is equivalent to the dimensional equation $F + T = x$, which is dimensionally heterogeneous and hence meaningless. Presumably what is involved here is a statement of the idea that a group of artifact assemblages having a high degree of formal resemblance to each other will usually or invariably show a compact clustering in time and in space, or in dimensional terms $\left[\dfrac{F_1}{T_1} = \dfrac{F_2}{T_2} \right]$. The dimensional equation

(put in brackets to indicate that it is not algebraic) states that a systematic relationship holds between degree of formal resemblance and length of time span; since form and time appear on both sides of the equation, it is homogeneous and can be given a determinate meaning. This illustration is intended to show that reasoning in terms of dimensional analysis can be something more than a sterile formality: it can be a safeguard against unclear thinking or exposition. The dimensional equation also points directly to a very real archaeological problem: if we are to substitute real data for the symbols of the equation, then we must develop objective scales for our dimensions.

The Formal Dimension

It is plain that the formal dimension cannot be dealt with by the application of any simple kind of scale, although it is a useful concept for broad theorizing. In practice formal descriptions and comparisons are made by analyzing artifact form into a number of discrete attribute systems: color, chemical composition, weight, various lengths (and the length relationships which describe shape), and so on. These attribute systems can be treated as dimensions in their own right, and from this point of view the formal dimension is a class of dimensions. I will not attempt more than a glance at some of the obvious characteristics of formal attributes.

Formal attributes can be divided into two classes, quantitative attributes (or measurements) and qualitative attributes. Quantitative attributes, weight and length for example, vary continuously, and they can be measured by ordinary scaling devices divided into equal units. Artifacts can be compared absolutely in terms of these measurements, that is, the difference between two artifacts can be expressed in equal units of the appropriate scale (x is 25 pounds heavier than y). Relative comparisons are also possible (x is twice as long as y) if the zero point of the scale is not arbitrary. To borrow an example from another dimension, it cannot be said that Hopewell is twice as old as Middle Mississippi because the age relationship is merely a function of an arbitrarily chosen reference point in time. Quantitative attributes can be described neatly in scale units, and the numerical properties of the measurements lend themselves to straightforward statistical description and inference.

Qualitative attributes cannot be described and compared by means of any familiar scaling device. They are thought of as discrete properties of artifacts, and the scale applied is no more than a notation of presence or absence. Recognition of the qualitative attributes of an artifact seems to be largely intuitive. The observer has a personal knowledge of human musculature and sensory apparatus and of the properties of materials, and he can judge at once that the addition of a pair of side notches to a flint projectile point represents a discrete segment of the total behavior involved in making the point. Qualitative attributes which are mutually exclusive can be grouped into a dimension; thus the projectile point may be made from white flint, argillite, or some other material. This grouping provides a three-position scale within the dimension of material for describing the point and for classifying a collection of points.

In an ultimate sense, the distinction between quantitative and qualitative attributes tends to break down because any real measuring instrument must be divided into discrete steps, however small they may be. Nevertheless, the distinction remains in practice; the fineness of recorded measurements is limited only by the precision of the measuring instrument and the nature of the number system in which the records are kept, but the nature of the attribute itself limits the observation of the qualitative attribute. It is sometimes possible to transform ostensibly qualitative attributes into continuously variable properties, as when personal judgments of shades of color are replaced by measurements with physical apparatus, and the resulting gain in objectivity may prove to be valuable. However, the essentially discrete nature of many attributes is plain enough to make such a translation superfluous for many purposes, and a wholesale attempt to replace with measurements the current presence-or-absence observation of recognized attributes would have no utility. No one questions the reasonableness or objectivity of describing a vessel as having four strap handles and contrasting it with other vessels having two or no strap handles.

The distinction between quantitative and qualitative attributes is operationally relevant in a fundamental archaeological problem, the preparation of an attribute list for the formal description of a collection of artifacts. The very nature of quantitative attributes ensures that no two artifacts will yield exactly the same measurement, but it is necessary to discriminate between the unimportant and presumably random variation expected of products made by hand from materials which are not uniform and the culturally meaningful variation resulting from significantly differing models held by the makers of the artifacts. The problem can be attacked by listing in order the individual values of some measurement (say projectile point length) in a collection. If the list seems to show a pronounced clustering of values around a central point with progressively fewer values toward the extremes of the observed range, the conclusion ordinarily reached will be that the variation is of the random type. If, on the other hand, there are two or more values around which the measurements cluster, then two or more categories will be distinguished, and each can be thought of as a separate qualitative attribute such as "large" and "small." The problem is purely statistical, although in many instances it can be solved by inspection rather than by formal statistical curve fitting.

Qualitative attributes are by definition those properties of artifacts which are already recognized as representing discrete segments of behavior, and accordingly they can be placed on the attribute list without further analysis. Subsequent study may show that a supposed qualitative attribute can in fact be split into two or more meaningful classes; for example, a description of a motif as an incised triangle may disguise a significant difference between large and small or scalene and isosceles triangles. Conversely, some distinctions may be quite objective but turn out to have a sharply limited utility for the purpose of describing significant variations in patterns of attribute association. Thus triangles, rectangles, or circles might appear as decorative elements on a group of otherwise identical pots, and on this basis it would make sense to group them as a class of geometrical decorative elements. These qualifications are essentially secondary, however, and do not override the basic distinction of continuity versus discontinuity which is the root of the quantitative-qualitative division.

Techniques for recognizing formal attributes logically precede the next problem, that of studying artifact interrelationships in terms of formal attributes. For this problem, the recognized attributes serve as linking constants from artifact to artifact: they are the units whose presences and absences constitute similarity or difference. In some respects attributes are analogous to linguistic phonemes. They represent minimal units of meaningful behavior; they are taken to be constant for comparative and descriptive purposes; and they are articulated to form the artifact, which can be regarded as the minimal independent unit of material culture. In the simplest terms, the problem is what to do with a collection of artifacts and a list of formal attributes which the artifacts exhibit. There appear to be three possibilities in ordering a collection of artifacts with respect to their formal attributes:

1. The collection can be characterized by tallying each appearance of every attribute recognized.

2. The particular combination of attributes exhibited by each artifact can be listed, and the list can be condensed by grouping and tallying identical combinations.

3. The artifacts can be classified in terms of attribute clusters; this is accomplished by mathematical manipulation of the data provided by Types 1 and 2. This process is referred to here as cluster analysis.

Classification of Type 1 results in a number of classes having no relationship to one another except that imposed by the nature of the attribute systems. The description offered by such a classification is of the general type: red pots, 50, other colors, 50; grit tempered pots, 35; sand tempered pots, 65; bowls, 30; jars, 30; plates, 40; and so on. Tallies in sets of mutually exclusive attributes must sum to the total number of artifacts, but no other relationship is expressed. The information on relationships furnished by the physical association of attributes on the individual artifacts is wasted; we are told in the example that 35 of the 100 pots are grit tempered, but we do not know how many grit tempered pots are red.

Classification of Type 2 requires a list of all observed attribute combinations as the categories within which the individual specimens are tallied. It contains all the information presented by the attribute count plus full information on attribute association. The categories of combinations divide the entire collection according to one principle so that there is no question of which of two or more possible piles a specimen belongs to. In short, it is a complete descriptive classification which wastes no information, although its completeness is, of course, relative to the adequacy of the underlying attribute list. However, some unexploited analytic possibilities involving the relationships of attribute and attribute combination frequencies remain, and these are dealt with by the Type 3 classification.

Classification of the third type, cluster analysis, is dependent on the data of the second, and it is specifically concerned with such questions as how many of the red jars are grit tempered. Its basic feature is the comparison of the observed count for each attribute combination with the count expected on a hypothesis of attribute independence. These comparisons result in a rating on a continuous scale for each attribute combination along the lines of less than expected, about the same as expected, and more than expected. The reasoning involved is more easily exemplified than stated abstractly. Calculation of the expected tally for a particular combination under the hypothesis of independence uses only the attribute frequencies. In the example given, we can ask how many red grit tempered jars can be expected if these attributes are independent. In the total of 100 pots, 50 are red, 35 are grit tempered, and 30 are jars; if these attributes have no tendency to

stick together, we can calculate that $\dfrac{50}{100} \times \dfrac{35}{100} \times \dfrac{30}{100} \times 100 = 5.25$ red

grit tempered jars will be expected. The observed tally for the combination can range from 0 to 30 pots under the conditions specified. If the tally is actually 0, it would appear that the combination was avoided by the maker of the pots; a tally of 5 or 6 would suggest that the combination was neither avoided nor sought after; and a tally of 25 or 30 would indicate a strong tendency to group the three attributes. The last case illustrates what is meant here by an attribute cluster — a strong positive association of two or more attributes. I have ignored for the sake of clarity the sampling uncertainties which are so troublesome in real problems.

So far as I can see, classification with respect to attribute clusters exploits fully the formal information presented by a collection of artifacts since it interrelates the entire list of discriminated attributes in terms of both attribute frequency and attribute combination frequency. In my opinion, it also offers an explicit, operationally useful model of the relationships comprised under the concept of artifact type. A distinctive cluster of attributes is the consistent pattern central to the idea of type in both ordinary usage and discussions in archaeological literature. Cluster analysis is simply a full-dress exposition of the reasoning implied in the shorthand statement that type classifications are accomplished by putting together the artifacts that look alike. It is important to note that cluster analysis does not create clusters when they are not implied by the empirical data, it does not of itself explain the cultural meaning of the clusters (or lack of them) revealed by the analysis, and it will not necessarily assign every artifact to a typological pigeon hole: some artifacts may be genuinely intermediate between two clusters and others may be aberrant hangers-on of a reasonably well-defined type. It is equally important to realize that artifact types are not necessarily the most convenient and economical units for investigating possible systematic formal relationships in a set of collections; for this purpose simple attribute or attribute combination relative frequencies may serve as well.

When a formal analysis of two or more collections has been completed, comparisons in terms of the attribute list, the attribute combination list, and the type list are possible. These orders of comparison provide increasingly sensitive scales of similarity. Thus on a presence-or-absence basis two components may have identical attribute lists but not identical attribute combination lists, and they may have identical attribute combination lists but not identical artifact types.

Still more sensitive comparisons are possible when category frequencies (reduced to proportions so as to provide standard values for collections of varying sizes) are considered. Obviously it may be possible to detect valid differences between two collections on the basis of attribute frequencies even though both possess the same list of attributes. Somewhat less obvious is the fact that two collections may differ in attribute combination frequencies although they have the same attribute list, identical attribute frequencies, and identical attribute combination lists. This situation is illustrated in Table I, in which three sets of attributes are symbolized by letters and subscripts with a total of 100 specimens and the following frequencies assumed for two collections:

A_1	35	B_1	50	C_1	25
A_2	65	B_2	50	C_2	75
	$\overline{100}$		$\overline{100}$		$\overline{100}$

Comparison of attribute combination frequencies is, in fact, the most sensitive possible because the combination tallies are a complete enumeration of the formal empirical data. Comparisons of type frequencies in the sense of the type concept used here would not add information to the formal likeness scale because any difference in the attribute clusters must be a reflection of differences in combination frequencies. The artifact type has no special value for formal comparison, although it does express objectively relationships inherent in or implied by the data. The attribute associations (or lack of them) revealed by cluster analysis are already contained, so to speak, in the attribute combination tallies. Cluster analysis brings into the open relationships which in many cases do not by any means leap to the eye from a simple inspection of the combination tallies; its purpose is to provide a basis for a culturally significant interpretation of differences in combination frequencies by ordering already existing data in a new way. It provides an escape from the dilemma of regarding everything as arbitrary (in which case "arbitrary" is robbed of any definite meaning) or neatly packaged (which is manifestly not true).

TABLE 1. VARIATION IN ATTRIBUTE/
COMBINATION FREQUENCIES IN TWO
COLLECTIONS

	Collection I						Collection II			
	A_1		A_2				A_1		A_2		
	B_1	B_2	B_1	B_2	Total		B_1	B_2	B_1	B_2	Total
C_1	15	8	1	1	25	C_1	3	2	9	11	25
C_2	10	2	24	39	75	C_2	15	15	23	22	75
Total	25	10	25	40	100	Total	18	17	32	33	100

Overall characterization and comparison of collections of artifacts can be conducted at a still more generalized level at which the entire body of empirical formal data is replaced by a single number. Ranking in terms of complexity is a familiar example. The basis for judging that, for example, a Hopewell assemblage is more complex than a Lamoka assemblage is usually not the result of a formal calculation, but it is plain that a simple comparison of the number of attributes, attribute combinations, or types in the two entities would support the judgment. If one were willing to assume that any attribute has about the same complexity as any other attribute, an attribute count would offer an objective measure of formal complexity. A second kind of overall characterization can be made in terms of the degree of attribute clustering shown by a collection. This sort of characterization in nonmathematical idiom takes the form of describing a collection in some such terms as rigidly stylized as opposed to unconstrained or imaginative. Possible mathematical devices to objectify judgments of this sort need not concern us in detail. A very simple example would be the ratio of observed attribute combinations to possible attribute combinations, and more complex statements based on contingency tables could be worked out.

The Spatial Dimension

Scaling of artifact loci is a familiar operation. It means no more than the application of a yardstick in the three ordinary directions of space to produce the latitude, longitude, and depth measurements which define a point uniquely. Spatial attributes in this sense are given; the measuring instrument can be applied directly to the artifact *in situ,* and the resulting measurements can be recorded and analyzed with the aid of all the techniques appropriate to a continuous variable.

There are, however, certain circumstances under which spatial units are given special meaning. These are the cases where artifacts occur in some sort of container, and there is consequently a relationship between them which goes beyond mere propinquity. The container may be culturally produced, examples being the grave goods of a single burial, a group of artifacts in a cache or storage pit, or the contents of a room in a pueblo. Here the entire collection of associated artifacts becomes a descriptive and comparative unit, and the spatial interrelationships of the component artifacts are presented in a formal description of the unit as a sort of superartifact. The container may be provided by natural action — a single gravel lens in a stream deposit, a stratum of debris sealed by a layer of volcanic ash, and so on — or it may be the result of combined cultural and natural activity, as in the case of strata produced by the abandonment of a site, development of an erosion surface, and reoccupation. These situations do not differ theoretically from that of the culturally produced container; the component artifacts again become a special unit of association, and for many purposes the significant spatial measurement may be simply whether a given artifact is within or outside of the container. When these special association units are present, spatial observations are interpreted in the light of the physical laws of superposition and intrusion applied to the contents of the entire unit. On the other hand, when visible strata or other boundaries yielding association units within an archaeological deposit are not present, the analysis of spatial relationships becomes an example of the general case. Thus the interpretation of vertical relationships in a massive deposit is a function of the actual vertically scaled position of each artifact.

Aside from these examples of special association, space scaling yields a set of coordinates on a continuously variable scale as another sort of attribute for each artifact, and collections of artifacts are characterized by lists of coordinate sets. One of the primary results of the analysis of such data is so obvious that it is usually thought of as simple observation rather than analysis. This result is the recognition of the very strong tendency for artifacts to occur in tight spatial clusters, that is, in archaeological sites. The site is ordinarily taken to be a given, and the assemblage of artifacts from a site is the customary unit of description and comparison. In many cases the vertical component is treated as if it were negligible; indeed, there is no other course for surface collections or thin deposits. If adequate vertical segregation is present, however, the site may be divided into two or more assemblages.

Actual techniques for analysis of the spatial coordinates of artifacts need not be described in full detail for the purposes of this paper. When strata or other boundaries giving immediately observable units are not present, the deposit can be divided into arbitrarily defined blocks for cluster analysis along the general lines discussed earlier. Excavations are often arranged to give such blocks immediately on the assumption that measuring the individual artifact coordinates would produce needlessly refined data. Such techniques in effect transform the quantitative space attributes into qualitative attributes for ease of control and statistical manipulation. It is possible to work directly with the individual coordinates treated as continuous variables if the underlying information is available and if it is judged that the expected gain in precision justifies the additional work. Finally, assemblages can be described and compared in terms of overall size and configuration.

The Temporal Dimension

Time itself is a continuum sensed as a succession of events. There are two types of time scales, relative and absolute. Relative time scaling is simply ranking an event as before or after some other event. Absolute time scaling means placing an event with respect to a sequence of events which are thought to occur at regular intervals and which are given a standard designation by reference to an arbitrarily chosen initial point. Our absolute scale is, of course, the calendar. As I noted above, all calendars are reckoned from an arbitrary starting period so that in a strict sense relative comparisons in terms of the calendar (x is twice as old as y) are not possible, although absolute comparisons (x is 500 years older than y) are. We can also make absolute and relative comparisons of time intervals between events and in consequence can make rate-of-change comparisons in relative terms. These aspects of chronology suggest that some confusion might be avoided if we adopt the term "time ranking" for the major type of time scale called "relative" above and generally referred to as relative chronology.

Since time scaling refers to events, not things, it is apparent that the temporal attributes of a prehistoric artifact must be prehistoric events whose occurrence is implied by the formal and spatial attributes of the artifact. The prehistoric events usually thought of as archaeologically significant — the targets of chronological inference — are the manufacture and primary deposition of the artifact. In most instances no serious question is asked about the time interval separating these two events; the general uncertainties of chronological scaling are such that the interval can be treated as negligible without serious difficulty. When the unit considered is a spatial cluster (an assemblage) of artifacts, as is usually the case, the question becomes still more complicated because a large number of events is involved. Here the goal is to define the assemblage so that the events represented by the component artifacts form a sufficiently tight cluster in time to permit the inference that no marked cultural changes took place during the time interval between the first and last events implied.

An equally plain consequence of the nature of chronological attributes is the fact that they cannot be observed directly in the way that formal and spatial characteristics can. All chronological judgments are inferences made by interpreting spatial and formal attributes in the light of physical, biological, or cultural principles. We have mentioned above the physical principles of superposition and intrusion, which allow spatial attributes to be transformed into temporal ranking. Similarly, measurement of radioactivity permits an estimate of absolute chronology based on a formal property of the artifact. These and other noncultural principles are of the highest importance because they provide a method of studying culture change over time without prior assumptions about the nature of cultural change. In short, they offer raw material for the construction of cultural theories. On the other hand, chronological judgments obtained by application of culturally derived theories of change merely illustrate what is meant by the theories; the judgments will be sound if the theories are sound and are applied correctly, but they will not be independent contributions to cultural theory. Thus one can arrange a group of assemblages in order of formal complexity of some class of artifacts common to all and infer that this arrangement is also a chronological ordering, but this procedure demonstrates nothing about formal changes in time because the ordering is a product of a prior theory about such changes.

A few remarks about chronological periods are probably in order here because of some apparent confusion in the literature and in archaeological discussions. It seems plain enough that a chronological period can be defined uniquely only by specifying unique sequent events for its boundaries in time. Nevertheless, examples of time periods defined by criteria which are actually an ambiguous succession of events are by no means unknown, and they have led to misunderstandings. Such "cultural periods" seem to have their origin in the observation that a number of assemblages in some geographical area have several artifact types in common while a number of other assemblages are characterized by quite different sets of types. In symbolic terms, there are ABCD sites (letters standing for types) and EFGH sites, and, since the spatial factor is limited, the observer falls into the habit of thinking of an ABCD period and EFGH period without further analysis. Sooner or later, however, a CDEF assemblage turns up, and it becomes apparent that something is wrong with the supposed chronological division. The new assemblage belongs to both or neither of the two original periods, and a new scheme is called for. This difficulty could have been avoided at the outset by more careful definition delineating a true division of time. If it is known that type A appeared before type E, then the periods could have been defined as: (1) from the appearance of type A to the appearance of type E, and (2) after the appearance of type E. Any assemblage having either E or A (or both E and A) can be placed in this scheme without ambiguity, and the periods can be subdivided if accumulating information makes it desirable.

INTERRELATIONSHIPS OF DIMENSIONS

The study of the interrelationship of the formal, spatial, and temporal properties of artifacts presupposes an independent scaling of each dimension considered. I have discussed in a very general way the characteristic scales and some of the scaling problems associated with each dimension, and I wish to consider now how the result of simultaneous classification in two or more dimensions leads to certain familiar archaeological concepts. The possible relationships are form-space, form-time, space-time, and form-space-time.

Form-Space

In the discussion of the formal characterization of collections of artifacts, it was asserted that artifact types could be defined solely on the basis of clusters of formal attributes. A minimum cluster is a close association of two formal attributes. But if we replace the intentionally vague concept of collection with the more restricted idea of assemblage (a spatial cluster of artifacts thought to represent something approaching a point in time), it may be possible to show a close association of a formal and a spatial attribute. Suppose that the problem at hand is a typological description of a group of vessels which are substantially identical except for the presence or absence of incised decoration on the lip, and suppose further that the collection consists of a number of assemblages. If an assemblage tally shows that plain and incised lips rarely or never occur in the same assemblage, then it would appear reasonable to recognize the two classes of vessels as distinct entities, and there is no objection to calling them artifact types. A cluster of a formal and a spatial attribute exists when the assemblage is treated as a unit of association.

Even within a single assemblage, it might be possible to show formal-spatial clustering and hence types if the special association units are considered as, for example, when the vessels with incised lips appear only as grave furnishings. Moreover, examination of the actual coordinates of the spatially segregated form variants can yield information for further inferences about the prehistoric behavior underlying the empirical data. The two types of vessels could be northern and southern or upstream and downstream variants, for example. Even the absence of any systematic arrangement of coordinates has definite implications for inferential reconstructions of behavior. A systematic time difference can be treated in the same manner; a cluster of a formal and a temporal attribute also provides satisfactory evidence for an artifact type.

A second level of form-space synthesis results from treating the assemblage as a unit of association of artifact types. The reasoning is very similar, perhaps identical, to that employed in discussing the concept of artifact type, with the assemblage playing the part of the artifact and the artifact type that of the attribute. The problem is to classify a group of assemblages with respect to their formal attributes (artifact types) so as to reveal the degree of clustering of artifact types, that is, to investigate the problem of assemblage typology. The essential raw material is a list of the artifact type combinations exhibited by each of the assemblages of the group being investigated. The method of investigation involves the familiar computing of an expected number of assemblages for various artifact type combinations under a hypothesis of independence and comparing the expected tally with the observed tally. As before, a substantial excess of observed over expected indicates a strong association of at least two artifact types, and this strong association defines a type of assemblage — a culture type. The culture type defined in this manner — as a group of assemblages possessing in common two or more artifact types having a strong positive association — seems very close to the old archaeological concept of "a culture," and it has the same faults and virtues. Specifically, it is noncommittal as to the number or nature of the artifact types forming the characterizing cluster. In fact, it implies no more than the existence of some sort of distinctive cultural entity, and the component assemblages might be virtually identical through a long list of complicated artifact types or they might barely fulfill the minimum requirements. It is plain that subclasses or subculture types can exist within a culture type. There is useful work for such concepts as the phase or the ranked (according to complexity of identifying criteria) scale of the McKern system.

A higher order of space-form relationship can be derived from the spatial position and formal typology of assemblages. If the loci of the assemblages comprising a culture type form a geographical cluster, then the area occupied by the cluster is a culture type area. Repeated examples of such culture type areas would lead to recognition of a principle of spatial coherence of the component assemblages of a culture type. Finally, the spatial clustering of culture type areas themselves can be investigated to discover whether or not there is repeated association of such areas with one geographical region. A geographical region that does show such a cluster of clusters can be considered an archaeologically defined culture area, one in which some factor is at work to produce a culturally distinct region independently of the particular types of culture characteristic of any given time period. The possibility of this kind of analysis has apparently never occurred to the archaeologists who argue that the culture area concept has no value to archaeology because variation in time inevitably produces more than one culture type in any area.

The foregoing discussion of space-form relationships is a more or less mechanical approach to some possible formulations in keeping with aims of this paper. I think it safe to hazard, however, that all archaeologists would agree to the general proposition that artifact form does in fact vary systematically in space. The relationship is a direct one: artifacts or assemblages which are formally close tend strongly toward spatial closeness. The explanation for this phenomenon is obvious, but it is drawn from observations of living cultures, not from the data of archaeology: most formal similarities are the result of person-to-person transmission of ideas and objects, and space is a barrier to this transmission. The converse of the relationship, that artifacts or assemblages which are formally distant tend strongly to be spatially distant, is no better than half true. Space is not the only barrier to transmission; time is equally effective. Hence, we expect two assemblages that are very much alike formally to be close both in space and in time. Two assemblages that are very different formally are expected to be distant in space, distant in time, or distant in both space and time.

The existence of a systematic relationship between formal similarity and spatial locus does not necessarily imply that there is any simple ratio of formal likeness to spatial distance (the time effect having been removed) which can describe the relationship adequately. If such a relationship did exist, cluster analysis would not indicate any special relationship of formal similarity to any bounded area. Similarities across all possible boundaries would be as great as similarities within boundaries. Indexes of likeness between assemblages would simply decrease at a regular ratio from any arbitrarily chosen starting point, or, if one conceded the spatial coherence of the component assemblages of a culture type, indexes of likeness of culture types would decrease at a regular rate. I am quite willing to argue that such a simple relationship does not represent adequately the empirical data. Formal similarities do tend to knot up in space, and culture areas are objectively demonstrable phenomena, not arbitrary descriptive conveniences. The explanation is again obvious, and again it is drawn from outside the limits of strictly archaeological observations. From the standpoint of human behavior, space is not a simple matter of x and y coordinates, of barriers to communication completely described in terms of miles. The real world not only presents special impediments to communication in the form of mountains, oceans, and the like, it also poses special problems of technological and social adaptation in the form of distinctive ecological areas.

Form-Time

Since time is not a directly observable artifact attribute, form-time relationships have necessarily been dealt with to some extent in the remarks on time scaling. The discussion here will consist of listing some assertions about the nature of form-time relationships and examining the empirical implications of the assertions. These assertions are that artifact form exhibits serial correlation, that formal innovations tend to cluster on the time scale, and that formal change through time tends to be unidirectional.

The principle of serial correlation of form implies that, other things being equal, there is an inverse relationship between the formal resemblance between two artifacts, assemblages, or culture types and the amount of time separating them. Put in a slightly different way, the best prediction of the formal characteristics of the material culture of a society for next year is that they will not differ much from the situation this year. The archaeological technique of seriation is a direct application of this principle; when a group of assemblages is arranged in order of formal likeness, the assemblages are also ranked in time. If a simple, consistent ordering in an index of likeness matrix or a graphic representation is not achieved, it is taken to mean that some factor other than time (sampling difficulties, spatial variation, and so on) is also represented. Evidence from living societies and stratified archaeological deposits offers ample testimony of the general correctness of the principle, and, so far as I know, there is no serious question of its applicability to time ranking.

The existence of clustering of formal innovations on the time scale is not so easily demonstrated, although the idea seems to be widely accepted and is implicit in many formulations. In the context of historic and proto-historic studies, the concept of cultural revolutions is a clear example. The view of cultural dynamics underlying the concept is that a typical mode of cultural change is the achievement of a key invention — a sort of quantum advance — followed quickly by a number of functionally related auxiliary innovations. The short periods of rapid change would be separated by relatively long periods of comparative quiescence, although not of total cultural stagnation, of course. If one accepts the view that social systems are devices for operating technological systems (as I do), there is a clear implication that the character of key inventions is technical; they are directed toward the natural environment and have a generative relationship to changes in social organization. This view is important to archaeology because archaeological data yield much fuller information on technological matters than they do on social systems. The empirical implications of such a developmental theory are clear enough: assemblages formally transitional between sequent and sharply distinctive culture types should be rare, and assemblages well within the formal boundaries of culture types should be relatively abundant. I think that the actual data do show this condition, and I suspect that the principle holds good for relationships of less spectacular dimensions than those of the grand culture types. It is this clustering tendency which makes the ambiguously defined "culture period" a useful concept in spite of its logical imperfections. The several events marking the opening or closing of the period are in fact clustered in time so that most assemblages do not seem to belong to two periods.

Unidirectionality of formal changes through time is simply the idea of cultural evolution. In strictly archaeological terms, sequent culture types in one region would be expected to show greater numbers of artifact types, not only through more formalized and more varied combinations of some stock of attributes but also through the addition of new attributes to the available list. One would also expect the sites of later culture types to be more numerous (or at any rate larger) than those of the earlier ones. These expectations are a translation into formal evidence of the behavioral concept that culture change is in the main rational: technological devices are modified and reorganized so as to increase productivity, and innovations are accepted if they are demonstrably superior with respect to productivity. Hence change tends strongly to be unidirectional. It is quite true that backsliding can occur, but it would be expected only under unusual circumstances such as climatic change. A change from an agricultural to a hunting and gathering economy in a restricted area can be imagined easily and it would not be difficult to suggest plausible explanations, but it is practically impossible to imagine circumstances short of total world disruption which would cause the abandonment of agriculture everywhere. The concept of a stage of cultural development is a combination of the ideas of unidirectionality and the key invention mode of change; there are stair-steps in culture change, and the steps lead consistently upward.

Space-Time

Time to space relationships, form being constant, are not the subject of much analysis in archaeology. Probably the most familiar generalization is that underlying the age-area concept. It is expected that the area of distribution of an artifact type will increase through time, and under some conditions a more widely distributed type is judged to have been invented earlier than a less widely distributed type. Judgments of this sort are necessarily precarious because of ecological and other conditions which can limit the spread of a type. No one expects snowshoes to be as widely spread as the use of fire, whatever their respective dates of first appearance may be. A few other remarks can be made about space-time relationships. If we consider the time-space distribution of artifacts as such, it is apparent that distribution increases in space through time, at least until the entire world is inhabited, and that space is more thickly studded with artifacts as time goes on. In short, both the quantity and the area of distribution of artifacts increases through time.

Form-Space-Time

The interrelationships of form, space, and time taken together have been foreshadowed by the discussion of the relationships of pairs of these dimensions. In a very broad sense, space and time are both expressible in terms of formal distance; the formal differences between two assemblages may be associated with either spatial distance or temporal difference or with both. If we assume that the rate of formal change has been constant in both dimensions, the interrelationship would be another example of the Pythagorean theorem. Plotting time on the vertical and space on the horizontal axis, the formal distance between a pair of points (representing two assemblages) on the graph would be the square root of the sum of squares of the time and space scales. From a dimensional point of view, such an operation implies that we have reduced time and space to the same dimension measured by a common scale calibrated in units of formal distance.

CONCLUSION

I have tried to make the common operations of archaeology somewhat more explicit than is frequently the case in archaeological discussions. The method used has been a translation of customary terminology into that of technically simpler and more elegant sciences, and the result has been a gain in precision and generality at the expense of realism. Certainly, to take an obvious example, there is a substantial discrepancy between my facile assumption of objective formal scales and the actual job of comparing the collections of artifacts from two assemblages. The question is whether or not such ideal formulations serve any useful purpose.

The answer is that these ideal formulations are implicit in actual archaeological research in any case, and there is no useful purpose served by not making them explicit. Indeed, failure to analyze the dimensional implications of statements about relationships has permitted formulations that are manifestly meaningless. Similarly, one may deny the possibility of objective formal scales, but the universally accepted judgment that Middle Mississippi culture is more complex than that of Indian Knoll inescapably implies that such scales are employed, however imperfect they may be. The sterile argument as to whether or not such scales exist can be replaced by a profitable discussion of ways and means to increase the sensitivity of formal scaling. The measure of success of any archaeological formulation is the degree to which it approaches the ideal, and the ideal is indispensable as an indicator of the direction and distance of the goals of archaeological research.

III
INTEGRATING
ARCHAEOLOGICAL
MATERIAL

ALBERT C. SPAULDING

*Albert Spaulding makes it clear that the formal dimension of
the artifact (its physical and chemical properties) is inherent
in the artifact. Unlike the spatial dimension (location) and
the temporal dimension (when and how long an object was
used), the formal dimension is defined by the object's
internal properties. An archaeologist can arrive at limited
formal classifications of artifacts without rigorous temporal
and spatial controls and still derive some cultural
information, but unless he is aware of the formal qualities of
artifacts, the other two dimensions are meaningless. For this
reason, problems in the classification of artifacts have long
occupied an important part in publications on archaeological
method and theory.*

*The fundamental question in establishing a taxonomy for
artifacts is whether or not the categories established by the
taxonomy are "culturally" realistic. Did the maker of the
artifact see it as the archaeologist does? If so, then the
archaeologist in creating typological categories is isolating
units of the world lived in by the man who made the object.
If not, then taxonomic exercises are ill-suited to produce
broader, behavioral descriptions of artifactual materials.*

*Albert Spaulding assumes that the type categories sought
by the archaeologist are inherent in the data, awaiting
discovery, and provides useful statistical techniques to aid
in their discovery. Thus the article illustrates one important
point of view in taxonomic discussions — the archaeologist
defines types that had reality for those who made them.*

4 Statistical Techniques for the Discovery of Artifact Types

Within recent years there appears to have been an increasing awareness on the part of archaeologists that certain statistical techniques offer economical methods of extracting information of cultural significance from archaeological data. The discussions of Kroeber (1940), Robinson (1951), and Brainerd (1951) have appeared in *American Antiquity*, and the last two even evoked a comment (Lehmer 1951). In addition to these papers, which are primarily devoted to exposition of method, a considerable number of special applications can be found in the literature. Archaeological research inevitably brings the researcher face to face with the problems of ordering and comparing quantities of data and of sampling error. There seems little doubt that the best approach to these problems involves a search of statistical literature for appropriate methods.

The discussion which follows is an attempt to apply certain statistical methods to the discovery and definition of artifact types and to suggest other applications to related problems. No effort has been made to explain such important statistical concepts as population, random sample, sampling error, and so on; these explanations are the proper function of textbooks, and any paraphrasing here would be presumptuous. I am indebted to Paul S. Dwyer, Consultant in the Statistical Research Laboratory of the University of Michigan, for reading and commenting on an earlier version of the manuscript.

The artifact type is here viewed as a group of artifacts exhibiting a consistent assemblage of attributes whose combined properties give a characteristic pattern. This implies that, even within a context of quite similar artifacts, classification into types is a process of discovery of combinations of attributes favored by the makers of the artifacts, not an arbitrary procedure of the classifier. Classification is further an operation which must be carried out exhaustively and independently for each cultural context if the most fruitful historical interpretations are to be made. It is the primary purpose of this paper to argue that with the aid of suitable statistical techniques the degree of consistency in attribute combinations can be discovered in any meaningful archaeological assemblage provided sufficient material is at hand, and hence that valid types can be set up on the basis of analysis of material from one component.

Reprinted, with the editorial changes noted, from "Statistical Techniques for the Discovery of Artifact Types" by Albert C. Spaulding, *American Antiquity* 18 (1953): 305–313, by permission of the author and the publisher. Tables are renumbered.

Wholesale acceptance of these views entails modification of a widely held concept of typology which has been clearly expressed by Krieger (Krieger 1944; Newell and Krieger 1949). Under this concept, the method employed to demonstrate the existence of a valid type is a site-to-site comparison to show consistency of the identifying pattern, range of variation, and historical relevance. In the absence of a method for investigation of consistency and range of variation within the site, this is indeed the only convincing technique available for validation of a proposed type. On the other hand, the presence of an adequate method for investigating consistency and range of variation within the site obviates a comparative study so far as the questions of the existence and definitive characteristics of a type are concerned. Historical relevance in this view is essentially derived from the typological analysis; a properly established type is the result of sound inferences concerning the customary behavior of the makers of the artifacts and cannot fail to have historical meaning. This is not meant to imply that corroborative evidence from the other sites would not be welcome in the case of a dubious type, i.e., one which is on the borderline of probability owing to a deficient sample or lack of clear evidence of attribute clustering, nor is it meant to imply that the classifier is relieved of the responsibility of avoiding synonymy. Finally, it is not intended to assert that artifact types are the only useful units of attribute association for site-to-site comparison; numerous examples of good comparative work with body sherds are sufficient refutation of such an assertion, although the common practice of failing to distinguish between kinds of body sherds and types of vessels is a stumbling block in understanding the cultural meaning of a comparison. It should be pointed out that this discussion owes much to the expositions of Rouse (1939: especially 9–23), Krieger (1944), Newell and Krieger (1949: 71–74), and Taylor (1948: especially 113–30).

The customary technique of classification consists of inspection and segregation of obtrusive combinations, or occasionally of attempting to describe all of the observed attribute combinations on an equal basis. Categories resulting from both of these methods are called "types," although they are not exactly comparable. Both methods fail to yield surely artifact types in the sense in which the term is used here. In the first case, segregation of obtrusive combinations, the cultural implications of the data are usually not exhausted, although under favorable circumstances all of the types may be discovered and described. In the second case, description of all combinations, the problem of typology is not faced at all; some of the "types" described will in all probability consist of combinations habitually avoided by the makers of the artifacts. Questions of typology arise, of course, only in a situation where a considerable variety exists within a group of generally similar artifacts — it is obvious that a stone projectile point and a pottery vessel belong in two separate artifact types. But within a group of similar artifacts the propriety of division into more than one type may be anything but obvious. It follows from the concept of the type adopted here that a pronounced association of two attributes is the minimum require- ment for the demonstration of the existence of an artifact type, since two is the smallest number which can be considered an assemblage.

Application of this concept to concrete material can be illustrated by a few simple examples. Inspection of a collection of 100 vessels which represent all the pottery from a component results in the noting of the following attributes: smooth surface, cord wrapped paddle stamped surface, grit tempered paste, and shell tempered paste. The question to be answered is whether the vessels represent one or two pottery types with respect to these attributes. The data necessary to answer the question are the frequen- cies of vessels in each of the four possible categories into which two pairs of alternatives can be grouped, here smooth surface and grit temper, smooth surface and shell temper, cord wrapped paddle stamped surface and grit temper, and cord wrapped paddle stamped surface and shell temper. Table 1 presents these frequencies in 2×2 form under the assumption that the count in each category is 25 vessels. It is evident by inspection that the 100

TABLE 1. FOUR-CELL FREQUENCIES
WITH NO ASSOCIATION OF ATTRIBUTES

	Grit Temper	Shell Temper	Total
Stamped Surface	25	25	50
Smooth Surface	25	25	50
Total	50	50	100

vessels cannot be separated into two types under these circumstances. The cord wrapped paddle stamped vessels are equally divided with respect to grit temper and shell temper, the same is true of the smooth surfaced vessels, and conversely both the shell tempered and the grit tempered vessels are equally divided with respect to surface finish. A mathematical statement to the same effect can be obtained by applying the simple and useful four-cell coefficient of association described by Kroeber (1940). If the upper left cell is designated a, and the upper right cell b, the lower left cell c, and the lower right cell d, the coefficient of association for the attributes grit temper and cord wrapped paddle stamped surface would be computed as

$$\frac{(a+d)-(b+c)}{a+b+c+d} = \frac{(25+25)-(25+25)}{25+25+25+25} = \frac{0}{100} = 0.$$

The same result would follow for the other three pairs. The opposite situation would be that of Table 2. Here there are plainly two types with respect to the traits considered, a cord wrapped paddle stamped and grit tempered type and a smooth surfaced and shell tempered type. The

TABLE 2. FOUR-CELL FREQUENCIES WITH
PERFECT ASSOCIATION OF ATTRIBUTES

	Grit Temper	Shell Temper	Total
Stamped Surface	50	0	50
Smooth Surface	0	50	50
Total	50	50	100

computed coefficient of association for the attributes grit temper and cord wrapped paddle stamped surface is

$$\frac{(50 + 50) - (0 + 0)}{50 + 0 + 50 + 0} = +1.0,$$

and the same coefficient would be obtained for the shell tempered, smooth surfaced category. On the other hand, the calculation for the smooth surfaced, grit tempered category shows

$$\frac{(0 + 0) - (50 + 50)}{0 + 50 + 0 + 50} = -1.0,$$

and this is also true of the cord wrapped paddle stamped, shell tempered category.

This discussion of four-cell coefficients has been introduced chiefly to illuminate the concept of the two attribute association as the minimum requirement for the establishment of an artifact type, although the simple four-cell coefficient of association and its more sophisticated relatives are by no means to be ignored as working methods under the proper conditions. One of the serious deficiencies of the four-cell coefficient is its failure to consider the vagaries of sampling, since a conservative interpretation of the material from any archaeological component requires that it be considered no more than a sample drawn from a universe of artifacts manufactured by a society over some vaguely defined period of time. Other precautions to observe when using four-cell coefficients are discussed by Kroeber (1940).

Methods do exist which give answers expressing the combined result of the error involved in sampling and the extent to which the observed data fit the expected with respect to a hypothesis. The remainder of this paper will be devoted to illustrating the application of these methods to typological problems and some other archaeological data. All of the techniques presented are drawn from the literature of biological statistics dealing with the analysis of binomial distributions, especially the discussions of Mather (1947: Chapter XI) and Snedecor (1946: Chapters 9 and 16), and the reader is referred to these sources for an adequate explanation of the underlying concepts. The most practical method of recording and subsequently extracting the variety and quantity of data needed for a thorough analysis of any sizable collection would appear to be one of the mechanically or electrically sorted punch card systems.

TABLE 3. FOUR-CELL FREQUENCIES
WITH INDEPENDENCE OF ATTRIBUTES

	Grit Temper	Shell Temper	Total
Stamped Surface	53	64	117
Smooth Surface	32	43	75
Total	85	107	192

Using Table 3 as an example, an analysis which fulfills the stipulated conditions can be made by means of a formula for computing a statistical entity known as chi square. The formula which is most convenient for a 2×2 table is

$$\chi^2 = \frac{n(ad - bc)^2}{(a + b)\ (c + d)\ (a + c)\ (b + d)},$$

or verbally, the number of specimens multiplied by the squared difference of the product of the diagonals divided by the product of the marginal totals. Substituting the values of Table 3 gives

$$\chi^2 = \frac{192[(53 \times 43) - (35 \times 64)]^2}{117 \times 75 \times 85 \times 107},$$

which reduces to

$$\frac{192 \times 231 \times 231}{117 \times 75 \times 85 \times 107} = 0.128.$$

With a χ^2 of 0.128 and one other argument, the number of degrees of freedom, it is possible to enter a table of χ^2 and read the probability of the occurrence of so large a χ^2 through the operation of sampling variation alone in a population having independent attributes in the ratios indicated by the marginal totals. The appropriate number of degrees of freedom is 1 because the computation imposes the restriction that the frequencies must add up to the marginal totals, so that as soon as a frequency is assigned to any cell those of the other three can be found by subtraction. The probability corresponding to a χ^2 of 0.128 with 1 degree of freedom is between .80 and .70, which means that a χ^2 this large would arise by chance alone between 70 and 80 times in 100 in a population having independent attributes. It seems reasonable to accept the hypothesis of independence of attributes and conclude that the marginal totals present a fair picture of the potters' habits, there being very little evidence that the individual cell frequencies fall outside the range expected in a random drawing from a homogeneous population having the proportions of attributes indicated by the marginal totals. In other words, there is no discernible tendency for the attributes to cluster into types. Here, in contrast to the coefficients of association mentioned above, it has been possible to make a statement in terms of numerical probability and a definite hypothesis, which reduces the data to their most comprehensible form.

Chi square for Table 2 would be computed as

$$\frac{100\,[\,(50 \times 50) - (0 \times 0)\,]^2}{50 \times 50 \times 50 \times 50} = 100,$$

a value exceeding by a large amount the tabled value of 10.877 for a probability of .001 for 1 degree of freedom, and the probability that the marginal totals fairly represent the potters' habits is astronomically remote. The attributes are not independent; inspection of the table shows that the sample is derived from two populations, one characterized by grit tempering and a cord wrapped paddle stamped surface, the other by shell tempering and a smooth surface. This is the same conclusion as that based on the coefficient of association, but again a numerical expression of the odds against the occurrence of such a distribution in a random drawing from a population having an independent distribution of the four attributes has been provided.

It is important to note that the proportions used in testing attribute independence or lack of it were derived from the sample, and consequently the calculations have not tested the proposition that the observed proportions exactly represent those of the population from which the sample was obained. What has been tested is the hypothesis that the two samples, those in the two rows or the two columns, were randomly drawn from a common binomial population. In the first instance (Table 3) the hypothesis was accepted, in the second (Table 2) it was rejected. Acceptance in the case of the data of Table 3 indicates that both cord wrapped paddle stamped and smooth surfaced vessels were randomly drawn from a population of vessels having grit temper and shell temper in a ratio estimated to be in the neighborhood of 85:107, or alternatively, both grit tempered and shell tempered vessels were randomly drawn from a population of vessels having cord wrapped paddle stamped and smooth surfaces in a ratio estimated to be 117:75. The estimated ratios are simply the marginal totals, and the inferences about the nature of the parent population can be completed by finding confidence limits for these estimates. This can be accomplished easily by means of a calculation or by reference to a table of confidence intervals such as that presented by Snedecor (1946:4). Rejection of the hypothesis of independence in the case of Table 2 leads to the conclusion that cord wrapped paddle stamped vessels were drawn from a population of vessels estimated to be exclusively grit tempered, and smooth surfaced vessels were drawn from a probably exclusively shell tempered population. Again confidence intervals can be assigned to the estimates.

The next question to be investigated is that of a suitable technique for situations involving combinations of more than two pairs of attributes. The method to be employed is closely related to that just illustrated, but the resemblance is obscured by the streamlined computing routine used for the 2×2 table. There are two basic steps required: (1) calculation of an expected frequency for the combination, customarily under the hypothesis that the combination in question does not constitute a distinctive type, i.e., that the attributes making up the combination have independent distributions; and (2) comparison of the expected frequency with the observed frequency to determine whether or not the difference between the two can be reasonably attributed to sampling error. If the observed frequency exceeds the expected frequency by an amount too great to be considered the result of mere sampling error, it will be concluded that a genuine tendency for the makers of the artifacts to combine the attributes in question has been discovered — that the existence of a type has been demonstrated.

The following data will be used to explain the working method: in a collection of 297 pottery vessels, it is suspected that a combination of grit tempering, stamped surface, and a collared rim occurs often enough to provide sufficient grounds for the definition of a pottery type. A count made of the frequency of the triple combination gives 83 vessels; of the frequency of grit tempering alone, 117 vessels; of stamped surface alone, 91 vessels; and of collared rims alone, 136 vessels.

Under the hypothesis of independent distribution of attributes (no type), the frequency of the combination would be expected to be a simple function of the relative frequencies of the component attributes. Calculation of the expected number is a straightforward problem in compound probability, here

$$\frac{117}{297} \times \frac{91}{297} \times \frac{136}{297} \times \frac{297}{1} = 16.42 \text{ vessels.}$$

In practice it is necessary to compute the proportion (p) characteristic of the combination for reasons to be explained below. The computation of p here is

$$\frac{117}{297} \times \frac{91}{297} \times \frac{136}{297} = .0553.$$

The next step is to obtain the deviation (d) of the observation from the expectation by subtracting 16.42 from 83.00, which results in a deviation of 66.58.

It is necessary here to introduce some new symbols required for the final comparison of the expected frequency (E) and the observed frequency (O).The proportion of vessels not expected to exhibit the combination will be designated q, which is simply $1 - p$ or $1.000 - .0553 = .9447$ in the example. The expectation for the various possible frequencies of two alternative types (in this example grit tempered, cord wrapped paddle stamped, collared rim vessels and vessels not having this combination) can be found by expanding the binomial $(p +q)^k$, where k is the symbol for the number of individuals in the group (297 vessels); in addition, and of immediate importance in the solution of the problem, is the fact that the variance of the expanded binomial distribution is pqk ($.0553 \times .9447 \times 297 = 15.52$). The standard deviation (σ) is $\sqrt{pqk}$, which makes it possible to compute easily either the deviate in units of standard deviation as

$$\frac{d}{\sigma}, \text{ or } \left[\frac{d}{\sigma}\right]^2 \text{ as } \frac{d^2}{pqk}. \text{ Both } \frac{d}{\sigma} \text{ and } \left[\frac{d}{\sigma}\right]^2 \text{ can be converted into state-}$$

ments of probability by means of widely available tables. In the case of d/σ, tables of areas of the normal curve or tables for t for infinite degrees of freedom may be used $(d/\sigma)^2$ is the familiar χ^2 for 1 degree of freedom. Choice of formula is a matter of individual preference since the answers obtained are identical; tables for χ^2 are less closely computed than those for d/σ owing to their two dimensional character, but the precision of the latter does not appear to have any advantage for archaeological purposes. In both cases the tables were computed on the basis of a continuous curve rather than the binomial curve with discrete steps used here, and consequently they are not exactly applicable. A widely recommended procedure for avoiding excessive distortion is to group categories so that the expected numbers are not too small, say 5 or less. A partial correction (the Yates correction) can be made by adjusting d, and precise methods of adjustment for small numbers can be found in statistical literature. The simple adjustments do not seem to change the results markedly, but anyone planning to use these techniques should be familiar with informed discussions of the subject.

Calculations for $(d/\sigma)^2$ for the example are

$$\frac{(66.58)^2}{15.52} = \frac{4432.90}{15.52} = 285.62.$$

Entering a table of χ^2 with this figure and 1 degree of freedom, a probability of finding a fit with hypothesis through chance at least as bad of very much less than .001 is noted. A similar calculation for d/σ indicates that the odds are actually less than 1 in 400,000,000,000 that so large a difference between observed and expected frequencies would arise through random sampling in the expanded binomial. It can be concluded that the chance of a sampling vagary as the explanation is exceedingly remote, and the large number of vessels exhibiting the combination must be attributed to the habits of the potters. The calculation does show that a pottery type exists. Further research would be necessary to investigate whether (1) on the basis of other attributes it might not be possible to identify a group of pottery types sharing the specified combination, or (2) whether there are other combinations differing by only one attribute which should be included in the type description as variants. The original conclusion — that the existence of a pottery type was demonstrated — is not modified by either case.

The evaluation of probability can perhaps be clarified by two other examples. Had the observed frequency been 24 vessels, χ^2 would have been computed as

$$\frac{(7.58)^2}{15.52} = \frac{57.46}{15.52} = 3.70,$$

which for 1 degree of freedom represents a probability of between .10 and .05, but much closer to .05. The conclusion is not at all clear. There is an appreciable chance that no real preference for the combination was exhibited by the potters, and the evaluation must be made with the aid of all the experience which the archaeologist can muster. If related sites plainly show that the combination is elsewhere a valid type, the interpretation would probably be that in this case the type was just appearing or disappearing. In the absence of other data, one could say only that there is a very good possibility that a type has been discovered. In certain types of statistical investigation a χ^2 of more than 3.841 (the .05 level of probability for 1 degree of freedom) is considered significant, or in our terms the hypothesis of independence would be rejected. It would appear unwise to carry over blindly such concepts into archaeology. Had the observed frequency of the combination been 8 vessels, d would have been 8.42 and $\chi^2 = 4.57$ with a probability between .05 and .02. The same general reasoning applies again, but here the situation is reversed because the expected frequency exceeds the observed frequency; there is a strong probability that the potters tended to avoid the combination, and the examples observed might best be considered the work of unorthodox potters.

A thorough investigation of a collection requires the calculation of d/σ or χ^2 for every possible combination of presumably important attributes. The number of combinations possible can be found by grouping the mutually exclusive attributes and multiplying together the number of attributes in each of the groups. If the groups of attributes consist of (1) smooth surface,

TABLE 4. COMPUTATION OF $\dfrac{d^2}{pqk}$ FOR
TWELVE COMBINATIONS OF ATTRIBUTES

Attribute Combination	O	E	d	d^2	pqk	$\dfrac{d^2}{pqk}$
Sm. surf., rect. sh., grit t.	0	11.51	−11.51	132.02	10.78	12.25
Sm. surf., curv. sh., grit t.	2	6.84	−1.85	23.52	6.59	3.56
Sm. surf, plain sh., grit t.	14	27.17	−13.17	173.45	23.21	7.47
Sm. surf., rect. sh., shell t.	38	19.07	+18.93	358.35	17.11	20.94
Sm. surf., curv. sh., shell t.	26	11.36	+14.64	214.33	10.66	20.11
Sm. surf., plain sh., shell t.	41	45.04	−4.04	16.24	34.13	0.48
St. surf., rect. sh., grit t.	3	6.18	−3.18	10.11	5.97	1.69
St. surf., curv. sh., grit t.	0	3.68	−3.68	13.54	3.61	3.75
St. surf., plain sh., grit t.	51	14.60	+36.40	1324.96	13.45	98.51
St. surf., rect. sh., shell t.	6	10.25	−4.25	18.06	9.69	1.86
St. surf., curv. sh., shell t.	0	6.10	−6.10	37.21	5.90	6.31
St. surf., plain sh., shell t.	5	24.20	−19.20	368.26	21.04	17.50
Total	186	186.00	0.00			

stamped surface; (2) incised rim, plain rim; (3) incised lip, plain lip; and (4) bowl shape, jar shape; the computation is $2 \times 2 \times 2 \times 2 = 16$ possible combinations. If the groups are (1) smooth surface, stamped surface; (2) rectilinear incising on shoulder, curvilinear incising on shoulder, plain shoulder; and (3) grit tempered, shell tempered; there are $2 \times 3 \times 2 = 12$ possible combinations. These 12 combinations will be used in an example with the following data given: total number of vessels (k), 186; frequency of smooth surface, 121 vessels; of stamped surface, 65 vessels; of rectilinear pattern incised on shoulder, 47 vessels; of curvilinear pattern incised on shoulder, 28 vessels; of plain shoulder, 111 vessels; of grit tempering, 70 vessels; and of shell tempering, 116 vessels. Combination counts and computations are shown in Table 4. The computations are exactly like those described above. For example, p in the first combination is

$$\frac{121}{186} \times \frac{47}{186} \times \frac{70}{186} = .0619.$$

The expected number (E) is $86 \times .0619 = 11.51$, and so on.

Table 4 is to be interpreted simply as a list of χ^2 values, each of which has its corresponding probability for 1 degree of freedom. The individual χ^2 values, computed as d^2/pqk, do not have additive properties in contrast to the contingency table discussed below. Interpretation in terms of pottery types follows the principles already discussed. Three combinations have large positive deviations and large χ^2 values with probabilities well beyond the .001 level. These are stamped surface, plain shoulder, grit temper;

smooth surface, curvilinear incised shoulder, shell temper; and smooth surface, rectilinear incised shoulder, shell temper. The last two combinations differ by only one attribute, and hence are to be lumped in one type. The same is true of the smooth surfaced, plain shouldered, shell tempered combination, which is important numerically but has a very small χ^2 value. Accordingly, there is definitely a smooth surfaced, shell tempered type having three kinds of shoulder treatment in a ratio estimated to be about 26:38:41. This can be confirmed by calculating a χ^2 for a 2×2 table testing the degree of association of smooth surface and shell temper. It will be found that they are very strongly associated, as are grit temper and a stamped surface. It can be inferred that the indifferent χ^2 value (0.48) of the shell tempered, plain shouldered, smoothed surface combination is the result of the fact that plain shoulders are shared with and are rather more characteristic of the stamped surfaced, grit tempered combination. This conclusion is at sharp variance with conventional type analysis, where the shell tempered, plain shouldered, smooth surfaced combination would almost surely be distinguished as a separate type, as would the other two smooth surfaced, shell tempered combinations. The calculations above are intended to be an objective demonstration that the fundamental pattern of the type is the smooth surfaced, shell tempered vessel. Shoulder treatment can be described only in terms of estimated ratios of a group of mutually exclusive attributes.

The stamped surfaced, plain shouldered, grit tempered vessels constitute a second definite type; χ^2 for the combination is very high (98.51) and it can be shown that stamped surface and grit temper are strongly associated. The 14 vessels having smooth surfaces, plain shoulders, and grit temper would not be assigned to either type; they are genuinely intermediate and would be so described. The same reasoning applies to the 5 vessels having stamped surfaces, plain shoulders, and shell tempering. The remaining few vessels share two attributes with one or the other of the types and would be assigned accordingly as somewhat aberrant examples. Combinations of this sort, characterized by negative deviations and crossing over of attributes from two types, offer interesting evidence on the degree of conventionality of the potters. In this connection the combinations with a frequency of 0 are highly informative.

A second sort of table can be computed which offers summary evidence on the total pottery making habits of the group. For this table, the individual contribution of each combination would be computed as d^2/E, which for the first combination of Table 4 is 132.02/11.51. The total of these contributions is a χ^2 value for the 12 combinations taken together, for which a probability can be found in the χ^2 table using 7 degrees of freedom. A verbal explanation of the appropriateness of 7 degrees of freedom is too cumbersome for inclusion here, and a clear graphic presentation of a

$2 \times 3 \times 2$ table is also difficult, but it can be stated that the particular restrictions imposed by the attribute totals used as basic data allow 7 of the 12 cells of the table to be filled in freely within the general limitations of the attribute totals. The remaining five can be determined by subtraction and hence do not contribute to the degrees of freedom. A χ^2 computed in this manner gives an overall measure of the tendency of the potters to group attributes and offers cogent material for comparison with other sites having the same categories. Other sorts of comparisons between sites can be made by using the observed number for each combination from one site as the expected number for the other and calculating the resulting χ^2 or by calculating a χ^2 testing the proposition that both sets of observed values could reasonably be considered random samples from a common population. The latter process is illustrated below in the example dealing with the problem of site homogeneity (Table 6).

All of the examples have been concerned exclusively with attributes which are physical properties of the artifacts. It is well known, however, that artifacts have other kinds of attributes, notably provenience, which can be pertinent evidence for the existence of a type. Thus a site might yield two kinds of vessels which differed only in the presence or absence of a single physical attribute, say a lip flange on one. If nothing but physical properties were considered, both kinds would be included in one pottery type because a difference of one attribute is not sufficient evidence for separation. But if the flanged lip appeared only on vessels found in graves and the plain lip was confined to village debris, it would be obvious that the potters had in mind two types with different functional connotations. Provenience furnishes the second attribute required to differentiate two types. The attributes "found in graves" and "found in village refuse" can be included in a probability calculation in exactly the same way as can any physical property of an artifact.

An example, this time not fictitious, of the application of this technique to a non-typological problem will be presented. The data of Table 5 are

TABLE 5. SURFACE FINISH OF BODY SHERDS BY PROVENIENCE, ARZBERGER SITE, SOUTH DAKOTA

Excavation Unit	Surface Finish		Total
	Grooved Paddle Stamped	Other	
House I	396	1,279	1,675
House II	135	546	681
House III	172	532	704
House IV	178	657	835
Ditch	0	4	4
Unknown	22	79	101
Total	903	3,097	4,000

from the Columbia University excavations at the Arzberger Site, Hughes County, South Dakota, and summarize provenience data of grooved paddle stamped body sherds and other types of surface finish. The problem to be investigated is one of site homogeneity. If the site is homogeneous, one excavation unit should be much like another within the limits of sampling error. With respect to the data given on surface finish of body sherds, a hypothesis of independence can be set up: the proportion of grooved paddle stamped sherds will be a function of the frequency of the totals and will be independent of the locus from which the sample is drawn if the site is truly homogeneous. Chi square is computed by the d^2/pqk method used above, although this is not the most common technique for a $2 \times n$ contingency table such as is given. The value of p is $903/4,000 = .2258$, $q = .7742$, and k is successively the total number of sherds for each sample. The values are shown in Table 6 (a few rounding errors have not been adjusted). The result is good evidence that the hypothesis of independence is correct. Individual values are small, and the total for 4 degrees of freedom (this is a 2×5 contingency table) corresponds to a probability of between .20 and .10, which does not give any very convincing reason to suspect significant differences in the various excavation units. It can be concluded that so far as the evidence at hand is concerned, the site may reasonably be considered the product of a single occupation over a restricted period of time.

An attempt to appraise the usefulness of this approach to typological and related problems should consider the amount of labor necessary in making the computations. In view of the general availability of computing machines, this seems trivial. The writing of the exposition was far more tedious than the computing of the examples. There is a great deal of work required in making, recording, and assembling the observations needed for a thorough study, but this is not the fault of the statistical methods. It is rather an inevitable part of any detailed study. The methods of calculation used here were selected on a basis of clarity of exposition, not economy of

TABLE 6. TEST OF HOMOGENEITY OF EXCAVATION UNITS, ARZBERGER SITE, SOUTH DAKOTA

	O	E	d	d^2	pqk	$\dfrac{d^2}{pqk}$
House I	396	378.21	17.79	316.48	292.81	1.08
House II	135	153.77	18.77	352.31	119.05	2.96
House III	172	158.96	13.04	170.04	123.07	1.38
House IV	178	188.54	10.54	111.09	145.97	0.76
Other[1]	22	23.70	1.70	2.89	18.35	0.16
Total	903	903.00				$\chi^2 = 6.34$

[1] The expected frequency for "Ditch" is less than 6, and accordingly it is incorporated in a new category by adding its value to "Unknown."

labor; those interested in computing routine are referred to the statistical textbooks cited.

With regard to the more serious question of general usefulness, these are the methods generally recommended for handling data of this sort, although no claim is made that the particular procedures illustrated here completely exhaust the resources of statistics. The information derived from them is important in an earnest attempt to discover the cultural significance inherent in archaeological remains, and there is no other way in which such information can be obtained. There is no magic involved, however; the usefulness of the result is entirely dependent upon the wisdom with which attributes are observed and investigated and on the relevance of the context to meaningful archaeological problems. Moreover, the inference to be drawn from a statement of probability is sometimes not altogether clear, but at least the degree of uncertainty is put into objective form.

A source of uncertainty which has been mentioned is the fact that the proportions on which the hypothesis of independence is evaluated are derived from the sample and hence are themselves subject to sampling error. This difficulty is inescapable; we can work only with the samples we have, and the observed proportions are surely the best estimate of the proportions of the population, the properties of which must be inferred from the sample. Nevertheless, the cautious student will interpret his results with one eye on a table of confidence limits. To add to this uncertainty, the dimensions of which can at least be estimated on the basis of statistical theory, there is the purely archaeological problem of the nature of the relationship of the sample to the living culture which produced the artifacts. The whole problem is summarized by the often repeated warning that statistics are never a substitute for thinking. But statistical analysis does present data which are well worth thinking about.

BIBLIOGRAPHY

Brainerd, George W.
    1951   "The Place of Chronological Ordering in Archaeological Analysis." *American Antiquity* 16, no. 4:301–13.
Krieger, Alex D.
    1944   "The Typological Concept." *American Antiquity* 9, no. 4:271–88.
Kroeber, A. L.
    1940   "Statistical Classification." *American Antiquity* 6, no. 1:29–44.
Lehmer, Donald J.
    1951   "Robinson's Coefficient of Agreement — A Critique." *American Antiquity* 17, no. 2:151.

Mather, K.
1947 *Statistical Analysis in Biology.* New York: Interscience Publishers.
Newell, H. Perry, and Alex D. Krieger
1949 "The George C. Davis Site, Cherokee County, Texas." *Memoirs of the Society for American Archaeology,* no. 5.
Robinson, W. S.
1951 "A Method for Chronologically Ordering Archaeological Deposits." *American Antiquity* 16, no. 4:293–301.
Rouse, Irving
1939 "Prehistory in Haiti, a Study in Method." *Yale University Publications in Anthropology,* no. 21.
Snedecor, George W.
1946 *Statistical Methods Applied to Experiments in Agriculture and Biology.* Ames: Iowa State College Press.
Taylor, Walter W.
1948 "A Study of Archeology." *American Anthropological Association Memoirs,* no. 69.

JAMES A. FORD

James Ford's statement about the nature and meaning of the archaeologist's typological categories contrasts strongly with Spaulding's view. Ford's writing belongs to the school of thought that believes "types" are made by the archaeologist, rather than inherent in the data, awaiting discovery. Discussing the complexity of formal variation in material culture, he points out the problems of any classificatory operation. Those complexities, whether or not a typological scheme is based on them, most often are ultimately cultural and behavioral. Although typologies may not reflect specific cultural realities, they may in some way have behavioral significance. That some typologies probably do approximate categories known by the makers of the artifacts is beside the point, however, if we view typology as primarily integrative, i.e., a way in which the archaeologist can relate his data to those observed by other workers. In this use of typology, it is a useful organizational device, but other methods and theories must be called upon when the archaeologist seeks to explain how his materials fit into the culture that produced them.

5   The Type Concept Revisited

Several years ago, Kluckhohn (1939) upbraided anthropologists in general and archaeologists in particular for failure to examine critically the assumptions and concepts which lie at the foundations of their methodologies. Perhaps this well justified censure has prompted the healthy introspection that has developed in the past decade and resulted in valuable papers such as those by Rouse (1939), Krieger (1944), Brew (1946), Taylor (1948), and Ehrich (1950).

Reproduced by permission of Mrs. James A. Ford and the American Anthropological Association from the *American Anthropologist*: Vol. 56, 1954, pp. 42–53. Footnotes are renumbered.

As soon as students of cultural phenomena cease to be satisfied with comparisons of mere qualities of cultural traits and begin also to treat their data quantitatively, it becomes apparent that the basic conceptual tool of cultural research is that of the type. To the present it is the archaeologists who have been most concerned with the formulation and use of cultural types, but this hardly redounds to the credit of this branch of the profession. Archaeologists have been forced into this position by the necessity for reconstructing cultural histories from a very limited range of cultural material. Although the term has been used indiscriminately, in practice the typological concept has been thoughtfully applied almost entirely to ceramics. The principles are the same, however, for all other aspects of culture, and we may expect to see it more widely used as sufficient evidence accumulates to make it possible and necessary.

To utilize the concept of type efficiently, it is very necessary that the cultural student have a clear idea of what a type is, how it is defined, and what purposes it may serve. At present there seems to be some confusion. The debate seems to center around the question of the "reality" of cultural types; a debate which is very similar to that carried on by the biologists for a number of years in regard to the significance of the species concept. To state it clearly, the questions may be put this way: "Do cultural types exist in the phenomena so that they may be discovered by a capable typologist?" This is an important question for the answer not only determines how investigators may proceed in identifying types, but it also determines how types may be employed in solving cultural problems.

Both Rouse (1939) and Krieger (1944) have given excellent discussion of the application of the concept of type but have failed to clarify this debated point. Neither am I entirely satisfied with the statement in Phillips, Ford, and Griffin (1951:61–64). Recently the question has again been brought up as a result of an article by A. C. Spaulding (1953) which describes a method for discovering cultural types by statistical methods. This discussion takes for granted the assumption that types do exist in culture and may be discovered by competent methodologies. This I doubt.

Perhaps it will clarify the problem to say a word about the history of the type concept, for the purposes of classification of archaeological material have undergone a change beginning in this country during the second and third decades of this century. Initially archaeological classifications were made for the purpose of describing collections, and the smallest divisions of the items were frequently called types. These groupings were defined without reference to the temporal and spatial coordinates of culture history. Where chronological information is lacking such descriptive classifications are the only sort that can be made and are extremely useful. A good example of such a classification is S. K. Lothrop's (1926) analysis of pottery collections from Costa Rica and Nicaragua.

The classifying of ceramics into type groupings that are designed to serve as measuring devices for culture history began in the southwestern United States and is now standard practice among American archaeologists. Descriptive systematization is subordinated to the necessity for emphasizing spatial and temporal change in the material. Perhaps it is unfortunate that the word "type" has been retained for this new function because to some it seems to carry a connotation of its earlier descriptive usage. Krieger (1944:272) has stated the current purpose of formulating types in the following words:

> Thus the purpose of a type in archaeology must be to provide an organizational tool which will enable the investigator to group specimens into bodies which have *demonstrable historical meaning in terms of behavior patterns*. Any group which may be labelled a "type" must embrace material which can be shown to consist of individual variations in the execution of a definite constructional idea; likewise, the dividing lines between a series of types must be based upon demonstrable historical factors, not, as is often the case, upon the inclinations of the analyst or the niceties of descriptive orderliness.

Spaulding (1953:305) seems to agree that to be useful each type must have historical significance: "Historical relevance in this view is essentially derived from the typological analysis; a properly established type is the result of sound inferences concerning the customary behavior of the makers of the artifacts and cannot fail to have historical meaning." I certainly am in agreement with both these authors that to be useful, each type must have a limited range in time and space and thus have historical significance.

The discussion that follows will retrace some of the same arguments set forth by Rouse and Krieger but will consider typology from a slightly different angle. Instead of emphasizing the problem from the point of view of archaeological specimens, I shall examine the concept as it would apply to a living culture. Further, to make the task easier and to attempt to clarify basic problems which the typologist must face, this will be fictitious culture history which has not been subjected to the complicating factors that operate in all actual histories. These factors are barriers to diffusion such as uneven population distribution, natural obstacles to communication, political and linguistic boundaries, or boundaries between competing cultural items of different geographic origin. Neither will it be subjected to the forces that speed and retard cultural change — wars, epidemics, alien cultures with high prestige, or advertising by influential innovators. Each culture bearer has been the normal minor innovator that has borne the responsibility for most of the change that has taken place in culture histories.

The fairy tale which follows is the sort of "stripped" description of phenomena which has proved very useful in more mature fields of science, such as physics. Every physical "Law" states that if certain modifying circumstances were nullified such and such would happen. In experience the modifying circumstances are always present and events never conform exactly to the "Law." This, then, is my excuse for introducing the Gamma-gamma people of the Island of Gamma, situated in the curious sea of Zeta.

A CULTURE IS A CLASSIFICATORY DEVICE

With no intention to disparage the work of fellow anthropologists, it may be said that the synchronous view of the ethnologist is the most simple way to consider cultural phenomena. When an ethnologist first arrives among the Gamma-gamma of the Island of Gamma, their culture will impress him as a confused conglomeration of absurdities. The Gamma-gamma will do strange, unreasonable things and on many occasions will appear to be lacking in common horse sense — an impression that has been shared by every tourist who has come into contact with people having a culture different from his own.

As the more-or-less impartial ethnologist becomes better acquainted and begins to acquire something of the point of view of the Gamma-gamma, social actions and cultural objects begin to fall into classes. It will be discovered that these classes are well organized to solve the problems that confront this group of human animals: procuring food, providing shelter and protection from enemies, regulating mating and other social relations, and magical techniques that affect otherwise uncontrollable forces such as diseases and the weather. There are patterned ways of dancing, of constructing a canoe, of clothing and decorating the body, etc. In addition, if the basic premises of Gamma-gamma thought are accepted, many of these cultural categories have a logical, apparently inevitable, relation to one another and these relations are cross-ties that reinforce and stabilize the entire cultural structure. Certain dances are necessary as a preliminary to catching fish; a man cannot marry until he has killed an enemy — human or shark — and has been tattooed; houses are the property of women because they build them; children belong to the mother's family for where is the child who can be certain of his father?

This compartmentalization and order are necessary and will be found in all other cultures. To add to the definitions recently listed by Kroeber and Kluckhohn (1952), it can also be said that culture is an organized system for handling human and social problems. However, different segments of a culture will vary as to the range of variability which is permitted as acceptable behavior. The Gamma-gamma group has very strict rules as to how a man may address his mother-in-law: he must face away to avoid seeing her and preface all remarks with polite formal phrases — to do otherwise would cause great scandal and what else no one knows for it has never been tried. However, there are a number of perfectly good ways to make an adze. Virtually any hard stone will serve as a blade, four varieties of hafting are used, and there are six shapes of handles. In addition, a man takes some pride in carving the handle in an original fashion, as different from those of his fellows as possible. Still, any ethnologist acquainted with the material culture of this region can recognize a twentieth-century Gamma-gamma adze at a glance. Despite the fact that it permits and even appears to encourage variability, this cultural trait is a classificatory device similar to the mother-in-law taboo and has wider but still rigid limits. The variation follows patterns and these people haven't thought of turning the blade around and making a hatchet of the tool.

It is this inherent order in culture of which archaeologists must be aware when they begin the search for types for this is the framework within which the typology must be constructed. This is certainly the order that will be revealed by applying statistical devices to the ceramics of prehistoric dwelling sites as recently advocated by Spaulding (1953). However, this order does not provide the historically significant grouping of traits which the archaeologist must have to measure culture history.

THE ETHNOLOGIST'S VIEW OF A CULTURAL TRAIT

The Gamma-gamma have each aspect of their culture well compartmentalized: pottery food-serving vessels have a limited range of shapes and decorations; water bottles have their appropriate range; and the containers in which the mild alcoholic drink is fermented have their range. However, the actual specimens that are manufactured for these various purposes are by no means identical duplicates such as would be turned out by a machine. Instead, each vessel is recognizably different from every other vessel in its class. As the ethnologist studies the pottery, and other aspects of the culture, he will observe that the variation in actual artifact tends to cluster about a mean, which he can then visualize as the central theme of the type.

The ethnologist cannot rely upon the culture bearers to define this central theme. They may or may not be aware of it, or may have rationalizations in regard to it which are at considerable variance with actual practice, as Dr. Kinsey's study of male sexual practices has demonstrated for our own culture. A statistical average must be arrived at, either by actual counting or by estimating. If desirable, the rationalizations may be considered apart for they are also cultural features and are subject to the same kind of analysis as actions.

The cultural trait, then, is an abstraction made by the ethnologist and derived from the cultural activity. It has a mean and a range of variation.

This range of variation may be visualized as a scatter diagram — a three-dimensional scatter diagram similar to a swarm of bees clustering about the queen might better represent the situation, but there are limitations to the printed page and a two-dimensional diagram will have to serve. In Figure 1, I have attempted to represent the variation in houses that was observed among the Gamma-gamma on the Island of Gamma in 1940. As the diagram shows, the majority of houses were medium-sized rectangular structures about 4 by 6 meters and 5 meters high, placed on low piers above the damp ground, and had gabled roofs, one room, and one door. Variations

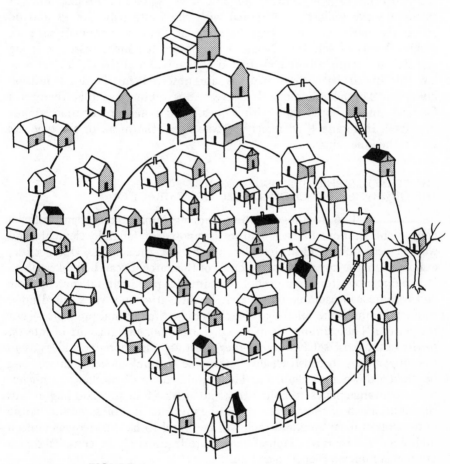

FIGURE 1

A diagram illustrating the frequency mean of a type at one point in time and space. The small houses grouped in the inner circle represent the mean. Variation from this mean is illustrated in four directions — a simplification of the variation that is found about the frequency means of actual types.

from this norm are observed in several directions. Houses illustrated toward the right of the diagram, mostly occupied by older people, were on high stilts, and one is in a tree. They tend to be smaller than the average. Toward the left side of the diagram, the houses are larger and are on very low stilts, or are built on the ground. A few have two rooms. Variation toward the top of the diagram tends toward larger size, and toward the bottom the houses are small, square, and the roofs approach the pyramidal in shape.

This description is an obvious simplification. As the diagram shows, there are all sorts of variations between the four poles described and, in addition, there are other variables which could also serve as poles in this diagram. For example, some buildings are roofed with the white palm fronds and on others the dark gray *kilea* grass is used. Still, these combinations have definite limits of variation. None of the houses has more than one living and sleeping room, all are constructed of bamboo and thatch, and no one has introduced bathrooms such as are observed in the local mission buildings. To the ethnological observer it is quite clear that there is a Gamma-gamma house type with a mean and range of variation as just described. In Figure 1, what may be considered the mean of the type lies within the inner circle.

THE ETHNOGRAPHIC TYPE IS FORMED BY THE OBSERVER AT A CHOSEN LEVEL OF ABSTRACTION

The dwellings of the Gamma-gamma at first glance offer a convenient segment of their culture composed of tangible elements and would seem to be ideal for the purpose of measuring. Upon closer examination, the apparent concreteness of this category can be broken down in two directions, for this aspect of the culture is part of an integrated whole and became a measurable unit merely because attention was focused upon it. First, it must be recalled that these buildings are cultural products — not the culture. These arrangements of wood, bamboo, and grass are of interest to the ethnologist solely because they illustrate the aborigine's ideas as to the proper ways to construct dwellings. The cultural concept "house" can be broken down into elements. There are a range of methods to anchor piers, to arrange plates, to lash rafters, and at least four standard methods of thatching. Each of these elements can be measured in the same way as the entire houses have been and each will be found to have a frequency mean and range of variation. "House" may quite legitimately be considered as a cultural complex rather than as a unit.[1]

On the other hand, the concepts dictating the proper ways to build a house are not isolated in the culture. For one thing, they are intimately

---

[1] This is comparable to what Irving Rouse and others have done when they have utilized ceramic traits as bases for comparison. Rouse termed such elements "modes."

connected with the form of the family. These people are monogamous and married children set themselves up in separate establishments. There is never need for more than one living room, nor is large size necessary. In turn, the single-room small houses tend to reinforce this pattern of family life. The house, then, might legitimately be considered as one element of the 1940 Gamma-gamma family type.

It is evident that "cultural types" are abstracted on different levels of apparent complexity by the observer.[2] One level is no more "real" than another. What the classifier must do is to select a level which will serve the purposes in view. If the objective is a comparison of religions, the student will set up religious types; if it is concerned with priestly paraphernalia, the types will be formed of cultural traits which are mere elements for the preceding purpose. The cultural scientist must be aware of this necessity and not allow chance focalization of interest to provide categories that are accepted as immutable units.

THE ETHNOGRAPHIC TYPE IS ABSTRACTED BY THE OBSERVER AT ONE POINT IN SPACE

So long as the ethnologist stays among the Gamma-gamma on the Island of Gamma, the house type described above appears to form a satisfactory unit. It seems to be a natural division of the culture. However, in the surrounding territory live people with the same general cultural tradition as the inhabitants of Gamma. After the ethnologist finishes his preliminary survey of Gamma and begins to visit their neighbors, he will discover that there is another reason why the house type which he has described for the Gamma-gamma is not a natural cultural unit.

In Figure 2 is illustrated the frequency distributions of dwellings on the islands that lie about the Isle of Gamma. This is a very simplified diagram. On each island the house in the center represents the mean as illustrated in Figure 1; the four buildings arranged about each mean represent the range of variation. It becomes apparent that the Gamma-gamma house type, illustrated in Figure 1, is not the cohesive cultural type which it appeared to be. The variants from the mean have to be assigned to house types typical of the neighboring peoples north, south, east, and west. As a matter of fact, this diagram shows that the polarity of Figure 1 was not correct. All the black-roofed houses are related to a type that centers to the eastward. Very few examples need be left to be classed in the Gamma-gamma type house.

Figure 2 illustrates the point that each locality will have a distinctive mean and a range about that mean which tends toward the means of

[2] "Apparent complexity," for all these levels are infinitely complex and it is the limitation of the observer's ability to perceive differences that set the limits. Ehrich (1950:468–81) gives an able discussion of this matter.

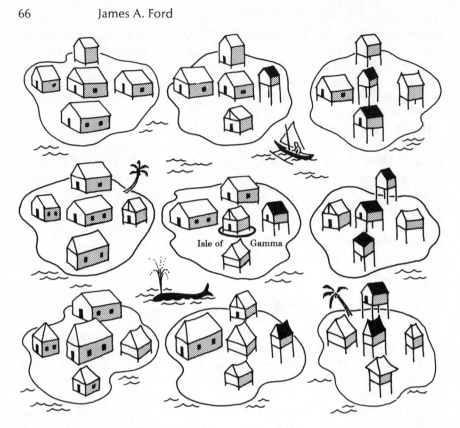

FIGURE 2

Diagram illustrating trait variation in geographical space. The
Island of Gamma occupies the center. The frequency of the
Gamma-gamma house type is in the center of this island and the
less numerous variations are grouped around it. On neighboring
islands mean and range are similarly indicated.

surrounding culture. However, Figure 2 is an unsatisfactory diagram in that
the geographical separation of the islands has created nodes in the pattern
of distribution. If the landscape had been undivided, the geographical
variation would be a more gradual function of space, similar to that shown
in Figure 3. Although this latter figure is designed to demonstrate the
nature of change with time, it will serve equally well for this discussion of
space-change. For this purpose it will be considered that each building
shown represents a local type. Variation about the mean in each locality is
not shown. The building near the upper center of the figure, just above the
hurrying female in a grass skirt, will represent the mean type at
Gamma-gamma. The gradualness of the change in means in all directions
becomes apparent.

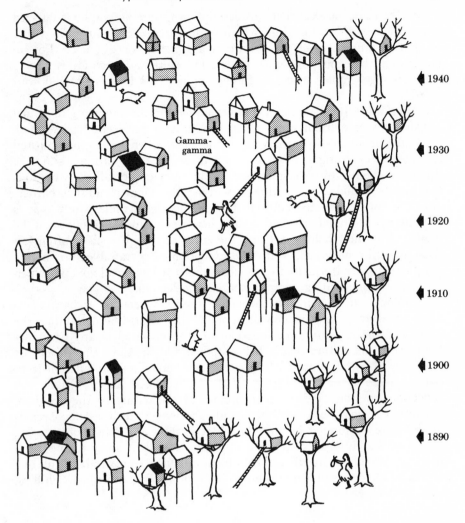

Gamma-gamma

1940

1930

1920

1910

1900

1890

FIGURE 3

This diagram will serve two purposes. First, it will represent geographical distribution of variation and for this purpose each house represents a trait mean. Location of the Gamma-gamma mean is shown and position of the houses represents geographical location. Second, this will serve as a chronological diagram. For this purpose time is the vertical ordinate of the figure and decades are indicated on the right-hand side. Variation is shown horizontally with frequency means in the center of the diagram.

Lest the reader suspect that this description is pure fiction, he is referred to an article by Wilhelm Milke which summarizes several illustrations that qualitative differentiation in culture is a function of distance.[3] For an illustration that the *popularity* of specific cultural categories is also a function of geographic space, see Phillips, *et al.* (1951:Figs. 6–12) and Ford (1952).

Setting aside the fictional Gamma-gamma for the moment, in actual distributions of cultural items change in form is accelerated by natural, political, and linguistic barriers, or at the zones where competing cultural items of different origins meet. For several reasons these barriers cannot be depended upon to furnish limitations to the spatial aspect of the variations that may be included in a cultural type. First, there may be no such barriers operating on the selected cultural item in the region under study — it is certainly not legitimate to assume that there were before their effect can be measured by the typology. Second, the effect of such barriers is often less than might be imagined. With the exception of impassable terrain, the effect of a barrier is usually to produce a more or less broad zone in which the rate of change with geographic space is accelerated.

It follows, then, that the particular locality where an archaeological collection chances to be made will be one of the factors that determines the mean and the range of variation that are demonstrated in any particular tradition in the culture that is being studied. On the same time level, the cord-marked pottery from a village site in northern Illinois is different from that on a site in southern Illinois. If the archaeologist has only these two collections to study and is not conscious of the nature of the problem, separate types may be "established" and considered as realities, unconscious of the favor performed by the chance geographic separation of samples. However, if additional collections, all of the same date, are available to fill in the intervening space, then the problem usually becomes the difficult one of fixing boundaries in a continuum which Phillips has described (Phillips, *et al.* 1951:66–68).

THE TYPE IS ABSTRACTED BY
THE OBSERVER AT A POINT IN TIME

The ethnographic view of a culture resembles a snapshot taken in the middle of a race for it is a static view of a very fluid process. Stretching back in time from each cultural element described and measured by the ethnographer there is a long history which must be traced if we wish to know why the trait assumes its particular form. For cultural traits that

[3] Milke 1949. The word "Quantitative" in Milke's title refers to the numbers of items in the compared cultures which are similar to the reference culture — not to relative popularity.

did not find expression in durable form, this is impossible; it can be done, however, for enough streams of thought to demonstrate the principle beyond reasonable doubt.

As illustration, again consider the mythical Gamma-gamma. In the 1940 static diagram, Figure 1, house structures are shown varying four ways from the mean of the type — already a simplification of the variation as explained above. To give a temporal picture of variation, it will be necessary to simplify still further and show only two directions of variation from the mean. This has been done in Figure 3, which now will be used for the purpose for which it was designed. From bottom to top this diagram represents the passage of time. Decades are indicated on the right-hand side. House form variation is shown horizontally and the frequency mean forms are illustrated down the center of the figure.

The phenomena of cultural drift with the passage of time is so well known to archeologists who have dealt with adequate samples of material culture representing appreciable time spans of culture history that it does not seem necessary to elaborate the illustration. Even in modern Western culture, with all of the acceleration of change that has developed, the well paid innovators who control design of automobiles, architecture, and clothing have learned that while minor innovations will sell new models, the buying public will tolerate no marked jumps in the development of stylistic patterns.

Figure 3 cannot fully illustrate the phenomena of time change among the houses of the Gamma-gamma for close inspection of these structures would show that not only did the gross outline of the structures change, but similar change was taking place in minor details such as systems for placing rafters, lashing, the methods of thatching, etc. The ethnologist's view of this cultural type in 1900 would have had the same order of mean and range as his 1940 view, but the types would have been recognizably different. A glance up and down the time scale demonstrates that there are no natural limits to temporal change in this cultural element which may be utilized as type boundaries.

In actual culture histories there are instances of major innovations which will cause one stream of cultural development to be replaced by another. An example is the addition of the gasoline motor to the buggy to make the horseless carriage. This is a different order of innovation from the numerous small changes that have occurred in the design of wheeled personnel carriers from the invention of the first cart to the rubber-tired buggy, or from Charles Duryea's automobile of 1892 to the 1953 Cadillac. Such major innovations are so rare that the archaeologist cannot depend on them to provide temporal limits for typology. They are of little use for the working out of *details* of culture history.

Abrupt change may also be caused by accidents, or profound shocks to the culture. For example, many Pacific island peoples have taken advantage of abandoned military establishments to change their dwelling types entirely. These are also relatively rare and typology based upon them would measure cultural change in great blocks, not in any detail.

To summarize the preceding discussion, there are four dimensions to the cultural type of which the archeologist must be fully aware if intelligent use is to be made of the concept. These are:

1. The inherent organization that exists in culture at all times and places. The cultural type will, to a greater or lesser degree, be a reflection of the boundaries to one stream of ideas which the cultural bearers considered related. This requires an analysis of the consistency of association of features which may, if necessary, be tested by statistical analysis.

2. The level of abstraction from the tightly interwoven cultural structure at which the typology is to be formulated. For archaeologists this may be at the level of the artifact, or, if desirable, features of artifacts may be utilized as Rouse has done for ceramics in the West Indies.

3. The cultural type will encompass variation due to cultural drift across geographical space. The apparent mean of the type is the function of the locality at which it is defined.

4. The cultural type will include variation that occurred with the passage of time. The apparent mean of the type is a result of the particular point in the history of the cultural stream at which it is selected.

In most archaeological research, chance has determined the form of the typological structure to a great extent. The fact that Site X was in a certain locality and represented a certain short span of culture history has determined the nature of the cultural types defined there. Permitting sampling chance to determine typology operates very well so long as the archaeologist has only a spotty sampling of the culture history. Types are easily separable and they look natural. However, when the gaps are filled in so that the history may be viewed as a continuum through time and across space, the naive typologist is certain to run into serious difficulties. Overlapping of types will render the typology a meaningless conglomeration. The artificiality of the groupings must be taken into consideration and type groupings consciously selected if a workable typology is to be developed.

The type concept as discussed in this paper is the working tool of the cultural student — the device which is used to examine the most minute fragments of culture which the student can grasp. This tool is designed for the reconstruction of culture history in time and space. This is the beginning and not the end of the archaeologists' responsibility. After culture history has been outlined various other methods of classification become possible and may be designed to measure different facets of the culture history. This, I think, is the place for classifications based on function as described by Steward. . . . For example, the functional classification which Gordon Willey (1953) applied to the prehistoric settlement patterns in Virú Valley, Peru, very neatly clarifies the history of this aspect of culture and permits comparison with the growth of communities in other parts of the world. However, the necessary prelude to this study of Willey's was the strictly morphological classification of thousands of potsherds.

REFERENCES CITED

Brew, J. Otis
    1946   "Archaeology of Alkali Ridge, Southeastern Utah." *Papers of the Peabody Museum,* Harvard University, vol. 21.

Ehrich, Robert W.
    1950   "Some Reflections on Archeological Interpretation." *American Anthropologist* 52:468–82.

Ford, James A.
    1952   "Measurements of Some Prehistoric Design Developments in the Southeastern States." *Anthropological Papers, American Museum of Natural History,* vol. 44, pt. 3.

Kluckhohn, Clyde
    1939   "The Place of Theory in Anthropological Studies." *Philosophy of Science* 6, no. 3:328–44.

Krieger, Alex D.
    1944   "The Typological Concept." *American Antiquity* 9, no. 3:271–88.

Kroeber, A. L., and Clyde Kluckhohn
    1952   "Culture, a Critical Review of Concepts and Definitions." *Papers of the Peabody Museum,* Harvard University, vol. 47, no. 1.

Lothrop, S. K.
    1926   *Pottery of Costa Rica and Nicaragua.* Vol. I: *Contributions.* New York: Museum of the American Indian, Heye Foundation.

Milke, Wilhelm
    1949   "The Quantitative Distribution of Cultural Similarities and Their Cartographic Representation." *American Anthropologist* 51:237–52.

Phillips, Philip, James A. Ford, and James B. Griffin
    1951   "Archaeological Survey in the Lower Mississippi Alluvial Valley, 1940-1947." *Papers of the Peabody Museum,* Harvard University, vol. 25.

Rouse, Irving
    1939   "Prehistory in Haiti, a Study in Method." *Yale University Publications in Anthropology,* no. 21.

Spaulding, Albert C.

1953   "Statistical Techniques for the Discovery of Artifact Types." *American Antiquity* 18:305–13.

Taylor, Walter W.

1948   "A Study of Archeology." *American Anthropologist,* vol. 50, no. 3, pt. 2 (*American Anthropological Association Memoirs,* no. 69).

Willey, Gordon R.

1953   "Prehistoric Settlement Patterns in the Virú Valley, Peru. *Bureau of American Ethnology, Bulletin* 155.

JOHN O. BREW

One set of data may be organized in many ways, if artifact types do not accurately and reliably reflect the classes of the artifact makers. John Brew's article is a classic in anthropological literature. It explores taxonomy's uses, as well as its misapplications. Brew emphasizes that type categories should accomplish certain ends, and that depending on one's purpose, one's data may be ordered in any number of ways. Thus there is no "true" typology for an assemblage, but rather many typologies, each of which may be of some use to the archaeologist.

6   The Use and Abuse of Taxonomy

Scepticism is a powerful aid to scientific thought. One must be bold enough to cast doubt both upon the theories of others and upon one's own, and even upon the foundations of one's own science and its method. — *Tallgren.*

Developments during the last ten years make it apparent that the time has come for a general consideration of cultural classification and taxonomic[1] determination, or systematics, as applied to archaeology. In a few recent articles, particularly by Kidder, Roberts, and Kluckhohn, critical discussion of our current Southwestern systematics has appeared. With the

Reprinted, with the editorial changes noted, from "The Use and Abuse of Taxonomy" by John O. Brew in *The Archaeology of Alkali Ridge, Southern Utah*, Papers, Peabody Museum, 21 (1946):44–66, by permission of the author and the Peabody Museum of Archaeology and Ethnology, copyright, 1946, by the President and Fellows of Harvard University. References and bibliography are omitted, and footnotes are renumbered.

[1] *Taxonomy* — "Classification, esp. in relation to its general laws or principles; that department of science, or of a particular science or subject, which consists in or relates to classification": definition in *A New English Dictionary on Historical Principles* (The Oxford English Dictionary), Sir James A. H. Murray, ed., Oxford, 1919. Some confusion has arisen in archaeological discussions from the practice, common east of the Rockies, of restricting the term "taxonomy" exclusively to phylogenetic or pseudo-phylogenetic classifications. It is herein applied in its basic meaning to all classifications. By those who use the restricted definition the title of this chapter should be read as "The Use and Abuse of Classification."

exception of the last named, this, however, has been very limited, largely because included in short papers or in introductions to monographs. A few writers have referred to difficulties in the application of systematic methods but have tacitly or expressly passed them off as unworthy of discussion longer than a few sentences or paragraphs. With this I do not agree. The present condition of archaeological research in the Southwestern field leads me to believe that a thorough and careful examination into the mechanical processes of classification, and into the logical assumptions behind it, is not only desirable but necessary.

When the reader has finished this section, I hope that I shall not be considered presumptuous in stating that a perusal of much of the recent archaeological literature of the Southwest leads me to believe that many archaeologists do not fully understand the meaning, applications, and technique of systematic analysis. I hasten to add that I do not claim a complete grasp of it myself, but I firmly believe that it does not and cannot do some of the things archaeologists seem to expect of it.

This is a statement which probably needs defense at the outset. That defense is simple and I believe forceful enough to justify the rather lengthy consideration which follows. It is, merely, that in biology, from which most of our systems are borrowed or adapted, the problems of taxonomic method are by no means settled, and much of current biological literature is occupied with attempts to solve those problems and to determine just what such techniques will and will not do in that branch of science.

Professionally, we are dealers in conceptual schemes, and we must keep before us at all times the realization that we are dealing with them. When a student says "Pueblo II," or "Mogollon," or "Vahki Phase," and fits cultural traits into them, he talks in terms of arbitrary concepts, and not of "objective realities."

These concepts we must have. We cannot get away from them because they are inherent in our processes of thought. They are the terms in which we think. In other words — and here I address myself to those among us who express distrust or disapproval of what they call "theory" as opposed to "fact" — we cannot get away from theory. We all use "theory," whether we admit it or not, *in all we do, in all our thinking.* Consequently, if we are not to waste our own time and that of others, we must analyze and attempt to understand it.

It is unfortunately the case, recently ably demonstrated, that while archaeologists are becoming more and more proficient in the gathering and presentation of "facts" they, for the most part, do not seem to have much understanding of the concepts which of necessity must be built up with those facts to give them significance.

This is not an attack on taxonomic methods as such. It is not an attack upon classificatory analysis of specimens or of culture complexes. It is a fervent plea for a better understanding of these methods and for scientific use of them.

The objections which I shall raise to parts of our current procedure are of such a nature that when clearly presented, they are usually admitted by most workers in the field. I contend, however, that the publications show that many archaeologists who in oral discussions admit the validity of these objections and recognize the limitations of their techniques do not carry those realizations into their actual work when they are deep in the analysis of their material.

In this connection I shall quote from a recent article on theory in anthropology, which in America includes archaeology.

> In any case the alternative is not, I think, between theory and no theory or a minimum of theory, but between adequate and inadequate theories, and, even more important, between theories, the postulates and propositions of which are conscious and which hence lend themselves to systematic criticism, and theories, the premises of which have not been examined even by their formulators. For I am afraid that many of our anthropologists who are most distrustful of "theory" are like Molière's character who spoke prose without knowing it, for a complex theoretical viewpoint is usually implicit in some of the most apparently innocent "statements of fact."

What I suggest, then, is a critical examination of our own thinking, including those archaeological concepts which at any given time we consider as "basic" or "established." Another quotation from the author cited above is appropriate here. "While in certain aspects of scientific investigation it is absolutely necessary we should take certain things for granted, it is equally necessary that at other times we should consider our subject, coming as close as we can to taking nothing for granted." The first part of this sentence is of supreme importance to our work. In building up a "theory," an "argument," and "historical reconstruction," we must make assumptions, must take certain things for granted. But we must also realize that we are doing so. We must know what we are assuming. And furthermore, it is our professional obligation to state those assumptions so that our readers may understand them, too. Otherwise we may mislead the reader. We shall be open to misconception, and, through this misconception, our work may be submitted to criticisms which would be unjustified were our assumptions clearly stated.

The quotation continues: "We must be eternally on guard against the insidious crystallization of dogma (unrealized as such) at the expense of that freshness of outlook which is surely a prerequisite to real scientific discovery." To maintain such a guard is extremely difficult, particularly for those of us who are also teachers. As teachers we must present our subject to untrained minds and in such a way that the enthusiasm of the beginner is not stifled and in such a way that he does not give up in disgust with the observation, "These archaeologists apparently do not know anything."

This is certainly not easy. During my first year in college, in a course designed to blast preconceived opinions and provide an introduction to science and scientific procedure, I was told to take nothing for granted. Yet a large part of my subsequent instruction, as an undergraduate, was nothing more than a piling up of dogma. That most of this dogma was arbitrary in nature was very rarely so much as intimated. In a large measure this report is an attempt to alleviate that situation in a way which may prove useful.

The primary problem has already been stated. There are certain very definite things which a student can accomplish by means of taxonomic studies and there are other things which cannot be done by such means. It is the latter group which is perhaps of most importance to us in 1945, for the failure to realize the limitations has created a large number of totally unnecessary problems in Southwestern archaeology which will take years to straighten out, thus occupying the energies of students who might otherwise have been more gainfully employed. I refer here, among other things, to the waste of time, energy, and space in publications spent in disputes as to the placing of a given trait in "Pueblo I" or "Pueblo II," the "identification" of a potsherd as belonging to one type or another, and, perhaps most important of all, the attempts to place cultural material, that is to say, specimens, in a single taxonomic system which will describe them completely and solve the problems of relationship in *one* operation. In order to show these limitations, it will be necessary to examine the very foundations of classificatory analysis.

The main points which this examination will attempt to establish are easily stated and had best be mentioned briefly here at the outset of the dissertation. Perhaps the basic one is the most readily admitted and the most thoroughly ignored of all; namely, that classificatory systems are merely tools, tools of analysis, manufactured and employed by students, just as shovels, trowels, and whisk brooms are tools of excavation. Upon this concept a number of others depend:

1. The system is "made" by the student, the diagnostic criteria are defined by him, and objects or cultures are placed in a particular class or type according to his designation: therefore:

2. Cultures are not "discovered," "types" are not "found." The student does not "recognize" a type, he *makes* it and *puts* the object in it. Objects do not "belong" or "fall into" types, they are *placed* in types by the student. Developing from this it can be stated that:

3. No typological system is actually inherent in the material. Systematic classifications are simplifications of and generalizations of the natural situation. The classes are entities and realities only in the minds of students, they have no other existence. Consequently:

4. There is no such thing as *the type* to which an object "belongs." The full implication of this is that:

5. There is no naturally or divinely created classificatory system in which the objects all have a place, so to speak, ex officio. This is of particular importance when considering attempts to design, let us say, a single taxonomic system into which all pottery may be placed, irrespective of the particular characters such as form, design, surface treatment, or paste composition being studied. Attempts to set up and use such a system introduce a series of insuperable difficulties which can best be stated by an example: given one hundred potsherds for analysis from a stratigraphic level in a site. These may be grouped according to determinations of paste composition and placed thereby in four classes of forty, thirty, twenty, and ten individuals, respectively. Then let us jumble them together again and classify them by certain criteria of surface finish, again for shape, again for design or any other series of characteristics. Do they "fall into" the same groups? Those who have handled such specimens can answer this immediately. Usually they do not! This brings our first positive conclusion as to the proper use of classification, namely:

6. A group of objects to be studied must be classified in a number of different ways depending upon the information the student wishes to obtain, and generally the classes will not coincide. The negative corollary to this is:

7. A student whose purpose is to find out all he can about his material restricts his findings to but a small amount of the possibilities when he uses only one classification.

Thus at the end of the first avenue of the subject explored we come to the conclusion that we advocate not less but *more* classification of a given series of objects, specifically more than one classification. The classifications, however, are personal to the student and his problem and are conditioned by the nature of the information he seeks to extract from his series.

The second avenue of thought to be followed throughout this discussion is perhaps not so clear-cut and straight. It has to do with a serious misconception, again denied as such, but continually used in practice. This is that relationships exist between cultural objects and between culture complexes which are either the same as or similar to the genetic relationships between living organisms. That this concept exists in the minds of many archaeologists is again apparent in their publications. It can be demonstrated, I believe, that it is fostered by the way in which systematics has been applied or, more specifically, by the misuse of systematics arising from a regrettable disregard of the fact that we are dealing with inanimate objects. This arises naturally because, as already stated:

8. Our systematics has been borrowed and adapted from biology. In this connection it will subsequently be shown that:

9. The authors of most of the outstanding classificatory systems in the Southwest were at one time biologists or received their early scientific training in a biological discipline. This will not be presented as a criticism of their attempts to apply their training to the new subject but, rather, as evidence providing a logical explanation of a source of this particular difficulty. Because of this:

10. Cultural material has been thought of and discussed in terms of kinds of relationships impossible in the nature of the material; and because of this:

11. There has been a tendency to ignore or subordinate certain relationships and phenomena which do exist. As J. H. Steward says in a recent review of Colton's adaptation of the Gila Pueblo Phase System:

> It is apparent from the cultural relationships shown in this scheme that strict adherence to a method drawn from biology inevitably fails to take into account the distinctively cultural and unbiological fact of blends . . . between essentially unlike types. . . . The inherent inability of this method to take cognizance of cultural blends is not surmounted in its application to archaeological data; it is ignored. . . . Those of us who have ventured to question taxonomic methods in archaeology are suspected of having disorderly minds. Obviously, our objection is not to order but to the supposition that classification is synonymous with order. We do not see the advantage of simplification, even for the general student and layman, when the method employed inevitably distorts true cultural relationships. If the purpose is to represent the development, interaction, and blending of diverse cultural streams, surely one can find a method that does not require the wholly unsuitable categories of biology.

It will also be shown that:

12. Serious doubt now exists that actual genetic relationships in biology are always properly presented in the taxonomic systems of that science. Consequently, it is absurd to expect that similar systems will show such relationships between objects which do not receive their characteristics through the transfer of genes; in other words, where actually such relationships do not exist.

Throughout the discussion the arbitrary nature of classificatory schemes will be emphasized and, I hope, established beyond doubt. The uses to which they may profitably be put will be presented along with considerations of their limitations. General problems of taxonomic nomenclature will be explored along with the difficulties encountered in establishing diagnostic criteria to distinguish groups and phases. And the dangers will be pointed out, in the so-called ideal or comprehensive schemes, of overemphasizing single criteria or selected groups of criteria which, although of value in studying those particular characters, cannot fail to give a warped picture of the whole.

In support of the various points to be made examples will be given and opinions will be quoted. The examples will, insofar as possible, be taken from archaeology; the opinions must perforce be quoted largely from the literature of biology because archaeologists, for the most part, have not turned their critical faculties in this direction.

I have mentioned before the necessity of examining the logical foundations of our work. Such examination should go on *all the time*, if we wish to be useful and to have our works withstand the increasingly critical judgments being brought to bear upon them, just as we continually examine the edge of a knife blade, the point of a drawing pen, or the effective member of any tool which we use. Because of developments in experimental physics and experimental biology, certain men engaged in these sciences have recently devoted themselves to epistemological studies, particularly to the manner in which scientists obtain their knowledge of the external world. A biologist, J. S. L. Gilmour, has recently published a paper which clearly shows the trend of these studies. I shall present the pertinent statements he makes about the nature of classificatory schemes, paraphrasing them to apply to our particular archaeological problems.

Citing H. Dingle, Gilmour believes there is a primary duality in our processes of obtaining knowledge. This consists of (1) a series of sense-impressions received through experience; (2) the mental processes which give order and coherence to these sense-impressions. To quote directly from Gilmour:

> This account of the thought-process gives an entirely different picture of the acquisition of knowledge from that usually accepted by working scientists. In both there is a duality. The commonly accepted picture is that of mind, on the one hand, and the objects of the external world, on the other, the business of science being to bring to the knowledge of mind an ever greater number of these objects. Mind in this picture plays no active part in *creating* the objects of the external world, but merely records what already exists. In Dingle's picture, however, the duality is not one between a passive, receptive mind and a pre-existing external world, but between an active, subjective, reasoning agent, and the countless sense-data of experience out of which reason builds that logically coherent pattern which we

call the external world. The "objects" of this "external world," therefore, consist of two distinct elements, one derived from sense-experience, the other supplied by the activity of the reasoning agent.

For example, a pot consists partly of a number of experienced sense-data such as color, shape, paste composition, and other qualities and partly of the concept *pot* which the mind of man has constructed to group these data together.

According to this, the process of classification is outlined by Gilmour as follows. The investigator experiences a large number of sense-data which he groups in classes, each defined in terms of certain specific data. Thus a class called "bowls" may be made for sense-data exhibiting a certain range of shape. Any series of data can be grouped in a number of different ways, depending on the purpose of the investigation. Thus the range of data placed under the class "pottery vessel" can be subdivided into colors, surface treatments, shapes, uses, and so on. The important thing here is that the making of these groups is an activity of reason and can and should be manipulated at will to serve the purpose of the student.

Concluding this argument Gilmour says: "Classification, then, has always a pragmatic element as well as an empirical and a rational one. Broadly speaking, the purpose of all classification is to enable the classifier to make inductive generalizations concerning the sense-data he is classifying."

This starts us fairly upon a consideration of the purposes of classification. It also casts grave doubts upon the possibility of obtaining that ideal of archaeological systematists, the "objective" classification of pottery or the "objective" classification of cultures.

The desire for "objectivity" in classification arises, I think, from the belief that the manufactured groups are realistic entities and the lack of realization that they are completely artificial. Thus the desire is essentially a paradox. Implicit in it is a faith, based upon the species concept of biology, in the existence of a "true" or "correct" classification for all objects, cultures, etc., which completely ignores the fact that they are all part of a continuous stream of cultural events.

It will be well here to examine the species concept in the context in which it was developed. Doubts as to the validity of species as real entities are not new, but difficulties encountered by many experimental biologists and physiologists in applying the concept, particularly to the smaller organisms, have recently brought them to the fore. Early expressions of the arbitrary nature of species are to be found in Darwin's writings. He regarded the term as one arbitrarily given and the furthest he ever went in his use of the concept was to regard species as "tolerably well-defined objects."

Later-day biologists have varied from complete denial of the concept to complete acceptance of it as representative of objective reality. E. Rabaud

denies its usefulness and declares that the individual is of greater consequence than species. At the opposite extreme Bateson believes that "specificity" is a universal attribute of organized life. Most zoologists and botanists
now hold beliefs somewhere between these two. G. C. Robson in his book
on the species problem says, "while many of the groups called 'species' by
the systematist are readily distinguishable one from another, there is no
universal criterion by which species as opposed to other systematic units
may be recognized." He believes the concept useful, though, for "while
there is no essential and absolute 'specificity' which can be attributed to
certain assemblages of individuals, but not to others, the groups which the
systematist treats as species have a tolerable degree of homogeneity. The
systematic status of such groups is generally recognized as a *purely conventional matter.*"

One of the common definitions of species, still held by many zoologists,
is that a species is made up of individuals capable of fertile union. This
definition has been repeatedly shown to be impractical and, because of the
difficulties of obtaining an acceptable precise definition, biologists are
gradually adopting a generalized one very similar to that by which the more
cautious archaeologists define their taxonomic categories; namely that a
species, as a useful classificatory tool, is a group of individuals resembling
each other more than they resemble the individuals of other groups.

The implications of this are important. The resemblances upon which
the groupings are made must be observed by the classifier. The relative
weight assigned to different characteristics of the individual vary and the
particular interests of students vary as well. This view of the species problem
does not arise from the study of such distinctive groups as the kangaroo and
giraffe but from small organisms such as insects of which approximately
10,000 new species are currently being described every year; a situation
somewhat comparable to that developing in the ceramic systematics of the
Southwest.

Thus, from a survey of biological literature, it seems that the various
taxonomic categories of that science, even the fundamental one of species,
are arbitrary. The diagnostic characteristics of each group are selected by
the student, the groups are arbitrarily defined by the student, and the
student puts the individual in the group.

Similar conclusions have been reached by certain archaeologists in the
Southwest and in other fields. Kidder in the introduction to the second
volume of "The Pottery of Pecos" says,

> The division of the Glaze ware of Pecos into six chronologically
> sequent types is a very convenient and, superficially, satisfactory
> arrangement. For some time I was very proud of it, so much so,
> in fact, that I came to think and to write about the types as if
> they were definite and describable entities. They are, of course,

nothing of the sort, being merely useful cross-sections of a constantly changing cultural trait. Most types, in reality, grew one from the other by stages well-nigh imperceptible. My grouping therefore amounts to a selection of six recognizable nodes of individuality; and a forcing into association with the most strongly marked or "peak" material of many actually older and younger transitional specimens.

Irving Rouse in his study of the prehistory of Haiti defines "types" as artificial concepts and devotes a large part of his paper to definition of his conceptual scheme and discussion of its utility and significance.

Likewise, Colton, though frankly adopting a scheme based upon biological taxonomy, says: "It must be stressed, however, that this is not a 'natural' classification but is purely artificial. The very nature of the material presupposes this."

It seems, therefore, that we can conclude that the classes in these systems are artificial; that they are part of our own devices for interpreting our observations; and that it is incorrect to believe that objects or cultures "fall into" a given place in a system or that we are able to "discover" an artifact type or a culture phase.

If this can be admitted, and I believe it must be, then we can view such systems in a different light. The most important result of this conclusion is that, if the systems do not exist in objective reality, that is to say, naturally, we are under no historical or scientific compulsion to "discover" or "record" them. Thus the question becomes one of method, and we can concern ourselves entirely with evaluation of the usefulness of the various systems; a study of what they do for us, how they do it, whether a given system "does more harm than good," that is, whether it introduces more problems than it solves, etc. In this regard, probably the most important part of the taxonomic technique is the way in which the various classes are defined, the criteria or diagnostics which are set up. These will be discussed at the end of the section when the specific application of this study to Southwestern archaeology will be made.

Before going on to a consideration of the genetic implications of current archaeological taxonomy, there is one more point which seems to merit further discussion. The fifth item in the list at the beginning of this section states that there is no ideal system of classification in which all objects or groups of objects have a place because of their natural characteristics. This is a very important consideration, for in recent years much time and energy has been spent in attempting to "find" or devise such schemes and in forcing objects into them. The attempts cover a great range of material, from fragments of artifacts, that is, potsherds, to large assemblages of traits called by various names such as "cultures," "periods," "phases," "aspects," etc.

Again I must emphasize that I do not criticize the manufacture of such schemes and their use in archaeological analysis and description. However, must we not condemn the practice of considering them as realities and above all of setting up one of many possible systems as the "true" classification of certain objects or of cultures?

This question, too, has been raised in biology; namely, is there a "final ideal classification towards which taxonomists are consciously or unconsciously striving"? In answer to this Gilmour writes:

> A natural classification is that grouping which endeavors to utilize *all* the attributes of the individuals under consideration, and is hence useful for a very wide range of purposes. . . . In so far as it is theoretically possible to envisage a classification on these lines, which does in fact embody all the attributes of the individuals being classified, it can be said that one final and ideal classification of living things is a goal to be aimed at. In practice, however, this aim would never be attained, owing both to the limitations of our knowledge and to the differences of opinion between taxonomists.

I wish particularly to draw attention to the final statement. If this is true of biologists who, after all, have in their hands the complete organism, how much more surely must it be true of archaeologists who deal, for the most part, only with fragments of objects or cultures. Even when the experimental biologist attempts to recreate natural situations of interaction between organisms he often feels that the behavior of his individuals is conditioned by the specializing factors of his laboratory set-up. With such exceptions as experimentation with pottery firing and with the reproduction of stone implements, even these controls are denied anthropologists. Our discipline is for the most part nonexperimental.

With regard to "final-ideal-complete-classifications" we must step for a few moments into what might well be considered the realm of absurdity. I do not think it is, for the two questions I am about to pose are asked time and again in oral discussions and are really of great importance. They are: (1) If we attain a classification in which "*all* the attributes of the individuals under consideration" are utilized, shall we not end up, provided our information be complete, with a situation wherein each individual constitutes a class by itself? and (2) If we arrive at a complete classification of all living things, of all pottery "types," of all "cultures" in the world, then what have we, and what do we do with it?

The first question is a hard one to answer. I believe we shall err if we agree to dismiss it as absurd, because so many systematists in different fields have published statements which seem to mean just that, or else they mean nothing. The logical conclusion of their published aims can result only in a reduction to the individual object in the case of artifacts and to the individual person in the case of "cultures."[2] Obviously there is something wrong here and we need better definition. The usual answer to this criticism is in terms of "significant criteria." In studying the differences between individuals which differences are significant and which differences insignificant in terms of taxonomy? No general answer seems possible. Here again is a manifestation of the arbitrary nature of these systems. We must agree which differences are significant, and the significance will again vary with the student and with the nature of his immediate problem. Bateson in his "Problems of Genetics" says: "They will serve Science best by giving names freely and by describing everything to which their successors may possibly want to refer, and generally by subdividing their material into as many species as they can induce any responsible journal to publish." This is an excellent and horrible example of the kind of thinking which brings discredit upon all scientific work and workers. If we follow Bateson we must describe our material according to the needs and interests of posterity, which we cannot possibly know, and in the final analysis the arbiters of the number of our groups, of the size of our classifications, are our publishers! What folly!

The only answer I can reach for the first question is a tentative one and not an answer, really, at all, but a negation of the whole proposition. At present, it seems to me that the "ideal-complete-classification" is an impractical concept because of the impossibility of arriving at standardized criteria which can meet the needs of actual study of the material with a view to solving particular problems. As has been said above and will be said many times below, the diagnostics of classificatory groups are too closely associated with the immediate problem in hand to permit a general classification which can be generally applied to a heterogeneous mass of problems. Lothrop in a recent critique of taxonomy says: "archaeological remains are human products, censored by destructive contact with the soil, and they therefore vary widely in quality and quantity. Furthermore archaeologists are individuals differing in character, training, ability and special interests. How then can there be any one . . . method which outranks all others?"

This verges upon the second question: if such an "ideal-complete-classification" can be worked out, what shall we have and how shall we use it? Some of my doubts as to its usefulness are already expressed. First let us consider what it is. By this ideal system we would have all of the pottery of the world, or the cultures of the world, arranged according to a single descriptive classification according to criteria arbitrarily agreed upon. This

2 The appropriateness of the question is attested by the following quotation from a recent botanical report. "In reading the original descriptions of Crataegus species one is impressed by the similarity of many of them in all but a few unimportant details. Some of the descriptions were so accurate that it would be difficult to find any tree or specimen except the type (specimen) that would fit them in every detail."

would be a nice orderly thing and to some workers, apparently, a sufficient end in itself. But what would it show? From it would appear certain real or fortuitous relationships, and I fear in most cases it would be impossible to tell which, based upon *the agreed criteria*. To establish other relationships and to check those suggested by the system itself it would still be necessary to reanalyze and reclassify the material according to other criteria. This would of necessity result in regrouping and in the production of various more limited classifications which would not conform to the basic one.

The famous McKern System (the Midwestern Taxonomic System) of culture classification in use in the eastern United States is, insofar as I am able to understand it, one of these "ideal-complete-classifications." There are those who claim that it has produced considerable order in the eastern field. On the other hand, it has also produced a tremendous amount of dispute, even acrimonious dispute, and confusion.

The most important single objection which has been raised against the McKern System is that its usefulness is greatly restricted or nullified by the ignoring of a time factor. Ford, with regard to his own system of classifying lower Mississippi cultures, says: "it is impossible to see, without chronology, how we can ever hope to rediscover the cultural history of the Indians of the Southeast."

Rouse, who used the McKern System in his earlier work in the West Indies and then devised one of his own to supplement it, says: "it will be seen, persistence is the logical counterpart to diffusion. One who traces the distribution of a type or mode only in space, thereby studying diffusion but ignoring persistence, reconstructs only part of the culture history." And vice versa, "A person must study both the diffusion and the persistence of culture traits if he desires to make a balanced historical reconstruction." He does not consider the McKern System to be useless but merely insufficient for his purposes. He says:

> The McKern technique made it possible to formulate static units of culture . . . and to point out the descriptive relationships between these units. The present technique (Rouse's system), on the other hand, has been used to reconstruct the history of certain individual traits of each cultural unit, and thereby to indicate how the traits changed from unit to unit. The dynamic nature of the present techniques seems to have been a good contrast to the static character of the McKern classification.

The same point is brought out by Colton in his "Prehistoric Culture Units and Their Relationships in Northern Arizona." He presents therein a system for classifying Southwestern cultures which is a combination of the Gladwin System and the McKern System. Colton writes:

> Although the various subdivisions of the Gladwin and McKern
> Systems seem superficially to be parallel, they really represent
> different dimensions of the same principle. The McKern System
> includes a horizontal or area dimension and omits time, while
> Gladwin includes area and a vertical or "time" dimension as
> well. The two systems, therefore, are not parallel but one may
> supplement the other.... Since archaeology is history and
> history involves the idea of chronology, the most satisfactory
> system of classifying phases or foci is one that also involves time.

I cite these objections not as specific criticisms of the McKern System but as objections to the concept of an "ideal-complete-classification" for which I have taken the McKern System as an example. I realize that I have come far from exhausting the subject, but I merely wish to emphasize at this point that such systems do not serve the purpose for which they seem to be designed but must be modified or supplemented to meet any particular problem. And when the modification is, itself, set up as an "ideal-complete-system" it, too, suffers from similar or other difficulties. For example, the current merger of the Gladwin and McKern Systems by Colton introduces the Gladwin "family-tree" concept which had been carefully and consciously avoided by McKern.

All of the above, I believe, serves to illustrate my point, which is that the McKern Classification, designed as a worldwide "single-ideal-complete" cultural classification is impractical and useless as such. To be used at all, it must be adapted to specific problems by each worker (other examples of adaptation of the McKern System can be found in the archaeological literature of the eastern United States), and these adaptations when made, constitute merely one of the classifications the particular student uses in the study of his material.

Consequently, I feel that we must express grave doubt that the "ideal-complete-classification," though perhaps superficially attractive, serves a useful end. If, however, it is used, as the McKern System is actually beginning to be used by the most advanced students, not as a "single-ideal-complete" classification but as merely one of a number of tools for the orderly presentation of a mass of data, then, indeed, it may be of value.

Since the question of the "family-tree" concept has arisen in connection with the Colton-Gladwin System above, it may perhaps be advisable now to get on with the second group of basis assumptions before attempting to analyze further the present systems.

The second major misconception I wish to discuss is that relationships exist between cultural objects and between culture complexes which are either the same as or similar to the genetic relationships between living organisms. Because of that belief, it has been thought, by some, that these relationships will "fall into" or can be described by taxonomic systems modeled after those of biological systematics.

In questioning the validity of this assumption I shall show:

1. That grave doubt has been cast *by biologists* upon the assumption that current biological taxonomic systems describe phylogenetic relationships.

2. That similar doubt has been raised by students in specialized fields closely allied to biology, such as paleontology, conchology, and oology.

3. That it is impossible for such systems to show phylogenetic relationships between inanimate objects since (a) they apparently do not show them between living objects, and (b) because phylogenetic relationships do not exist between inanimate objects.

The statement that biological systematics does not actually record and describe evolutionary relationships will occasion more surprise to many archaeologists than it will to biologists. Among the latter it has long been a question for discussion. The more critical among them even go so far as to doubt whether the real significance of the term "phylogenetic relationship" is yet fully understood, and this is something to be kept in mind while we are considering the firmness of the ground upon which our archaeological systematics is based.

The purpose of this section, however, is not to argue the theory of evolution nor to discuss biological relationships. I shall merely present statements of current workers in biology which will be sufficient for my point and refer to their publications for the benefit of those readers who wish to go deeper into the matter.

In so far as this question affects biological taxonomy, it arises through the transfer by the student of the inheritance mechanisms of the individual to the taxonomic groups. In essence, it is a concept of group rather than of lineage phylogeny. According to Gilmour this arose from a false analogy between taxonomic groups and individuals and was based upon the objective existence which both were supposed to possess. From this analogy came the belief that there is a relationship between groups analogous to the genealogical relationship between individuals. Gilmour concludes his argument with the statement, "It is only when taxonomic groups are seen to be collections of individuals classed together because of the possession of certain attributes in common that the falseness of the . . . analogy becomes clear."

This does not imply that members of a group are not physically related, since in most cases biological groups are composed of closely related lineages. The point made by Gilmour is that this is not always so and that it is not implicit in the system. Therefore he believes that phylogeny does not form the basis for the "single, ideal natural classification" but that it is actually one of the many "classifications constructed for the purpose of special investigations."

This position, as intimated above, is not new. In 1877, T. H. Huxley wrote, "The things classified are arranged according to the totality of their morphological resemblances, and the features which are taken as the marks of groups are those which have been ascertained by observation to be the indications of many likenesses or unlikenesses." He definitely denied any attempt, on his own part, to base classification on phylogeny.

I shall cite only one other statement on the side of general biology. Those who wish to explore it further will find numerous bibliographic references in the papers already cited. Discussing the problem of the "origins of species" Lancelot Hogben says,

> We name assemblages as such for two reasons. One is disconti-
> nuity of pattern among living creatures. The other is that it is
> necessary to have a convenient card index of distinguishable
> types. The procedure we adopt in making it has little to do with
> *experimental inquiry* into the nature of hereditable variations;
> and there is no necessary reason for expecting a close connexion
> between categories of resemblance based on the architecture of
> the germ-cells and categories of resemblance appropriate to the
> practice of taxonomy.

Later in his paper Hogben gives an example which is not only amusing but foreshadows some of the factors we must consider when taxonomy is applied to archaeology.

> Several local "species" of the dog family, like races of mankind,
> are interfertile products of geographical specialization. In so far
> as extrinsic barriers separate them into distinct assemblages, they
> may be given taxonomic rank as species, and they remain so as
> long as the extrinsic barriers are there. So the taxonomic
> distinction is relative to a certain level of transport industry. In
> so far as this is so, the origin of dog species is less a problem of
> biology than a problem of economic history. The sterility of
> discussing the polyphyletic origin of man is analogous, and also
> illustrates how difficult it is to think clearly about matters which
> involve social preferences.

At this point I merely wish to point out the possibly even greater role played by preference in the selection of a design to be painted on a pot. And it has a looser rein, for the preference in the latter case must needs apply to only one of the parties to the transaction.

Before going on I believe it will be useful to quote a few recent definitions of "species" published by biologists, as follows:

A community or number of related communities, whose distinctive morphological characters are in the opinion of a competent systematist sufficiently definite to entitle it, or them, to a specific name.

A practical and convenient unit by which fossils are distinguished.

A species is a group of individuals which, in the sum total of their attributes, resemble each other to a degree usually accepted as specific, the exact degree being ultimately determined by the more or less arbitrary judgement of taxonomists.

All of these point one way, all of them exclude phylogeny, and all of them definitely state that the determining factor is the opinion of the classifier.

Many more citations could be made to the same end, but I believe these are sufficient to establish our right to question the assumption that biological taxonomic systems represent phylogenetic relationships.

There is one other biological concept, widely used by anthropologists and archaeologists which we *must discard,* even if we persist, as I hope we shall not, in using a system based on biology. This is the simple "family-tree" concept by which the development of a graduated series of classificatory groups is represented by a diagram in the form of a tree, with parent stem, major forks, major and minor branches, etc. The more critical biologists believe a diagram which is an interlocking network to be a better indicator of genetic relationships, and perhaps a three-dimensional diagram of this kind is an even closer approximation than a two-dimensional one.

So much, for the present, for general biology. There are a number of very interesting scientific disciplines which are part way between pure biology and archaeology, in terms of the problem we are discussing. These are sciences which deal with certain characteristics of organisms without dealing directly with the organism in its entirety. I shall mention three of these in the natural sciences and one striking development in a field closely bound up with anthropology and history. First, paleontology, where the scientist has only the fossil bones of the organism; second, conchology, where the student deals with the shell of the organism; third, oology, where the investigator studies the eggs of birds, especially their shape and color, in other words the visual, external characteristics of the temporary housing of the organism in its embryological stage; and fourth, a specialized study which has been made of medieval human armor.

In all of these cases I shall point out that, although classifications have been made and presented as representing evolutionary development, they do not necessarily describe or even parallel the phylogeny of the actual organisms.

Taxonomic troubles are not new in paleontology. In 1927 F. A. Bather presented doubts that phylogeny is a sound basis for paleontological classification. In 1931 C. E. B. Bremekamp denied that it is useful at all for this purpose. W. J. Arkell and J. A. Moy-Thomas have recently published a detailed consideration of the problem from which I shall quote at some length because much of the difficulty they experienced is present in archaeological systematics. With regard to traditional procedure in paleontology they say,

> The method of classification now used by the majority of palaeontologists is the phylogenetic one, in which fossils are arranged as nearly as possible in accordance with the supposed course of their evolution. Thus classification has come to aim, not only at providing an easy means of recognizing fossils, but also at giving a summary of existing knowledge of phylogeny. It is because these dual objects frequently tend to produce conflicting results that the problems of taxonomy have arisen.

This conflicting duality will be understood by those who have attempted to use the recently developed ceramic taxonomy of Southwestern archaeology. The latter aims not only at providing an easy means for recognizing pottery and for placing the specimens in time and space, but also at providing an outline for the development of cultures and the movement of peoples.

The next statement I shall quote from Arkell and Moy-Thomas is equally applicable to archaeological systematics. The paleontologist is "torn between two irreconcilable endeavors; for as a phylogenist he strives to reveal closer and closer relationships, while as a systematist he must point out differences and divide up his material into units bearing distinct names." Here we have a statement of the basis of the conflict between the so-called "lumpers" and the "splitters" in archaeology which will be treated more fully later.

The crux of the paleontologist's difficulty is expressed in the next quotation. "It is part of the paleontologist's business to unravel phylogeny by the study of fossils; but he can only arrive at an approximation to the truth, for he has only a fraction of the material to work on, the hard parts which alone have been preserved by fossilization." Even if we disregard for the moment the fact that objects of material culture are not sexually reproductive, I believe that the reader will agree that this objection applies equally well to systematic schemes built upon a study of potsherds.

Because of this situation, these two paleontologists feel free to state that: "At the best of times his (the paleontologist's) results are hypothetical and more or less subjective, and it may be questioned whether such results form a suitable foundation on which to build a classification and a nomenclature."

If this is true in the case of fossil bones it is even more obviously the case with the shells of mollusks. That the morphology of these shells, arranged in a taxonomic classification, does not parallel the morphological classifications of the organisms which inhabit them has been sufficiently demonstrated. An interesting analogy might be drawn here between the development of house type and the evolution of human beings.

In oology I believe the disparity between the classificatory system and the genetic history of the organism is even more apparent. The differences in eggshells are even more minute and the range is smaller than in the shells of mollusks, while the differences in the organisms, in this case birds, are more gross and the range is greater. In any case, the same arguments apply and I think we must conclude that classifications of form and color of birds' eggs do not "reveal" genetic relationships between groups of birds.

The fourth case is of a different nature but is inserted here to help in the transition from "natural" to "cultural" objects. Bashford Dean was an ichthyologist whose interest led him to specialize in armored fishes. From that the step to human armor was made, and it is natural that Dean carried with him into his cultural study the taxonomic system he had learned in his biological work. The result is a series of amazingly detailed "family-trees" of armor which are published in the catalogue of the Metropolitan Museum in New York, and which are used by T. H. Morgan to illustrate certain points in his critique of the theory of evolution. The epistemological fallacy here is quite apparent. The only defense there can be for a classification of armor based upon phylogenetic theory is that the individual objects were made and used by man. Yet the connection between the object and its user is even less close than that between the shell and the mollusk or between the egg and the developed bird. And since this correlation does not exist, then armor has no phylogeny and a "family-tree" classification is not only meaningless but actually misleading.

This brings us close to one of the most dangerous examples of complaisance I have encountered among archaeologists. I refer to the use of biological concepts and terms with the knowledge that they do not apply. This means one of two things: either the concepts and definitions must be greatly modified for archaeological usage or else they are in fact either meaningless or false. Such usage is perhaps worse then in the case of the workers who really believe that biological rules of taxonomy are absolute and that they do apply to cultural matters. For it means that the user is either lazy or indefinite in his pursuit of knowledge.

In this connection I would, had I sufficient faith in the probability, express the hope that I should never again hear or see the term "evolution" applied to an artifact or to a "culture." I hasten to state that I realize that many humanists and historians who use this term do not imply by it genetic relationships. Of them I ask, in that case, of what use is the term? And I further charge them with this responsibility: that, even though they do not intend such implication, the general association of the term with the genetic history of living organisms leads their hearers and readers to make such implications themselves, to the detriment of progress in the understanding of cultural development.

I also wish to state that I realize that the phylogenetic implication has been added to the word "evolution" by the biologists and that the first meanings given in most dictionaries are of such general nature as to permit the term to be applied to cultural development. My interests, however, are in the ideas which the use of the term brings forward in our minds. In other words, I believe the recent modification of meaning introduced by biologists to be so widely accepted that, if we wish to free ourselves entirely from genetic concepts false to the processes we are studying, it will be necessary to abandon the application of the term to inanimate objects.

In support of this plea I shall quote again from the biologists who are responsible for the present specialized meaning of the word. T. H. Morgan, in his critique of the theory of evolution, says: "There is an obvious and striking similarity between the evolution of man's inventions and the evolution of the shells of molluscs and of the bones of mammals, yet in neither case does a knowledge of the order in which these things arose *explain them.*" I have added the italics. This is a most important point, and I wish to emphasize here that one of the leading proponents of the biological theory of evolution does not believe that it, or a taxonomic system based upon it, can be usefully adapted to the study of fossil bones, shells, or the cultural products of human beings.

In criticizing general usage of the term "evolution," Morgan writes:

> We use the word evolution in many ways — to include many different kinds of changes. There is hardly any other scientific term that is used so carelessly — to imply so much, to mean so little.
>
> We speak of the evolution of the stars, of the evolution of the horse, of the evolution of the steam engine, as though they were all part of the same process. What have they in common? Only this, that each concerns itself with the *history* of something. Clearly no more (in common) than that from a simple beginning through a series of changes something more complex, or at least different, has come to being. To lump all these kinds of changes into one and call them evolution is only to assert that you believe in consecutive series of events (which is history) causally connected (which is science).

Morgan concludes that our aims as scientists should be to find out actually what kind of causes produced the stars in the heavens and the steam engine in the mind and works of man. To confound these causes with the genetic mechanisms which have produced the modern horse does not assist that aim.

It has now been shown that many competent biologists do not believe that the taxonomic system is a proper tool for describing genetic relationships in living organisms. It has also been shown that the use of taxonomic systems for this purpose in the fields of paleontology, conchology, and oology has been questioned by some of those who, nevertheless, believe it is a useful tool in descriptive biology. If there is, as there certainly seems to be, a reasonable doubt of the usefulness of phylogenetic classification for fossils, how much greater must the doubt be of the usefulness of a pseudo-phylogenetic classification of artifacts and cultures.

The defense has been offered that such systems are useful, because artifacts and cultures are made by man and closely associated with man, who as an animal is subject to the processes of phylogeny. This can be most effectively exposed as false in two ways. (1) The arguments presented above in the case of conchology, etc., apply even more patently to cultural objects. In other words, although the objects were made by man, there is no necessary or causal connection between the form of the object and the shape and color of the man. (2) It may also be effectively pointed out in this connection that although the objects were made by men, the classifications were not made by the same men. And, although the archaeological "cultures" are simplified expressions of life led by men, those expressions were not made by the men who lived the "cultures." A number of ideas (probably most of them) in such classifications were not present in the minds of the makers of the objects and the possessors of the "cultures." This is admirably stated by Rouse in the following quotation:

> If the aborigines had been trained to think in cultural terms, they might possibly have conceptualized the artifacts in terms of community standards of behavior, as the writer has done. It is not within the power of the writer, however, to determine whether or not they did so. He can only assume that the types and modes are products of his own mind, whereas the artifacts were objects made by the aborigines.

Consequently, since the relationships are expressed in terms of these classifications produced in the minds of students, they can not be assumed to be identical with the phylogeny of mankind through association. To speak of "polished pottery people," "Folsom people," or even — I almost hesitate to write it — "Bell Beaker people" on the basis of the presence in archaeological sites of a single distinctive artifact type is an epistemological solecism which can and has warped our studies. Tallgren considers this one of the major weaknesses in archaeological procedure. He describes it as "the tendency to see ... a uniform population or ethnic group behind cultural phenomena, that is behind the forms of material culture; we have also been too apt to see, in cultural connections and particularly in cultural transmissions, the movements and migrations of *peoples* instead rather of the products of different social classes and of commerce." A good example of this tendency can be found in the American field. Because of the great amount of red ochre found with caches of certain distinctive artifacts in Maine, the complex constructed on the basis of these artifacts was called the "Red Paint Culture." In usage, many archaeologists as far west as the Mississippi Valley speculate upon the presence of the "Red Paint people" whenever red ochre appears in a site or a burial. Yet red ochre was generally used by most North American Indians. This, again, is not a criticism of the application of the term to the arbitrary complex, though a better one certainly could have been devised, but it is a criticism of the use of the term in a large measure out of context and in such a way as to suggest migrations and associations of physical type not justified by the evidence.

Before proceeding further with discussion of the use of this concept by archaeologists, it may be profitable to examine briefly the history of the application of biological classificatory schemes to Southwestern archaeology.

With the development of stratigraphic technique in the second decade of the twentieth century, the accumulating mass of data from excavations and surveys, still for the most part disjointed, presented a complicated picture which defied the ordinary descriptive approach current until then. The preliminary Kidder-Guernsey and Morris classifications were designed to bring order into this mass and eventually resulted in the Pecos System as described above. A definitely evolutionary concept provided the skeleton for the system, but it lacked sufficient precision to satisfy men familiar with more exacting disciplines. In an attempt to supply this precision a binomial taxonomic system for the classification of pottery was invented and, based primarily upon it, there developed a "family-tree" concept of culture classification designed to describe all Southwestern prehistory.

Colton outlines the development of this system in Hargrave's original presentation of the taxonomic studies of the Museum of Northern Arizona. "The present situation of pottery nomenclature and classification resembles biology before the days of Linnaeus. In this paper the general rules of biological nomenclature have been followed and a biological classification adopted. . . . At a conference at Gila Pueblo, April 1930, several Southwestern Workers tentatively agreed to adopt a biological method in the classification of Southwestern pottery types."

Present at this conference were Mera, Colton, Hargrave, Renaud, and Gladwin. From this system of pottery classification came Gladwin's phase system, even more strictly biological, if possible, in that it emphasized the evolutionary nature of the scheme in graphical representations of "lineage," "family-trees" of culture.

The biological background is further emphasized by Hargrave in his taxonomic outline which included the following groups: Kingdom, Phylum, Class, Order, Ware, Genus, Type, or Subtype. The genetic basis was confirmed by the introduction of hybrid genera and types. The continued use of the term "hybrid" in connection with artifacts by many Southwestern taxonomists seems to me to be one of the best reasons for a thorough examination of our concepts of cultural processes.

That these ideas are still current, despite disavowals, can be shown by a quotation from the latest taxonomic manual of Southwestern pottery. "A Series, therefore, is a group of pottery types within a single ware in which each type bears a *genetic relation* to each other, including all those types and only those types that occur ... in the *direct line* of *chronological genetic development* from an original primitive or *ancestral* type to a late type." The italics are mine; in the original the entire passage is in italics.

An accompanying statement that pottery objects are inanimate does not remove the definite phylogenetic implications of the above quotation. I believe it is impossible to think in those terms without implying race history concepts of physical causal relationships.

That I am not waving a "red herring" in emphasizing this point is perhaps best shown by the following quotation. In an article entitled "The Family Tree of Chaco Canyon Masonry," F. M. Hawley says:

> Southwestern Pueblo pottery of the prehistoric periods has been studied, named with dozens of geographic appellations, and traced back from period to period with *genealogic* thoroughness. "And La Plata Black-on-White *begat* Red Mesa Black-on-White, and Red Mesa Black-on-White *begat* Escavada Black-on-White, and Escavada Black-on-White *begat* Gallup Black-on-White." But the *family tree* of prehistoric Southwestern walls has not been cultivated with the ardor of the potsherd horticulturalist; the relation of roots to branches has been largely conjectural.

This was apparently written in all seriousness. The italics are mine.

Most of the men closely associated with this development had received a major part if not all of their scientific training in the biological sciences. Colton was a well-known biological systematist at the University of Pennsylvania; Hargrave, his assistant, was a competent ornithologist; and Mera holds a medical degree. Their energetic application of their own specialized knowledge to archaeology is extremely commendable and follows the best archaeological in the manner of their discovery, we can learn about the techniques developed in other fields of learning. In this category are geochronology, dendrochronology, pollen analysis, soil analysis, etc. In the case of artifacts and cultures, however, there is an important difference, and it seems to me that this difference *must* be considered; namely, although applied to archaeological problems, glacial geology still deals with geological phenomena, dendrochronology still deals with the growth mechanism of trees, pollen analysis still deals with plant remains, etc. That is, the materials which these techniques analyze are still the materials they were designed to handle before they were adapted to archaeological ends. The question we must ask is simply: Is this the case with biological classifications applied to artifacts and culture complexes? The answer, it seems to me, is a negative. The systematics of biology was designed to classify living organisms. Even though we disregard the doubts presented above of the value of the technique in biology itself, we still are faced with the fact that, with the exception of skeletal material, the objects and concepts of archaeology are not living organisms or parts of living organisms. Consequently, their development is not properly represented by a classificatory technique based upon the genetic relationships of living organisms.[3]

In the foregoing pages I have attempted to show, principally, two things: (1) that all classification is arbitrary, that the classes are made by students for their own use; and (2) that the biological implications inherent in certain archaeological systems of taxonomy are dangerous in that they may introduce concepts at variance with the anthropological and historical processes with which we are dealing.

The question before us now is, what can we do? How should we proceed in the analysis of our data? I repeat that we must have conceptual schemes. We can do nothing without them, because we cannot think without them. We need them to help make accessible and comprehensible a mass of otherwise disorganized material. The statement, often made at present by those who are dissatisified with taxonomy, that we must abandon classificatory methods and substitute a "purely historical" scheme based upon tree-ring chronology means not what it at first appears to mean but only that one conceptual scheme is suggested in place of another. The "historical" method of classifying cultures by centuries or by dynasties is just as much an arbitrary scheme as is the McKern System of archaeological taxonomy.

The way in which we handle our material must, first of all, be related to certain basic concepts of the nature of this material. Duncan Strong, in his essay on anthropological theory and archaeological fact conceives anthropology as "midway between" the biological and social sciences, in that it deals with two "definitely historical" processes: (1) biological evolution and (2) cultural development. The former has to do with the animal nature of man

---

[3] Archaelogists of the Old World, notably Childe and Tallgren, also warn against the noncritical application of the systems of other disciplines to our problems. In "The Irish Stone Age," H. L. Movius writes, "But with the exception of the primary rule of stratigraphy, the laws of the natural sciences are far too rigid to provide an adequate interpretation of human culture. . . ."

and is physical anthropology. The latter has to do with the products of the minds, hands, and nerves of men and includes archaeology.

Here, then, is a basic scheme, which seems as good as any to serve as a point of departure for archaeological research. It assumes that we deal with a succession of human deeds and relationships. In archaeology we study the material manifestations of these deeds and relationships and attempt to reconstruct the latter. If we can then go beyond the historical task and interpret our material so that it can make contributions to the specialized divisions of modern life, so much the better for our justification before the world at large.

This reconstruction can not, it seems to me, be done solely on the basis of schemes for the classification of artifacts, or of groups of artifacts placed together in "periods," "complexes," "phases," etc.

With regard to this, Tallgren in his paper on the method of prehistoric archaeology says:

> Brilliant systematization, regarded as exact, has not led and does not lead to an elucidation of the organic structure of the whole life of the period studied, to an understanding of social systems, of economic and social history, to the history of religious ideas. In short, forms and types, that is, products, have been regarded as more real and alive than the society which created them and whose needs determined these manifestations.

However, it should be noted here that systematization when not regarded as exact is not only useful but also necessary in the handling of our multitudinous evidence. When the various systematizations are regarded simply as bits of evidence themselves, though of a different kind from the actual objects, and when they too are submitted to analysis, they then serve as profitable tools. In much current work I seem to see the misconception that systematic arrangement, that is, classification, is in itself analysis.

At present for the final summing up at the end of a study I see no alternative to the so-called "narrative approach" which, currently, is sometimes decried. The kind of simplification and systematization introduced by the usual classificatory schemes brings about a distortion which must be corrected by proper interpretation, and proper interpretation of such things demands narrative, not charts and diagrams, which are simplifications themselves. Improper interpretation and lack of understanding of these simplifications has definitely hampered advancement of our studies in many instances.

As an example of this distortion I shall cite the reasoning used by Gladwin in dating the "Vahki Phase" of the Hohokam culture at 300 B.C. I hasten to assert that I do not say that the objects classified as Vahki are not that old. I am perfectly willing to admit that I think it unlikely, but that is beside the point; our interest here is the argument by which Gladwin attempts to establish the date.

During the study of the material excavated at Snaketown a scheme of phases was set up based upon typological variations in pottery, house form, and other artifacts. The later phases in this sequence were cross-dated by means of intrusive potsherds with certain periods in the Pecos Classification of Pueblo cultures. The uncertainty in the minds of students over the number of years which should be assigned to the Pueblo periods is well known. However, for the sake of convenience it has become customary for many workers to consider a "period" roughly and loosely to represent two hundred years. Gladwin, then, accepts this time unit for a Pueblo period, asserts that Hohokam phases are equivalent to Pueblo periods, and concludes as follows: "By using these methods at Snaketown, we have been able to define seven phases, the last of which ended about 1100 A.D. Since each of the two latest phases lasted two hundred years, we may assume that the occupation of Snaketown, from first to last, was fourteen hundred years, which would place the beginning of the Vahki Phase at 300 B.C." As pointed out . . . the Vahki date was revised by Gladwin shortly after the first part of this paragraph was originally written in 1941. My statement is left as written because, although the new date for the Vahki Phase, A.D. 600–650, is considered by many to be a more reasonable date for that phase, Gladwin has arrived at it by exactly the same method. He has merely changed the time value of a phase from two hundred years to fifty years.

As with all his theories, Gladwin quite properly states it as an assumption and allows that it may be questioned. At the same time he submits that the assumption is not arbitrary, a proposition with which I cannot agree. What he has done is to correlate one set of arbitrary phases, defined by himself, in the Gila Basin, with another set of arbitrary phases, defined by the Pecos Conference and called Periods, on the Colorado Plateau. He then assumes that his phases represent a constant rate of culture change, that, if the last two represent the span of two hundred years, all other phases existed over the same length of time. Yet there is more variation in house type assigned to the Pueblo I period alone than in the whole range of the Snaketown phases. The differences in diagnostic pottery types are also relatively smaller between most of the Snaketown phases than they are between Pueblo periods. Most workers in the Pueblo area would consider many of his phases to be merely minor variations within periods, which is just another way of saying that another student might, quite legitimately, make different phase divisions, with correspondingly different results in dating by this method. It might also be pointed out here that a much different result as to date would be obtained if the original Hohokam "periods" (Pioneer, Colonial, Sedentary, Classic, etc.) should be used in the correlation instead of the later Hohokam phases.

Gladwin's assumption that his "phases" can be considered all to be equivalent to two hundred years in the time-scale, in the argument given above, can even be questioned on the basis of his own published work. . . . he adapts the Pueblo cultures to his phase system, assigning phases throughout the Pueblo area. In the charts published in that paper he presents sixty-two phases in columns adjacent to the listing of Pueblo periods. However, only sixteen of those sixty-two are equated with Pueblo periods and therefore equivalent to two hundred years, in terms of his Hohokam argument. But there are nine instances where two phases are equivalent to one period, that is, following the same reasoning, eighteen phases are only *one hundred years long*. Similarly, eighteen more come at the rate of three to a period, or *sixty-seven years* per phase; eight more are at the rate of four to a period, or *fifty years* per phase; and two phases are listed as equivalent to two Pueblo periods each, or *four hundred years* per phase. Thus only 25.8 percent of these phases are equal to Gladwin's two hundred years to a phase, according to his own system of reckoning. An even smaller number, only 12.9 percent, equal fifty years, which is the new time value of a phase assigned in Gladwin, 1942, the Snaketown revision. And this, indeed, is what we should expect. Except for one special case, phases, by reason of what they are and how they are made, are not and can not be equivalent in time-span. The exception is in classifications like the one we often use for our modern European cultures, dividing them by centuries, with chronology as the sole determinant of period or phase. Some students are now trying to use the period names of the Pecos Classification this way, in conjunction with tree-ring dates. We can have no quarrel with this, if the dates are well established and if the original period diagnostics of the Pecos Classification are completely abandoned.[4]

I have taken my example from Gladwin's work, above, merely because of the present importance of the Snaketown dating. We have all had similar trouble and have made similar mistakes. I believe that a better understanding of the nature of classificatory systems will save us from this kind of fallacy in reasoning. We have here an illustration of one of the things which such schemes do to us, against which we must ever be on guard. The *force of the scheme* itself produces a new type of archaeological conservatism, the conservatism of false reality which, after all, is nothing but dogma dressed

---

[4] However, in this case, since Pecos period diagnostics loom so large in our thinking, and since tree-ring dates are now for the most part expressed in terms of our calendar, it might be better to apply the "century" system in the Southwest, where successfully applied it will only serve as a convenient time-scale. Classifications based on other cultural factors will still be necessary.

up in modern terminology. These schemes often lead us into what A. N. Whitehead calls the fallacy of misplaced concreteness.

The above discussion brings us to the most important taxonomic question in Southwestern archaeology. We have already decided that major conceptual schemes are not only necessary but unavoidable, and that minor classificatory schemes are also useful if properly used and understood. The greatest difficulties with them in practice have to do with the criteria or diagnostics by which the various divisions are set up.

Outstanding here is the vexing question of where to place a trait, a group of traits, a site, or part of a site. As has already been shown, the things, unfortunately, do not "fall into" categories by themselves, but must be put in them. The taxonomic rules by which the placing can be done are far from clear.

Three questions posed by Kluckhohn will serve to introduce these problems. He asks:

1. "Is it absolute presence or absence of the criteria which counts or merely predominance — or does the answer to this question vary in the case of various traits?

2. "Must the culture or 'culture period' check with all or with how large a majority of the diagnostics?

3. "Are certain of the criteria indispensable and others not?"

To point the question he cites a hypothetical problem. Suppose there are eight criteria generally accepted for Pueblo I and we agree that six of them must check before the period designation may be applied. Then "will we still call a site Pueblo I if six of the eight criteria are found indubitably associated with a masonry type or a pottery complex which has been accepted as diagnostic of Pueblo II?" The answer to this, in terms of contemporary usage, is usually no. This problem presents the question of the weighting of criteria and, as all Southwestern classification systems are used at present, despite statements of cultural inclusiveness, pottery type, primarily, and house type, secondarily, are the most significant factors. The only important exceptions to this are two: (1) the few workers who continue to use the extremely unsatisfactory criterion of physical type as the most important diagnostic and (2) those who attempt to use tree-ring chronology alone.

This situation is recognized by Kluckhohn who discusses it with particular insight into the problems of systematics. His statements are worth quoting at considerable length, as he has gone further into the problem than any other writer in the Southwestern field. With regard to the weighting of criteria he says:

> Observation of the actual operations of archaeologists suggests
> that in many cases the classification of a site is actually made on

the basis of pottery complex or architectural style (including masonry type) alone. If this fact is explicitly stated, this procedure may well be the most convenient and quite unobjectionable. If, however, there is assertion or implication that the classification has been made on the basis of total culture complex, some confusion results.

Here again we are faced with the difference between statement and practice, so characteristic of archaeological systematics.

Kluckhohn goes on to say:

> For what occurs is that the other culture elements found associated with the critical pottery complex or architectural style are simply dragged in after the crucial step has been taken. If we are really operating with pottery or masonry-architectural complexes (or a combination of these two) only, it would be in the interests of clear thinking if this circumstance were brought into the open, either through terminology or explicit statement. It seems possible that classificatory operations frankly based solely upon these apparently somewhat more sensitive and more consistent criteria would be most useful. The associated culture elements (not used in cultural classification) could then be studied apart from the prejudice of a question-begging nomenclature. . . .
>
> It would, then, be necessary to make clear how great a proportion of traits otherwise regarded as diagnostic of, let us say, Pueblo II could be admitted *seriatim* in a Pueblo I site. It would likewise be imperative to state if any criteria are to be weighed as of greater importance and which differentiae are to be applied first. Because, as in physical anthropology, two investigators can use the same diagnostic traits in making a classification and yet get different results, depending on the order in which they are applied (with resultant eliminations). It follows, also, that the relative significance to be attached to positive and negative evidence would have to be specified.

Such analysis of our current practice is certainly necessary at present. Kidder and Guernsey worked much with sandal types, Haury and F. H. Douglas have made detailed studies of textiles, Bartlett has written a paper on metate types, R. B. Woodbury is studying stone and bone implements, respectively, but very little indeed is known about the chronological and geographical distributions of artifact types in the Southwest aside from pottery and, to a much smaller extent, architecture. Surely it is better procedure to recognize this and to govern ourselves accordingly than to cover our systems with a camouflage of completeness, admittedly a desirable ideal, but one which is far from attained. The very admission not only eliminates current misconceptions but emphasizes the urgent necessity of intensive study of the lesser-known divisions of material culture.

There is another factor here which may help us to a better understanding of our difficulties with criteria. In order to give a heterogeneous mass of data orderly classification, it is necessary arbitrarily to set up definitions of groups and to determine certain characteristics which will be considered as diagnostics for these groups. But after this is done it seems always to be the case that a number of objects cannot be satisfactorily placed. And the more material and the more knowledge the investigator gathers, the greater this difficulty seems to become.

The difficulty applies to detailed classifications of artifacts and to the broader concepts of culture classification as well. In the former case the so-called "intermediate types" cause the trouble. And the glib answer, "Make a new type," does not solve the problem, because, as in the case of Jeddito Black-on-orange and Jeddito Black-on-yellow pottery in the Hopi country, when a large number of specimens is obtained, a complete series marked by almost imperceptible gradations appears between the two types.

In the latter case, that of the broader concepts of culture classification, the difficulty is that when a large number of sites have been excavated, it is found that the criteria do not change simultaneously, like the change of billing for a vaudeville show, but tend to change individually and to present a varied picture of lag and overlap in individual traits. In my own experience I have never seen a Southwestern site which did not present, in a single "occupation-level," criteria of at least two major cultural periods. The only unnatural thing about the hypothetical problem presented by Kluckhohn above was the small number of overlapping criteria.

It is this situation, shown admirably by trait charts in Rouse's first report and present in the reports of all major Southwestern digs, which impels Kidder to look upon all arbitrary classifications as temporary and to say: "our investigation has now reached a point at which formal classifications, such as the Pecos nomenclature, are not only of lessening value, but are often . . . positively misleading."

In biology, taxonomy has also encountered this difficulty. Robson, discussing the species problem, says: "The only conclusion at which we can arrive is that there is no criterion by which we can define and delimit separate units of the status required by the species-concept. There may be a general sense in which the four criteria we have discussed are simultaneously applicable. But the degree to which in any one instance differentiation is manifested in respect of these is so variable that it defies organization in the sense required by the concept. It is not only impossible to find a standardized type of group by applying any single criterion; but also the various main criteria do not give the same results, the same indications of affinity."

On the cultural side consider a wealthy modern Hopi trader in his house which has windows purchased in Holbrook, Arizona, but a roof similar to that of a prehistoric dwelling. Imagine him seated on a stone loom weight, facing a coal range of the vintage of 1890, smoking a "tailor-made" cigarette, wearing triangular turquoise earrings, and listening to a dance orchestra from Havana, Cuba, on the short wave band of a new radio, while his son drives up in a ten-year-old Ford and his wife grinds corn in a primitive mealing bin, using, for sentiment's sake, a mano which she has picked up at the old Sikyatki ruin. This is an extreme case, but such cases can be demonstrated any day in the year. In some degree or other, it is situations like this we are called upon as archaeologists to handle. But, at the outset of any given problem we do not have in hand the information which enables us to evaluate the archaeological case as we can the modern case just cited. So, we make our schemes, and, if we are wise, as our knowledge of that particular set of problems advances, *we change our schemes.*

The overlaps are not necessarily, as some would have us believe, unimportant and of only a few years' duration. Some of them last for centuries. The "intermediate types" are *not* unimportant, to be eliminated, as is often done, by disregarding them. We are dealing with a constant stream of cultural development, not evolutionary in the genetic sense, but still a continuum of human activity.

It is quite apparent, now, that we are facing a much larger question than the one so frequently asked, "Should the Pecos Classification be abandoned?" My answer to that question perhaps points the way to the general suggestions as to procedure with which this section will be concluded. I do not believe that the Pecos Classification should be abandoned. I do, however, believe that we should abandon the practice of treating it as the only classification applicable or useful to the phenomena we group under the term Pueblo or Anasazi culture. My contention is that it is very useful in certain stages of our studies. In many parts of the region and in many aspects of our investigations its definitions and terminology provide an extremely handy mechanism. On the other hand, in certain districts and in certain divisions of the development of material culture our accumulated knowledge now renders that sort of classification unnecessary. In his consideration of the situation in Chaco Canyon, Kluckhohn says:

> But we must remember, as Whitehead has so often reminded us, that a classification is, at best, "a half-way house." A classification is useful so long as the facts fall without violence into it. So soon, however, as their greater bulk, greater complexity, or greater subtleties of discrimination make the classification a Procrustean bed into which the maimed and helpless facts are forced, the classification should be abandoned or radically modified.

This process is going on all the time, in actuality. The Museum of Northern Arizona, the University of New Mexico, the University of Arizona, the Laboratory of Anthropology at Santa Fe, and the Field Museum all use the Pecos Classification in conjunction with concepts borrowed from Gladwin's system and concepts of cultural development by centuries based upon tree-ring chronology. Yet many of the workers in the field express dissatisfaction with the lack of precision involved in such procedure and continue to feel that they should adopt a single system and "stick to it." My contention is that to adapt and change classifications and to make new ones as needs arise is correct procedure provided it is implemented with a better understanding of the nature of systematics, a more critical examination of new systems for dangerous distortions (like the "family-tree" concept in the Gladwin System), and accompanied in the published reports by *a statement of the various assumptions used.* To adopt a single system and to stick to it would be fatal to scientific progress.

In certain minds approval of such technique will be denied because it is not precise. Admittedly, it is not. And for that very reason it is practical and scientific. We are not able to treat precisely the material with which we are dealing. Whether or not we shall in part ever be able to do so in future can not be decided now. The fact is that the processes which govern the deeds and beliefs of any group of people at any particular time are conditioned by a large number of variables, many of which we do not understand and many of which we as archaeologists are not able to deduce from our fragmentary evidence. A flexible, nonprecise technique is more useful and more "scientific" for the kind of evidence we have of the kind of phenomena with which we deal than is the pseudo-precision which, at this time, is the only alternative.

We must make our choice between these two alternatives. Shall we maintain a fluid technique which can be changed as our needs change and as our knowledge develops or shall we fix our technique into a pseudo-precise system which by its very dogmatism will bar all progress beyond its level? Fortunately, we probably can not do the latter, even should we wish it. The vigorous spirit of inquiry in the mind of man certainly will not be satisfied with it for long. But why waste our time trying it on?

Thus we come to what may be a positive rule of procedure. All classificatory schemes, it seems, are arbitrary and designed to fill an immediate need. If research prospers, there comes a time, and this is what Kidder says in the quotation above, when the information gathered goes beyond the simplifications of the given systems. *The systems then become obsolete,* to use them longer is awkward and definitely warps the results. We should then pass on to new systems which will absorb all the known "facts" and systematize the new and more "advanced" unassimilated data.

Our systematics, then, must be flexible, too, as are the materials with which we deal. In all of this we must remember, as Tallgren points out, that it is the *use* and not the *form* of artifacts which is important to us. Variations in form, treated systematically, can aid us greatly in prosecuting our research, but when we can fit the object into its economic or social environment, into the system of production of which it is an instrument or the ceremonial system of which it is a part, we should readily dispense with the purely morphological classification.

That is going a long way, probably further than most of us will ever get in our lifetimes, but all our work should tend toward such an end. Similarly with "cultures"; when we can show, as I think we can in this report, the gradual development of houses, kivas, pottery, and a few other objects by numerous small changes over a period of six hundred or more years, it will not advance our cause to present them in only four periods, which we must do if we discuss them only in the terms of the Pecos Classification.

What, then, should our procedure be? It is easy to offer destructive criticism and fashionable to leave it at that. And I am not one of those who feel that we are not entitled to indulge in destructive criticism unless we also offer constructive suggestions. But in this case I shall offer suggestions which I hope will prove to be constructive. I do this because I believe the subject of our analytical method to be of supreme importance to us and because I believe I can see some ways in which our methods can be improved and in which some current difficulties can be avoided. On the other hand, most of the suggestions I am about to make are so simple that I distrust them somewhat myself. I present them for consideration, if they seem worthy of that, and above all with the hope that this discussion will induce some further examination into the basic assumptions and analytical methods of our subject.

With regard to taxonomy, then, I believe we can say this. As archaeologists we must classify our material in all ways that will produce for us useful information. I repeat, we need more rather than fewer classifications, different classifications, always new classifications, to meet new needs. We must not be satisfied with a single classification of a group of artifacts or of a cultural development, for that way lies dogma and defeat. We are, or should be, in search of all of the evidence our material holds. Even in simple things no single analysis will bring out all that evidence.

We must continually analyze not only our material but also our methods, we must continually check our concepts for distorting factors, and we must always remember to advise the reader thoroughly of the concepts we are using.

We need have no fear of changing established systems or of designing new ones, for it is only by such means that we can progress. At the same time we must not present our new system or systems as a standard to be used and adopted by everyone and forevermore. We must recognize that any given system in its entirety will probably be applicable only to the given set of problems it was designed to meet. The main value of a published description of a given system is that it may then be *adapted* by another student to his problems, not that he should force his material into it.

Above all, we must remember that we are dealing with a cultural continuum which is *continually changing*. Even the products of the automotive assembly line are not identical, and this is probably the greatest material standardization yet achieved by mankind. We must ever be on guard against that peculiar paradox of anthropology which permits men to "trace" a "complex" of, let us say, physical type, pottery type, and religion over 10,000 miles of terrain and down through 10,000 years of history while in the same breath, or in the next lecture, the same men vigorously defend the theory of continuous change.

Before concluding this chapter, in which I have so greatly emphasized the subject of taxonomy, it will be well to dig even deeper than we have dug already and to consider the ultimate objectives of archaeology. For the devices discussed above certainly do not constitute the end of our studies. They are merely a part of the tool kit we must use in achieving that end, whatever it may be.

Although to add to our store of accumulated knowledge may be in itself satisfactory to many, I believe that our objective should be much more than the systematic amassing of information and the conjectural reconstruction of past events. Beyond that, as I see it, the aim of archaeology is to relate our newly gathered information scientifically to the immediate problems of human life and society, through an analysis of the problems and achievements of other peoples, toward a better relationship with our physical and social environments. We must broaden our cultural horizon by showing to ourselves the accomplishments of these others in the various fields of human endeavor, both material and artistic.

There are those who will object to the inclusion of the aesthetic aspects of prehistoric cultures along with the material on the grounds that, while the latter is objective, the former is purely subjective and cannot be brought to life from the past. It will be said that I am injecting the personal equation, something no good scientist should ever do. It may even be said with vehemence, as though I could keep the personal factor out if I wished to do so. In this chapter I have deplored dogmatic statement but I shall now offer one for my critics to work on. *Those who say these things will be wrong.* As I have pointed out time and again in the preceding pages, the personal element is necessarily implicit even in the most mathematical systematics. To present our results so that they will be useful to men at large we must, at times, leave our systematics with our test tubes in the laboratory. If we fail to do so, every once in a while, we shall fall short of our aim.

Such presentation, which I believe to be necessary, involves the "narrative approach" and subjective picturization. This must be done with any body of archaeological data, if those data are to be of use to anyone besides archaeologists. Our obligation to society, our aim which I defined two paragraphs above, has been stated much more simply by a friend of mine, a lawyer — "A reasonable degree of humanizing is the only justification for archaeological research, carefully stopping short, of course, of fanciful romance." That statement contains a challenge we must meet. We are on the defensive. Our research is costly and its products must be useful. To make them so we must vastly improve our systematics and then go beyond them. We must present much more than our systematics to society.

IRVING ROUSE

All classes of artifact types are multi-attribute constructs, i.e., they are created by describing a given type by its constituent features or attributes — called "modes" in this article by Irving Rouse, who distinguishes between a conceptual mode (material, shape, and decoration) and a procedural mode (customary procedures followed in making and using the artifact). This excellent discussion focuses on points covered in earlier selections: (1) different typologies may be used to do different things, made explicit in Rouse's historical and descriptive types; (2) the behavioral significance of type categories may be vague simply because the usual type embraces too many attributes. A number of recent studies in which detailed behavioral inferences have been made are based on more minute analysis of artifacts. An example is James Hill's article on Broken K Pueblo in Part III.

7   The Classification of Artifacts in Archaeology

A number of recent papers, such as Phillips (1958), Wheat, Gifford, and Wasley (1958), and Sears (1960), have been concerned with particular methods used by archaeologists to classify artifacts. The present paper is instead an attempt to survey the range of current methods. It is intended to differentiate the various methods, to discuss their theoretical basis, and to assess their relative utility.

According to the dictionary (Nielson, Knott, and Earhart 1940:496), the word *classification* refers to "the act of assigning [artifacts] to a proper class." If the class is a new one, it will have to be defined by listing the

Reprinted, with the editorial changes noted, from "The Classification of Artifacts in Archaeology" by Irving Rouse, *American Antiquity* 25 (1960):313–323, by permission of the author and the publisher.

criteria used to form it and will also have to be given a name or a number. If pertinent classes had previously been established, it will be enough to determine that the new artifacts have the criteria diagnostic of one of the classes, and to give them the name of that class.

Classification, like statistics, is not an end in itself but a technique by means of which to attain specified objectives, and so it must be varied with the objective. The main opportunity for variation comes in selecting the criteria which are to be considered diagnostic of one's classes. In my experience, archaeologists select these criteria to meet one of two alternate objectives; either to form modes or to establish types. If modes are the objective, the classification is called "analytic" (Whiteford 1947). If, instead, the purpose is to form types, then the classification becomes "taxonomic" (Phillips 1958). I shall discuss these two kinds of classification in turn.

ANALYTIC CLASSIFICATION

By the term "mode" is meant any standard, concept, or custom which governs the behavior of the artisans of a community, which they hand down from generation to generation, and which may spread from community to community over considerable distances (Rouse 1939). Such modes will be reflected in the artifacts as attributes which conform to a community's standards, which express its concepts, or which reveal its customary ways of manufacturing and using artifacts. Analytic classification focuses on these attributes and, through them, attempts to get at the standards, concepts, and customs themselves. In effect, it attempts to read such modes out of the artifacts.

Not all the attributes of the artifacts are indicative of modes. Some attributes will instead express personal idiosyncracies of the artisans. A unique design, which occurs only once, may be cited as an example. Other attributes fall within the realm of biology, chemistry, or physics rather than culture. The atomic structure of artifacts is an obvious example. The white color of shell artifacts is another. This whiteness does not appear until after the artifacts have been in the ground for some time, it is as prevalent among natural as among worked shells, and hence it must be considered a purely biological trait which has no part to play in cultural studies.

Analytic classification, then, must single out modes, which are cultural, and exclude those traits which are purely biological, chemical, or physical. One way to do this is to examine a collection in terms of the artisan's procedure, starting first with the materials he used, continuing with his techniques of manufacture, and then considering shape, decoration, and uses. At each stage in the procedure one may find that the artisan had some choice of standards or customs (Fig. 1). This makes it possible, for example,

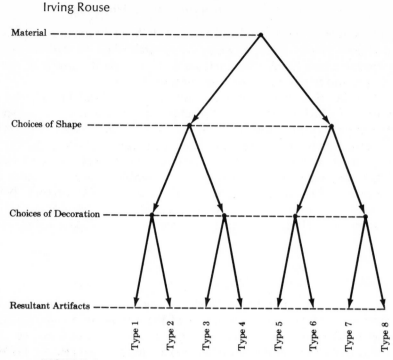

FIGURE 1

Procedure of making artifacts.

to divide a given collection into one or more series of classes on the basis of the materials used. One can then redistribute the same specimens into other series of classes on the basis of techniques, elements of shape and decoration, and uses (Fig. 2). Each class will have one or more diagnostic attributes, and those attributes will be indicative of a single mode.

For example, an archaeologist may take a collection of potsherds and divide it into two classes, one consisting of sherds with inclusions of grit and the other, of sherds with inclusions of shell. He thereby determines that the potters had two alternative customs of tempering their vessels, one with pieces of stone and the other with pieces of shell. Then, he may pick out the sherds which are from rims and regroup them into a second series of classes, each characterized by a different set of rim attributes. In this case, he will have established a series of standards to which the potters conformed in making rims. He may repeat this process of reclassification with other aspects of material, shape, decoration, and use, ending up, as I have done in the case of my Antillean collections, with as many as eighty modes of material, shape, and decoration (Rouse 1939, 1941, 1952).

It is not necessary, of course, to be so systematic and all-inclusive as this in doing analytic classification. Various authors have concentrated upon

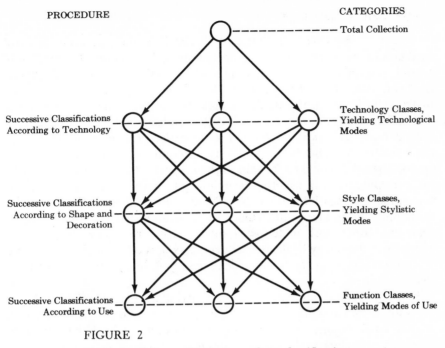

PROCEDURE

CATEGORIES

Successive Classifications According to Technology

Successive Classifications According to Shape and Decoration

Successive Classifications According to Use

Total Collection

Technology Classes, Yielding Technological Modes

Style Classes, Yielding Stylistic Modes

Function Classes, Yielding Modes of Use

FIGURE 2

Example of the analytic approach to classification.

technology (Matson 1942), upon shapes (Black and Weer 1936), upon designs (Amsden 1936), or upon uses (C. S. Ford 1937). The important point is that the author be interested in establishing independent modes and not in studying the manner in which those modes are combined on the artifacts.

The modes may be of two kinds: (1) concepts of material, shape, and decoration to which the artisans conformed and (2) customary procedures followed in making and using the artifacts. In the case of conceptual modes, the archaeologist need only designate one or more attributes of his artifacts to be diagnostic of each class, but in the case of procedural modes he must also infer behavior of the artisans from the diagnostic attributes. The process of inferring procedural modes has been well described and illustrated by other authors (Osgood 1942; Thompson 1958).

Once modes have been set up — whether conceptual or procedural — and their diagnostic attributes have been determined, one may identify these modes on new artifacts simply by looking to see whether the proper diagnostic attributes are present, without actually grouping and regrouping the artifacts. Many archaeologists (Waring and Holder 1945, Fig. 1) have found it helpful to make drawings of the more complex conceptual modes, such as rim profiles or designs, to assist in identification.

TAXONOMIC CLASSIFICATION

We have seen that analytic classification concentrates on the attributes of the artifacts which indicate modes. Taxonomic classification is instead concerned with those attributes which indicate types (Gladwin and Gladwin, 1930, 1931, 1933; Haury 1936; Sayles 1936). As in the case of analytic classification, the attributes indicative of types must be chosen for their cultural significance (Gifford 1960). Indeed, if the archaeologist is being completely logical, he should first do analytic classification in order to form modes and should then classify taxonomically in terms of those modes, instead of going back again to the original attributes. In such a case, for example, he will use the technique of incision as a criterion for taxonomic classification, rather than the attribute of incised lines. In order to simplify the following discussion, I will assume that the archaeological taxonomist does work in terms of modes rather than raw attributes, in which case a type may be defined as a complex of modes which is diagnostic of a certain class of artifacts and which serves to differentiate that class from all other classes.

There are several different ways of classifying a collection to form types. The most systematic one is to divide the specimens into two or more classes on the basis of one set of modes, for example, of materials; then to subdivide each class on the basis of another set of modes, such as shapes; and to continue this process until all the artifacts of the same kind have been separated into a single sub-subclass (Fig. 3). Another way is to work intuitively by simply sorting and resorting the artifacts until they end up in relatively homogeneous classes (Krieger 1944, Fig. 25). A third is to work statistically, for example, by noting the taxonomically significant modes of each artifact on a punch card and sorting out the cards according to the most frequent combinations of modes (Shepard 1956:322–32). In all cases the end result is the same: a single series of classes or subclasses rather than the successive series which result from analytic classification (compare Figs. 2, 3).

In all cases, the classifier must decide how many modes he is to consider diagnostic, that is, how many are going to end up in the type. He must select more than one, since by definition a type consists of two or more modes. On the other hand, he cannot expect to use all the modes; to do so would result in too large a number of types, especially if the artisan was permitted choices of modes during the course of the manufacture of the artifacts (Fig. 1). The proportion of modes which it is practicable to use as the criteria for taxonomic classification varies with the complexity of the artifacts and with the number of alternatives open to the artisan. Simple artifacts with few alternatives, for example, no decoration, can be classified

PROCEDURE CATEGORIES

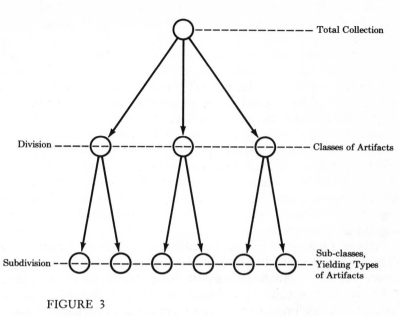

FIGURE 3

Example of the taxonomic approach to classification.

in terms of almost all their modes, whereas complex artifacts with many alternatives, such as elaborately decorated pottery, require selection of only a few modes from among many. The type "stone ball" may be cited as an example of the former extreme; here the three diagnostic modes, use of stone, grinding, and spherical shape, are practically the only ones which can be analyzed from the specimens. Pottery types illustrate the other extreme; for example, Ritchie and MacNeish (1949:99, Fig. 36), in their study of pre-Iroquoian pottery, explicitly limited the diagnostic modes they used to rim profiles, designs, and decorative techniques, excluding all the other modes which were analyzable from the sherds.

The personality of the taxonomist may also have an effect upon the number of modes which he selects to be diagnostic. If he is a "lumper," he will group the artifacts into large and inclusive classes, each of which will contain so much variation that relatively few of its modes can be considered diagnostic. If, on the other hand, he is a "splitter," he will establish many more classes, there will be less variation within each class, and as a result the ratio of diagnostic to non-diagnostic modes will be considerably higher.

The current tendency on the part of some archaeologists to subdivide pottery types into varieties (Gifford 1960) seems designed to meet this problem. It permits one to select a relatively small number of diagnostic modes for one's types and thereby to satisfy the lumper, and at the same time to define varieties in terms of larger numbers of diagnostic modes, thus satisfying the splitter as well.

The distinction between diagnostic modes, which form part of the type or variety, and non-diagnostic modes, which do not, is frequently obscured by the practice of "describing types" (Ford and Willey 1949:71–78). In the terminology of the present paper, such descriptions amount to a presentation of the modes analyzable from the artifacts of each class. Some of these modes will be diagnostic and, as a result, form part of the type; but others — and in many cases the majority — will not. Ritchie and MacNeish (1949:100–116) provide a good example. In the case of each type, these authors specify only three "diagnostic features" and then proceed to list a much larger number of other modes of "paste," "surface finish," "decoration," and "forms." The latter modes are not part of the type, as the word is used in the present paper.

The selection of modes has a qualitative as well as a quantitative aspect. The taxonomist must decide not only how many but also what kinds of modes are to be considered diagnostic of his classes and hence constituents of his types. Our colleagues in biology solve this problem by selecting the diagnostics which best show the course of organic evolution. We archaeologists are not so consistent. In the case of pottery and sometimes also projectile points, we select those modes which best indicate differences in time and space (Ford and Willey 1949:40). Otherwise, we tend to select modes which best express the intrinsic nature of the artifacts (Rouse 1952:327–29). This difference is reflected in the names of our types, for example, "Glades Plain" in the case of pottery and "semilunar knife" in the case of stonework — or "problematical form" when the nature of the artifact is not known.

This difference must be kept in mind if we are to think clearly about classification. It leads me to make a distinction between (1) historical types, whose modes have been selected, consciously or unconsciously, for their time-space significance and (2) descriptive types, composed of modes referring primarily to the nature of the artifacts.

Once types have been established — whether they are historical or descriptive — they may be used to identify new artifacts without the necessity of actually grouping the artifacts into classes. One need only determine that the new artifacts have the modes comprising a certain type and then apply the name of that type. This is easy enough to do if the types are simple. In the case of more complex types, containing a greater number of diagnostic modes, it has sometimes proved helpful to establish a key to assist in comparison. As in biology, such a key consists of a list in outline form of the modes comprising all of the types. To identify an unknown artifact, one need only trace it down through the key by means of its modes (Colton and Hargrave 1937:36–41; Colton 1952, 1955).

Another device to assist in the identification of new material is the "type artifact(s)." Not to be confused with an artifact type, this consists of the most typical artifact(s) in a class. To identify unknown artifacts or to check identifications made by means of a key, one may compare the unknown artifacts with the type artifacts and thereby, in effect, assign them to the classes typified by those artifacts (Osgood 1942:22–25).

MODES VS. TYPES

We have now distinguished the two principal ways in which archaeologists classify artifacts, analytic and taxonomic. Analytic classification is done by forming successive series of classes, focusing on different features of the artifacts. Each class is characterized by one or more attributes which indicate a procedure to which the artisan conformed, such as a technique of manufacture, or a concept which he expressed in the artifacts, such as an element of shape or decoration. Each custom or concept constitutes a mode.

Taxonomic classification is done by formulating a single set of classes, which differentiate the artifacts in one's collection according to type. Each taxonomic class is characterized by two or more modes, selected from among the total number of modes obtainable by means of analytic classification. The modes diagnostic of each class constitute its type.

Types, then, consist of selected modes. We have seen that the nature of the selection will vary from type to type depending upon the complexity of the artifacts, the number of alternatives which the culture offered to the artisans, the personal inclination of the taxonomist (whether he is a "lumper" or a "splitter"), and the purposes for which he plans to use the types.

To put this in another way, modes are inherent in one's collection. If two archaeologists analyze the same collection and do an equally good job of it, they should produce the same modes (Taylor 1948:129–30). Types, on the contrary, are imposed on the collection. If two taxonomists classify the same collection and decide, for whatever reason, upon different diagnostic modes, they will produce different types (Brew 1946:46). The mode, therefore, is a natural unit of cultural study, whereas the type is an arbitrary one.

It does not follow from this that types are any less demonstrable than modes. An archaeologist can validate types equally well by grouping them into classes and demonstrating that the artifacts of each class share the same diagnostic modes. The point is that he can then regroup the artifacts according to another set of diagnostic modes and thereby produce other types which will have equal validity.

It should not be implied, either, that a type consists merely of the sum of its constituent modes. The fact that all these modes recur from artifact to artifact gives them a reality above and beyond that of the individual modes.

We have distinguished two kinds of modes: (1) conceptual modes, consisting of ideas and standards which the artisans expressed in the artifacts, and (2) procedural modes, consisting of customs followed by the artisans in making and using the artifacts. Conceptual modes are directly indicated by the attributes of the artifacts whereas procedural modes have to be inferred from the attributes. Hence, the distinction between the two is primarily a matter of relative reliability.

Two kinds of types have likewise been distinguished: (1) historical types, formed in order to establish differences of time and space, and (2) descriptive types, formed in order to express differences in the nature of the artifacts. There may be some overlapping between these two, but generally they will be distinct, because the modes comprising each will have been chosen for different reasons. Here, we have a good example of the arbitrary nature of types.

A comparison with ethnology may perhaps help to clarify these distinctions. One of the things an ethnologist does in studying material culture is to ask or observe how his informants make and use their artifacts. Such observations enable the ethnologist to distinguish various techniques of manufacture and uses of the artifacts. In the terminology of the present paper, the latter are procedural modes.

It is likewise possible for the ethnologist to ask his informants to identify the various parts of their artifacts. If the informants go on to distinguish different kinds of handles, for example, or if the ethnologist himself does so, they will be producing the units here called conceptual modes.

A third possibility is for the ethnologist to ask his informants to identify the artifacts as complete objects by saying, for example, that they are "knives" or "scrapers." If either the informant or the ethnologist goes on to define the resultant categories by listing the modes diagnostic of each, he will be producing the units which we have termed descriptive types.

Finally, the informants may refer to certain artifacts as being "old-" or "new-fashioned" and to others as being of a local or foreign style. If either the informant or the ethnologist should define these categories by listing their distinctive modes, he would be producing what are here called historical types.

In other words, the ethnologist as well as the archaeologist may do both analytic and taxonomic classification. The ethnologist, however, is able to do so with the assistance of informants, whereas the archaeologist is forced to rely entirely upon his own judgment and experience in formulating modes and types.

UTILITY OF THE METHODS

Brew (1946:65) has observed that "we need more rather than fewer classifications, different classifications, always new classifications, to meet new needs." If Brew is correct, we ought to be able to list the needs for classification in archaeology and to state the kinds of classification which best meet each need. The remainder of the paper will be devoted to this task. It will be done in terms of the products of our two kinds of classification, conceptual and procedural modes and historical and descriptive types.

Identification of Artifacts. There is probably no professional archaeologist who has not, at one time or another, had an amateur come up to him, take an artifact out of his pocket, and ask for an identification. When the amateur does this, he expects to be answered in terms of descriptive types, that is, to be told that the artifact is a "knife" or a "scraper," for example. If the artifact is a potsherd, the professional will probably answer instead in terms of historical types, calling it "Sebonac Stamped," for example. In my experience the latter answer is not so satisfying to the amateur. He does not understand it, unless he is unusually sophisticated, and tends to look upon it as an affectation of the professional. The amateur is probably right in this, insofar as he is interested purely in identification and not in the historical significance of the potsherd. It would be more appropriate for the professional to identify the sherd descriptively as "a fragment of a cooking pot" instead of terming it "Sebonac Stamped."

Interest in such descriptive identification is, of course, not limited to amateurs. The professional must do it in cataloguing his artifacts and in preparing museum exhibits, where specimens are grouped according to types. Descriptive identification is also basic to several more academic pursuits of the archaeologist, which are discussed below. It is fortunate that taxonomy has not lost prestige among archaeologists as it has in the other natural sciences, for it is a vital part of our research.

Determination of the Culture of a Component. Following the lead of Taylor (1948:197), I would suggest that, when archaeologists determine the culture of a component, that is, of a culturally homogeneous site unit, they would do well to conform to ethnographic practice. As already indicated, ethnographers handle their collections in two different ways: (1) they identify the artifacts, usually in terms supplied by their informants, and (2) they discuss the manufacture and use of the artifacts. (Thompson 1958: 65–146). From the standpoint of the present paper, (1) corresponds to descriptive types and (2) to the modes produced by means of analytic classification. (Ethnographers seem to emphasize procedural modes, but many of them also pay some attention to conceptual modes.) Accordingly, I would suggest that the best way to determine and present the culture of a component is in terms of descriptive types and of procedural and conceptual modes. I doubt that historical types are necessary for this particular purpose, so long as the descriptive approach is applied to pottery and projectile points as well as to other kinds of artifacts, since the historical types will overlap the descriptive types, and anyway they are designed for a different purpose.

The descriptive types and modes will, of course, suffice only to present the material culture of the component. They must be combined with other traits and complexes inferred from the non-artifactual content of the component, for example, the settlement pattern, in order to establish the total culture of the component. The various types, modes, and other traits may simply be listed or they may be grouped into culturally meaningful categories. For example, Fairbanks (1942:228–29) has organized them about the activities of the people inhabiting the Stallings Island component, in accordance with the concept of activity proposed by Linton (1936:397).

Classification of Components to Form Cultures. Many archaeologists find it advisable to group their components into cultures, known variously as foci, phases, complexes, industries, or styles. This requires a form of taxonomic classification. The common practice is to compare the components in terms of their "traits" and, as in the taxonomic classification of artifacts, to select certain traits to be "determinants" of each culture (Cole and Deuel 1937:207–23). When one examines such determinants from the standpoint of the present paper, one finds that they consist of varying combinations of procedural and conceptual modes and of descriptive and historical types. The four appear to be used indiscriminately, without thought as to which units, if any, would be more suitable. To my knowledge, the only author who has attempted to discriminate among the various kinds of determinants is Phillips (1958:123–24), who advocates the use of types as the primary basis for classifying components but would supplement them with modes.

Phillips does not distinguish among the various kinds of types and modes but, if the suggestions made above for the presentation of the culture of a component are correct, it would be appropriate to use descriptive types and both kinds of modes. Personally, I would hesitate to state categorically, as Phillips does, that types should be given priority over modes. I suspect that this will depend on the nature of the cultures being studied. In fact, I can conceive of cases in which modes might suffice by themselves. I do not believe that it would do merely to use single modes, but types are not the only available kinds of combinations of modes. It has been possible, for example, to establish structural relationships among modes, such as Amsden's (1936) correlation of "design vocabulary" and elements of shape. Such structural relationships have proved to be effective as determinants in other branches of anthropology, for example, in the classification of folktales

(Propp 1958), and I wonder whether they might not work better in the classification of some archaeological components than typological complexes of modes, whether selected for their historical or their descriptive significance.

Alternatively, there may well be cases in which neither types nor modes are the best criteria to use in classifying components. Non-artifactual traits, such as settlement patterns and means of subsistence, may sometimes prove to be superior.

In any case, I am certain that artifact types alone cannot provide an adequate basis for the classification of components, if only because they do not cover enough of the culture of the components. For example, Brew (in Tax and others 1953:245) has argued that there is no such thing as a Folsom culture (complex) because practically nothing is known of it but the Folsom type of projectile point. Even assuming that we have only the one type of point, the situation looks better when viewed in terms of modes and non-artifactual traits, for we know the kinds of material used; the techniques of manufacture; distinctive elements of shape; a characteristic, if assumed use; and something about the means of subsistence. All these are separate traits which Brew obscured by limiting himself to the type concept.

Dating of Components and Cultures. Historical types are unquestionably the most effective kind of unit to use in dating components and cultures. The fact that their constituent modes have been selected for time-space significance makes them superior to descriptive types; and the fact that they consist of multiple modes gives them greater reliability than individual modes. This is true whether the types are used as "time markers" with which to correlate strata (components) in the manner of paleontology or are studied in terms of their relative popularity in a more purely archaeological fashion (Heizer 1958:112–13, 114–15).

Definition of Cultural Periods. By the same token, historical types should be most suitable for defining local cultural periods. J. A. Ford's various chronological studies may be cited as examples; his lettered "time scale" and the correlated periods are measured against the frequency changes of pottery types (Phillips, Ford, and Griffin 1951, Fig. 17–21). If, on the other hand, one wishes to work with chronology on a regional, multi-areal basis, modes are likely to be more practicable, whether used singly or in combinations, since they tend to have a broader distribution than types (Cruxent and Rouse 1959).

Studies of Cultural Distribution. Following J. A. Ford's lead (1952:319), I would suggest that modes are the best unit to use in studying cultural distributions. One may trace their persistence and their relative popularity through time (Rouse 1939, Fig. 6) or their diffusion from area to area (Wendorf 1953:163–70). By so doing, one will not only be able to reconstruct the histories of the individual modes but also one will find that certain modes tend always to occur together and hence to form discrete historical complexes. Some of these complexes will correspond to types, that is, they will consist of the same modes as those comprising types, but other complexes will cut across the types. The structural relationships discussed above provide one example. The "traditions" and "horizon styles" of Peruvian archaeology are another (Willey 1945).

An archaeologist who studies the distributions of individual modes, then, will be in a position to reconstruct the histories of those modes and also the histories of types and of non-typological complexes of modes. On the other hand, the archaeologist who studies only the distributions of types will be unable to get at the histories of the other kinds of units. Southwestern archaeology, where it is customary to concentrate on the distribution of types (Colton and Hargrave 1937, Fig. 1), is a case in point. Several authors (Rouse 1954:223) have commented on the lack of horizon styles in the Southwest. This may well be a peculiarity of the culture history of the Southwestern area, but there is also a possibility that it reflects failure on the part of Southwestern archaeologists, in their preoccupation with types, to trace the distribution of enough individual modes.

Studies of Cultural Change. If one is interested in the problem of how one complex (whether typological or not) or one culture has changed into another, modes are again the proper unit to use. As Barnett (1953:185) has put it,

> in order to understand the innovative process, we must be prepared to analyze ideas in any fashion and without limit ... so that we may follow the ramifications of recombination as they actually occur. We cannot deal with the gross stereotyped wholes [i.e., types] only.... We must treat conventional ideas, such as those of tables and men, merely as more or less stable organizations of experience that can be torn down and reassembled in the wink of an eye.
>
> In all the sciences we have come to expect very detailed analyses of data for purposes of classification. This lead, however, has not been followed by students of [culture change].... In trying to understand invention it is common practice to deal with such gross units as automobiles and buggies or [pottery types] and spinning wheels. The attempt to understand one of these complex wholes in terms of the whole of another will give us no insight into their true relationships. We must view the inception of each one in terms of an analysis of its component parts.
>
> The linguists long ago recognized this necessity, and students of linguistic change do not hesitate to break down sentences, words, parts of words, and parts of these parts.... There can be no question that linguists are far ahead of the rest of us in their understanding of the mechanics of cultural change.

Barnett might have added that archaeologists are also accustomed to do analysis and to study culture change in terms of the resultant modes. Gladwin's (1957:282–84) final report on Southwestern archaeology may be cited as an example. Linguists cannot claim sole credit for this kind of approach, nor to have produced the only significant results from it.

CONCLUSIONS

In the foregoing section I have attempted to indicate some of the situations in which it is better to use modes, resulting from analytic classification, or types, resulting from taxonomic classification. I do not pretend to have fully covered the subject; rather I have intended to call attention to it as a problem which deserves the consideration of archaeologists. Too many of us, in my experience, fail to discriminate between modes and types, treating them as equivalent units and substituting one for the other whenever it is convenient to do so (Webb and Snow 1945:16–28). We need to think more about when the various kinds of modes, types, or combinations thereof will be the most effective units to use.

This paper has likewise been intended to call attention to the way in which analysis and taxonomy complement each other as methods of classification. I think we should beware the tendency of some archaeologists to become preoccupied with one to the neglect of the other.

As already indicated, taxonomic classification has received particular emphasis in the American Southwest. We appear at the moment to be witnessing the diffusion of certain Southwestern taxonomic developments to the Southeast (Phillips 1958) and Mesoamerica (Smith, Willey, and Gifford 1960). I do not criticize this diffusion; indeed, I would recommend that it be expanded to include other Southwestern taxonomic devices, such as the key and the type artifact.

On the other hand, I share with Sears (1960) the belief that the analytic approach likewise needs to be strengthened and applied more widely. We need more studies of individual modes and of their non-typological combinations, such as the recent work of Wasley (1959) in the Southwest.

The fact is that both analytic and taxonomic classification must be done in order to make a full study of any collection. Neither, by itself, will supply a complete picture of the culture of the collection, nor will either be able to furnish all the data needed to formulate cultures or to reconstruct culture history.

BIBLIOGRAPHY

Amsden, C. A.
    1936   The Structural Analysis of Pottery Design. In his "An Analysis of Hohokam Pottery Design," *Medallion Papers*, no. 23, pp. 1–17. Globe, Ariz.: Gila Pueblo.

Barnett, H. G.
   1953   *Innovation: The Basis of Cultural Change.* New York: McGraw-Hill.
Black, G. A., and P. Weer
   1936   "A Proposed Terminology for Shape Classification of Artifacts." *American Antiquity* 1, no. 4:280–94.
Brew, J. O.
   1946   The Use and Abuse of Taxonomy. In his "Archaeology of Alkali Ridge, Southeastern Utah," *Papers of the Peabody Museum,* Harvard University 21:44–66.
Cole, Fay-Cooper, and Thorne Deuel
   1937   *Rediscovering Illinois: Archæological Explorations in and around Fulton County.* Chicago: University of Chicago Press.
Colton, H. S.
   1952   "Pottery Types of the Arizona Strip and Adjacent Areas in Utah and Nevada." *Museum of Northern Arizona, Ceramic Series,* no. 1.
   1955   "Check List of Southwestern Pottery Types." *Museum of Northern Arizona, Ceramic Series,* no. 2.
   ———, and L. L. Hargrave
   1937   "Handbook of Northern Arizona Pottery Wares." *Museum of Northern Arizona, Bulletin,* no. 11.
Cruxent, J. M., and Irving Rouse
   1959   "An Archeological Chronology of Venezuela." *Pan American Union, Social Science Monographs,* no. 6.
Fairbanks, C. H.
   1942   "The Taxonomic Position of Stalling's Island, Georgia." *American Antiquity* 7, no. 3:223–31.
Ford, C. S.
   1937   "A Sample Comparative Analysis of Material Culture." In *Studies in the Science of Society,* G. P. Murdock (ed.), pp. 225–46. New Haven: Yale University Press.
Ford, J. A.
   1952   "Measurements of Some Prehistoric Design Developments in the Southeastern United States." *Anthropological Papers of the American Museum of Natural History,* vol. 44, pt. 3.
   ———, and G. R. Willey
   1949   "Surface Survey of the Virú Valley, Peru." *Anthropological Papers of the American Museum of Natural History,* vol. 43, pt. 1.
Gifford, J. C.
   1960   "The Type-Variety Method of Ceramic Classification as an Indicator of Cultural Phenomena." *American Antiquity* 25, no. 3:341–47.

Gladwin, H. S.
  1957   A *History of the Ancient Southwest*. Portland, Maine: Bond, Wheelwright.

Gladwin, Winifred, and H. S. Gladwin
  1930   "Some Southwestern Pottery Types, Series I." *Medallion Papers*, no. 8. Globe, Ariz.: Gila Pueblo.
  1931   "Some Southwestern Pottery Types, Series II." *Medallion Papers*, no. 10. Globe, Ariz.: Gila Pueblo.
  1933   "Some Southwestern Pottery Types, Series III." *Medallion Papers*, no. 13. Globe, Ariz.: Gila Pueblo.

Haury, E. W.
  1936   "Some Southwestern Pottery Types, Series IV." *Medallion Papers*, no. 19. Globe, Ariz.: Gila Pueblo.

Heizer, R. F., ed.
  1958   A *Guide to Archaeological Field Methods*. 3rd rev. ed. Palo Alto, Calif.: National Press.

Krieger, A. D.
  1944   "The Typological Concept." *American Antiquity* 9, no. 3:271–88.

Linton, Ralph
  1936   *The Study of Man*. New York: Appleton, Century.

Matson, F. R.
  1952   "The Contribution of Technical Ceramic Studies to American Archaeology." *Prehistoric Pottery of the Eastern United States*, no. 2, pp. 1–7. Ann Arbor.

Neilson, W. A., T. A. Knott, and P. W. Earhart, eds.
  1940   *Webster's New International Dictionary of the English Language*. 2nd ed. Springfield, Mass.: G. & C. Merriam Co.

Osgood, Cornelius
  1942   "The Ciboney Culture of Cayo Redondo, Cuba." *Yale University Publications in Anthropology*, no. 25.

Phillips, Philip
  1958   "Application of the Wheat–Gifford–Wasley Taxonomy to Eastern Ceramics." *American Antiquity* 24, no. 2:117–30.

————, J. A. Ford, and J. B. Griffin
  1951   "Archaeological Survey in the Lower Mississippi Alluvial Valley, 1940–1947." *Papers of the Peabody Museum*, Harvard University, vol. 25.

Propp, V.
  1958   "Morphology of the Folktale." *Publications of the Indiana University Research Center in Anthropology, Folklore, and Linguistics*, no. 10.

Ritchie, W. A., and R. S. MacNeish
    1949   "The Pre-Iroquoian Pottery of New York State."
            American Antiquity 15, no. 2:97–124.

Rouse, Irving
    1939   "Prehistory in Haiti: A Study in Method." *Yale
            University Publications in Anthropology*, no. 21.
    1941   "Culture of the Ft. Liberté Region, Haiti." *Yale
            University Publications in Anthropology*, no. 24.
    1952   "Porto Rican Prehistory." *The New York Academy of
            Sciences, Scientific Survey of Porto Rico and the
            Virgin Islands* 18, nos. 3–4:307–578.
    1954   "On the Use of the Concept of Area Co-Tradition."
            American Antiquity 19, no. 3:221–25.

Sayles, E. B.
    1936   "Some Southwestern Pottery Types, Series V." *Medal-
            lion Papers*, no. 21. Globe, Ariz.: Gila Pueblo.

Sears, W. H.
    1960   "Taxonomic Systems and Eastern Archaeology." *Amer-
            ican Antiquity* 25, no. 3:324–29.

Shepard, A. O.
    1956   "Ceramics for the Archaeologist." *Carnegie Institution
            of Washington, Publication*, no. 609.

Smith, R. E., G. R. Willey, and J. C. Gifford
    1960   "The Type-Variety Concept as a Basis for the Analysis
            of Maya Pottery." *American Antiquity* 25, no.
            3:330–40.

Taylor, W. W.
    1948   "A Study of Archeology." *American Anthropological
            Association Memoirs*, no. 69.

Tax, Sol, L. C. Eiseley, Irving Rouse, and C. F. Voegelin, eds.
    1953   *An Appraisal of Anthropology Today*. Chicago: Uni-
            versity of Chicago Press.

Thompson, R. H.
    1958   "Modern Yucatecan Maya Pottery Making." *Memoirs
            of the Society for American Archaeology*, no. 15.

Waring, A. J., Jr., and Preston Holder
    1945   "A Prehistoric Ceremonial Complex in the Southeast-
            ern United States." *American Anthropologist* 47, no.
            1:1–34.

Wasley, W. W.
    1959   "Cultural Implications of Style Trends in Southwest-
            ern Pottery: Basketmaker III to Pueblo II in West
            Central New Mexico." Ms, Ph.D. dissertation, Univer-
            sity of Arizona.

Webb, W. S., and C. E. Snow
    1945 "The Adena People." *The University of Kentucky Reports in Anthropology and Archaeology*, vol. 6.
Wendorf, Fred
    1953 "Archaeological Studies in the Petrified Forest National Monument." *Museum of Northern Arizona Bulletin*, no. 27.
Wheat, J. B., J. C. Gifford, and W. W. Wasley
    1958 "Ceramic Variety, Type Cluster, and Ceramic System in Southwestern Pottery Analysis." *American Antiquity* 24, no. 1:34–47.
Whiteford, A. H.
    1947 "Description for Artifact Analysis." *American Antiquity* 12, no. 4:226–37.
Willey, G. R.
    1945 "Horizon Styles and Pottery Traditions in Peruvian Archaeology." *American Antiquity* 11, no. 1:49–56.

JAMES C. GIFFORD

Another approach to how artifact types are used as behavioral indicators appears in this article. James Gifford has modified the type category to include a finer level of variation, the "variety." He then employs types and varieties in Spaulding's sense of "type," as essentially inherent in the data. At the same time, Gifford is sensitive to attribute variation and its significance, but explains this within the framework of a larger type construct. His article illustrates how the type-variety method can explain certain cultural phenomena, based on data from a collection of pottery.

8   The Type-Variety Method of Ceramic Classification as an Indicator of Cultural Phenomena

One of the primary reasons why the archaeologist finds it advantageous to analyze pottery in terms of typological concepts is that a pottery type, once recognized and described, will inevitably repay the analyst by providing him with certain information otherwise unavailable or only available in part. Over thirty years ago Vaillant (1930:9) observed "that the backbone of most of the New World chronologies is variation in pottery types and that the arrangement of a tribal ceramic into chronological divisions is not only very technical but also highly interpretive and impressionistic." The minimum elemental information now held to be usually bound up in a type is that the ceramic entity, such as Benque Viejo

Reprinted, with the editorial changes noted, from "The Type-Variety Method of Ceramic Classification as an Indicator of Cultural Phenomena" by James C. Gifford, *American Antiquity* 25 (1960):341–347, by permission of the publisher and Dr. James C. Gifford, Associate Professor of Anthropology, Department of Anthropology, Temple University, Philadelphia, Penn.

Polychrome, a type, is a specific kind of pottery embodying a unique combination of recognizably distinct attributes, and that this pottery, as well as being the product of a certain cultural configuration, has a definable areal distribution and temporal significance. When the analyst has set down a pottery type description, then the taxonomic device, or pottery type name, he attaches to the described ceramic entity, comes to stand for the entire set of recognizably distinct attributes plus a particular cultural affiliation, areal distribution, and temporal connotation.

In addition anthropological schemes of classification such as this should be means to define and weigh the relative importance of variation and regularity in human society. Most classifications used in anthropology find their rationale in that part of the scientific method which subscribes to the basic assumption that out of what may appear to be a mass of variation, regularities or laws of (cultural) process may be discerned, delineated, and described.

A scheme of ceramic classification has been proposed in three recent papers that is geared especially to the analysis of material aspects of human culture and that also provides a foundation upon which theoretical cultural considerations can be based. These three papers outline and define what is called the "type-variety concept" (variety, Wheat, Gifford, and Wasley 1958; type, Phillips 1958; type-variety concept, Smith, Willey, and Gifford 1960). In the following discussion whenever the term "type" is used, it is intended strictly as defined by Phillips. His usage corresponds to the "type cluster" in the Wheat-Gifford-Wasley nomenclature. For present purposes the terms "type," "variety," and "type-variety concept" are words with a special meaning not to be construed in settings other than those set forth in the three interpretations cited.

Within the context of the type-variety concept, variation as a recognizable reality can be thought of as the product of the individual or of relatively small social groups in human society. "Individual and small social group variation" is meant to encompass not only (at a minimum) actual individual variation, but also variation due to the activities of potters in a village segment, a village, a group of small villages, a community, or a series of communities (at a maximum). When entire cultural configurations are taken into account certain regularities are discernible that are due to the interaction of individuals and small social groups within a society, and these are observed as types. Types in this sense are material manifestations of the regularities of human behavior. Furthermore, theoretical conceptions such as "horizon style" (Willey 1945), "tradition" (Thompson 1956; Willey and Phillips 1958:34–40), "ceramic system" and "ceramic sequence" (Wheat, Gifford, and Wasley 1958) are based on the assumption that on higher levels of societal integration, currents may be discerned which represent the very generalized responses of human groups as determined by recurrent situations and pressures of an even higher order of regularity in human behavior (Fig. 1). The type-variety concept accepts the premise that "cultural phenomena, by definition, have other than a chance distribution" (Kluckhohn 1958b:40) and that there is discoverable order in the data. If the behavioral regularities of societies are documented by means of ceramic and other schemes of classification, some of the laws of human behavior which may exist will become apparent. Classificatory schemes applied to archaeological materials are in part useful as a means toward this end.

These views come to center in particular about the idea that the "type" as an entity is meaningful from the standpoint of cultural interpretation. In the most general terms and to varying degrees, this sentiment is adhered to by many others who have conducted and written about ceramic analyses. Nevertheless, there are competent analysts who do not concur with this view; they believe it tends too far in the direction of interpretive inference. Most previous discussions of ceramic data, however, have been severely limited because the type was the only accepted unit of analysis. Limitations have also come about through an insufficiently coordinated use of theoretical conceptions having to do with other factors in the cultural context under investigation.

The possession of a more flexible definition of the type in conjunction with the variety as well as other ideas such as those embodied in the "ceramic system" and the "ceramic sequence," makes it possible to add new dimensions to a discussion which previously of necessity had to revolve about notions restricted to ceramic units of equivalent status. Within the type-variety concept analysts do not need to refer to all entities as types, and the newer levels of analytical deliberation introduced by an application of more than one theoretical conception upon the ceramic material open up avenues of greater freedom in our thinking. It may thus be possible to bring under one roof viewpoints and opinions previously thought to incline toward opposite poles and be irreconcilable.

When conducting a ceramic analysis utilizing the type-variety concept, the ceramic units involved in the interim sortings are designated "potential varieties." These potential variety units are useful because they are separable on the basis of attributes which are recognizably distinct from one another, but at this stage in classification, these units may or may not be contrivances or artificial constructs of the student. Nevertheless, as any pottery analysis proceeds and as other studies are conducted involving like materials, knowledge concerning each variety increases to the extent that those varieties which *are* only artificial constructs can be discarded on the basis that they have no cultural reality and therefore virtually no further utility. Varieties which survive each addition to knowledge concerning them more and more closely approximate actual material ceramic manifestations of individual and small social group variation in a society. Consequently one may admit that some preliminary variety units indeed prove to be creations of the worker, but in accord with the underlying premise that classification for classification's sake alone is not justifiable, those variety units which expanded knowledge does reveal as having been without cultural meaning are discarded. The more we know of varieties and types, the better we are able to formulate them into units that approximate what were meaningful entities in whatever cultural context we are endeavoring to illuminate.

Types generally include several or many varieties, and as a result are summations of individual and small social group variation. The basic attributes involved in any type came together in the combination of a mental image plus the motor habits of the prehistoric artisans of a culture in such a way that when executed in clay, they fulfilled the requirements of the ceramic and stylistic values of that culture. As noted by Kluckhohn (1958a:474): "In the last analysis it is clearly from individual variability that new cultural values take their origin." And so it is that "types," having grown out of a blending of individual variation, both reflect cultural values and are determined by them. A type is regarded as being the material outcome of a set of fundamental attributes that coalesced, consciously or unconsciously, as a ceramic idea or "esthetic ideal" — the boundaries of which were imposed through the value system operative in the society by virtue of individual interaction on a societal level. These ceramic ideas occurred in the brains of the potters who made the ceramic fabric that constitutes a type, and they are not by any means creations of an analyst.

The distinction of one variety from another within a type rests upon differences having to do with one or several minor characteristics. In contrast with those particulars which distinguish one type from another, such minor ceramic differences were the result of work produced within the confines of relatively small social groups or by individual potters who indulged preferences as to the locale where temper or clay must be gathered or who were able to give vent to artistic flairs and so on. As such, varieties cannot be held as representing any cultural configuration in its entirety. Varieties are apt to reflect "individual and small social group variation" rather than whole-culture phenomena, while the type portrays a combination of a number of pottery traits that were acceptable not only to the potter but to most others adhering to a given culure pattern (Fig. 1). Here we approach certain important observational points that bear upon the reasons why types do represent cultural phenomena.

> There are psychological causes or mental conditions — generally considered physiological — which might also be called "tendencies." Such are the tendency to fatigue, the tendency to form habits, the tendency toward imitation by suggestion, and others.

> These exist nearly identically in all men, whatever their degree of civilization. . . .The tendencies of which we have spoken are at the root of all anthropological phenomena (Kroeber 1952:18).

The "tendency to form habits" and "the tendency toward imitation by suggestion" are intimately connected with the basic causal factors intertwined in the cultural validity of the type.

In the words of a passage contained in a theoretically oriented study by Rands and Riley can be found a pertinent statement of this validity. Cultural phenomena and processes can be documented in the identification of varieties and types because "culture growth often involves a great deal of elaboration — those embellishments which so often impress the student by their number and variety. At the same time, habit channeling, together with the nature of the complex nucleus, will tend significantly to delimit the forms of embellishment that are likely to take place" (Rands and Riley 1958:276). Applying the first of these remarks to prehistoric pottery, the "ceramic variety" represents elaboration and embellishment, whereas the second statement refers to that which results in a combination of abstracted elements that in pottery is represented by the "ceramic type."

It is plain that a pottery type has a cultural basis because the implicit values inherent in the cultural configuration as a whole cast serious limitations upon what in the realm of ceramic products will be acceptable to the participants in that cultural configuration. At the same time the cluster of values also imposes serious strictures upon the ceramic mental images that the potters will draw upon. The potters respond to value-sanctioned, culturally defined images and not to others that could be encompassed by their abilities or imagination because most people, due to economic necessity and for reasons of greater psychological comfort having to do with reduction of social stress, tend to conform to the demands of a majority of the norms that are a part of their culture at a particular time in history. "To speak of 'values' is one way of saying that human behavior is neither random nor solely 'instinctual' . . . the individual gets abstract, perduring standards primarily from the culture or sub-culture as mediated by parents and other persons from whom he learns" (Kluckhohn 1958a:474). Types, therefore, equate themselves with the crystallization of conscious or unconscious ceramic esthetic images conditioned by values. In this regard, the scheme of classification discussed approaches a definition of the ceramic value system which pertains to any given archaeological culture. In other words, when recognizing and defining types, the analyst is describing the material manifestations "of preferred paths of behavior that take their direction from varying concepts of the desirable" (Kluckhohn 1958a:473).

In speaking of artifacts Leslie White says, "We do not customarily call these things human behavior, but they are the embodiments of human behavior; the difference between a nodule of flint and a stone axe is the factor of human labor. An axe, bowl, crucifix — or a haircut — is congealed human labor." White maintains artifacts are the result of acts which cumulatively, in this sense, are human behavior and the concern of psychology. "If, however, we treat them [artifacts] in terms of their relationship to one another, quite apart from their relationship to human organisms, i.e., in an extra somatic, or extraorganismic, context, the things and events become *culture* — cultural elements or culture traits." The difference between the two "derives from the difference between contexts in which their common subject matter is treated" (White 1959:232–33).

Tacit recognition is accorded these well-stated contextual observations in the implications of the type-variety concept. The situation, however, is treated not as a dichotomy but as a duality (one flowing from the other) in that the "variety" is a reflection of concrete individual human behavior while a "type" represents an abstraction from individual or small social group behavior that is the ceramic unit most useful in showing relationships of one kind of pottery (one ceramic cultural element) to another. Further-more when viewed in this light the type-variety concept tends to be consonant with the definition of culture by Kroeber and Kluckhohn (1952:155) who say it " is an abstraction from concrete human behavior, but it is not itself behavior." By analyzing pottery within the framework of the type-variety methodology we move from a consideration of human acts to the consideration of theoretical abstractions that can be used in various ways to increase our understanding of cultural processes (Fig. 1). It is an analytical progression from the specific to the general, from percepts to concepts, and in this case from appreciable examples of human behavior (in pottery making) to concern with abstract cultural elements.

In the light of the foregoing remarks as they pertain to innate human tendencies, the archaeologist, in his capacity as a student of material culture, seems to come more directly into contact with what may be subsumed under two particularly fundamental tendencies. These two tendencies are to be found as components of elemental human nature in the form of (1) stability, as expressed by type persistence and continuity through time, a condition essentially embodied in the concept of tradition (Thompson 1956; Willey and Phillips 1958:34–40); and (2) change, as encompassed by the constant regrouping of artifact attributes into new types. In each individual craftsman there is a rudimentary desire for a measure of both stability or continuity (manifested by habits and a clinging to the old) and change (manifested by the desire for something new). The extent to which either of these is satisfied or emphasized is conditioned by the total value system of the society in which the individual finds himself. Some societies emphasize fast moving change accelerated to such a point as to be constantly disturbing to the individual. Others emphasize stability to such a degree as to be almost dormant. On his own the individual seems to incline

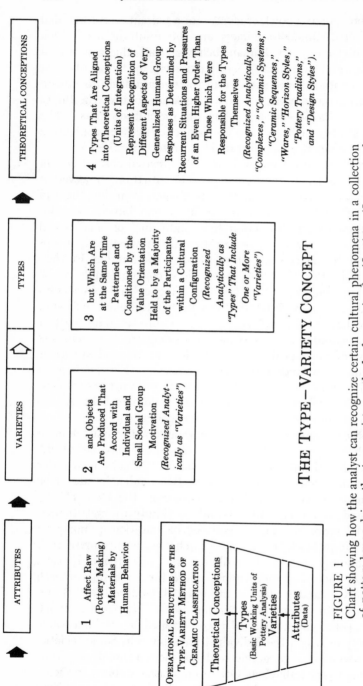

THE TYPE–VARIETY CONCEPT

FIGURE 1

Chart showing how the analyst can recognize certain cultural phenomena in a collection of pottery by applying the type-variety method of ceramic classification. (In terms of absolute theory: within a cultural matrix where the individual motivation of all participant pottery makers coincides completely with the ceramic and stylistic values of that culture, all types would tend to be exclusively one-variety types with a certain range of variation in each case as determined by participant diversity in skills and so forth; on the other hand, within a cultural matrix where no value orientation obtains concerning pottery or where the value orientation has for some reason been totally shattered, the products of every pottery-producing individual would be a distinct variety and the number of varieties within a type would be limited only by the number of pottery-producing individuals within the cultural configuration.)

toward a fine balance of change and stability, and his desires would be met under ideal conditions by a rhythmic pattern of new types within established traditions. Actual situations deviate from the ideal in accord with the degree to which stability or change is emphasized within a cultural matrix. In trying to describe and observe the tendency in any given configuration toward one or the other extreme we approach an understanding of the underlying mechanisms of human nature and the societal values that produce types as observable realities. In describing types and recording the material traditions within a society we are indicating the tempo of that society as reflected in its material culture.

Cultural anthropology has consistently drawn attention to tendencies of this kind and there has been an effort to delineate them with regard to value orientations. A recent paper (Colby 1958:317–22) pinpoints the problem in the context of an equilibrium theory of behavioral redundancy. In any cultural configuration

> predictability of tomorrow's events and of what people may do or think is of paramount importance. . . . For predictability to be constantly maintained at a high level of efficiency, value systems must be changeable, must always be in process. . . . But there are other trends in the opposite direction which temper the dread of the unexpected. These are trends toward disorganization, toward the unknown, and toward experimental innovations. . . . By maintaining some sort of equilibrium between order and disorder or rigidity and fluidity [man] can stay at peak adjustment. Such is the maturation process in culture and in personality. . . . One may say then that life in general, like language, seeks . . . an equilibrium between the new (unexpected) and the old (predictable); between disorganization and organization.

In consequence of these underlying tendencies of human behavior as discussed by Colby, there is in any cultural continuum a "process of constant reformulation, reassessment, and affirmation of value structure regulated by the movement either toward or away from organization." It is this interesting aspect of human nature that provides a considerable explanation of the "why" and the cause of dynamics in cultural process. The archaeologist sees and documents it when he describes gradual change within a cultural or artifact "tradition." The ceramic analyst has observed similar circumstances when he elucidates a "ceramic sequence."

The fact cannot be overemphasized that it is due to the results of the combined value forces of the total cultural configuration (indeed the inherent cultural bias) that particular kinds (types) of pottery become widely acceptable and are striven for as desired norms in ceramic manufacture. Awareness must be exercised that any normal "human act, even in its first expression in the person of a single individual, is a group product to begin with" (White 1959:244). The individual craftman is never really "free" to "create" the entity recognized as a variety or type because although he may be free to produce an entity of some sort, his production may either be accepted or rejected by the culture in response to its particular bias. And since the individual did not by himself create the bias, the cultural acceptance of his product is beyond his immediate control. The results of his work may, in terms of the culture, merely go down as experiment, thereby resulting only in one or a few expressions of individual variation, or it may "catch on," that is, be compatible with the bias of a major portion of the culture and thus have an appeal which is pleasing or advantageous in one way or another to a majority of the participants in the culture. And of course, due to the mechanisms of culture change through time, the cultural bias shifts with time and what will please at one time may not please at another — so it is that a type is a true indicator of time and a complex of types (a ceramic complex) is a valid delineation of the ceramic content of a phase.

To repeat the substance of many an earlier discourse, a potsherd is surely not a biological entity and therefore cannot in a biological sense be related to or evolve into another kind of potsherd. But let me reiterate my view that pottery types are manifestations of ceramic ideas, ceramic images, held originally in the minds of human beings. The ideas are human concepts and as such can be and are indeed related to one another areally and do indeed, as ideas or conceptions develop one into another through time. Relationships of this order are recognized by the analyst through the medium of theoretical conceptions such as "ceramic systems" and "ceramic sequences" (ceramic micro-traditions).

Ideas, mental images, are the "genes" of culture. These ideas or mental images, and in particular ceramic ideas or mental images, while being in no way biologically related to other mental images, can be and often are related within cultures and cross-culturally within a cultural frame of reference (see Osgood 1951:202–14). Therefore, anthropological classifications having to do with ideas or mental images as recognized in objects of material culture find their basis and justification within the processes of culture itself. Such classifications as these should not in any sense be viewed as biological classifications. They are cultural classifications. As a result, even though man is a biological organism, the "type-variety" methodological approach is a cultural classification because it is concerned with the analysis of man's nonbiological *culture products*.

An interesting point has been raised by Kluckhohn to the effect that classifications which are to be of use to anthropology should be typologies. He defines a typology as

> a classification that has an intent, that is, has a direction. The ways one may classify things are limitless and therefore any number of classifications may be conceived, but a typology has

an explicit theoretical basis and the typologist is interested in using a given classification in order to shed light upon the reasons beneath the occurrence of some observable phenomena. . . . A classification is no more than a set (or sets) of empirical groupings established for convenience. A typology, however, is a theoretically oriented classification that is directed toward the solution of some problem or problems (Kluckhohn, in press).

Following this distinction I view the type-variety methodological scheme as a typology. In addition, when an analyst subjects a collection to study by means of the type-variety concept, I believe he accomplishes both what Rouse (1960) calls "analytic classification" and "taxonomic classification."

In conclusion, let us review the query, should an anthropological typology be an end in itself? Absolutely not. Any classification of use to anthropology, whatever the medium, must be but a means whereby cultural processes are described and elucidated. Within such a frame of reference cultural classifications (anthropological typologies) are some of the instruments which anthropologists must use if they are to chart reliably the actualized and potential dimensions of human nature through time and space.

This is not by any means to say that it is desirable to adopt blindly any one scheme and stick to it come what may. It is rather my feeling that ultimately a classificatory scheme or group of compatible schemes will be refined which will accurately reflect the regularities and irregularities, the similarities and dissimilarities, of cultural processes, perhaps on a worldwide basis, and that our present efforts are but steps in this direction.

BIBLIOGRAPHY

Colby, B. N.
    1958   "Behavioral Redundancy." *Behavioral Science* 3, no. 4:317–22.
Kluckhohn, Clyde
    1958a "The Scientific Study of Values and Contemporary Civilization." *Proceedings of the American Philosophical Society* 102, no. 5:469–76. Philadelphia.
    1958b "The Scientific Study of Values." *University of Toronto Installation Lectures*, 1958, pp. 25–54. Toronto: University of Toronto Press.
    [1960] "The Use of Typology in Anthropological Theory." In *Selected Papers from the Proceedings of the Vth International Congress of Anthropological and Ethnological Sciences*, Anthony F. C. Wallace (ed.). Philadelphia: University of Pennsylvania Press.
Kroeber, A. L.
    1952   *The Nature of Culture.* Chicago: University of Chicago Press.

————, and Clyde Kluckhohn
1952 "Culture: A Critical Review of Concepts and Definitions." *Papers of the Peabody Museum,* Harvard University, vol. 47, no. 1.

Osgood, Cornelius
1951 "Culture: Its Empirical and Non-Empirical Character." *Southwestern Journal of Anthropology* 7, no. 2:202–14.

Phillips, Philip
1958 "Application of the Wheat-Gifford-Wasley Taxonomy to Eastern Ceramics." *American Antiquity* 24, no. 2:117–25.

Rands, R. L., and C. L. Riley
1958 "Diffusion and Discontinuous Distribution." *American Anthropologist* 60, no. 2:274–97.

Rouse, Irving
1960 "The Classification of Artifacts in Archaeology." *American Antiquity* 25, no. 3:313–23.

Smith, R. E., G. R. Willey, and J. C. Gifford
1960 "The Type-Variety Concept as a Basis for the Analysis of Maya Pottery." *American Antiquity* 25, no. 3:330–40.

Thompson, R. H., ed.
1956 An Archaeological Approach to the Study of Cultural Stability. In "Seminars in Archaeology: 1955," Robert Wauchope (ed.), pp. 31–57. *Memoirs of the Society for American Archaeology,* no. 11.

Vaillant, G. C.
1930 "Excavations at Zacatenco." *Anthropological Papers of the American Museum of Natural History,* vol. 32, pt. I.

Wheat, J. B., J. C. Gifford, and W. W. Wasley
1958 "Ceramic Variety, Type Cluster, and Ceramic System in Southwestern Pottery Analysis." *American Antiquity* 24, no. 1:34–47.

White, L. A.
1959 "The Concept of Culture." *American Anthropologist* 61, no. 2:227–51.

Willey, G. R.
1945 "Horizon Styles and Pottery Traditions in Peruvian Archaeology." *American Antiquity* 11, no. 1:49–56.
————, and Philip Phillips
1958 *Method and Theory in American Archaeology.* Chicago: University of Chicago Press.

GEORGE L. COWGILL

The preceding articles on artifact classification dramatize the complexities involved in ordering data before further analysis and explanation. Spaulding's earlier discussion of statistical techniques strongly suggests that complex data must be matched by equally complex and sophisticated techniques of data storage, ordering, and manipulation. In the decade since computers were first used to process archaeological data, exciting progress has been made in this field through the capability of treating vast quantities of data efficiently. Yet the computer is only a machine that greatly speeds up the various operations on data, which are determined by the archaeologist. The computer cannot perform explanatory tasks — this the archaeologist alone can do. In this article, George Cowgill surveys the current uses and potentials for automatic data-processing equipment — one of the most important advances in archaeology in recent years.

9   Computers and Prehistoric Archaeology

I should begin by explaining that by prehistoric archaeology I do not mean the study of peoples who are necessarily remote from us in time, but rather work on cultures of any era which have perished without leaving written records. My topic is limited in this way because I do not wish to discuss the roles of computers in dealing with ancient texts. This is an important use for computers, but my preference is to concentrate on applications which I would not expect historians or linguists to deal with. I will merely remark that for the archaeological study of historic cultures, computers could be used for everything the prehistorian can use them for, in addition to their uses for textual materials.

An inherent condition of archaeological research is that it produces vast amounts of data, and much of an archaeologist's life is spent in coping with

From "Computers and Prehistoric Archaeology" by George L. Cowgill in E. A. Bowles (ed.), *Computers in Humanistic Research*, pp. 47–56, © 1967. Reprinted by permission of the author and Prentice-Hall, Inc., Englewood Cliffs, New Jersey. Footnotes are renumbered.

masses of details; keeping track of them, organizing them, taking many relevant things into account at once, and extracting some kind of orderly interpretations. Considering how much effort has recently gone into developing electronic equipment intended to deal with data processing problems in general, it seems inevitable that these new machines can lighten some of the archaeologist's burdens, and very probable that some quite new horizons in data analysis can be opened up.

Broadly, I see three major roles for computers in prehistoric archaeology. First, they can be used to do the tabulating, more or less "bookkeeping" jobs, more quickly, accurately, and neatly, which are normally done anyhow. There is little to be gained by using them for this purpose alone. Archaeologists do not usually work under the time pressure that businesses do, and there are often adequate alternatives, including desk calculators (many of which are portable enough to be usable in the field while work is in progress) and the relatively simple and accessible machines which punch and sort cards, make tabulations, and print card data or tabulation results. If anything, archaeologists could profit by making more use than they do of extremely simple aids in the field, such as slide rules (to figure percentages and ratios). The point about computers in relation to this role is that, if a computer is set up to do something more sophisticated with the data, for which simpler equipment is inadequate, it is very easy to use it in addition for producing routine tabulations.

A second role for computers in archaeology is in the general field of data storage and retrieval. What I have in mind here is making it easy for the archaeologist to inspect all the available data relevant to some specified topic, or relevant to objects or sites of some specified category. When emphasis shifts to what the archaeologist does with the data he inspects, one moves out of data retrieval and into data analysis. Of course the two fields are intimately linked, and one cannot always make a sharp distinction between them.

In part, the archaeological data retrieval problem is simply the need for fast and comprehensive indexing of the literature in a way that is flexible and informative enough to be helpful to users with many different specific interests. There is nothing distinctively archaeological about this problem; it is just one aspect of the growing bibliographic difficulties of scholarly literature in general, and by and large the same methods and machines that come to be adopted for other fields should also work well for archaeologists.

A more specifically archaeological problem is involved when the data search is aimed less at finding publications relevant to a given topic than at discovering other objects comparable to a given specimen, or objects comparable to any or all of a given collection of specimens. At present, anyone trying to do this, using published literature, unpublished manuscripts and notes, or museum collections faces a discouraging mess.

Much less comparative work is done than might be, and what is done takes too long and is often needlessly spotty and inconclusive.

What is crucial for any real progress with this problem, whether computers are used or not, is a great clarification and standardization of the concepts and terms used in archaeological description and classification. Nearly twenty years ago, long before archaeologists thought of computers, J. O. Brew pointed out, in one of the few truly important discussions of archaeological theory, that there is really more to good archaeological classification than a certain intuitive astuteness as to which things "go together" and which things are best put into separate categories.[1] Brew argued for a multiplicity of different classifications in order to serve different purposes. I agree with this, and would emphasize that what we must standardize are the concepts and terms themselves, not the classifications. One great opportunity that computers offer us is that, rather than forcing greater rigidity upon us (as I suspect many archaeologists assume), they will make possible much more of the flexibility that Brew asked for.

In particular, one controversy has involved "lumpers" and "splitters." Several different points are at issue here, but one of them is the "lumper" argument that some systems of artifact typology are so complicated that they can only be learned by a few specialists, and that therefore they should be simplified. To this I would reply that one task of archaeological reporting is to describe historical phenomena; that historical phenomena are inherently complex and "messy"; and that there is just no such thing as a simple model of them which does not oversimplify to the point of falsification. Simple schemes and broad outlines are vital for introducing a student to an area and for the edification of the interested person without research interests in the area. But, for research by the area specialist, and, also, for most research involving comparisons between areas, we absolutely require systems of handling the data which are compendious and expressive of minor contrasts, yet systematically organized, and not merely lists of item-by-item descriptions.

To some extent this dilemma can be resolved by hierarchical taxonomies, using a "fine-grained" system of numerous categories based on minor differences for the experts, and lumping these into a smaller number of more inclusive, higher level categories for nonspecialists. This is not entirely satisfactory either, for the hierarchy itself has a simple structure in which there is no easy provision for expressing multidimensional relationships in which a given category resembles a second in one way, a third category in a different way, a fourth in still another, and so on. Here again, there is a built-in pressure toward oversimplification and a Procrustean treatment of historical complexities.

[1] J. O. Brew, "The Archaeology of Alkali Ridge, Southeastern Utah," *Papers of the Peabody Museum*, Harvard University, no. 21 (1946).

With a computerized data file, any feature that is recorded can be used as a basis for searching the file, and one can retrieve data in a form that groups together all specimens which share any one of the enormous number of different logically possible combinations of features. Different sets of searching criteria imply different systems of classification, and a limited number of criteria can be combined in several different ways to generate a great many schemes of classification. The only limitation is the obvious one that the file cannot be searched for any features that were never recorded in it in the first place.

This raises a related problem in the retrieval of archaeological data. To what extent is it feasible or desirable to establish a single basic code for describing all specimens of a given class of material, such as pottery? No matter what varying philosophies about the defining of types they adhere to, all archaeologists would surely agree that features which mark important contrasts in the material of one area or period may be of very little importance for other times or places. A code designed to be useful both for Mississippian pottery of the eastern United States and for Anasazi pottery of the Southwest would have to provide for many attributes which would be observed exclusively in one area, and never in the other. It would probably also force one to record a number of minor details which were important in one area, and trivial by any possible criteria in the other. For many purposes it would be simpler to use different codes in each area.

But what about the person who specifically wants to search for similarities in the pottery of these two areas? Or suppose one wanted to do a comparative study of a north Texas collection which had affiliations in both directions. Must one make separate computer runs, coping with two or more distinct coding systems? This coding problem will require much study, and its outcome will depend upon the extent to which archaeologists in different areas can agree not to make things needlessly difficult for one another. At the very least, there should be no more disparity between systems than is really required by disparity in the data.

In this connection, the work of the New World Lithic Typology Project sounds like exactly the sort of thing that is needed, and something similar should be begun for ceramics.[2] I suggest that we develop on paper a large and extremely detailed "master code" for ceramics, including provision for every descriptive variable which may be important anywhere; provision for infinite subdivision of all measurable or rankable variables; and provision for unlimited additions to the range or number of states ("attributes") of all variables. Undoubtedly, new variables and new ranges or states for old variables will have to be added from time to time, but I believe this could

[2] See A. D. Krieger, "New World Lithic Typology Project: Part II," *American Antiquity* 29 (1964):489–93; and E. M. Weyer, Jr., "New World Lithic Typology Project: Part I," *ibid.*, pp. 487–89.

be done in an orderly way such that every new thing has a new designation, and all old designations are either unchanged in meaning or totally discarded.

One could then set up files of data which, depending on circumstances, could cover anything from one component of one site to the whole world, using as an actual working code whatever simplification of the master code was most convenient. Under no circumstances should the working code provide *more* detail than the master code; it should always be some simplification, in which some master code variables are ignored, and in which some ranges or states of the variables used are lumped together (for example, in the case of length, by rounding off exact values to the nearest whole centimeter).

A vital individual responsibility will be to specify for every working code *exactly* how it relates to the master code. By doing so, the codes used for any two files, however different in themselves, will be related to one another through the one underlying master code, and one could be specific about the extent to which data from two or more files were unambiguously similar. One could also be specific about the nature and extent of ambiguities in such comparisons. To avoid needless ambiguities, it should be required that all working codes *must* provide at least information on some minimum list of variables and states or intervals of these variables, whatever else is provided in addition.

The master code is roughly analogous to the linguistic concept of a universal system for describing phonetically all possible speech sounds, but I would stress that the working codes need not, and often will not, approximate the criteria which were "important" in the cognitive systems of the makers or users of the artifacts. That is, in the terms of Pike, all our codes may be more or less "etic" rather than "emic."[3] It may become possible to convincingly demonstrate in some cases that we are close to the categories important for a prehistoric people, but even if we could we would still want for many purposes to take account of other features in our analyses.[4]

As in the case of tabulation, there are some simpler alternatives to computers for data retrieval, including hand-sorted, edge-punched cards[5]

---

[3] K. Pike, *Language in Relation to a Unified Theory of the Structure of Human Behavior* (Glendale, 1955).

[4] For an excellent discussion of this, see J-C. Gardin, "On a Possible Interpretation of Componential Analysis in Archaeology," in *Formal Semantic Analysis*, E. A. Hammel (ed.), pp. 9–22, pt. 2 of *American Anthropologist*, vol. 67, no. 5 (1965).

[5] See A. O. Shepard, *Ceramics for the Archaeologist* (Washington, 1957); and E. L. Davis, "Three Applications of Edge-Punched Cards for Recording and Analyzing Field Data," in *Contributions of the Wetherill Mesa Archaeological Project* (assembled by D. Osborne, edited by B. S. Katz). *Memoirs of the Society for American Archaeology* 19 (1965):216–26.

and optical coincidence cards.[6] In my experience they are less desirable than computers, either if one wishes to put all important data directly into the punched code, or to integrate data-searching directly with statistical analysis; or indeed, any time that the data are really numerous. Their best use is for multiple indexing of a few hundred items, including illustrations, descriptive text, or both, where the records themselves are to be inspected for much detail that is not included in the coding system *per se*.[7]

Formerly, another advantage of hand-operated systems was their much greater accessibility. It appears that this is being greatly changed by the development of remote time-sharing computer services; whereby a number of users at consoles many miles apart can simultaneously run their problems on the same large high speed computer. Archaeological data retrieval would require scanning, perhaps repeated scanning, of files containing several hundred thousand to several million characters, and I am not sure whether this is feasible with present time-sharing facilities. At any rate, it seems reasonable to expect that it will become possible soon. Certainly it will be possible to write programs for searching such that the individual user need know nothing about programming, and need only supply the machine with a request for specific data files and a specification of the criteria to be used in searching. It should be possible for an archaeologist to learn a system about as complicated as that he now must know in order to get one book out of a library (assuming the book is not already out or lost), go to a console within a few yards or a few blocks of his office, and in a few minutes do a comparative study that would take him months by precomputer methods.

This assumes that the archaeological data are stored in a computer facility which is used primarily for business or scientific purposes, which has the advantage that the same facility could be used very easily for data analysis. In some cases it may be better to use one of the microfilm machines being developed for library or archival purposes, and this might especially be true if high-resolution pictures of artifacts are desired as part of the search output.

Whatever kind of machine is used, the big and costly bottleneck will be getting the data into the file to begin with. Besides working out a suitable code, much tedious, meticulous, and rather skilled labor will be required to produce good descriptions of the material in a language readable by the machine. There is not much hope of automating this process. One can, for instance, imagine an electronic scanner automatically sensing and recording minute color variations in an object, but the day is still very distant when a

[6] J. D. Campbell and H. S. Caron, "Data Processing by Optical Coincidence," *Science* 133 (1961):1333–38; and J. Christophe and J. Deshayes, *Index de l'outillage sur cartes perforées: outils de l'âge du bronze des Balkans à l'Indus* (Paris, 1964).

[7] Krieger, in *op. cit.*, expresses a similar opinion.

computer can cope with the problem of deciding which colors on a pot are properly characteristic of it, and which best ought to be recorded as "firing clouds," "altered due to erosion," or the like.

The third role for computers in archaeology is in the statistical or mathematical analysis of data. Archaeologists have not very often gone much beyond intuitive interpretations based on inspection of tabulated counts or percentages. There have been some instances of ill-founded judgments based on statistically inadequate evidence (too small a sample, a badly selected or biased sample, or inadequately defined or poorly chosen variables) but probably most interpretations have been valid as far as they went. The exciting things about statistical methods are the possibilities they offer for new and richer interpretations of data; especially for better methods of generating categories and taxonomies, for dealing with complex interactions between different traditions, and for convincingly validated reconstructions of prehistoric social and cultural systems.

Archaeologists have been making some use of statistical techniques at least since Spier's work at Zuñi[8] but the use has always been very limited.[9] However, since 1955, statistically oriented papers have appeared with increasing frequency. Perhaps there has been some justification for this lack of enthusiasm, for most of the really interesting problems for archaeologists require multivariate techniques for dealing simultaneously with many variables, such as cluster analysis, factor analysis, multiple correlation, etc., which are discouragingly tedious without a computer.

Today the stumbling block is not in the execution of the computations, but in the education of archaeologists in the methods, so that we can have some idea of what technique or techniques might be available for a given problem, and of what interpretations are justified, and not justified, on the basis of a given computer result. There is probably still too much of a tendency for most archaeologists either to flatly reject the notion that "a machine can do your thinking for you" or else to put a somewhat premature and excessive trust in computer results. My own position was expressed when I earlier used the phrase "exciting . . . possibilities."

Roughly, three general things can happen in any particular study. First, the mathematical model may fit the data so poorly that actually wrong results are obtained, even though the computations themselves are technically correct. Second, the results may not be wrong, but may yield so

[8] L. Spier, "An Outline for a Chronology of Zuñi Ruins," *Anthropological Papers of the American Museum of Natural History* 18 (1917):200–331.

[9] Particularly influential studies include the work of Bordes, as reported by H. L. Movius, Jr., "Old World Prehistory: Paleolithic," in *Anthropology Today*, A. L. Kroeber (ed.) (Chicago, 1953), pp. 163–92; also W. S. Robinson, "A Method for Chronologically Ordering Archaeological Deposits," *American Antiquity* 16 (1951): 293–301; and A. C. Spaulding, "Statistical Techniques for the Discovery of Artifact Types," *American Antiquity* 18 (1953):305–13.

little beyond what was already apparent that the effort is not worthwhile. Finally, the results may be both valid and an important addition to what can be obtained by more familiar methods.

I believe that results of this kind are beginning to appear in print.[10] To my mind the greatest weakness in these, and in all other studies to date, is that archaeologists have been too dependent on statisticians whose own outlooks have mostly been derived from experience in other social sciences, particularly psychology and educational testing. In many ways it is true that multivariate data are *multivariate data,* and there are many logical and formal similarities whether they concern archaeological assemblages, responses to a battery of tests, or anything else. But there are problems peculiar to archaeological data, and, especially, the formal, logical structures of the kinds of interpretations we want sometimes differ importantly from what a psychologist wants from his data. As long as we just borrow multivariate techniques which have been developed primarily to meet the needs of psychologists and educators, we are almost certainly missing many of the possibilities of these methods for specifically archaeological problems.

Clearly, one thing which is needed is that at least a few archaeologists learn enough statistics to be able to talk to, and sometimes talk back to, the statisticians. Equally, the bulk of mathematics-allergic archaeologists must learn, in a general qualitative way, what the names of the various multivariate techniques are, what assumptions about the data each presupposes, what general sorts of problems each is useful for, and what major peculiarities, pitfalls, and ambiguities are associated with each. As far as I can tell, many archaeologists who are tackling problems by less suitable methods are not consciously rejecting multivariate techniques but simply are unaware that anything better than their present methods is available.

One final point about the role of computers in archaeology should be made. It has become quite common for most anthropology departments to have a few students who already have substantial computer programming and operating experience. This competent and motivated student energy is a major resource for the fuller and more effective use of computers by archaeologists.

I have made no attempt to review specific current computer projects, but I should mention briefly my own work, which is more fully reported elsewhere.[11] Since the spring of 1965 I have been collaborating with René

[10] For example, W. A. Longacre, "Archaeology as Anthropology: A Case Study," *Science* 144 (1964):1454 f.; J. A. Brown and L. G. Freeman, Jr., "A UNIVAC Analysis of Sherd Frequencies from the Carter Ranch Pueblo, Eastern Arizona," *American Antiquity* 30 (1964):162–67; and J. Deetz, *The Dynamics of Stylistic Change in Arikara Ceramics* (Illinois Studies in Anthropology, no. 4), Urbana, 1965.

[11] G. L. Cowgill, Computer Analysis of Archaeological Data from Teotihuacan, Mexico, paper delivered at the Annual Meeting of the American Anthropological Association, Denver, Colo., November 1965.

Millon in a pilot study for computer analysis of data obtained by him and his associates in the course of a detailed mapping and surface reconnaissance of Teotihuacan, a huge prehistoric city in central Mexico.[12] It has been clear for many years that gross contrasts exist between different parts of the city, and, like any other preindustrial city, it must have been occupied by a complex and richly differentiated society. One major aim of the mapping project has been to bring the evidence on differentiation into sharper focus and to get a better idea of the city as a going concern. Much that is new can already be said without recourse to computers, but given the enormous quantity and the detailed character of the data which are being accumulated, not all its implications can be brought to light by ordinary inspection.

One important use for multivariate analysis involves treating each artifact as a "case" and generating a typology or classification of the artifacts, based on comparisons of their attributes. So far we have not been working on this level, but have instead been treating each of the roughly 5,000 separate tracts from which we have materials as a "case." The variables used to characterize these cases include architectural and other features which may be observed as present or absent, rankings of extent or intensity of other features, and counts of various categories of pottery and other materials collected from the surface.

At present, it is often difficult to say if a feature is worth including in our code or not. We have been guided by the idea that in a pilot study we should run the risk of including too much rather than too little, and have developed a code which requires eight eighty-column punched cards for each site. We think of this as primarily a format for data storage, which can be recorded by machine in many different ways, to serve as input data for many alternative statistical programs. In recording we have great freedom to select or omit different variables, to build new variables as functions of the old, or to collapse or simplify variables in different ways; all far more easily than if we had to return to the original data sheets each time.

We have not, of course, any intention of trying to provide in the code for everything observed in each site. Data on features which are unique or extremely rare are best retrieved by merely listing the sites which have them, and are too sparse to be useful for multivariate analysis.

Much of our work so far has been concerned specifically with the development of a code which retains a good deal of the detail of the original data without becoming impossibly cumbersome. We have also been very concerned with establishing the validity and reliability of our data. Comparisons of frequencies and ratios of materials collected and analyzed

---

[12] . . . For a preliminary report on this project, see Millon, "The Teotihuacan Mapping Project," *American Antiquity* 29 (1964):345–52.

from the same tracts by different workers at different times have so far turned out to show surprisingly good reliability. However, sampling problems inherent in scarce categories require that for some things we must do our studies on the basis of aggregates rather than individual tracts and thereby lose some sharpness of detail for these categories. This is one of the inescapable limitations of surface-collected data that can be overcome only by digging and not by computing.

Our major goal is to search for clusters of features (including artifact types) which are similar in their *distributions,* and for clusters of tracts which are similar in their *features.* The first procedure is what in factor analysis is called R technique, while the second is Q technique. We plan to compare results and costs of various clustering techniques.

We do not expect all the resulting clusters to be self-evident in their interpretation (although some of them probably will be). Rather, they are to be seen as themselves important kinds of data which will demand the fullest exercise of intuition, judgment, and control of both mathematical and anthropological concepts and materials for their best interpretation in cultural terms.

Other useful applications of the computer include simple tabulation of the data, and the machine production of distribution maps. For the latter purpose, the SYMAP program of Howard T. Fisher, of the Graduate School of Design, Harvard University, looks most promising. For tabulations and statistical analyses, the DATA-TEXT system of programs being developed for use on the IBM 7094 by Arthur S. Couch, Department of Social Relations, Harvard University, has many very attractive features, including great flexibility in recoding variables.

RAYMOND H. THOMPSON

Whether the archaeologist employs conventional typology, mode or attribute analysis, or any other method of classification, and whether he uses a computer to order his data or works them up by hand, he reaches a point where he must seek cultural or processual explanations from his data. This search is the crux of archaeology. We could excavate, describe, and classify artifacts in their spatial and temporal contexts for a lifetime and not derive any anthropological information, and such a pursuit would, of course, be sterile.

To find the significance of the data to prehistoric man, his lifeways, and his cultural development, we need a body of explanatory theory, and the past decade has witnessed a strong development of such theory and its methods. The following selections state some foundations of this theory and illustrate its applications.

Raymond Thompson's article on the subjective element in inference covers several critical problems. To be sure, we are all subjective when dealing with culture, since we participate in it; to deny subjectivity is unrealistic, and in evaluating any cultural data, we should make proper allowances for it. But a corollary problem that has recently been the subject of considerable discussion involves the distinction between deductive and inductive approaches to archaeological explanation. In a deductive process, the distinction revolves around the degree to which the archaeologist brings a problem to his material — in the form of a hypothesis to be tested — before he has excavated it. In this approach, the "fit" of the hypothesis to the data is determined by what is observed, and the data are rejected, retained, or modified accordingly. Alternately, a site can simply be excavated, with no preconceived problem, and the explanation of the data, after classification and comparison to other data, can be based largely on itself and its relationships.

Both approaches have value since the subjectivity of the archaeologist intrudes in both cases. The deductive approach merely removes subjectivity by one step, because the hypothesis to be tested is derived by an inductive process from analogous ethnographic data. Thus, while Thompson suggests that in the case of inductive archaeology, the work

*may be evaluated by our estimation of the integrity and skill
of the archaeologist responsible, the results of an
archaeologist working deductively also must be judged, at
least in part, by the integrity of his initial hypothesis.*

10   The Subjective Element in Archaeological Inference

Willey[1] has described the two large problem fields of archaeology as the spatial-temporal arrangement of cultural materials and the reconstruction of cultural and ecological contexts. He points out that archaeology already has the methods and techniques for the first of these. It is in the second that methodological explorations are necessary for it is here that the archaeologist operates by inference from the ethnographic present. There seems to be a healthy although sometimes overzealous appreciation of this need, but at the same time a surprising lack of interest in the equally important need for an examination of the conceptual tools for remedying the situation. This paper is a first step toward such an examination; it is an attempt to find out what an archaeologist does when he operates by inference.

There are two related procedures involved in the establishment of an archaeological inference. First, the material evidence must be examined for suggestions or indications that an inference is possible. But an indicated conclusion cannot be established as an inference until its probability has been tested. Thus, the second process consists of the introduction of the probative material which contributes to this evaluation. The first step is a

Reprinted, with the editorial changes noted, from "The Subjective Element in Archaeological Inference" by Raymond H. Thompson, *Southwestern Journal of Anthropology* 12 (1956):327–332, by permission of the author and the publisher. Footnotes are renumbered.

[1] Gordon R. Willey, in Sol Tax, Loren C. Eiseley, Irving Rouse, and Carl F. Voegelin (eds.), *An Appraisal of Anthropology Today* (Chicago: University of Chicago Press, 1953), p. 229.

recognition of the indicative quality of the evidence; the second a full utilization of the probative analogy.

THE INDICATIVE QUALITY

An indication is that quality of the basic data which describes their inferential possibilities. The recognition of this quality is the starting point for any inference, for it is the indication which suggests that the inference is possible. The ability to recognize the indicative quality of the data is therefore a first requisite for the archaeologist who hopes to reconstruct the context of the specimen which he recovers. This ability is of course subjective. It is often described as the "feel" which an investigator has for the material.

The failure of archaeologists to define this individual sensitivity has caused other social scientists, and even some archaeologists, to seriously question its methodological validity. Attempts have been made to replace this subjective ability with more objective approaches. However, a devotion to objectivity cannot be substituted for the ability of the investigator to recognize that a certain cluster of the objectively described data is susceptible of yielding additional information.

Contrary to the folklore of the discipline, this sensitivity for the indicative quality is not an uncanny and inexplicable ability which only certain gifted individuals possess. Rather, it is the combination of the investigator's anthropological background or training in fact and theory, his archaeological experience which is often called familiarity with the material, and his intellectual capacity. It is the subtle combination of these three variables which makes the recognition of the indicative quality a subjective matter. This combination becomes such an intimate part of the individual archaeologist's analytical thinking that he is not conscious of the exact sources of the impression or indication that he expresses other than the cluster of data which initiated the indicative process.

The ability is therefore subjective or individual in that each investigator brings a different combination of skills to bear on any given problem. This does not mean that the ability to recognize the indicative quality is inexplicable, but it does mean that this ability is hard to define. It would be quite unnecessary to ask each archaeologist to set forth the details of his background, experience, and intelligence for the benefit of those who may wish to judge his work. It is not, however, too much to ask that he define the segment of the combination which contributes to a particular indication.

But as soon as an investigator begins to ask himself how and why he arrived at a particular indicated conclusion, he shifts from the indicative to the probative phase of the inferential process. This phase consists of specific statements of the evidence which enters into the substantiation of the inference. Some of them are explicit formulations of the indicative data; others are statements of entirely new material. In many cases the archaeologist would find it difficult to distinguish between the indicative material and the new evidence. In practice, the probative data represent a transition from the explicit declaration of the indicative background to the introduction of the new information, such that the documentation of the indicative reasoning leads to additional probative evidence. These observations parallel John Dewey's remark[2] on the conjugate relationship of the indicative and probative qualities of data, which I paraphrase: It is important that the material from which an inference is drawn should also be suitable as far as is possible to test the inference that is made, to indicate what new kinds of data are required, and to give some suggestion as to how they are to be obtained.

THE PROBATIVE ANALOGY

The archaeologist who formulates an indicated conclusion is suggesting that there is a correlation between a certain set of archaeological material objects and a particular range of sociocultural behavior. He must test this conclusion by demonstrating that an artifact-behavior correlation similar to the suggested one is a common occurrence in ethnographic reality. What actually happens is that he compares an artifact type which is derived from archaeological data with a similar type in a known life situation. If the resemblance in the form of the two artifact types is reasonably close, he infers that the archaeological type shares the technique, behavior, or other cultural activity which is usually associated with the ethnographic type.

Thus the archaeologist proceeds from descriptive data to contextual inference by demonstrating the existence and validity of various degrees of relation of likeness. This similarity or parallelism of relations is called analogy. Archaeological inference is impossible without recourse to analogy.

It is of considerable theoretical importance to recognize that archaeological analogy is based on a comparison of abstractions rather than a resemblance between individual artifacts. In the translation of archaeological data into general anthropological terms artifacts are classified according to concepts which are designed to produce groupings of potential cultural significance. An artifact is not treated as an individual object but as a member of a group of objects called a type. A type, then, is an abstraction derived from a group of artifacts of similar form. The type, not the single object, serves as the basis for analogy.

2 John Dewey, *Logic, the Theory of Inquiry* (New York: Henry Holt, 1938), p. 428.

Since the starting point of an archaeological analogy is an abstraction, it is a logical necessity that the other elements in the analogy be formulated as abstractions also. Thus, a type of archaeological objects must be compared with a type of ethnographic objects.

Just as the objects themselves, whether archaeological or ethnographic, are treated as types, so the associated cultural activity must be considered in terms of ranges and abstractions. The analogy cannot be established by invoking a single item of behavior any more than it can be based on an individual object. It can only be accomplished by the correlation of generalized ranges of behavior with types of artifacts.

Although a correlation between the artifact types and various cultural generalizations is the ultimate goal of an archaeological reconstruction the first inferences must be based on technological generalizations. The material bias of the basic archaeological evidence dictates this technological beginning of the inferential construct. The technical and ecological factors which condition the properties, source, and availability of raw materials define a specific range of possibilities for the manufacture of a class of artifacts. These technological possibilities have to be evaluated in terms of the archaeological evidence in order to narrow the range to fit the individual situation.

However, the information which is abstracted in a generalization is useless for analogy until it is organized to emphasize its relationship to the archaeological evidence. The probative value of any generalization is a function of the closeness of this relationship. It is therefore important that these abstract summaries be stated in precise and carefully chosen language. Technical data especially must be well organized not only because they begin the inferential construct but also because the significance of much technological information is often not readily apparent. Whenever an archaeologist receives technical or noncultural information from another discipline he accepts the responsibility for identifying and exposing its interpretive significance.

The results of an analysis of the raw materials from which a group of artifacts is made are usually presented in terms of the properties of the materials. These data, like any other kind of non-cultural information, must be related to the archaeological problem. The archaeologist must shift the emphasis from a description of the technical property to a statement of some use which man makes of this property. In effecting this shift he introduces a cultural factor.

This transition from a technological to a cultural orientation is a fundamental step in archaeological inference because it establishes a cultural context for all of the probative material. But, the mere demonstration that this context exists does not define the nature or closeness of the relationship between the probative generalizations and the indicative archaeological evidence. This lack of definition results in a serious restriction of the probative value of these generalizations. Failure to recognize that culture is but one of three elements present in all archaeological concepts is responsible for this situation. These three basic properties are space, time, and culture. Phillips and Willey discuss the importance of this combination to archaeological theory:

> It is impossible to imagine an artifact type or a cultural "unit" that is not defined with reference to specific forms and does not also have distribution in space and duration in time. However, though invariably present, these three diverse properties may and do vary enormously in proportion one to the other. . . . It becomes essential, therefore, in the definition and use of archaeological concepts of whatever nature to understand precisely what quantities of space, time, and formal content are involved in the mixture.[3]

These remarks have a particular significance for the related problems of the comparability of the ethnographic data used for analogy and the probability of the resulting archaeological inference. Both the indicative and the probative data are stated as abstractions in order to reduce all of the ingredients of the comparison to the same level of organization. But the system used to organize these data is also important. The abstractions must be formulated according to a single set of organizational criteria. Since the point of departure for the analogy consists of archaeological evidence, the same theory and system used in the arrangement of this evidence must be used in formulating the comparative generalizations. It is, therefore, not enough to demonstrate the cultural nature of the probative information. The spatial and temporal boundaries must also be clearly defined before the generalizations can be used to maximum advantage for analogy with archaeological material.

Thus the archaeologist injects a subjective element into his inferential reconstruction at least twice. The importance of the archaeologist's particular skills and views in the recognition of the indicative quality has been particularly emphasized. These same faculties are employed in the probative phase of the inferential process, first in the search for analogous data, and then in the demonstration of the nature of the relationship between this material and the archaeological evidence. In both the indicative and probative phases the archaeologist makes increasingly greater use of the subjective element as he attempts inferences into the social and mental associations of his excavated material.

[3] Philip Phillips and Gordon R. Willey, "Method and Theory in American Archeology: An Operational Basis for Culture-Historical Integration," *American Anthropologist* 55 (pp. 615–33, 1953):617–18.

The subjective element serves as a kind of common denominator for archaeological inference. The individual investigator with his unique combination of interpretive skills provides the only possible means for the reconstruction of the cultural context of an archaeological collection. The final judgment of any archaeologist's cultural reconstructions must therefore be based on an appraisal of his professional competence, and particularly the quality of the subjective contribution to that competence. Our present method of assessing the role of this subjective element by an appraisal of the intellectual honesty of the archaeologist who makes the inferences is certainly inadequate. But, there does not seem to be any practical means of greatly improving the situation despite the insistence of many of the critics of archaeological method. We can only hope for improvements in the methods of measuring the amount of faith we place in an individual's work.

Fortunately, intellectual ability and integrity are not the only variables in an investigator's approach to a problem of archaeological reconstruction. These native qualities cannot be properly exploited without a rich background in anthropological theory and fact and a reasonable amount of familiarity with archaeological materials. Consequently, the best course to follow seems to be a continuation of the educational philosophy that an archaeologist is a general anthropologist who happens to prefer to pursue the study of man through an analysis of the unique documents of past human activity which can be found in prehistoric rubbish heaps.

LEWIS R. BINFORD

*One of the most eloquent spokesmen for the deductive
approach, which he combines with general systems theory, is
Lewis Binford. His excellent article surveys the new
directions of archaeology today, and contrasts these new
perspectives with those being supplemented or replaced. The
article appropriately introduces the following articles, since
in its original context it served as an introductory statement to
selections by archaeologists deeply involved in the new
directions of method and theory.*

11 Archaeological Perspectives

... This paper does not attempt an exhaustive historical
analysis of the field of archaeology but is rather the selective treatment of
several general areas of archaeological concern put into historical
perspective. ...

THE AIMS OF ARCHAEOLOGY

⌐The most profitable inquiry [of archaeology] is the search for
the origin of epoch-making ideas in order to comprehend the
history of civilization (Mason 1893:403).⌐

⌐Archaeology, by etymology the study of beginnings, has historical reconstruction for its objective (Kroeber 1937:163).⌐

These early statements summarize the generally accepted view on the
aims of archaeology. Taylor (1948:26, 207) has thoroughly documented the
fact that reconstruction of culture history was widely accepted as the end of
archaeological research. Since Taylor's publication, this aim has been

Reprinted, with the editorial changes noted, from "Archeological Perspectives" by
Lewis R. Binford in Sally R. and Lewis R. Binford, Editors, *New Perspectives in Archeology* (Chicago: Aldine Publishing Company, 1968), pp. 5–32, by permission of the
author and the publisher; copyright © 1968 by Wenner-Gren Foundation for Anthropological Research, Inc.

reiterated frequently and continues to be stated in very recent publications (Rouse 1965:2; Meggers, Evans, and Estrada 1965:5; Willey 1966:2–3; Deetz 1967a:3).

If seeking origins and tracing the history of culture was one task of archaeology, some researchers considered a further aim to be the reconstruction of the lifeways of the peoples responsible for the archaeological remains. Such an aim appears early in the literature — for example, in H. I. Smith (1910) and Sollas (1924). Concern with the reconstruction of lifeways of extinct peoples has been expressed by many, but probably the most influential advocate for more attention toward this end has been Taylor:

> The conjunctive approach . . . has as its primary goal the elucidation of cultural conjunctives, the associations and relationships, the "affinities," within the manifestation under investigation. It aims at drawing the completest possible picture of past human life in terms of its human and geographic environment (1948: 95–96).

Most archaeologists would agree that we should not lose sight of "the Indian behind the artifact" (Braidwood 1959:79) and would accept as a major aim of archaeology the reconstruction of lifeways.

While these aims of reconstructing culture history and lifeways cannot be said to have been satisfactorily achieved, a few archaeologists during the 1930s began to suggest aims reaching far beyond these:

> Some day world culture history will be known as far as archaeological materials and human intelligence permit. Every possible element of culture will have been placed in time and space. The invention, diffusion, mutation and association of elements will have been determined. When taxonomy and history are thus complete, shall we cease our labors and hope that the future Darwin of Anthropology will interpret the great historical scheme that will have been erected? . . . Candor would seem to compel the admission that archaeology could be made much more pertinent to general cultural studies if we paused to take stock of its possibilities. Surely we can shed some light not only on the chronological and spatial arrangements and associations of elements, but on conditions underlying their origin, development, diffusion, acceptance and interaction with one another. These are problems of cultural process . . . (Steward and Setzler 1938:5–7).

And one year earlier a Scandinavian archaeologist also urged that his colleagues take stock of where they have been and where they were going:

> It appears that archaeology, in spite of its remarkable achievements, has got into a cul-de-sac. . . . The whole subject consists

merely of a comparison of forms and systematization. . . . Brilliant systematization, regarded as exact, has not led to and does not lead to an elucidation of the organic structure of the whole life of the period studied, to an understanding of social systems, of economic and social history. . . . Forms and types . . . have been regarded as much more real and alive than the society which created them and whole needs determined these manifestations of life. . . . Have we reached a crisis where the procedure and aim of our science must be revised? (Tallgren 1937:154–55).

Statements urging archaeologists to concern themselves with problems of process appeared with increasing frequency in the literature of the next twenty years (Steward 1942:139; Bennett 1943:208; Childe 1946:248; Clark 1953a, 1953b; Barth 1950; and especially Caldwell 1959). As recently as 1958 this concern with process was still being defined and distinguished from other aims of archaeology:

So little work has been done in American archaeology on the explanatory level that it is difficult to find a name for it. . . . In the context of archaeology, processual interpretation is the study of the nature of what is vaguely referred to as the culture-historical process. Practically speaking, it implies an attempt to discover regularities in the relationships given by the methods of culture-historical integration. . . . On this explanatory level of organization . . . we are no longer asking merely what but also how and even why (Willey and Phillips 1958:5–6).

Willey and Phillips' statement about so little work having been done on the explanatory level was made despite such efforts as Steward's (1937) investigation of settlement patterns which were later elaborated on in the Viru Valley project. Willey himself had expressed great optimism about the possibilities for "processual interpretation" as well as for the reconstruction of cultural institutions (Willey 1953:1). Some of the other efforts made between the late 1930s and the late 1950s toward gaining an understanding of cultural process were White's arguments on the role of energy in the evolution of culture (White 1943:335–56), Steward's "Cultural Causality and Law . . ." (1949), and Steward and Wittfogel's study of irrigation (Steward, *et al.* 1955).

In his 1962 Presidential Address to the American Anthropological Association, Willey again commented on the lack of progress in gaining a processual understanding of culture history:

Certainly the answers to the . . . causal questions as to why the ancient American civilizations began and flourished as they did and when they did still elude us, and what I can offer . . . will do little more ... than describe and compare certain situations and series of events (Willey 1962:1).

There began to appear in the literature a general dampening of enthusiasm of those who some twenty years earlier had called for the archaeologist to turn his attention to processual investigations. There was a similar pessimism expressed in the writing of British scholars despite the work of such authors as Childe (1936), Crawford (1953), and Clark (1951, 1953):

> We have lost the confidence of the nineteenth century, and are children of an age of doubt.... We must recognize that in archaeology ... there are no facts other than those which are ... "observational data." ... What we have at our disposal, as prehistorians, is the accidentally surviving durable remnants of material culture, which we interpret as best we may and inevitably the peculiar quality of this evidence dictates the sort of information we can obtain from it (Piggott 1965b:4–5).

The linking together of the limits of archaeological interpretation with the fragmentary nature of the archaeological record is a phenomenon we examine in some detail later . . . but the points to be made here are: (1) there was general acceptance of the three aims of archaeology — reconstruction of culture history, reconstruction of lifeways, and the delineation of cultural process; and (2) there has been increasing despair over the feasibility of achieving the third aim.

THE METHODS OF ARCHAEOLOGY — TRADITIONAL APPROACHES

This section examines the methods traditionally used in attempts to achieve the aims of archaeology. We shall deal with each of the aims separately, attempt to describe the methods employed, and analyze some of the problems underlying the application of method to problem.

Reconstructing Culture History

Reconstructing culture history consists of arranging cultural units in a way which accurately reveals their generic affinities. Archaeologists have generally operated on the basis of the following two assumptions:

(1) The degree of genealogical affinity between two cultural units varies directly with the similarities they exhibit in generically related characteristics (for example, whole culture traits or complexes, design elements on artifacts, etc.).

(2) The degree of genealogical affinity between two cultural units can be measured by the ratio of shared generically related characteristics to the number of such traits not shared.

It is evident that each culture trait tabulated in obtaining the ratio which measures degree of genealogical affinity must be evaluated to determine whether the similarity between traits arose as a function of lineal transmission, diffusion between cultural units, or independent development within each cultural unit. It is here that a basic, unsolved problem lies: How can archaeologists distinguish between homologous and analogous cultural similarities?

As early as 1896 E. B. Tylor concerned himself with this problem and suggested a procedure for analyzing observed similarities by

> ... division into constituent elements showing so little connection with one another that they may be reasonably treated as independent. The more numerous such elements, the more improbable the recurrence of the combination (1896:66).

In other words, Tylor suggests that one might calculate the probabilities of independent occurrences of identical combinations among a set of independently varying characteristics.

Other workers worrying over the same problem offered similar suggestions. For example, Graebner (1911) cites two criteria for evaluating cultural similarities: the criterion of form, and that of quantitative coincidence. For Graebner the criterion of form consisted of the degree to which there was a coincidence of characteristics which did not necessarily stem from "the nature of the objects compared"; the criterion of coincidence lay in determining whether or not the trait or item under study occurred as an isolated similarity or as an element of a greater cultural complex. On the basis of the criterion of form, this greater cultural complex could not reasonably be viewed as having arisen independently.

Robert Lowie pointed out some of the shortcomings of Graebner's reasoning: "The comparison of form can never do more than establish the identity of forms; that such identity is to be explained by genetic relationship is an hypothesis" (1912:28). He also noted that Graebner's quantitative criterion was not probabalistic as was Tylor's but was simply the criterion of form raised to a higher level of abstraction and was therefore not an independent criterion for judgment (1912:27).

A recent evaluation of the applications of Tylor's probability method notes that probability calculations of concrete cases have seldom been performed accurately, and in many instances the apparent accuracy of probability reasoning has been a semantic rather then a methodological addition to the anthropological literature (Erasmus 1950:374–75). A more basic flaw in Tylor's procedure is the assumption of a worker's ability to recognize constitutent elements which are in fact independent variables. This problem has been discussed (Erasmus 1950:375–87; Rands and Riley 1958; and indirectly by Sackett 1966), but no methods have been advanced for the solution of the problem other than the intensive analysis of the distribution and patterns of covariation demonstrable among selected characteristics. Such studies have rarely been conducted by archaeologists and certainly have never been a routine analytical component of the works of archaeologists proposing historical reconstructions. This particular problem has been the almost exclusive concern of ethnographers, and is one of which archaeologists involved in reconstructions of culture history have seemed deliciously unaware.

Lowie (1912:24–27) pointed out another problem in method — that while some workers have attempted to identify similarities which arose from genetic connections between cultural units, no one had considered the means for evaluating the alternative of independent development, except by lack of ability to demonstrate historical connections. Without first gaining some understanding of laws of cultural development, such independent means for evaluating particular cases will continue to be lacking.

Despite these unsolved problems of method and our consequent inability to distinguish accurately between analogies and homologies, archaeologists have continued to formulate reconstructions using the procedures set forth by Tylor and Graebner on a common sense level, often adding distributional criteria. The principles of interpretation which have guided archaeologists' reconstructions of culture history can be summarized as follows:

1. The probability of diffusion having taken place increases directly with the degree of formal resemblance between items and traits (Jennings 1957:265; Linton 1936:372) and with the degree of componential complexity of the traits compared (Linton 1936:372).

2. The probability of diffusion having taken place decreases with the amount of temporal and spatial separation between the traits being compared (Linton 1936:370; for relevant discussions see Wallis 1928; Meggers, Evans, and Estrada 1965:157–78; and Rowe 1966:334–37).

Such guides to interpretation ignore the inherent unsolved problems of method and epistemology, and most taxonomic schemes proposed as aids to historical reconstruction also fail to cope with them. For example, McKern in his discussion of the Midwestern Taxonomic System made it quite clear that classifications are to be made with respect to a list of culture traits undifferentiated as to the likelihood of their representing analogies or homologies:

> All the traits characteristic of a given culture manifestation comprise the culture complex for that manifestation.... In any comparison of this manifestation with another, made for purposes of classification, certain traits may be demonstrated as present in both complexes, and these linked traits [serve] to show cultural similarity between the two culture variants (1939:205).

Numerous cases of the application of the Midwestern Taxonomic System (Smith 1940; Cole and Deuel 1937:207–19; Griffin 1943; Morse 1963) demonstrate that there was no attempt made to distinguish between analogous and homologous traits. (It should be pointed out, however, that the McKern system is internally consistent and logical; most of the problems with it have arisen from those who have misused it.) Other schemes have also employed summations of observations whose relevance to discussions of cultural phylogeny and contact might well be questioned (Gladwin 1934; Colton 1939). Rouse (1955) recognized the difference between classification based on gross measures of similarity and "genetic correlations"; he went on to suggest that for the purpose of historical reconstruction

> . . . it would seem advisable first to eliminate all those resemblances which do not appear to have been accompanied by contact. Next, one must decide which of the remaining resemblances are due to genetic connection rather than to some other factor such as adaptation to a similar environment or attainment of the same level of cultural development. Only then will it be safe to choose from among two various possible forms of genetic connection (1955:719).

However, Rouse offers no guidelines for deciding which traits are generically related and which ones might exhibit similarity from other causes. In short, Rouse's statement shows an awareness of many of the shortcomings of taxonomic schemes but offers no solution to one of the major underlying methodological problems.

It is argued here that the accomplishment of the reconstruction of culture history is predicated upon an overhaul of method and theory, that traditional methodology and analytical procedures are inadequate for the successful achievement of the stated aims of the field. Given our current sophistication in dating techniques, we can fairly accurately place archeological remains in their proper chronological relationships to one another. We can inventory the remains and discuss additions, deletions, and "hybridizations" in the inventories of sites through time. We can also formulate classifications of assemblages on the basis of summary measures of formal similarities between recovered items (see Ford 1954); we can also measure likenesses by comparing the total composition of the sample of recovered materials (see Bordes 1953). Arguments can then be formulated about the probability of one such taxon being the cultural ancestor, descendant, or collateral relative of another taxon (see Hodson, *et al.* 1966; Doran and Hodson 1966), or whether another unit might be more appropriately considered (see Warren 1967:168–85; Sanger 1967:186–97; Aikens 1967:198–209; and Schlesier 1967:210–22).

These procedures, however, do not help to achieve the stated aims of archaeology. An accurate and meaningful history is more than a generalized narrative of the changes in composition of the archaeological record through time (see, for example, Griffin 1967); it is also more than a reconstruction from that record using interpretive principles such as those discussed above which can be shown to have inherent flaws. If we hope to achieve the aim of reconstructing culture history, we must develop means for using archaeological remains as a record of the past and as a source of data for testing propositions which we set forth regarding past events, rather than as a record we can read according to a set of a priori rules or interpretive principles whose application allows the skilled interpreter to "reconstruct" the past. We know much too little about both archaeological data and processes of cultural development to make "reading the archaeological record" anything but a shallow and suspicious pastime. What we seek to investigate is cultural process, and only with an understanding of such processes can we reconstruct the events which form the context in which the archaeological record was produced.

Reconstructing Past Lifeways

The reconstruction of the lifeways of extinct peoples is the second aim of archaeology which we will examine in order to evaluate traditional methods. The standard operating procedure for achieving this aim is set forth in the following quotation:

> Everyone is aware of the fact that it is impossible to explain and to give absolute meaning to all the discoveries which are made while digging ancient villages. All we can do is to interpret what we find in the light of our knowledge of modern . . . [peoples].
> . . . In this way, it is possible to moderate our conjectures, and piece them together by means of reasonable imagination. Thus, the cold, unrelated and often dull archaeological facts are vivified and the reader may have some sort of reconstruction in his mind's eye of what [past peoples] . . . were like and how they lived. (Martin and Rinaldo 1939:457. [This statement is one of the first in the literature of American archaeology that deals with the reconstruction of lifeways. Paul Martin was in the avant–garde of archaeological thought in the 1930s, and he still is today. This quotation should in no way be considered a statement of his current views, which have grown and changed remarkably in thirty years. — Eds.]).

Most archaeologists would agree with this statement (see Willey 1966:3; Chang 1967a:109; Ascher 1961). Analogy to living peoples has been the traditional answer to the question of how one goes about reconstructing lifeways (see Randall-MacIver 1932:6-7; Hawkes 1954:157-58; Vogt

1956:175; Piggott 1965b:12; Rouse 1965:10; Willey 1966:3–4). The major controversy has concerned the appropriateness of a given ethnographically known group or set of conditions as a model for the lifeways of the groups under archaeological study (see Lowie 1940:369–70; Slotkin 1952; S. R. Binford 1968).

Given the method of analogy to living peoples, appeals have been made by archaeologists to explore the record in search of units which can be meaningfully compared in analogies to living peoples. One obvious plea has been for archaeologists to excavate the remains of entire communities, to concern themselves with the comparative study of settlement, as well as with the internal organization of sites. Taylor (1948), in appealing for archaeologists to study in detail the contextual relationships among the archaeological remains, asked for a search for order demonstrable among the elements in an archaeological deposit. Willey (1953, 1956), Chang (1958, 1967a), and Trigger (1967) among others, have stressed the desirability of the investigation of settlement patterns, since these are observable among living peoples and are said to be informative about social organization.

Pleistocene archaeologists also are increasingly viewing sites as the remains of activities conducted by social units; this kind of data collection is stressed in the search for living floors and in attempts at fairly complete excavation of sites.

> The living places of Pleistocene peoples are capable of yielding the same kind of evidence as to the behavior and ecology as do those of much later times when the appropriate techniques of exposure and excavation are applied to their recovery.... Such field studies ... of ... Paleolithic sites [are] infinitely more rewarding and significant, as can be . . . appreciated from papers . . . relating to living floor excavation (Clark and Howell 1966:v–vi).

Another aspect of data collection which has been dealt with in recent years is the problem of sampling. There has been frequent discussion of the use of sampling techniques which are designed to increase the probability that archaeological samples taken are in fact representative of what remains from the past (see L. R. Binford 1964; Rootenburg 1964).

Along with these refinements in data collection, there has been a growing interest in the study of living peoples by archaeologists (Crawford 1953; Kleindienst and Watson 1956; Thompson 1958; Ascher 1962; Watson 1966). Such studies have as their aim the delineation of behavioral correlates for material items (Chang 1958; Robbins 1966), and the purpose of archaeologists undertaking such research has been to maximize their interpretive powers by increasing their knowledge of living peoples — that is, to make more secure the analogies they draw between lifeways of peoples known archaeologically and those known ethnographically.

While we applaud all attempts to increase the reliability of data collected archaeologically, and while we certainly favor a firmer basis for determining the behavioral correlates of material culture, both refinements in data collection and increased ethnographic knowledge cannot by themselves increase our knowledge of the past. Facts do not speak for themselves, and even if we had complete living floors from the beginning of the Pleistocene through the rise of urban centers, such data would tell us nothing about cultural process or past lifeways unless we asked the appropriate questions. We can infinitely expand our knowledge of the lifeways of living peoples, yet we cannot reconstruct the lifeways of extinct peoples unless we employ a more sophisticated methodology. Fitting archaeological remains into ethnographically known patterns of life adds nothing to our knowledge of the past. In fact, such a procedure denies to archaeology the possibility of dealing with forms of cultural adaptation outside the range of variation known ethnographically (see S. R. Binford 1968). In view of the high probability that cultural forms existed in the past for which we have no ethnographic examples, reconstruction of the lifeways of such sociocultural systems demands the rigorous testing of deductively drawn hypotheses against independent sets of data.

This perspective is in marked contrast to the epistemological basis of traditional method, whose implications can readily be seen in a recent statement:

> As to analogy, archaeology as a whole is analogy, for to claim any knowledge other than the objects themselves is to assume knowledge of patterns in culture and history and to apply these patterns to the facts (Chang 1967a:109).

I have criticized this view elsewhere (L. R. Binford 1967a, 1967b, 1968) and would state here that so long as we insist that our knowledge of the past is limited by our knowledge of the present, we are painting ourselves into a methodological corner. The archaeologist must make use of his data as documents of past conditions, proceed to formulate propositions about the past, and devise means for testing them against archaeological remains. It is the testing of hypotheses that makes our knowledge of the past more certain, and this is admittedly a difficult business. Archaeology as part of anthropology and anthropology as a social science are often guilty of the charges made against them by the "harder" scientists:

> The most important feature about a hypothesis is that it is a mere trial idea ... [and] until it has been *tested*, it should not be confused with a *law*. ... The difficulty of testing hypotheses in the social sciences has led to an abbreviation of the scientific method in which this step is simply omitted. Plausible

hypotheses are merely set down as facts without further ado (Wilson 1952:26–27).

Traditional archaeological methodology has not developed this final link in scientific procedure. For this reason, reconstruction of lifeways has remained an art which could be evaluated only by judging the competence and honesty of the person offering the reconstruction (Thompson 1956).

The Study of Cultural Process

Different authors have referred to different phenomena in their discussions of culture process. The phrase has been used to refer to the dynamic relationships (causes and effects) operative among sociocultural systems, to those processes responsible for changes observed in the organization and/or content of the systems, or to the integration of new formal components into the system. The term cultural process has been used by others to refer to patterns or configurations in the temporal or spatial distributions of the archaeological materials themselves (see Wauchope 1966:19–38). The first set of meanings — that of dynamic relationships operative among cultural systems — is the one used by this author. . . .

Let us examine the methods and procedures traditionally followed in seeking an understanding of culture process, regardless of the meaning given to the term. Most often, the procedure has been to equate process to a transformational sequence of forms, normally summarized in a stage classification. A second, or sometimes an alternative, procedure has been to pursue a comparative study of temporal and spatial changes of archaeologically known cultural forms, to note certain trends or regularities. These trends are then stated as empirical generalizations which, in turn, are taken as statements regarding culture process (see Steward 1949; Braidwood 1952, 1960; Braidwood and Reed 1957; Willey and Phillips 1958; Willey 1960; Beardsley, *et al.* 1956). The criticism to be offered here is that any stage classification is simply an ordeal scale for measurement. The application of such a scale to innumerable empirical cases, or even the ultimate systematization of all archaeological materials, can never provide us with an understanding of the processes operative in the past which resulted in the stadial sequence. An empirical generalization of data — no matter how accurate it is — is never an explanation for the data. The ordering of forms of life, the end-products of evolution, by Linnaeus, did not describe or define the process of organic evolution.

Steward has suggested that the comparative study of distribution of cultural forms in space and through time will reveal certain trends, regularities, or patterns for which historical or generic interpretations are appropriate; he suggests further that these tends or patterns reflect cultural process (Steward 1949:3). This suggestion is, however, predicated on our ability to discriminate between cultural analogies and homologies. As pointed out above ... methods for such discrimination have yet to be developed. Even if we were capable of making this distinction, the demonstration of empirical "regularities" simply documents similarities which need to be explained; it is to be hoped that the explanations offered would deal with cultural or ecological processes operative in the past.

Rouse (1964, 1965) has offered archaeologists an "out," and his ideas undoubtedly have great appeal for those who would like to study cultural processes but lack the methods for doing so. He states that since we recognize a difference between the *process* of evolution and the *products* of evolution, that the study of the process should properly be the domain of ethnologists, "who are able to observe change as it is still going on" (Rouse 1964:465). He suggests further that the archaeologists might more appropriately study the products of evolution in systematic terms — by descriptive taxonomic and distributional schemes. In this view, processes of cause and effect cannot legitimately be studied by archaeologists, since they are not part of the archaeological record, cannot be dug up, and are not available for direct observation.

Others, working within the traditional framework, have stated that archaeologists *can* gain understanding of cultural process, and that the means for doing so is to interpret data from the past in the light of our understanding of the present. An example of this approach can be seen in what Willey and Phillips term "developmental interpretation" — a process which allows the archaeologist to "abstract ... certain characteristics that seem to have significance from the point of view of the general development of ... culture" (Willey and Phillips 1958:77).

However, the decisions as to which characteristics are significant in the general development of culture do not derive from the data themselves; they are given meaning by the ideas we hold about the processes of cultural development. If we simply employ these ideas for interpreting aracheological remains, then no new information can be gained from the archaeological record about processes which operated in the past. In short, traditional archaeological studies have often recognized the desirability of investigating process, but methods for successfully conducting such studies have not been developed. . . .

ARCHAEOLOGICAL THEORY AND METHOD — NEW PERSPECTIVES

We have offered a brief review of the methods commonly employed for achieving the stated aims of archaeology. In this section we hope to compare and contrast some aspects of traditional method and theory with very recent developments in the field which are substantively illustrated in this book. This discussion of theory and method will be conducted under several problem headings.

Induction and Deduction

One striking feature of traditional archaeological method, regardless of the aims of the research, has been the lack of any rigorous means of testing, and thereby gaining confidence in, propositions about the past. Statements about the historical, functional, or processual significance of observed characteristics of the archaeological record have been evaluated by two criteria: (1) the degree to which our knowledge of contemporary peoples might justifiably be projected back to extinct sociocultural systems, and (2) the degree to which we might have confidence in the professional competence and intellectual honesty of the archaeologist advancing interpretations (see Thompson 1956:33). Traditional methodology almost universally espouses simple induction as the appropriate procedure, and the archaeological record is viewed as a body of phenomena from which one makes inductive inferences about the past. Such inferences are to be guided by our knowledge of contemporary peoples and also by certain principles, such as mechanical principles which govern the fracture of flint. The application of ethnographic knowledge and of guiding principles are the traditional means for increasing confidence in our inferential generalizations about the past.

> Inference is the key or the methodological pivot of archaeology, for it is only through inference that inanimate objects are reassembled into the milieu of life. Inferences are drawn from analogies... (Willey 1966:3).

> At the inferential level, the archaeologist is at last providing the flesh for the bare bones of his data, and, if done with care and imagination, such a procedure makes possible the delineation and ultimate understanding of past cultures (Deetz 1967a:11).

The changes in archaeology which are documented in this book are more than simply new methods and new theories; the changes consist of theories and methods developed in the context of a new epistemological perspective on such basic issues as the appropriate scientific procedures to be followed in investigating the past. In this perspective, a central point to be made concerns the role of induction in science:

> There can be no general rules of induction; the demand for them rests on a confusion of logical and psychological issues. . . . What determines the soundness of a hypothesis is not the way it is arrived at (it may have been suggested by a dream or a hallucination), but the way it stands up when tested, i.e., when confronted with relevant observational data (Hempel 1965:6).

In stressing induction and the drawing of sound inferences, then, the stress falls on the psychological issue, as pointed out by Hempel, of how to make meaningful statements about archaeological remains and what they represent from the past. What is argued here is that the generation of inferences regarding the past should not be the end-product of the archaeologist's work. While an awareness of as great a range of variability in sociocultural phenomena as possible and the citation of analogy to living peoples are not belittled here, the main point of our argument is that independent means of testing propositions about the past must be developed. Such means must be considerably more rigorous than evaluating an author's propositions by judging his professional competence or intellectual honesty.

We assert that our knowledge of the past is more than a projection of our ethnographic understanding. The accuracy of our knowledge of the past can be measured; it is this assertion which most sharply differentiates the new perspective from more traditional approaches. The yardstick of measurement is the degree to which propositions about the past can be confirmed or refuted through hypothesis testing — not by passing judgment on the personal qualifications of the person putting forth the propositions. The role of ethnographic training for archaeologists, the use of analogy, and the use of imagination and conjecture are all fully acknowledged. However, once a proposition has been advanced — no matter by what means it was reached — the next task is to deduce a series of testable hypotheses which, if verified against independent empirical data, would tend to verify the proposition.

The shift to a consciously deductive philosophy, with the attendant emphasis on the verification of propositions through hypothesis testing, has far-reaching consequences for archaeology. As an example of such consequences I will discuss briefly two topics commonly treated in presentations on archaeological theory and method: the limitations of the archaeological record, and the appropriate units of archaeological observation.

Limitations of the Archaeological Record

The arguments on this topic generally begin by citing the fact that much of the material content of an ongoing sociocultural system is lost through decay or the action of other physical agents (such as fire) before the time the archaeologist can make his observations. It is then asserted that our knowledge of the past is limited to those classes of data which survive and that, depending on variations in past behavior, our knowledge of the operation of the sociocultural system in question may be enormously distorted (see, for example, Piggott 1965a:8). Such arguments also frequently take the form of asserting that since we can never know what is missing from the archaeological record, we can never correctly evaluate what *is* present. How can we know that an empirical generalization about

archaeological data is accurate, since there may be pertinent and noncon-
forming evidence that has been lost? (See M. A. Smith 1955:6; Heider
1967:62; Deetz 1968.)

An excellent example of reasoning of this kind is found in a recent
discussion of the proper historical interpretation of distributions of African
art styles:

> It is a curious fact that, with certain exceptions in Tanganyika,
> little rock art in the form of either painting or engraving, has
> been found north of the Zambezi. . . . It would appear that there
> is an almost complete break between the painting and engraving
> traditions of southern Africa and those of the Sahara. If this is
> so it makes the similarity between the two groups . . . appear as a
> striking example of parallel development. This would be a very
> hard case to prove . . . in view of the practice in many parts of
> the world of painting and engraving on such perishable sub-
> stances as wood. . . . Indeed there is no reason to suppose that
> Late Stone Age man in East Africa and in the Congo did not
> paint or draw or engrave, simply because his work has not been
> preserved (Allchin 1966:41).

Allchin's dilemma arises directly and inevitably from the fact that she is
offering an empirical generalization directly from the data and makes use of
an a priori principle for interpreting the historical-cultural significance of
the generalization. In this case the unstated principle would be that an
interrupted distribution signifies a cultural boundary and independence for
the two traditions represented. If one accepts the interpretive principle, the
only possible way of invalidating the interpretation is to question the
validity of the empirical generalization itself (namely, that there is a
geographical break between the painting and engraving traditions of southern Africa and those of the Sahara). The validity of the generalization can
be destroyed by citing an empirical case to the contrary (an instance of
painting or engraving in the "empty zone"). The generalization can also be
challenged, and this is what Allchin does, by suggesting the possibility of
such an empirical case to the contrary.

The possibility of an undocumented case to the contrary normally takes
the form used in Allchin's argument — speculation about conditions under
which data might be destroyed, overlooked, or "hidden." The validity of all
generalizations may be questioned if this procedure is followed, since the
possibilities for speculation about "hidden data" are infinite. Further, the
validity of the interpretive principle itself can never be independently
tested, since its accuracy is tested only by reference to the empirical
generalization it is said to cover. Extension of the generalization to cover
new cases simply provides more instances for which the principle might be
relevant; it in no way tests the principle itself. Cases to the contrary of the

generalization only show that the data generalized are inappropriate to the principle employed; they in no way serve to test the principle itself. This is one of the crucially weak points of a purely inductive methodology. Thus, Allchin's principle implicitly used for interpretation of her generalization cannot, with the methodology employed, be validated or refuted, and the generalization itself can always be questioned by the possibility of citing hidden data on the incompleteness of the archaeological record.

The procedure we would advocate as a way out of Allchin's dilemma would be as follows:

Observations:

1.) There is a geographical break in the archaeological distribution of rock paintings and engravings between southern Africa and the Sahara.

2.) The styles of paintings and engravings from the two areas are very similar.

Proposition:

The geographic break is the result of there having been two independent cultural traditions in the respective areas.

Deduction:

Therefore, the similarity in form of painting and engraving is the result of parallel development.

Prediction:

We would expect a similar break in the distribution of stylistic attributes of other items — for example, bead forms, decoration on bone implements, projectile point forms, etc.

Bridging Arguments:

Here we would attempt to establish the relevance of some classes of archaeological data to our deduction and prediction. We would try to establish that certain formal characteristics of artifacts, other than rock paintings and engravings, were stylistic and would therefore vary as a function of tradition.

Hypothesis:

The distribution of the data whose relevance has been argued will exhibit interrupted distributions between southern Africa and the Sahara.

If the hypothesis were confirmed, then arguments about hidden data would be irrelevant since the existence of cultural boundaries would have been established by independent data. If the hypothesis were refuted, arguments of hidden data, while possibly relevant to the original generalization, would in no way place limits on our ability to gain knowledge of cultural boundaries from the archaeological record.

High-probability statements covering a broad range of phenomena are the aim of science, not empirical generalizations which can be destroyed by the citation of a single empirical case to the contrary. The endless search for data in harmony with empirical generalizations is a wasteful procedure at best, and the data can never serve to validate the generalization. Propositions can be evaluated by deducing hypotheses which must be tested against independent data. The argument of hidden data can always be made about generalizations, but it is significant only insofar as it prompts testing the validity of propositions made regarding the significance of the generalization. The citation of possible hidden data has no inherent value as a statement of limitation of our knowledge of the past, nor is it applicable to the truth or falsity of propositions. Confidence in any given proposition can be evaluated only with respect to the history of hypothesis formulation and with testing relevant to that proposition.

Another common argument on the limitations of the archaeological record asserts that the reliability of conclusions reached by an archaeologist varies directly with the degree to which the subject is removed from discussions of artifacts themselves (see MacWhite 1956:4–6; Hawkes 1954:161; M. A. Smith 1955:3–4, Piggott 1965a: 10–11).

> Artifacts and the study of artifacts — including typologies — are placed at the lowest level, and historic interpretations based upon such studies are considered to be of the greatest reliability. Moving into the socio-cultural system is moving up the levels of abstraction with increased use of inferences, and moving down the ladder of reliability. . . . Those who want to make inferences and to step beyond the limitations of archaeological remains can do so and engage in the fancy game of socio-cultural reconstruction (Chang 1967a:12–13).

A frequent way of stating this argument is to propose a formal ladder of reliability:

> 1) To infer from the archaeological phenomena to the techniques producing them I take to be relatively easy. . . .
> 2) To infer to the subsistence-economies of the human groups concerned is fairly easy. . . .
> 3) To infer to the socio/political institutions of the groups, however, is considerably harder.
> 4) To infer to the religious institutions and spiritual life . . . is the hardest inference of all (Hawkes 1954:161–62).

These statements are predicated upon two major premises: first, that the archaeological record is incomplete, that many items of the material culture have been lost through decay, destruction, etc.; second, that the archaeological record is lacking in all the nonmaterial features of the sociocultural system under study. The conclusion is then drawn that the reliability of our interpretations will vary directly with the degree to which we can justify the acceptance of a partial record as representative of the total material culture, and also with the degree to which we can believe that the nonmaterial components of any sociocultural system are reflected in the imperfectly preserved material items.

This reasoning is functionally linked to a methodology that limits the archaeologist to generalizing about the "facts" he uncovers. Since preservation is always imperfect, inferences from the facts of material culture to statements about the nonmaterial culture move us away from the primary data and thus diminish the reliability of our statements.

There has been a wide range of opinion expressed on this latter point — the degree to which nonmaterial aspects of culture can be inferred from material facts; the ultraconservative range of this spectrum can be seen in the following statement:

> Since historical events and essential social divisions of prehistoric peoples don't find an adequate expression in material remains, it cannot be right to try to arrive at a knowledge of them through archaeological interpretation (M. A. Smith 1955:7).

Most of the authors in this volume* would take strong exception to this statement. In the first place, the argument that archaeologists must limit their knowledge to features of material culture is open to serious question; and second, the dichotomy between material and nonmaterial aspects of culture itself and the relevance of this dichotomy for a proposed hierarchy of reliability have also been the subject of critical discussion (Service 1964; L. R. Binford 1962, 1965). It is virtually impossible to imagine that any given cultural item functioned in a sociocultural system independently of the operation of "nonmaterial" variables. Every item has its history within a sociocultural system — its phases of procurement of raw material, manufacture, use, and final discarding. . . . There is every reason to expect that the empirical properties of artifacts and their arrangement in the archaeological record will exhibit attributes which can inform on different phases of the artifact's life history.

Many different determinants which were operative in the past might be cited as proper explanatory variables for archaeologically recovered items. For example, pottery vessels manufactured in two different communities for use in identical tasks may vary significantly in form, depending on local habits of ceramic manufacture and on local design and decorative concepts. On the other hand, different forms of vessels made for different uses (for example, cooking vs. storage) might be produced with the same techniques and have similar decorative elements. In this latter case, the formal properties of the vessels relating to use would vary independently of formal properties relating to local ceramic techniques. It is conceivable that many other independently varying classes of attributes in combination might characterize the final form of any given class of item. Each kind of independently varying attribute might be relevant to a different set of

* [Reference is to the authors of *New Perspectives in Archeology*, L. Binford and S. Binford (eds.). — Ed.]

determinants and would thus require independent explanation for their form and distribution in the archaeological record. Each such independent explanation would, upon verification, inform us about the operation of different variables in the cultural system under study. It is highly improbable that the multiple, independent variables which determined the form of any item or the distribution of items should be restricted to only one component of a cultural system. This means that data relevant to most, if not all, the components of past sociocultural system *are* preserved in the archaeological record. (L. R. Binford 1962:218–19).

Our task, then, is to devise means for extracting this information from our data, and this demands more than making summary generalizations about items of material culture. There is no reason to expect that our explanations of the archaeological record should necessarily refer to the same order of phenomena as that being explained. If this is so, it follows that we cannot be restricted to the knowledge of "material culture"; rather, to explain our observations from the archaeological record, we must deal with the full range of determinants which operate within any sociocultural system, extant or extinct.

There has been as yet no attempt to assess the limitations of the archaeological record for yielding different kinds of information; nor does there seem to be the means of accurately determining these limits short of total knowledge of all the systematic relationships which characterized past cultural systems. Thus, present discussions of limitations of reliability are inappropriate and are based on speculation. And it is speculation which the more conservative exponents of such arguments have sought to avoid!

The position being taken here is that different kinds of phenomena are never remote; they are either accessible or they are not. "Nonmaterial" aspects of culture are accessible in direct measure with the testability of propositions being advanced about them. Propositions concerning any realm of culture — technology, social organization, psychology, philosophy, etc. — for which arguments of relevance and empirically testable hypotheses can be offered are as sound as the history of hypothesis confirmation. The practical limitations on our knowledge of the past are not inherent in the nature of the archaeological record; the limitations lie in our methodological naiveté, in our lack of development for principles determining the relevance of archaeological remains to propositions regarding processes and events of the past.

Units of Observation and Units of Relevance: A Basis for Analysis

The shift to a rigorous hypothetico-deductive method with the goal of explanation implies changes also in our perception and use of the archaeological record. Archaeologists have normally accepted certain observational units — such as the item, the industry, or the assemblage — as the appropriate units for comparative investigation. Such investigation gererally proceeds by breaking down archaeological remains into categories based on raw materials: bone, stone, ceramics, basketry, etc. Or, in other cases, the investigator may use functional classes, such as projectile points, knives, axes, etc. Whatever the breakdown used, such analysis serves only to clarify information already available; it cannot increase our knowledge. After his initial comparative analysis, the archaeologist may offer descriptive generalizations regarding his analytical categories; he may also offer some kind of synthetic statement, assigning categories to proposed events which presumably were the context in which the materials in question were produced. The end-product of this kind of analysis is normally comparison, either by verbal generalizations or summary statistics, among a series of sites in order to evaluate differences and similarities which are then used to reconstruct culture history or formulate statements about culture process.

One of the assumptions underlying such a procedure is that the analytical categories used are adequate and useful components of a nominal scale for measuring cultural differences and similarities. By definition the categories of a nominal scale are mutually exclusive and presumably part of an exhaustive scale which can accommodate all archaeological observations (see Siegel 1956:21–30; Blalock 1960:11–16, for a discussion of scales for measurement). One other linked assumption is that information tabulated by such a scale is additive (this is well documented in Thompson, *et al.* 1956:42–45). Stated another way, the assumption is that culture consists of a single class of phenomena which can be accurately measured by our analytical units and about which accurate summary statements, based on those analytical units, can be made. When we compare the summary statements or statistics from a number of sites and observe differences or similarities, these are generally taken as indicators of degrees of cultural relationship.

We can criticize this kind of analysis on two grounds. First, it is highly questionable that the analytical categories used by archaeologists actually measure a single class of phenomena; we would argue that they are measuring along several dimensions simultaneously, that culture is neither simple nor additive. Second, intuitively established analytical units, whose significance is not specified, can at best be of limited utility in testing hypotheses. For in hypothesis testing we must always be able to justify our observations as relevant measures of the variables identified in the propositions we have formulated (see Nagel 1967:10).

With respect to the first criticism — that culture is not additive and consists of more than summed traits — we would argue further that culture is a system of interrelated components. The archaeological record must be viewed as the byproduct of the operation of such a system, and any single facet of the record can be referred back to multiple variables or components of that system. The determinants which operated to produce one part of the archaeological record need not be, and probably are not, the same determinants which produced another part of the archaeological record.

We may explain changes or differences in certain attributes of artifacts or features in terms of variations in prehistoric economy; such explanations may be largely irrelevant for explaining variations in motor habits as documented in the same artifacts. If we treat both these kinds of variation as undifferentiated measures of cultural difference, we are scarcely getting reliable information about past cultural systems. This same criticism is applicable to consideration of a single attribute and also to generalizations about summed attributes. A single characteristic observed in the archaeological record might well be the compounded by-product of a number of codeterminant variables.

An example of the confusion produced by treating independent variables as though they were one compounded variable can be seen if we take the case of measuring attributes of people rather than of artifacts. Let us assume that what we wish to explain is variation in human size, and the attribute we select as informing most economically on size is that of volume. We might proceed to measure a large number of people and even work out a taxonomy based on variation as measured by volume. The next step would be to attempt to explain variability in size and the distribution of size among human groups. We might investigate the degree to which size as measured by volume tends to covary with other variables such as environment, diet, disease, etc. Any such attempt would necessarily be doomed to failure, since at least two independent variables — height and weight — were being observed compounded into a single variable — volume. Someone who is six and one-half feet tall and very thin might yield an identical value for volume as someone who is five feet tall and exceedingly stout. In studying the archaeological record, there is no reason to expect that our units of observation are, in their form and distribution, referrable to the operation of a single variable in the past.

The crucial question for archaeology is the relationship of our observations to the operation of past cultural systems. What are we measuring when we apply various scales to the archaeological record: either nominal scales (typologies) or ordinal scales (stage classifications)? Do our stone tool typologies, for example, measure function or style, or do the attributes which define types involve two or more variables? At each juncture of explaining observations from the archaeological record, we must question anew to what variables operative in the past our observations refer. Any explanatory proposition must be reasoned in terms of relevance to the operation of the cultural system under study (see Spaulding 1957:87). These arguments of relevance frequently result in the modification of our analytical units and the generation of further analytical categories. This procedure insures the expansion of our knowledge of the past, since it facilitates the testing of propositions. With the acceptance of a hypothetico-deductive method for archaeology and the use of a multiple-stage scientific procedure — observation and generalization, formulation of explanatory propositions, testing these against the archaeological data — it becomes evident that the analytical units employed in the initial stage may not be very useful during the final stages of testing. The sets of phenomena selected for observation, from the infinite number of possible observations, are not most profitably determined by the formal structure of the archaeological record itself. On the contrary, they are data which we must justify as relevant to the particular propositions advanced and as useful for hypothesis testing. A crucial role is thus given to the development of analytical techniques and to the generation of increasingly accurate analytical units for measuring cultural and environmental variables. During the past thirty years archaeologists have warned against the mixing of levels and inaccurate partitioning of archaeological deposits; the warning offered here is against the analytical mixing of variables and against the partitioning of our observational universe into irrelevant analytical units.

Relevance is established by reference to the propositions being advanced and by the theoretical context of those propositions. We can anticipate that progress toward achieving the goals of archaeology will be marked by continued refinement of the units of observation by which the archaeological record can be summarized and by the development of more accurate and less multivariate scales for measurement.

CONCLUSIONS

I have attempted to point out rather specifically what is new about the new perspectives. In doing so, I have made several points of contrast with more traditional approaches. I have noted that most archaeologists of whatever theoretical persuasion would agree on the triple aims of the discipline — reconstruction of culture history, reconstruction of extinct lifeways, and the delineation of culture process. There are, however, major differences among archaeologists when it comes to theory and method, and it is argued that revamping traditional theory and method is essential for achieving any or all of the generally agreed-upon aims of the field. The major methodological and theoretical points of contrast involve distinctions between cultural analogies and homologies, between culture viewed as a summation of traits and culture viewed as a system, between units of observation and units of analysis, between inductive and deductive approaches to the archaeological record. A basic underlying problem involves the use of scales of measurement. It was argued that traditional archaeological measures compound variables which probably operated independently in the past, and that a solution of the problem of measuring along several dimensions simultaneously must be reached in order to determine just what it is we *are* measuring. Despite remarkable advances in data collection techniques and in techniques of analysis, so long as the data from the past are considered within the framework of traditional theory, they can bring nothing new to bear on our knowledge of the past. It is a concern with the nature of knowledge, with the testing and verification of hypotheses, and with the relevance of questions asked that distinguishes much of the work in this book.* We assume that the past is knowable; that with enough methodological ingenuity, propositions about the past are testable; and that there are valid scientific criteria for judging the probability of a statement about the past besides ad hominem arguments or "common sense."

The problems raised by the relationship of theory, method, and question-asking were elegantly dealt with fifteen years ago by Sherwood L. Washburn. Although Washburn was writing specifically about physical anthropology, his statement seems uncannily relevant for archaeology in the 1960s:

> The assumption seems to have been that description (whether morphological or metrical), if accurate enough and in sufficient quantity, could solve problems of process, pattern, and interpretation. . . . But all that can be done with the initial descriptive information is to gain a first understanding, a sense of problem, and a preliminary classification. To get further requires an elaboration of theory and method along different lines (Washburn 1953:714–15).

The elaboration of theory and method which characterizes much of the recent work in archaeology consists minimally of two elements: First, the active search for understanding variability in the archaeological record — all of the variability and not just that judged a priori to be significant; second, an attempt to explain variability scientifically, rather than by conjecture or by "hunch." Some variability may be more apparent than real and may reflect sampling error, partial erosion, redeposition, etc. Only with the self-conscious use of sophisticated method can this "noise" be factored out. Many kinds of variation will be shown to be the result of the normal functioning of internally differentiated cultural systems; others may document evolutionary changes within cultural systems. Still other kinds of variation may reflect changes in content within an essentially stable cultural system. In our search for explanations of differences and similarities in the archaeological record, our ultimate goal is the formulation of laws of cultural dynamics.

* [*New Perspectives in Archeology.* — Ed.]

Many of the authors in [*New Perspectives*] would agree that advances in achieving the aims of archaeology necessitate the enforced obsolescence of much of traditional theory and method, and thus many of the papers in this book are radical in the original sense of the word. If we are successful, many traditional archaeological problems will prove to be irrelevant, and we will see an expansion of the scope of our question-asking which today would make us giddy to contemplate. Despite a recent statement that one should not speak of a "new archaeology" since this alienates it from the old (Chang 1967a:3), we feel that archaeology in the 1960s is at a major point of evolutionary change. Evolution always builds on what went before, but it always involves basic structural changes.

In a rather caustic analysis of the field of archaeology, Spaulding has stated that apparently

> ...truth is to be determined by some sort of polling of archaeologists, that productivity is doing what other archaeologists do, and that the only purpose of archaeology is to make archaeologists happy (Spaulding 1953:590).

We think that this statement was more appropriate in 1953 than it is today, and its inappropriateness today is a rough measure of the extent to which our field has advanced.

REFERENCES

Aikens, C. Melvin
    1967   "Plains Relationships of the Fremont Culture: A Hypothesis." *American Antiquity* 32:198–209.
Allchin, Bridget
    1966   *The Stone Tipped Arrow, Late Stone Age Hunters of the Tropical Old World*. New York: Barnes and Noble.
Ascher, Robert
    1961   "Analogy in Archaeological Interpretation." *Southwestern Journal of Anthropology* 17:317–25.
    1962   "Ethnography for Archeology: A Case from the Seri Indians." *Ethnology* 1:360–69.
Barth, Fredrik
    1950   "Ecologic Adaptation and Cultural Change in Archaeology." *American Antiquity* 15:338–39.
Beardsley, R. K., et al.
    1956   "Functional and Evolutionary Implications of Community Patterning." In Robert Wauchope (ed.), *Seminars in Archaeology*, a special publication of *American Antiquity* 22, no. 22, pt. 2:129–57.

Bennett, John W.
  1943 "Recent Developments in the Functional Interpreta-
        tion of Archaeological Data." *American Antiquity* 8:
        208–19.
Binford, L. R.
  1962 "Archaeology as Anthropology." *American Antiquity*
        28:217–25.
  1964 "A Consideration of Archaeological Research Design."
        American Antiquity 29:425–41.
  1965 "Archaeological Systematics and the Study of Culture
        Process." *American Antiquity* 31:203–210.
  1967a "Smudge Pits and Hide Smoking: The Role of Anal-
        ogy in Archaeological Reasoning." *American Antiquity*
        32:1–12.
  1967b "Comment on K. C. Chang's 'Major Aspects of the
        Interrelationship of Archaeology and Ethnology.'"
        Current Anthropology 8:234–35.
  1968 "Methodological Considerations of the Archeological
        Use of Ethnographic Data." In Richard B. Lee and
        Irven DeVore (eds.), *Man the Hunter*. Chicago:
        Aldine Publishing Co.
Binford, Sally R.
  1968 "Ethnographic Data and Understanding the Pleisto-
        cene." In Richard B. Lee and Irven DeVore (eds.),
        Man the Hunter. Chicago: Aldine Publishing Co.
Blalock, Hubert M., Jr.
  1960 *Social Statistics*. New York: McGraw-Hill.
Bordes, François
  1953 "Essai de classification des industries 'moustériennes.'"
        Bulletin de la Société Préhistorique Française 50:457–
        66.
Braidwood, Robert J.
  1952 "The Near East and the Foundations for Civilization."
        Condon Lectures. Eugene: University of Oregon.
  1959 *Archeology and the Evolutionary Theory*. In *Evolution
        and Anthropology: A Centennial Appraisal*, pp. 76–89.
        Washington: Anthropological Society of Washington.
  1960 "Levels in Prehistory, a Model for the Consideration
        of the Evidence." In Sol Tax (ed.), *The Evolution of
        Man* (vol. 2 of *Evolution after Darwin*). Chicago:
        University of Chicago Press.
  ———, and Charles Reed
  1957 "The Achievement and Early Consequences of Food
        Production." *Cold Spring Harbor Symposia in Quanti-
        tative Biology* 22:19–31.
Caldwell, Joseph R.
  1958 "The New American Archeology." *Science* 129:303–
        307.

Chang, Kwang-Chih
   1958 "Study of the Neolithic Social Grouping: Examples from the New World." *American Anthropologist* 60:298–334.
   1967a *Rethinking Archaeology.* New York: Random House.
   1967b "Major Aspects of the Interrelationship of Archaeology and Ethnology." *Current Anthropology* 8:227–34.
Childe, V. Gordon
   1936 *Man Makes Himself.* London: Watts and Co.
   1946 "Archaeology and Anthropology." *Southwestern Journal of Anthropology* 2:243–51.
Clark, Grahame
   1951 *Star Carr.* Cambridge: Cambridge University Press.
   1953a "The Economic Approach to Prehistory." *Proceedings of the British Academy* 39:215–38.
   1953b "Archaeological Theories and Interpretation: Old World." In A. L. Kroeber (ed.), *Anthropology Today.* Chicago: University of Chicago Press.
Clark, J. Desmond, and F. Clark Howell
   1966 Preface. In J. Desmond Clark and F. Clark Howell (eds.), *Recent Studies in Paleoanthropology,* a special publication of the *American Anthropologist* 68, no. 2, pt. 2.
Cole, Fay-Cooper, and Thorne Deuel
   1937 *Rediscovering Illinois.* Chicago: University of Chicago Press.
Colton, Harold S.
   1939 "Prehistoric Culture Units and Their Relationships in Northern Arizona." *Bulletin* 17. Flagstaff: Museum of Northern Arizona.
Crawford, O. G. S.
   1953 *Archaeology in the Field.* London: Phoenix House.
Deetz, James
   1967 *Invitation to Archaeology.* Garden City, N.Y.: American Museum Science Books, Natural History Press.
   1968 "The Archeological Visibility of Food-Gatherers." In Richard B. Lee and Irven DeVore (eds.), *Man the Hunter.* Chicago: Aldine Publishing Co.
Doran, J. E., and F. R. Hodson
   1966 "A Digital Computer Analysis of Palaeolithic Flint Assemblages." *Nature* 210:688–89.
Erasmus, Charles J.
   1950 "Patolli, Parchisi, and the Limitation of Possibilities." *Southwestern Journal of Anthropology* 6:369–87.
Ford, J. A.
   1954 "The Type Concept Revisited." *American Anthropologist* 56:42–54.

Gladwin, Harold S.
   1934   "A Method for Designation of Cultures and Their
          Variations." *Medallion Papers,* no. 15. Globe, Ariz.:
          Gila Pueblo.
Graebner, Fritz
   1911   *Methode der Ethnologie.* Heidelberg: Universitätsbuch-
          handlung.
Griffin, James B.
   1943   *The Fort Ancient Aspect.* Ann Arbor: University of
          Michigan Press.
   1967   "Eastern North American Archaeology: A Summary."
          Science 156:175–91.
Hawkes, Christopher
   1954   "Archeological Theory and Method: Some Suggestions
          from the Old World. *American Anthropologist*
          56:155–68.
Heider, Karl G.
   1967   "Archaeological Assumptions and Ethnographical
          Facts: A Cautionary Tale from New Guinea." *South-
          western Journal of Anthropology* 23:52–64.
Hempel, Carl G.
   1965   *Aspects of Scientific Explanation.* New York: The Free
          Press.
Hodson, F. R., P. H. A. Sneath, and J. E. Doran
   1966   "Some Experiments in the Numerical Analysis of
          Archaeological Data." *Biometrika* 53:311–24.
Jennings, Jesse D.
   1957   "Danger Cave." *Memoir of the Society for American
          Archaeology,* no. 14, *American Antiquity* 23, no. 2, pt. 2.
Kroeber, A. L.
   1937   "Archaeology." In *Encyclopedia of the Social Sciences,*
          vol. 2.
Kleindienst, Maxine R., and Patty Jo Watson
   1956   "Action Archeology: The Archeological Inventory of a
          Living Community. *Anthropology Tomorrow* 5:75–78.
Linton, Ralph
   1936   *The Study of Man.* New York: Appleton-Century-
          Crofts.
Lowie, Robert H.
   1912   "The Principle of Convergence in Ethnology." *Journal
          of American Folk-Lore* 25, no. 45:24–42.
   1940   *An Introduction to Cultural Anthropology.* 2d ed.
          New York: Farrar and Rinehart.
McKern, W. C.
   1939   "The Midwestern Taxonomic Method as an Aid to
          Archaeological Culture Study." *American Antiquity*
          4:301–13.

MacWhite, Eóin
    1956   "On the Interpretation of Archeological Evidence in
            Historical and Sociological Terms." *American Anthro-
            pologist* 58:3–25.
Martin, Paul S., and John Rinaldo
    1939   "Modified Basket Maker Sites Ackmen-Lowry Area
            Southwestern Colorado." *Anthropological Series, Field
            Museum of Natural History*, vol. 23, no. 3, Publication
            444:307–444.
Mason, Otis T.
    1893   "The Birth of Invention." In *Annual Report Smithso-
            nian Institution for 1892*. Washington: Smithsonian
            Institution.
Meggers, Betty J., Clifford Evans, and Emillio Estrada
    1965   "Early Formative Period of Coastal Ecuador: The
            Valdivia and Machalilla Phases." *Smithsonian Contri-
            butions to Anthropology*, vol. 1. Washington: Smith-
            sonian Institution.
Morse, Dan F.
    1963   "The Steuben Village and Mounds: A Multicompo-
            nent Late Hopewell Site in Illinois." *Anthropological
            Papers*, no. 21. Ann Arbor: Museum of Anthropology,
            University of Michigan.
Nagel, Ernest
    1967   "The Nature and Aim of Science." In Sidney Morgan-
            besser (ed.), *Philosophy of Science Today*. New York:
            Basic Books.
Piggott, Stuart
    1965a   *Ancient Europe: From the Beginnings of Agriculture
            to Classical Antiquity*. Chicago: Aldine Publishing Co.
    1965b   *Approach to Archaeology*. New York and Toronto:
            McGraw-Hill Paperbacks; Harvard University Press.
Randallh-MacIver, David
    1932   "Archaeology as a Science." *Antiquity* 7:5–20.
Rands, Robert L., and Carroll L. Riley
    1958   "Diffusion and Discontinuous Distribution." *American
            Anthropologist* 60:274–97.
Robbins, Michael C.
    1966   "House Types and Settlement Patterns: An Applica-
            tion of Ethnology to Archaeological Interpretation."
            The Minnesota Archaeologist 28:3–35.
Rootenberg, S.
    1964   "Archaeological Field Sampling." *American Antiquity*
            30:111–88.
Rouse, Irving
    1955   "On the Correlation of Phases of Culture." *American
            Anthropologist* 57:713–22.

1964 "Archaeological Approaches to Cultural Evolution." In Ward Goodenough (ed.), *Explorations in Cultural Anthropology*. New York: McGraw-Hill.

1965 "The Place of 'Peoples' in Prehistoric Research." *Journal of the Royal Anthropological Institute* 95:1–15.

Rowe, John Howland
1966 "Diffusionism and Archaeology." *American Antiquity* 31:334–37.

Sackett, James R.
1966 "Quantitative Analysis of Upper Paleolithic Stone Tools." In J. Desmond Clark and F. Clark Howell (eds.), *Recent Studies in Paleoanthropology*, a special publication of the *American Anthropologist* 68, no. 2, pt. 2:356–94.

Sanger, David
1967 "Prehistory of the Pacific Northwest Plateau as Seen from the Interior of British Columbia." *American Antiquity* 32:186–97.

Schlesier, Karl H.
1967 "Sedna Creek: Report on an Archaeological Survey of the Arctic Slope of the Brooks Range." *American Antiquity* 32:210–24.

Service, Elman R.
1964 "Archaeological Theory and Ethnological Fact." In Robert A. Manners (ed.), *Process and Pattern in Culture: Essays in Honor of Julian H. Steward*. Chicago: Aldine Publishing Co.

Siegel, Sidney
1956 *Nonparametric Statistics for the Behavioral Sciences*. New York: McGraw-Hill.

Slotkin, J. S.
1952 "Some Basic Methodological Problems in Prehistory." *Southwestern Journal of Anthropology* 8:442–43.

Smith, Benjamin L.
1940 "The Midwestern Taxonomic Method and Its Application to an Eastern Massachusetts Group." *Bulletin of the Massachusetts Archaeological Society* 2:1–13.

Smith, H. I.
1910 "Prehistoric Ethnology of a Kentucky Site." *Anthropological Papers of the American Museum of Natural History*, vol. 6, no. 2.

Smith, M. A.
1955 "The Limitations of Inference in Archaeology." *Archaeological Newsletter* 6:3–7.

Sollas, W. J.
1924   *Ancient Hunters and Their Modern Representatives.* 3d rev. ed. New York: Macmillan.

Spaulding, A. C.
1953   "Review of 'Measurements of Some Prehistoric Design Developments in the Southeastern States' by James A. Ford." *American Anthropologist* 55:588–91.
1957   "Review of 'Method and Theory in American Archaeology,' by Gordon R. Willey and Philip Phillips." *American Antiquity* 23:85–87.

Steward, Julian H.
1937   "Ecological Aspects of Southwestern Society." *Anthropos* 32:87–114.
1942   "The Direct Historical Approach to Archaeology." *American Antiquity* 7:337–43.
1949   "Culture Causality and Law: A Trial Formulation of the Development of Early Civilizations." *American Anthropologist* 51:1–28.
1960   "Evolutionary Principles and Social Types." In Sol Tax (ed.), *The Evolution of Man* (vol. 2 of *Evolution after Darwin*). Chicago: University of Chicago Press.

Steward, Julian H., and Frank M. Setzler
1938   "Function and Configuration in Archaeology." *American Antiquity* 4:4–10.

Steward, Julian H., *et al.*
1955   "Irrigation Civilizations: A Comparative Study." *Social Science Monographs I.* Washington: Pan American Union.

Tallgren, A. M.
1937   "The Method of Prehistoric Archaeology." *Antiquity* 11, no. 42:152–61.

Taylor, Walter W.
1948   "A Study of Archeology." *American Anthropologist*, vol. 50, no. 2, pt. 2. Memoir no. 69.

Thompson, Raymond H.
1956   "The Subjective Element in Archaeological Inference." *Southwestern Journal of Anthropology* 12:327–32.
1958   "Modern Yucatecan Maya Pottery Making." *Memoirs of the Society for American Archaeology*, no. 15, *American Antiquity*, vol. 23, no. 4, pt. 2.

Trigger, Bruce G.
1967   "Settlement Archaeology — Its Goals and Promise." *American Antiquity* 32:149–59.

Tylor, E. B.
1896   "On American Lot-Games as Evidence of Asiatic Intercourse before the Time of Columbus." *Internationales Archiv für Ethnographie*, vol. 9.

Vogt, Evon Z.
1956   "An Appraisal of 'Prehistoric Settlement Patterns in the New World.'" In Gordon R. Willey (ed.), *Prehistoric Settlement Patterns in the New World.* Viking Fund Publications in Anthropology no. 23. New York: Wenner-Gren Foundation for Anthropological Research.

Wallis, Wilson D.
1928   "Probability and the Diffusion of Culture Traits." *American Anthropologist* 30:94–106.

Warren, Claude N.
1967   "The San Dieguito Complex: A Review and Hypothesis." *American Antiquity* 32:168–85.

Washburn, S. L.
1953   "The Strategy of Physical Anthropology." In A. L. Kroeber (ed.), *Anthropology Today.* Chicago: University of Chicago Press.

Watson, Patty Jo
1966   "Clues to Iranian Prehistory in Modern Village Life." Philadelphia: University Museum of the University of Pennsylvania.

Wauchope, Robert
1966   "Archaeological Survey of Northern Georgia, with a Test of Some Cultural Hypotheses." *American Antiquity*, vol. 3, no. 5, pt. 2. Memoir no. 21.

White, Leslie A.
1943   "Energy and the Evolution of Culture." *American Anthropologist* 45:335–56.

Willey, Gordon R.
1953   "Prehistoric Settlement Patterns in the Virú Valley, Peru." *Bureau of American Ethnology, Bulletin 155.* Washington: Smithsonian Institution.

1956   (ed.) "Prehistoric Settlement Patterns in the New World." Viking Fund Publications in Anthropology, no. 23. New York: Wenner-Gren Foundation for Anthropological Research.

1960   "Historical Patterns and Evolution in Native New World Cultures." In Sol Tax (ed.), *The Evolution of Man* (vol. 2 of *Evolution after Darwin*). Chicago: University of Chicago Press.

1962   "The Early Great Styles and the Rise of the Pre-Columbian Civilizations." *American Anthropologist* 64:1–14.

1966   *An Introduction to American Archaeology.* Vol. 1: *North and Middle America.* Englewood Cliffs, N.J.: Prentice-Hall.

————, and Philip Phillips
   1958   *Method and Theory in American Archaeology.* Chicago: University of Chicago Press.
Wilson, E. Bright, Jr.
   1952   *An Introduction to Scientific Research.* New York: McGraw-Hill.

STUART STRUEVER

*The new approaches to archaeological thinking outlined by
Lewis Binford in the preceding article must, of course, be
applied to problems facing the archaeologist in the field, in
the laboratory, and in the preparation of reports, and Stuart
Struever's selection sums up these problems. Struever looks
again at some of the more recent methodological approaches,
and provides insights into the fundamental problems of
fieldwork. Most important, the author reflects a realization of
the magnitude of work all archaeologists must perform to
accomplish their aims efficiently, and recognizes the
compromises they face. For example, to excavate and analyze
a single site as thoroughly as possible would involve
prohibitive expenditures of time and money, so to achieve
realistic programs, the archaeologist must make optimum use
of resources and yet not lose sight of the relevant problems
and solutions. The challenge is an imposing one.*

12   Problems, Methods, and Organization: A Disparity in the Growth of Archaeology

As general anthropological theory has advanced, new and
exciting problems have been conceptualized for archaeology. Chronology-
building is an initial step to the solution of broader problems, not an
end-result of research. The introduction of cultural ecology, general systems
theory and more sophisticated evolutionary concepts have made the quest
of cultural process, not a slogan (or a form of Hippocratic oath taken on
entrance to graduate school) but an operational problem for archaeologists.

Reprinted, with the editorial changes noted, from "Problems, Methods and Organization: A Disparity in the Growth of Archeology" by Stuart Struever in Betty Meggers
(ed.), *Anthropological Archeology in the Americas* (Washington, D.C.: Anthropological
Society of Washington, 1968), pp. 131–151, by permission of the author and the
publisher.

187

If problems have changed, so have the tools for their solution. Attention is now focused on translating problems into research design (Binford 1964). More importantly, with help from the physical and biological sciences, we are witnessing a marked increase in the diversity and sophistication of methods that expand our capacity for translating research design into concrete fieldwork and analysis (cf. Brothwell and Higgs 1963, for a partial inventory of recent developments in archaeological method). For example, models in population growth and demography developed in animal ecology have been adopted by prehistorians concerned with explaining human evolution. Advances made in the studies of soil, pollen and geomorphology enable reconstruction of climatic history; this information is critical for developing models to describe and explain the history of human adaptations. There have been dramatic innovations in techniques to increase the completeness of data recovery (e.g., mechanical screens and flotation techniques); in techniques for analyzing the content of raw materials (e.g., optical emission spectroscopy); in computer technology that greatly extends our capacity for observing often subtle relationships between classes of artifacts (e.g., programs in factor analysis); in dating techniques (e.g., archaeomagnetism and thermoluminescence); and in ethnobotanical and -zoological methods that expand our understanding of prehistoric subsistence practices.

Organization of archaeological research, however, has changed little. New World archaeologists work in departments of anthropology, either in a university or museum. The departments are internally undifferentiated, i.e., all members occupy research and/or teaching roles. The *only* recognized roles are professor and student. All faculty members have professional status, and particularly in the larger institutions all are expected to pursue research, self-directed and largely independent of each other. Archaeology is and always has been basically a one-man undertaking, a form of scholarship in which individual autonomy has high priority. Research is not executed by one person, but the extent and sophistication of problems conceived, of excavation and analytical methods used to solve these problems, and the capital outlays of equipment and facilities seldom exceed the resources or resourcefulness of a single investigator or the longevity of his personal interest. The scope of the problems investigated, then, is limited by the personal commitment of a single archaeologist and by the restrictions imposed on or by the funding organizations in providing capital to carry out a project. This results in formulation of relatively small-scale problems dependent on limited and voluntary (and often irregular) cooperation of collateral specialists, and calling for small capital outlays that restrict the number and completeness of technical studies that feed basic information into the research. To be sure, many projects today involve the temporary collaboration of archaeologists and other specialists, but these are based on expediency. Not long after the joint effort begins to work smoothly it often dissolves, with each specialist turning to his own interests again.

Therefore, while archaeological funding has increased today along with the level of informal cooperation, the basic organizational structure within which research is carried out has changed little. The thesis of this paper is that, given a certain theoretical framework and the problems deriving from it, role-undifferentiated departments of anthropology no longer provide an adequate institutional base for undertaking archaeological research.

The description of culture as an adaptive system, the description of culture history as a shift from simple to complex cultural systems, the appearance of regularities in development between independent traditions, and the *explanation* of these documented changes and regularities — explanations which are aimed at isolating the processes of culture change — require that archaeology itself undergo a shift to a higher organizational level.

What is called for is the development of an archaeological organization complex enough to enable formulation of broad and important problems, while at the same time providing *an institutionalized means* of assembling the personnel, the capital equipment, and the special bodies of knowledge necessary to plan a research design and to carry out fieldwork and analysis. The value of this approach is that the formulation of problems and undertaking of research will still basically depend on the combined capabilities of the investigators, but the institution within which the research is organized will itself provide a way of combining a greater number of intellectual skills, a greater repertoire of excavation and analytical techniques, and greater capital resources. Most importantly, it will help to insure long-term continuity without which such a program could not succeed.

This paper will show that, if a major purpose of archaeology is to elucidate cultural process by *explaining* prehistoric episodes of change or stability, then the strategy of archaeology must shift to long-term programs of fieldwork and analysis. This will be illustrated in terms of a specific explanatory problem on which we are currently working; I will outline a research design that, were it translated into actual fieldwork, would enable us to build a corpus of data from which hypotheses can be generated and tested. I will also show that execution of this design is not feasible within the organizational limitations of archaeology today.

THE PERSPECTIVES OF CULTURAL EVOLUTION, CULTURAL ECOLOGY, AND GENERAL SYSTEMS THEORY: FOUNDATIONS FOR EXPLAINING CULTURE CHANGE

The job of archaeology, as conceived here, is to describe and, more particularly, *to explain* the total range of cultural similarities and cultural differences observable in space and through time. An evolutionary perspective is essential to the explanation of these similarities and differences. More efficient and more differentiated cultural forms replace less efficient ones, and higher levels of integration replace lower ones in the history of culture change. Structural diversity of cultures is consistent with adaptation to widely varying social and natural environments, and history bespeaks of increasing cultural diversity through time as cultures become more closely geared to differing environments. Rates of cultural evolution are not uniform, but change with shifting selective pressures.

Culture is a system of functionally interdependent parts in which change in one aspect is related in specifiable ways to changes in others. Explanations for change in a cultural system require understanding these linkages. Variations between cultures are responses to differing adaptive requirements of specific environments; accordingly, varying ecological potentialities are linked to different exploitative economies and the latter, in turn, to differing integrative requirements met by differing forms of social structure, etc.

Archaeology seeks, first, to reconstruct historical sequences of cultural systems with focus on the linkages between variables involved in the structural modification of these systems through time. And secondly, though controlled comparative studies between sequences, it seeks to elucidate the functional relationships pertaining between these variables.

Binford (1962) suggests that material culture relates in a systematic way to the structure of the total culture. Archaeology — and social anthropology — are faced with the task of correlating the structure of material elements of a cultural system with the structure of behavioral attributes of that same system. The structure of material remains is observable in terms of the qualitative and quantitative representation and spatial configurations of all classes of debris.

North America has been a major focus of archaeological research for more than fifty years. The resultant body of literature documents three broad objectives in this work:

a. The definition of prehistoric cultures in terms of an undifferentiated list of mixed functional and stylistic-formal traits. A newly recovered archaeological assemblage is attributed to one or another previously-defined culture on the basis of number of shared traits.

b. The alignment of these cultures within a chronological framework.

c. Discrete historical explanation for cultural similarities and differences. Attempts are made to show specific historical ties between different cultures through time and space; local cultural manifestations are "explained" in terms of influences emanating from other locales.

Significantly, through most of this archaeological research there has been little attempt to describe prehistoric culture in structural — that is quantitative and spatial, as well as qualitative — terms, without which the archaeological equivalents of cultural systems cannot be defined.

In recent years, there has been increasing discussion of the importance of delineating *culture types* from archaeological remains. Braidwood (1960), Willey (1960), Steward (1955), and others conceive definition of types in structural, not stylistic-formal, terms. The culture types sought must be cross-culturally valid, i.e., they can be expected to appear again and again in historically unrelated traditions perhaps separated by thousands of miles.

Many archaeologists who espouse these aims acknowledge technology as the most accessible aspect of the total cultural system. They seek to describe prehistoric subsistence patterns in terms of exploitative and maintenance technologies utilized and the resources exploited. The settlement pattern, that is, the manner in which a society is segmented and partitioned to exploit the environment — is an essential corollary of subsistence.

DEFINING A SUBSISTENCE-SETTLEMENT SYSTEM FROM MATERIAL REMAINS

Given a systemic view of culture, it can be expected that the material elements of an extinct subsistence-settlement system will reveal a structured set of relationships, just as social anthropology has demonstrated these relationships in the behavioral aspect of the system. This "structure of material culture" can be described by the archaeologist within various analytical frames, e.g., the site, the region, etc. Within a site, such structure might manifest itself in the definition of *activity areas* (e.g., cooking locality) and *areas of social distinction* (e.g., locus of a kin-defined residence unit). Each will have a formal definition based on correlations of material cultural elements. A cooking locality, as one type of activity area, might be defined in terms of one or more *tool kits* or *activity sets*, themselves defined on the basis of the spatial clustering of certain artifact types (e.g., pestles and slab grinding stones), kinds of life-maintenance by-products (e.g., fire residues and plant remains), and structural feature types (e.g., hearths and earth ovens). In addition, each activity area can be expected to have a spatial dimension, since activities tend to be localized and to a degree spatially segregated within the area of a community.

The analysis of kind, number, and distribution of material elements recovered from an archaeological site, therefore, enables the archaeologist to define tool kits, activity sets, and hopefully, activity areas. These are the building blocks upon which *settlement types* are defined. Sites in which a particular configuration of exploitative and maintenance activities were carried out will disclose a similar structure of material elements; all such sites are representative of a single settlement type. If focus shifts to a regional universe, the structure of an extinct settlement system should be reflected in the kind, number, and distribution of settlement types, each defined as indicated above.

An underlying assumption here is that the biophysical environment is itself structured, and that as an adaptive system, a culture articulates with this environment through a highly complex set of patterned relationships. Aspects of biophysical environment include topography, water sources, animal life, vegetation, etc.[1] Each may be expected to have a highly variable distribution within the total geographic area encompassed by a single settlement system. Given that types of plant associations in an area have a variable distribution, and that placement of settlements of a certain cultural phase was in part determined by the location of specific natural plant foods, correlations noted between habitation sites and these resources should provide important clues for understanding the subsistence-settlement system characteristic of that phase.

Though archaeologists have turned to study of subsistence-settlement systems, research designs are seldom planned and carried out explicitly to maximize recovery of data pertinent to defining these systems. The literature is replete with intuitive assessments of archaeological complexes in deriving subsistence-settlement patterns, but descriptions are usually qualitative, lacking analysis of the quantitative-spatial relationships between classes of artifacts, features, etc., on which firm definitions hinge.

Recently, there have been several efforts to excavate and analyze prehistoric sites with the express purpose of describing the structure of material remains (e.g., Binford and Binford 1966; Clark 1954). However, a sequence of structurally-defined subsistence-settlement systems still does not exist for any region. Only when such information becomes available can hypotheses be developed that explain changes between systems from one cultural phase to the next within a tradition. And only after similar hypotheses have been tested, changed, and strengthened in several regional traditions can regularities in change between them be recognized and explained.

THE CONTRIBUTIONS OF CULTURAL EVOLUTION, ECOLOGY, AND SYSTEMS THEORY TO DEFINITION OF ARCHAEOLOGICAL PROBLEMS: A SUBSTANTIVE EXAMPLE

As viewed here, the explanatory problems of archaeology, and therefore the research designs and fieldwork strategies necessary to investigate them, are rooted in three postulates on the nature of culture and of culture change:

---

[1] Together these define one of two segments that comprise the *total adaptive milieu* of any culture. For a moment we are ignoring adaptive pressures stemming from other cultural systems, which might be regarded as constituting the *social* environment of a culture.

1. The history of culture change is one of increasing structural diversity and higher levels of integration.

2. Culture is analyzable as a superorganic system.

3. Culture is an adaptive form within two environmental milieus, one biophysical, the other social.

Accepting these premises, I believe we can validate our thesis that the development of archaeological problems and methods has outstripped the organizational means for carrying out research by outlining the strategy appropriate to solving a specific problem. The problem is one of explaining an episode of rapid culture change that took place at a specific time and place in prehistory.

A. The Problem

Archaeological work in the principal river valleys immediately south of the western Great Lakes in midwestern United States documents a major period of culture change beginning ca. 100 B.C., the advent of Hopewell Culture (cf. Caldwell and Hall 1964 and Struever 1965 for recent comments on this development).

The evidence for a shift to higher levels of complexity is threefold: (1) an extension and intensification of "interaction" between cultural groups, sometimes widely separated from each other and scattered over much of eastern United States, involving development of a widespread trade or exchange network within and far beyond the midwestern riverine area. Exotic raw materials (e.g., obsidian) and selected artifact styles (e.g., animal effigy pipes) moved between groups in widely separated localities; (2) a rapid and marked increase in population density in certain restricted locales within the riverine area; and (3) an increase in social complexity (specifically, increased status differentiation) as reflected in a broadening of differences in access to goods and services, expressed in the context of ceremonial-mortuary activity. Hopewell mounds in the Mississippi Valley typically contain a central log tomb with a few burials accompanied by artistically elaborate goods and scarce raw materials seldom found with apparent lower status individuals interred in and around the earth mound that was placed over the tomb.

Importantly, this synchronous emergence of style-sharing and raw material exchange over a wide area; of mortuary practices reflecting increasing status differentiation; and of rapid population expansion *was confined to certain localities within the Illinois, Mississippi, and a few other major valleys* within the Great Lakes–Riverine area. Contemporary cultural groups located outside these valleys apparently participated little or not at all in this interaction. This and the absence of the distinctive Hopewell mortuary forms suggests they remained on a lower level of complexity (cf. Struever

1965:216). In short, the archaeological evidence for Hopewell during the Middle Woodland Period suggests that these three developments were interrelated aspects of a single phenomenon of culture change largely restricted to segments of a few river valleys. The problem poses itself: Are these in fact interdependent phenomena? If so, what model of systemic change best explains the available evidence for this episode of cultural development?

B. The Hypothesis

An attempt to answer these questions began by noting a relationship between known Hopewellian mound groups in the western Great Lakes and several important ecological variables, including temperature clines, major waterfowl migration routes, and variants of a particular river valley ecosystem. From this it was inferred that a change in subsistence practices was an important aspect of the Hopewellian development and, further, that the degree to which Woodland groups in different locales underwent a shift to a higher level of complexity, as manifested in increasing population densities, larger settlements, intensification of interaction, and increased status differentiation, was closely related to the extent to which they experienced these economic changes. It remained to identify these changes.

Several seasons of survey and excavation in one river valley make it possible to argue (Struever, n.d.) that these developments at the outset of the Middle Woodland period could in one sense be "explained" by a sharp and documentable increase in economic productivity. In certain riverine localities, this productivity increase was based on development of an "intensive harvest collecting" subsistence base featuring exploitation of plant and animal species that could be taken in large quantities with relatively small labor output. This technology appeared only in those environments supporting a number of regularly renewed, harvestable natural foods. Localities fitting this description are geographically restricted within the Great Lakes–Riverine area. In addition, recent studies of plant remains suggest that increased productivity in some localities during the Early and Middle Woodland periods also involved the first *effective* food production in the riverine area (Black 1963; Yarnell 1965). Cultivars included squash (*Cucurbita pepo*), and perhaps certain native weeds, particularly pigweed (*Amaranthus* sp.), lamb's-quarter (*Chenopodium* sp.) and marsh elder (*Iva annua* var. *macrocarpa*).

The fact that all local Hopewell expressions in the riverine area represent cultures that underwent marked change does not mean these regional cultures changed at equal rates or achieved comparable levels of complexity by the end of the Middle Woodland period (ca. A.D. 400). Nor does it indicate they underwent similar changes in subsistence base. In fact, our best evidence suggests that the mixed harvest collecting-agricultural subsistence base was *not* characteristic of the majority of Great Lakes–Riverine Woodland groups that experienced socioeconomic-demographic change about 100 B.C. For example, Prufer (1965) argues that the elaborate Hopewellian developments in the Scioto Valley of Ohio occurred in the context of a shift from collecting to major dependence on agriculture. The configuration of harvestable natural foods, described earlier as characteristic of *certain localities* in the riverine area, may not have existed in the Scioto. Also, the extent and richness of bottomland soils in the central Scioto may have provided particularly favorable conditions for a more rapid and more complete shift to cultivation.

To say that a documented shift to higher levels of productivity, whether based on effective agriculture or harvest collecting, accounts for and explains culture change in the various local Hopewell expressions is incorrect. It only identifies one of the variables in a linked series of changes whose explanation remains our primary research objective. Increased production may have been prerequisite to subsequent changes in population density, social structure, and between-group interaction, but the problem is still to explain the initial shifts in subsistence base that resulted in higher productivity. To say that the biophysical environment *allowed* intensive harvest collecting or productive agriculture to develop is not to explain this development. Cultures do not necessarily represent maximizing adaptations; maximization is a phenomenon of intensified selection. Our problem remains to identify and explain changing selective pressures in either the biophysical or social environments, or both, of each culture under consideration by isolating shifts in the natural habitat and "social habitat" in each of several regional sequences of Early and Middle Woodland cultures.

It is hypothesized that sometime during the last two centuries B.C. the coping situations changed for various regional Woodland cultures; important changes in subsistence base and social structure were adaptive responses to these changes. To test this hypothesis we must have information, first, on change in the biophysical and social environments of these various cultures, and secondly, on change in the cultural systems themselves.

Today, liaisons between archaeologists, biologists, cultural geographers, and pollen and soil specialists have made reconstruction of early biophysical environments increasingly possible. From these data, changes in climate, vegetation, and animal populations can be assessed in order to determine their effect on the selective pressures exerted on a given Woodland culture. Analysis of change in the social environment is a task of enormously greater magnitude. Hopewell expressions cover several thousand square miles of eastern United States; many cultures from the Genessee River in western New York State to Kansas City, Missouri, participated in a system of exchange. Exotic raw materials and finished goods made from them, along with ideological rationalizations for their use (and probably ownership), were moved through this system. The specific form of relationship between any two societies within the total "interaction sphere" is an important problem. Prufer (1964) suggests this interaction involved the spread of a "religious cult" and paraphernalia associated with it; Winters (n.d.) interprets it as an economic phenomenon, probably centering on the reciprocal exchange of staple raw materials, such as flint and perhaps food.

To explain culture change at 100 B.C. in any locality from New York to Kansas City requires us to understand changes in the relationships between a host of cultures which directly or indirectly impinged on each other in this interaction system. In short, a number of cultural systems underwent various degrees and kinds of change at about 100 B.C. with a highly complex net effect on the relations between any two of them.

C. Testing the Hypothesis:
Design of a Research Program

We may now outline the major steps in an archaeological field program appropriate to testing the initial hypothesis that important changes occurred in the technoenvironmental adaptations of various Early and Middle Woodland groups within the Great Lakes–Riverine area. This will point up the discrepancy today between the resources available and those required for such a research program.

The first step is to describe culture change in *one* region within the riverine area. This requires reconstruction of a series of cultural systems (or, more specifically, subsistence-settlement systems) existing prior to, during, and following the period of change.

The tactical problems in carrying out such a program are illustrated by our current research. Focus of the work is a 2,800-square-mile area that centers on a 70-mile stretch of the lower Illinois River Valley. Eighty years of archaeological work show that major culture change occurred here between the Early and Middle Woodland periods, and that local Middle Woodland groups participated actively in the Hopewell interaction system.

The first objective in the Illinois Valley project was to understand the Black Sands (Early Woodland period) and succeeding Havana-Hopewell (Middle Woodland period) subsistence-settlement systems, attempting to document the shift between them (c.f. Struever, n.d.). Once accepting the proposition that Black Sands and Havana-Hopewell systems were adapting in two environmental contexts, explanation of culture change at the beginning of the Middle Woodland period in the lower Illinois Valley makes it necessary not only to reconstruct subsistence-settlement changes there, but also to understand the history of culture change in adjacent regions insofar as cultures in those regions constituted part of the social environment for the lower Illinois Valley Black Sands and Havana-Hopewell groups.

PALEOENVIRONMENTAL RECONSTRUCTION

Since cultures are closely tied to the physiographic, botanical, and other conditions of their surroundings, reconstruction of the biophysical environments characteristic of the Early and Middle Woodland periods is the first step in our research design. Plant ecologists, working in conjunction with soil and pollen specialists, reconstruct the prehistoric botanical environments, perhaps establishing microvegetation zones. An animal ecologist, drawing on climatological and botanical data, infers the spatial and temporal organization of each species on the landscape and its relative productive potential for men. The soil specialist and geomorphologist collaborate on regional physiography and hydrography. At the same time, they contribute to paleo-climatological interpretation.

The object of these combined studies is, of course, reconstruction of all aspects of the biophysical environment specifically pertaining to Black Sands and Hopewellian adaptations in the lower Illinois Valley. The success of these studies will depend on close contact between the archaeologist, ecologist, and physical scientist, since the criteria used in the paleonenvironmental reconstruction must be appropriate to the primary objective of describing a series of Woodland cultural-ecological adaptations.

FIELDWORK STRATEGY: SURFACE SURVEY

The first phase of archaeological fieldwork — surface survey — cannot be planned effectively until the environments to which the Woodland subsistence-settlement systems were adapted are understood. The object of survey is to learn prehistoric site distribution in the region. Since the geographic area encompassed by the research is great, some form of sampling is required. Once the internal variability in soils, land forms, water sources, flora, and fauna are understood, these data will be used to design a sampling pattern appropriate to covering each microenvironment that may have played a part in the Early and Middle Woodland exploitative economies.

It is assumed that Woodland settlements were situated partly in terms of the distribution of certain natural resources. If the biophysical environment is structured, and the Woodland cultures exploited the various recognized microzones differentially, then a different range of exploitative maintenance activities can be predicted for settlements located in these different microzones. These serve to differentiate settlement types. The occurrence of more than one settlement type in a subsistence-settlement system may reflect: (a) necessity of moving the settlement in terms of these distributions in order to exploit resources when they become maximally available; (b) aggregation or dispersion of the population to meet seasonally shifting requirements for resource exploitation; and (c) formation of task-specific groups to carry out particular subsistence activities.

Geographic relationships between sites and the various previously defined microenvironments provide a clue to recognizing settlement types. To obtain this information, the 2,800-square-mile area is stratified in terms of these microenvironments, and a method of sampling each is devised. A microenvironment is gridded off and selected squares within the grid are surveyed completely. It is expected that the number and distribution of sites thus located within the sampled units of each microenvironment will closely reflect the actual number and distribution of sites in that niche.

Analysis of the surface collections resulting from the site sample survey is then undertaken for (1) identification of all sites attributable to the Black Sands and Havana-Hopewell phases; and (2) recognition of differences between sites in kinds and quantitative representation of functional artifact types and other classes of materials relating to subsistence activities. Differences in "debris profiles" based on survey data alone serve as initial guidelines for distinguishing settlement types. This is based on the premise that variations in natural resource distribution should correlate with the locations from which activities relating to these resources were carried out by man, and the latter should be reflected in the geographic distribution of artifacts and debris used in or resulting from these activities.

When sites representative of these tentative settlement types are plotted against the distributions of the various microenvironments, correlations may appear. Sometimes, however, surface evidence fails to reveal the qualitative and quantitative differences between sites necessary to establish tentative settlement types. Both repeated plowing of the site surface, which reduces to small fragments all classes of debris, and the continuous activity of relic collectors, has a tendency to remove selected artifact classes, thus biasing the artifact composition of the surface collections. If collectors walk the plowed surface of a habitation site for many years, picking up projectile points, both whole and broken, subsequent archaeological survey will produce a debris profile with low point frequencies. Nonetheless, careful analysis of the survey collections should produce the first signs of between-site differences that will eventually emerge as the basis of a settlement typology.

By employing "controlled surface pickup" it may be possible to recognize what, following excavation, will be defined as different *activity areas* in a prehistoric community. For this purpose the entire site surface must be laid out in a grid system. If the site is small, the archaeologist can literally "vacuum clean" its surface, i.e., collect all debris from all squares in the grid. Otherwise an adequate sampling procedure will produce data from selected squares that closely approximate the relative frequencies of the total populations of all classes of artifacts and debris on the site surface. When distributions of all classes of debris relating to exploitation and maintenance have been plotted on the grid, density variations may appear that reflect localization of task performance. These first clues of activity variation within the Woodland community can be investigated in each of three subsequent excavation phases.

FIELDWORK STRATEGY WITHIN A SINGLE SITE: EXCAVATION

A detailed description of a single habitation site is the next step in our study of the Black Sands or Havana-Hopewell subsistence-settlement systems in the lower Illinois Valley. Controlled sampling within a site should yield data to describe the internal structure of this community. This structural description of a single site provides us with one example of one settlement type within the total settlement system; this excavation program must then be extended to several sites representative of each tentative settlement type, to test the initial definitions and to alter them if necessary.

Binford outlines an excavation strategy, pointing out why such a strategy is essential to the above objectives:

> The sampling and field-observation procedures utilized do not affect our ability to analyze items formally, but they greatly affect our ability to study the distribution, form, and structure of *a population of cultural items* (Binford 1964:430).

It is upon the distribution, form, and structure of the *populations* of cultural items that our settlement type definitions will ultimately depend. To illustrate: Different economic and social activities comprising settlement life may be in part spatially localized. Indeed, the division of work and living space within the community precincts is often a formal expression of role and status differentiation. Therefore, a uniform distribution within the site area of artifacts, constructions, and other debris relating to the performance of various economic, ceremonial, and other tasks would not be expected. This leaves it to the archaeologist to sample the total site area in a manner that enables determination of: (1) the total range of variability in all classes of cultural items; (2) the frequency representation of every variant in each class; and (3) what cultural items cluster spatially with others. In this way only, can he isolate the various complexes of artifacts and features that constitute the remnants of different activities. These artifact-feature complexes — "activity sets" — reflect the kinds and relative importance of different exploitative and maintenance activities in community life, and therefore serve as the criteria for defining settlement types.

Binford (1964:438ff) proposes a three-phase excavation program to achieve these ends. For purposes of clarity, the hypothetical site considered here is assumed to represent a one-period occupation; this eliminates from concern the important problem of assigning cultural items to a specific period in a multi-occupation site.

TEST EXCAVATIONS

The first phase of excavation is a series of small test squares spaced over the site surface in some randomized fashion to sample the populations of artifacts, features, and maintenance by-products within the site precincts. Once analyzed, these will serve to test, and certainly expand, the preliminary settlement type definitions, since remains of structures (features) and other classes of debris normally absent from surface collections will be recovered.

Test excavations also disclose something of the depositional history of soil and cultural remains on a site. If more than one occupation occurred, the geographic extent of each within the site can be determined. The field archaeologist will also note if post-occupation sheet wash has covered part of the site, or whether wind or water erosion has cut away areas of deposit and thereby disturbed the original context of debris. It will be important to learn if the local Black Sands or Havana-Hopewell group lived on a stable or "floating" ground surface. A floating surface is one that gradually rises as water carries soil down the talus slope into the living area. Deep, stratified sites often reflect occupation of a floating surface over a period of time. This information on the stability of the living surface is essential for planning the final stage of excavation.

Test excavations reveal, not only the range of formal variation in all classes of debris at the site, but also the distribution and relative frequencies of all artifact and feature types over the site surface. When plotted on a site map, these may be used to define tentative "activity areas" within the prehistoric settlement. Butchering, cooking, burial, storage, and ritual are among activities reflected in test excavation data that may show a localized distribution, both within and between settlements. Because these excavated materials come largely from below the level of modern agricultural disturbance, a more accurate picture of the kinds and relative frequencies of debris should emerge than that based on surface evidence alone. Accordingly, test excavation materials reflect more accurately the relative importance of various activities in the totality of community life.

Analysis of test-excavated materials from two or more sites representative of each tentative settlement type will test the initial subsistence-settlement model, altering it to fit the combined surface and excavation data. Predictions based on this model are then tested by means of large-scale, "block" excavations.

BLOCK EXCAVATION

Sites representative of each proposed settlement type within the lower Illinois Valley Black Sands and Hopewell subsistence-settlement systems are selected for intensive excavations.

While a major object of test excavation is to sample populations of all classes of debris over the entire site surface, these pits may be too small to allow exposure and identification of larger constructions such as house floors. Block excavations are planned for each tentative activity area defined on the site. Such an excavation provides a broad exposure of living surface, enabling recovery of the total population of cultural items resulting from activities carried on in that particular precinct. Block excavations also seek: (a) to establish the spatial relationship between these formal classes of remains, and (b) to determine the relative quantitative representation of each. Repeated configurations of certain artifact and feature types may enable definition of activity sets[2] which serve to sharpen our delineation of an activity or "use" area. Test excavation enables general recognition of activity variation within the settlement, but will not normally yield large enough samples of artifacts and features, or indicate their relative positioning to each other. It is left to block excavations to recover the more extensive data necessary for specific interpretation of the activities carried out in each locality.

Lacking time and money, many field programs do not proceed beyond test excavation, and the investigator is left to make inferences on community life on too little evidence. It may be impossible to accurately assess the function of feature types from their sparse occurrence in test squares: often features must be recovered in quantity and in particular spatial relationships, as disclosed by block excavation, before their function in maintenance or other activities becomes clear.

STRIPPING EXCAVATIONS

The third and final stage in excavation strategy — "stripping" — is seldom undertaken in archaeology, largely because money and equipment are inadequate. Stripping involves use of power machinery (e.g., road

[2] An activity set refers to a number of features and associated artifact types utilized in, and by-products resulting from, performance of one or several related maintenance tasks.

grader with hydraulic blade) to remove extensive areas of midden down to the level where cultural features can be observed. This can be achieved only in areas of the site where a stable ground surface was maintained during the period of prehistoric occupation. If frequent episodes of sheet erosion blanketed the site with a mantle of silt and thus gradually elevated the ground surface within the habitation area, the upper limits of features will occur at progressively higher elevations consistent with the rising surface level. With such a "floating surface," it is almost impossible to strip away midden to a horizontal plane that would represent the upper limits of all or most features. Where test and block excavations reveal a stable land surface during the period of occupation, however, a road grader can rapidly expose a population of features over an extensive area. Excavators then hand-scrape the living surface to highlight feature outlines, which are plotted on a field map and subsequently excavated.

The value of stripping excavations is that they greatly increase the sample size in all classes of artifacts and features, thus reducing distortion due to a sampling error.

FIELDWORK STRATEGY WITHIN A REGIONAL UNIVERSE

Thus far focus has been on a three-phase excavation strategy applied to a single archaeological site. Test, block, and stripping excavations are carried out, and stage-by-stage analysis of the recovered materials enables definition of exploitative and maintenance tasks that serve as criteria for defining settlement types. This strategy must then be extended to all sites whose excavation is necessary to reconstruct a sequence of subsistence-settlement systems from Black Sands through Havana-Hopewell phases. This reconstruction is itself prerequisite to solving our initial problem, that of explaining change marking the advent of the Hopewellian phase in the lower Illinois Valley ca. 100 B.C.

Analysis of surface survey data from sites within all recognized microenvironments throughout the region enables us to establish a number of tentative settlement types. Test excavations in sites representative of each type will likely necessitate revision of this original model. Block excavations carried out in several sites of each settlement type in this revised model provide a definitive picture of internal community structure for each site. Two block-excavated sites representative of one settlement type should disclose similar debris profiles, and if comparative analysis shows important differences between sites grouped into one settlement type, then the subsistence-settlement model must be altered to fit the more complete evidence.

No matter how detailed the information on internal community structure, however, and no matter how clear the debris profile from one site, this site cannot be treated as representative of a firm settlement type within a total subsistence-settlement system until comparable fieldwork has been carried out in other sites. It must be demonstrated that all reflect the same range and importance of exploitative and maintenance activities, and therefore can be legitimately grouped into one settlement type. Finally, stripping excavations should be carried out in several sites representative of each settlement type in the refined model, thereby expanding the type definition.

Since our problem is to explain culture change between Black Sands and Havana-Hopewell phases, our task includes description of *two* subsistence-settlement systems. This means a three-phase excavation strategy must be applied to sites of both phases. Immense resources are needed for such a program.

PRACTICAL HANDICAPS

In the Illinois Valley Project, we have had neither the perspective nor financial resources to carry out a scheme like that described here. A jerry-built program is however, gradually recovering much of the information sought in the above research design. From survey and excavation data we have thus far defined two Black Sands and four Havana-Hopewell settlement types. Since our problem is to describe the Black Sands and Havana-Hopewell settlement systems, to compare them, and to generate a hypothesis to explain their observable differences, it is necessary to apply the three-phase excavation program to several sites grouped into each of these six tentative settlement types. We have thoroughly investigated (test and block excavations only) one Havana-Hopewell site, the Apple Creek site. Apple Creek required two excavation seasons of three months each, with field crews of from fifteen to twenty persons each season. Excavation was completed in the fall of 1963 and analysis of the data still continues. Typologies are largely completed, but the many steps of correlational analysis necessary to define tool kits, activity sets, and activity areas within the Apple Creek settlement, still remain to be undertaken. When the Apple Creek analysis is finished, we will have described a single example of one settlement type in a Havana-Hopewell subsistence-settlement system. It then remains to undertake three-phase excavation in additional sites of the same settlement type in which Apple Creek is placed, not to mention work in sites of each of the three remaining tentative settlement types defined from survey evidence.

Recently, I attempted (Struever, n.d.) to develop a lower Illinois Havana-Hopewell settlement model from the Apple Creek and survey data.

However, as I have emphasized, one thoroughly excavated site does not make a settlement type and certainly does not make a subsistence-settlement system!

My own, like many other subsistence-settlement reconstructions today, can be reduced to evidence from one, or at best, two extensively excavated sites. The archaeologist attempts to project the structure of the total system from what he has learned in one or two excavations. Research programs commonly terminate at this point, that is, with *suggesting* the form of a prehistoric settlement system. We have argued here that what is needed is a fieldwork strategy enabling *demonstration* of such a system.

Even if the full research design and fieldwork strategy is carried out step-by-step, and the Black Sands and Hopewell settlement systems are described, this still does not *explain* the change from one to the other. An orthogenetic argument, one that sees inherent qualities of human nature as the vital elements responsible for a directional series of events, is not adequate. The shifting adaptation from Black Sands to Hopewell is not a "natural" outcome of the increasing familiarity of man with his environment. Instead, we must look to changes in selective pressures stemming from *both* the biophysical and social environments of the relevant cultures if we are to explain the observed cultural change. Therefore, even if a research design like that described here could be operationalized in the lower Illinois Valley, it is unlikely that we could explain the shifts in technology, population, and social structure from Black Sands to Hopewell. These changes cannot be explained without reference to a much broader intercultural environment. Knowledge of this intercultural environment requires similar in-depth programs for reconstucting Early and Middle Woodland culture history in those regions where cultures may have undergone changes that subsequently intensified old and created new selective pressures on lower Illinois Valley groups.

CONCLUSIONS

If the objective of an archaeological program, on the historiographic level, is to delineate a series of prehistoric subsistence-settlement systems, then a research design of the kind set forth in this paper is necessary. Hopefully, this discussion has dramatized two points:

1. From paleoenvironmental reconstruction to three-phase excavations in each of numerous sites, the magnitude of resources (funds, personnel, and facilities) required greatly exceeds those available to archaeologists in the United States today.

2. More basically, the organization of archaeological research no longer reflects accurately, either what are seen as today's important research

problems, or the continually expanding array of methods developed to solve them. Problems and methods have changed, but the institutional basis for executing research has not.

This disparity in development between problems and methods on the one hand, and organization on the other, is reflected in the great increase in new excavation and analytical techniques without a comparable increase in their application in actual research.

The past few years have seen a literal "methods explosion." Excavation technology has greatly improved with introduction of power machinery for earth-moving and screening. Water separation and chemical flotation techniques sharply increase our ability to recover small-scale food remains on a site. More efficient archaeological prospecting is possible with new resistivity equipment and the proton magnatometer. Experiments in new dating techniques are too numerous to mention. A civil engineer is attempting to demonstrate the limits of prehistoric mathematical capability by analyzing remains of houses and other constructions (Marshall, n.d.). And proliferation of techniques in physics and chemistry have refined our analyses of prehistoric raw materials; centers now exist for the development of these techniques (e.g., the Applied Science Center for Archaeology at the University of Pennsylvania). Less novel, but no less important, are the myriad developments in ethnobotany, -zoology and palynology that have expanded our capacity to understand prehistoric climate and ecology on the one hand, and subsistence practices on the other.

With all of this, there is remarkably little use of new methods as standard archaeological procedure. This gap between innovation and application, this failure to incorporate known technology and bodies of knowledge into archaeological research, is a critical problem. So long as reconstruction of prehistoric cultural-ecological adaptations is the objective, we must have popular access to new methods which, practically speaking, are unavailable to most archaeologists. The capital outlay required for equipment and space exceed the sources of most institutions carrying on archaeology today. No less important, the expertise required to perform the analyses has far outstripped the capacity of any individual.

The problem of describing a subsistence-settlement system is complex enough, as this paper attempts to show. But when explanation of culture change is a primary objective, and it is accepted that a culture is adapting to a social as well as a biophysical environment, then the scope of the problem increases many times. Often no adequate explanation for a particular episode of culture change can be obtained by analyzing only the technoenvironmental adaptations of a series of cultures in a region. Explanations may lie in new selective pressures emanating from the social environment. The changing relationships of the culture with all other cultures impinging on it is an essential part of the adaptive situation requiring analysis.

Failure to attempt such analyses results, not so much from limitations in our methods for testing these models, but from our inability to employ the methods and bodies of knowledge that exist. As organized today, archaeology lacks the institutional framework within which archaeologists, natural scientists, and technicians can work together in a continuing program with the facilities and funding necessary to employ the full range of available methods in attacking an explanatory problem. A sharp increase in our capacity to explain culture change will occur if and when we find a way to increase the complexity of archaeological research institutions.

LITERATURE CITED

Binford, Lewis R.
    1962   "Archaeology as Anthropology." *American Antiquity* 28:217–25.
    1964   "A Consideration of Archaeological Research Design." *American Antiquity* 29:425–41.
———, and Sally R. Binford
    1966   "A Preliminary Analysis of Functional Variability in the Mousterian of Levallois Facies." In *Recent Studies in Paleoanthropology*, J. Desmond Clark and F. Clark Howell (eds.). American Anthropological Association Special Publication, pp. 238–95.
Black, Meredith
    1963   "The Distribution and Archaeological Significance of the Marshelder Iva Annua L." *Papers of the Michigan Academy of Science, Arts and Letters* 48:541–47.
Braidwood, Robert J.
    1960   "Levels in Prehistory: A Model for the Consideration of the Evidence." In *The Evolution of Man* (*Evolution after Darwin*, Sol Tax [ed.], vol. 2), pp. 143–51. Chicago: University of Chicago Press.
Brothwell, Don, and Eric Higgs, eds.
    1963   *Science in Archaeology*. New York: Basic Books, Inc.
Caldwell, Joseph R., and Robert L. Hall, eds.
    1964   "Hopewellian Studies." *Illinois State Museum Scientific Papers*, vol. 12.
Clark, J. G. D.
    1954   *Excavations at Star Carr*. Cambridge: Cambridge University Press.
Marshall, James A.
    [1969]   "Engineering Principles and the Study of Prehistoric Structures: A Substantive Example." *American Antiquity*, 34:166–71.

Prufer, Olaf H.

1964 "The Hopewell Cult." *Scientific American*, 211, no. 6:90–102.

1965 "The McGraw Site: A Study in Hopewellian Dynamics." *Cleveland Museum of Natural History Scientific Publications*, vol. 4, no. 1.

Steward, Julian H.

1955 *Theory of Culture Change*. Urbana: University of Illinois Press.

Struever, Stuart

1965 "Middle Woodland Culture History in the Great Lakes-Riverine Area." *American Antiquity* 31:211–23.

1968 "Woodland Subsistence-Settlement Systems in the Lower Illinois Valley." In *New Perspectives in Archeology*, Lewis R. and Sally R. Binford (eds.). Chicago: Aldine Publishing Co.

Willey, Gordon R.

1960 "Historical Patterns and Evolution in Native New World Cultures." In *The Evolution of Man* (*Evolution after Darwin*, Sol Tax [ed.], vol. 2), pp. 111–41. Chicago: University of Chicago Press.

Winters, Howard D.

n.d. "The Hopewell Interaction Sphere." Paper delivered at the 1964 Annual Meeting of the Society for American Archaeology, Chapel Hill, N.C.

Yarnell, R. A.

1965 "Early Woodland Plant Remains and the Question of Cultivation." *Florida Anthropologist* 18, no. 2:77–82.

JAMES DEETZ

Archaeological theory and method can be refined by the employment of more controlled and thus more accurate testing procedures and experiments. Although it is not likely that archaeology will ever achieve such stringent techniques as physics or chemistry have developed, historically controlled data can be used as one means. James Deetz deals with historic archaeology and shows its potential in producing results of historical and ethnological value.

13   Late Man in North America: Archaeology of European Americans

Most laymen think of archaeology as concerned with the old, the buried, and the exotic. From this identification comes a de facto definition of archaeology as the study of excavated remains of ancient cultures quite different from our own. Until recently, such a definition would not have encountered serious criticism, even from members of the anthropological profession. However, a developing interest in the archaeology of European culture in North America has brought us to reject all three of the above criteria, and has even led to some fundamental reconsiderations of the basic structure of archaeology.

Although a specific designation has not yet been applied to such studies — historic, colonial, or historic site archaeology all have been suggested and used — they have developed to a point where a new national organization has been founded to coordinate their results. Annual meetings of the Society for American Archaeology also now regularly include sessions

Reprinted, with the editorial changes noted, from "Late Man in North America: Archeology of European Americans" by James Deetz in Betty Meggers (ed.), *Anthropological Archeology in the Americas* (Washington, D.C.: Anthropological Society of Washington, 1968), pp. 121–130, by permission of the author and the publisher.

on historic studies, and a large body of literature on the subject has accumulated over the past several years.

This paper will consider various applications of the archaeological study of European Colonial culture in North America through numerous examples. These applications range from the direct use of results in the development of outdoor museums to quite sophisticated refinements in the method and theory of modern archaeology and anthropology, and include results of historical and ethnological value as well.

Archaeological investigations of seventeenth- and early eighteenth-century house sites in southeastern Massachusetts have been of considerable value to the reconstruction of Colonial Plymouth by Plimoth Plantation, an educational organization which is devoted to educating the public in Colonial culture through outdoor museum exhibits and research and publication. Many complex problems of detailed reconstruction of early seventeenth-century households are solved through the study of documentary evidence, contemporary paintings, museum collections, and excavation. Archaeological studies in the Plymouth area represent a long tradition. What is almost certainly the earliest example of controlled scientific archaeological excavation was done in 1853 by James Hall, who exposed the foundations of Miles Standish's home in Duxbury, Massachusetts. The records and artifacts from this remarkable project came to light only in 1963, when they were sent from Mexico to the Pilgrim Society of Plymouth by a descendant of Hall's. Included was a detailed scale plan of the excavations and a portion of what had been a complete, well-catalogued collection of artifacts. The plan showed the location of each artifact, indicated its *in situ* position, and notes included statements of the stratigraphic relationships of deposits within the house foundation. The excavations were tied to *two* datum points. Cataloging was meticulous, each artifact bearing a tag identifying it and relating it to the plan.

Later work included the excavation of the Aptucxet trading post by Lombard in the 1920s (Lombard 1933), of an early seventeenth-century house site in Kingston by Strickland in the 1930s, Hornblower's work at the Winslow site in Marshfield and the R.M. Site in Plymouth in 1940 and 1941 (Hornblower 1943, 1950), and Deetz's excavations of the Bartlett site in Plymouth, and the Bradford and Howland sites in Kingston from 1959 through 1966 (Deetz 1960a, b). The collections from most of these excavations are stored at Plimoth Plantation where they function as a valuable corpus of data on which to base details of architectural reconstruction and house furnishing. Whether the problem involves hinges, nails, window cames, pottery, glass, or cutlery, there is usually a series of artifacts on which to base one's reconstruction or corroborate evidence from other sources. The collections are not only of the usual material culture inventory, but include extensive faunal samples, which will be of great value to the reconstruction of a mid-seventeenth-century farm complex soon to be built on the plantation site. While it might be argued that one need not excavate so many sites just to determine the general form of seventeenth-century colonial culture, since documentary evidence is in fact rather rich, the latter approach only tells us what was available to the early settlers and not what was actually used. There are significant differences between the archaeological collections from Jamestown and Plymouth, although both colonies were drawing from the same larger pool of European materials. One striking difference is seen in the occurrence of forks and Chinese porcelain in a seventeenth-century context at Jamestown, while both artifact types are totally lacking from contemporary Plymouth, a difference which probably reflects the difference between the socioeconomic backgrounds of the settlers in each case, with the Plymouth plantation deriving from a more humble background than that of the Jamestown planters. There are also similarities in domestic crafts between both colonies which seem to transcend their common cultural heritage. In both colonies, bricks used in construction exhibit the same trends in dimensional changes through the seventeenth century, even though there was little contact between the colonies of a type which would account for the similarity. In each case, bricks become shorter, wider, and thicker (Deetz 1960b), changing from an earlier presumably common set of dimensions shared by both groups in England prior to their removal to the New World. A possible explanation of this pattern is found in an additional shared feature, mortar prepared from shells, oysters in Jamestown and clams in Plymouth. Shell mortar is inferior to that made from commercial lime, and as a result, wider brick would provide a better bearing sufrace. Thickening the bricks would permit fewer courses to obtain a wall of the same height. These two changes would then make the bricks heavier, but shortening them would be one way to retain the same volume. In Plymouth, even though all three dimensions change through the century, the cubic content remains unchanged. This pattern of identical change from a common form after isolation, brought about by a similar set of external factors, is reminiscent of the process of drift as it has been perceived in language, and may well be a legitimate analogy.

The archaeological program at Plymouth has applications of a broader nature than simply aiding in restoration and reconstruction. It has frequently been said that archaeology can serve as a valuable supplement to history, since each discipline has a quite different emphasis. As the number of excavated sites in the Plymouth area increases over the coming years, the pattern of settlement and expansion of the colony will be made clear in a way not available from other sources. Since the dating of these early house sites is quite accurate, we can confidently expect to obtain a detailed pattern not only of the location but duration of various farmsteads. Many of these are now located in wooded areas, although they certainly occupied cleared and cultivated land at the time of their use. Another advantage gained from the Plymouth sites results from their relatively brief occupation. The cellars of most of these early houses are sealed samples of twenty to thirty years' duration. Since they are rarely stratified, and are isolated in areas which even today have seldom been plowed, very accurate dates can be assigned to various artifact types within them. At a recent meeting of the Society for Post-Medieval Archaeology in London, it was apparent that the occurrence of certain pottery types in closely dated contexts in Plymouth serves as a source of refinement of the chronology of ceramic manufacture in England, since English sites seldom if ever have such clear temporal limits.

In addition to supplementing the historical record, archaeological study of European sites in this country frequently sheds light on the process of acculturation of the aboriginal population. An excellent case in point is provided by recent work at La Purisima Mission in Lompoc, California, fifty miles north of Santa Barbara (Deetz 1963). Following the destruction of the original mission, Purisima Vieja, in 1812 by severe earthquake, the fathers moved to a new site and rebuilt. By 1814 they had constructed a long barracks building formed of contiguous two-room units to house the neophytes, each unit occupied by a nuclear family group. The only Indians not housed in this structure were unmarried adolescent girls, who were confined to separate quarters. Brief mention of this Indian barracks was made by the resident padre, but it was not until the Civilian Conservation Corps restorations of the 1930s that it was discovered archaeologically. A portion of it was excavated at that time, and the remainder by Norman Gabel in 1950 and by James Deetz in 1962. Final mapping of the feature showed it to have been 540 feet long, of heavy adobe brick construction with a tile roof. The artifact content of this structure was extremely rich, consisting of both aboriginal materials and European trade objects.

Careful analysis and comparison of the inventory from the barracks with assemblages from contemporary aboriginal village sites in the same area produced a striking pattern. Aboriginal artifacts from the barracks were divided into two categories: those reflecting male activity and those representative of female activities. Artifacts of male association were extremely rare; only a scant handful of stone knives, points, and scrapers were encountered in the entire structure. Furthermore, waste flakes which would have resulted from the on-the-spot manufacture of stone tools were virtually absent. Female-associated artifacts on the other hand were just as common as in contemporary aboriginal village sites. Bowls, mortars, pestles, baskets, manos, and metates form the vast majority of the aboriginal assemblage from the barracks. Since we know from the historical record that adults of both sexes occupied the barracks, and since the walls and floors of the structure provided close spatial control, the explanation of the differential rate of material culture loss could be made with confidence. Indian males underwent a rather profound change in roles, with herding, farming, and crafts replacing the older hunting and fishing pattern. Females on the other hand probably continued to perform domestic tasks not too different from those of pre-contact days. The result is seen in the assemblage from the barracks, with almost total loss of material culture reflecting aboriginal male roles and little if any change or loss in the female-associated sub-assemblage. In fact, in comparison to contemporary village sites near the mission, female industries almost seem elaborated, possibly the result of a more sedentary lifeway in the mission compound. A final support of this explanation is provided by a small measure of chronological control within the boundaries of the structure, since it could be shown that the majority of the few male-associated artifacts recovered was from the older portion of the barracks.

The examples thus far cited indicate that there is considerable anthropological and historical value to the archaeological study of European sites in North America. Although recent and not particularly exotic, such sites are as relevant as older or less familiar cultural remains. Another kind of research that can be legitimately included in historic archaeology is the work currently being done on Colonial mortuary art in New England (Deetz and Dethlefsen 1965, 1967; Dethlefsen and Deetz 1966). In this case, we are not dealing with excavated evidence; all of the artifacts are on the surface, and field equipment is limited to pencil, paper, and camera. In a one-hundred-mile-square area centering on Boston, there are over 100,000 gravestones of the late seventeenth, eighteenth, and early nineteenth centuries. These artifacts constitute a unique and powerfully controlled context in which to refine and develop archaeological method and elaborate archaeological theory. They are particularly suited to this purpose since they were the products of a folk culture, and their spatial, temporal, and formal dimensions can be controlled to a very high degree. Each stone has a date inscribed, the location of manufacture is known, and relationships between styles can be clearly delineated through our knowledge of their carvers. With such control on the primary dimensions of archaeological variation, it is possible to measure diffusion rates (Deetz and Dethlefsen 1965), to relate stylistic change as it reflects social differences (Deetz and Dethlefsen 1966), to measure religious change in time and space (Dethlefsen and Deetz 1966), and to postulate and test a host of other aspects of variation in a class of artifacts as it reflects changes in the producing culture. Although a complete description of the results of this study is far beyond the scope of this paper, an example will serve to emphasize its relevance to archaeological method (Earle 1966).

In eastern Massachusetts, between 1700 and 1820, three styles of mortuary design were popular in gravestone art, each during a particular period. Earliest was the winged death's head, and its gradual decline and ultimate disappearance has been shown to be a function of the decline of orthodox Puritanism in Massachusetts Bay Colony. This motif is replaced during the eighteenth century by a cherub design, and cherubs dominate the mortuary art of the middle and late eighteenth century until they are replaced by a third design, the urn and willow motif, which rapidly becomes universal in the early years of the nineteenth century. Graphs showing stylistic sequence and replacement in each cemetery studied provide solid support to the traditional "battleship" shaped curve of seriation method. Although the rates and times of replacement vary considerably from community to community, the overall sequence is repeated in practically every cemetery in the study area.

One area provides a notable exception, and in this case, the death's head design, when plotted against time, forms a wasp-waisted curve that violates the general assumptions underlying proper seriation (Fig. 1). However, since our controls are so rigorous, there is no question that the hour-glass form is indeed an accurate reflection of the popularity career of the death's head design in this case. One must then ask why this distortion occurs, and what one might learn from attempting to explain its existence.

The area where this divergent style curve is seen is Cape Cod, and in those communities further out on the Cape the effect is more pronounced. The degree of constriction of the curve is thus a function of the distance from the point of attachment of the Cape to southeastern Massachusetts. A study of stylistic sequences in other communities of eastern Massachusetts provides us with a clear and convincing explanation of this pattern. Before considering why the death's head has such a peculiar temporal distribution on the Cape, we must first examine the differences in its rate of disappearance elsewhere.

The death's head motif has its longest duration in and around Boston, where it did not vanish completely until the first decades of the nineteenth century. This is probably a function of the strength of residual Puritan values and their accompanying symbols in the conservative folk element of urban Boston. Communities further removed from Boston show a progressively earlier date of final death's head disappearance, and in the Plymouth area, fifty miles south of Boston, they had vanished completely by the 1750s. This rapid disappearance was a function of a change in religion and mortuary symbolism generated by the great awakenings of the mid-eighteenth century combined with a differential in the date of appearance of the first locally produced cherub motifs in the area. Cherub designs, strongly correlated with the more cosmopolitan elements of the population in Boston and especially in Cambridge, diffuse slowly into the surrounding countryside at a rate of roughly one mile per year, reaching the

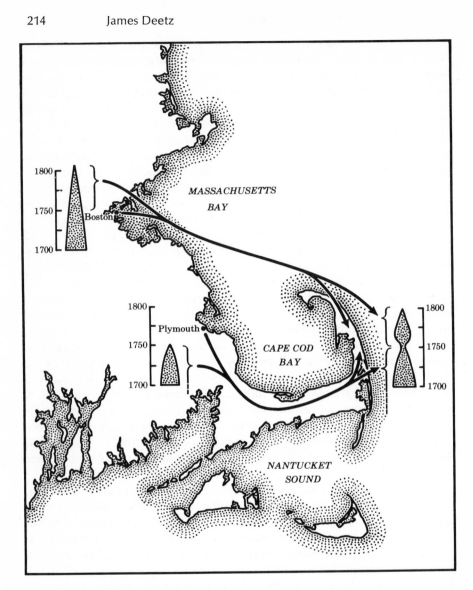

FIGURE 1

Changes in tombstone style in eastern Massachusetts during the
eighteenth century. This abnormal double climax in the popularity of the death's head style on Cape Cod, which contrasts
with the normal frequency curves of its popularity at Plymouth
and Boston, is explainable by a mid-eighteenth-century transfer of
trade relations and consequently of tombstone importation from
Plymouth (where the style was nearly extinct) to Boston (where
it still remained popular).

Plymouth area in the late 1750s. A time-space line marking the last use of death's head designs would slope downwards (earlier) as it moved outward from Boston in any direction on a spatial axis.

Cape Cod, with its sandy soils and absence of good quarries, had no resident stone carvers, and all gravestones were imported to the Cape from elsewhere in eastern Massachusetts. By the mid-eighteenth century, the soils of the Cape had lost much of their agricultural potential, and populations were increasing. Communities began to turn to fishing as a primary means of subsistence and economy. The further out on the Cape a community was located, the more pronounced was the change from an agrarian to a marine economy. Communities such as Sandwich, almost on the mainland portion of southeastern Massachusetts, were hardly affected by soil exhaustion.

When the distorted style curves for the death's head motif are examined closely, the date of maximum constriction coincides with the time of establishment of the first fishing fleets on the Cape. This in turn provides us with an understanding of the reasons for the distortion. When the communities turned to a maritime occupation, they also changed their market orientation. While farming was the primary occupation, all Cape communities participated in the Plymouth market area, a pattern which probably reflects an earlier political grouping of the Cape with Plymouth Colony until its absorption by Massachusetts Bay Colony under the New Charter in 1692. This shift from agrarian to marine economy meant a shift from the Plymouth market sphere to that of Boston. Gravestones, being entirely imported, were a commodity brought in along the lines of broader market trade, and the change of orientation simply meant that they were being brought in from Boston rather than Plymouth after the mid-century market change. However, while the death's head design was no longer being produced in Plymouth by the time this change occurred, stones with death's heads were still nearly universal in Boston. The final result was a style curve for the type marked by near disappearance and then a sudden return to popularity, which in such communities as Truro and Eastham on the outer Cape approaches 100 percent in the years after 1760, and does not return to the earlier popularity low point until ca. 1800.

Operating on purely formal criteria of classification, there is relatively little difference between the death's heads of Plymouth and those of Boston. What is important in this consideration is that local preferences were overshadowed by availability. Had there been resident stone cutters in the Cape communities, a normal distribution of the style across time almost certainly would have occurred. But since all preferences were ultimately primarily a function of those held elsewhere, a distortion is introduced which in less rigorously controlled circumstances would almost certainly be the source of controversy and possible improper ordering of individual samples in time.

If an analysis such as that just described is essentially archaeological, and I would insist that it is, then the last of the three criteria cited in the introduction of this paper has been disposed of. We are now dealing with recent and familiar objects that are not even buried. Such a study in turn suggests that perhaps the role of archaeology in the broader framework of anthropology be reexamined.

The precise relevance of the archaeology of Colonial America to anthropology is that it is an area in which a certain unification of data can be brought about to the desirable end of making more powerful our various integrative methods and inferential theories. The twin aims of archaeology are the writing of culture history and the explanation of extinct cultures in a synchronic sense. The former is dependent on the latter, much in the way that historical linguistics must ultimately be based on sound structural linguistic theory. The essence of sophisticated theoretical treatment of past cultures in order to derive meaningful inferences lies in our understanding of the manner in which the patterning of cultural behavior is reflected in that part of his physical environment which man manipulates, forms, and modifies. From this it follows that archaeology must concern itself with material culture regardless of provenience, be it archaeological in the excavated sense or ethnographic in terms of present use. Colonial archaeology, in the broadest of terms as defined here, bridges the gap between these extremes, and because of its documentary support, gives the archaeologist an area in which to develop general theory treating the relationships between culture and its tangible products.

Once such a position is taken by the archaeologist — if he still thinks of himself as such — other avenues of approach become readily apparent. Recent activity in the areas of transformational grammar as it applies to style and the basic structural aspects of material assemblages based on structural linguistic theory can be and are applied to all of material culture regardless of provenience (Deetz 1967). Freeing oneself from reliance solely on imperfect excavated data but not rejecting it, and adding to it from areas of more rigorous control is certain to advance the area of archaeology far more significantly than digging alone ever would. The term "New Archaeology" is very much in fashion at present, but perhaps it is an unfortunate choice, in that much of what is old in this sense is quite significant. Instead of the emphasis on "new" versus "old," with the implication of one replacing the other, it would seem a wiser course to expand the field to include certain subject areas, in this way stressing additive rather than replacive change. This problem might seem to be simply a matter of semantic quibbling, but as anthropologists we are all aware of how our labels tend to shape our world.

In a semi-serious vein, I would suggest the formal area of "Late Man" in this connection, since it derives from the precedent of the formal reified concept of "Early Man." In fact, Late Man studies are more sharply bounded in a temporal sense, with their earlier limit coinciding with the first written records in North America. By comparison the limiting date of Early Man studies lies somewhere in a five-century limbo.

By whatever term it is known, the area of historical archaeology holds promise for the refinement and advancement of archaeology and anthropology. Only recently have anthropologists developed a broad and lively interest in this field, and as they work more and more in the expanding horizons of the recent and familiar, buried or not, deeper understandings which can only sharpen our theoretical tools are bound to result.

REFERENCES CITED

Deetz, James
1960a "Excavations at the Joseph Howland Site (C-5), Rocky Nook, Kingston, Massachusetts, 1959: A Preliminary Report." *Howland Quarterly*, vol. 24, nos. 2–3.
1960b "The Howlands at Rocky Nook: An Archaeological and Historical Study." *Howland Quarterly*, vol. 24, no. 4.
1963 "Archaeological Investigations at La Purisima Mission." *UCLA Archaeological Survey, Annual Report for 1962-63*, pp. 165–241.
1967 *Invitation to Archaeology*. New York: Natural History Press.
————, and Edwin Dethlefsen
1965 "The Doppler Effect and Archaeology: A Consideration of the Spatial Aspects of Seriation." *Southwestern Journal of Anthropology* 21:196–206.
1966 "Some Social Aspects of New England Colonial Mortuary Art." Paper delivered at 65th Annual Meeting, American Anthropological Association, Pittsburgh, Pa.
1967 "Death's Head, Cherub, Urn and Willow." *Natural History* 76, no. 3:29–37.
Dethlefsen, Edwin, and James Deetz
1966 "Death's Heads, Cherubs and Willow Trees: Experimental Archaeology in Colonial Cemeteries." *American Antiquity* 31:502–10.
Earle, Timothy
1966 Chatham, Massachusetts: A Study in Death. Unpublished paper prepared for Anthropology 112, Harvard University.

Hornblower, Henry, II
    1943   "The Status of Colonial Archaeology in Massachusetts in 1941." *Massachusetts Archaeological Society Bulletin* 4:41.
    1950   "Pilgrim Sites in the Old Colony Area." *Eastern States Archaeological Federation Bulletin*, no. 9, pp. 9–10.
Lombard, Percival
    1953   *The Aptucxet Trading Post*. Bourne, Mass.: Bourne Historical Society.

EÓIN MacWHITE

*A constant theme in archaeological literature concerns the
articulation between the archaeologist's data and the society
whose remains they comprise. The earlier selections treating
problems of typology relate to part of the question: to what
degree is the archaeologist's type equivalent to some reality
held by the man who made the artifact? An exact fit between
archaeological and ethnological materials is probably an
impossible goal because of problems like imperfect
preservation and uncertain analogy. Yet if archaeologists are
to explain their material in behavioral terms, they must find
an answer to the above question, and many have been
working on the problem. Eóin MacWhite surveys several
views on interpreting archaeological material historically and
sociologically, and presents his own. Some topics covered in
other articles appear here — induction vs. deduction, the
reality of types, the archaeological definition of culture — as
well they should, since the bridge between artifacts like
potsherds and projectile points and the society that made
them is the most critical connection in archaeology.*

14 On the Interpretation of Archaeological Evidence in Historical and Sociological Terms

I. INTRODUCTION

Hawkes (1948:5) has rightly remarked that archaeology belongs to "history not only in operational practice, but in philosophical
theory likewise."[1] In practice, however, history is based on documentary
evidence and is highly personalized in the sense that we can usually see the
individual person playing his part. On the other hand, archaeological
evidence is limited to the portions of material culture which time and
circumstance have permitted to survive until at least the moment of

Reproduced by permission of the author and the American Anthropological Association
from the *American Anthropologist*: Vol. 58, 1956, pp. 3–25. Footnotes are renumbered.
   [1] Cf. Marrou 1954:35–36.

discovery, and because of its medium archaeology tends to be impersonal since the individual, as a person, can but very rarely be discerned. Professional historians, forgetting that philosophically, as Devoto (1946:9–10) reminds us, history is coterminous with mankind, tend to limit themselves to the study of literate societies. From the various sources of documentary evidence, of which some like inscriptions, papyri, etc., are also archaeological in the manner of their discovery, we can learn about the nonmaterial aspects of that society's culture, such as language, social organization, religion, historical events, and even the personal reactions of its members to the problems of life as expressed in myth, chronicle, tale, prayer, poetry, or drama. The archaeology of these societies is, to use Hawkes's (1954:156–57) term, "text-aided": in German it is sometimes called *archäologie*, as distinct from V*or-* and U*r-geschichte*, which is "text-free." Hawkes's (1951:3ff.; 1954:159ff.) cognitional system of nomenclature for prehistory serves as an excellent instrument whereby we can measure the validity of applying inferences based on documentary evidence, in practice mainly philological, to predocumentary periods. Such inferences can sometimes be extended back through protohistoric to parahistoric times but with decreasing validity. But in these periods we are mostly, and in the purely text-free zones of human history we are completely, dependent on archaeological evidence and archaeological reasoning for our knowledge of human activity and achievements.

During the past century archaeology has developed a rather impressive form of reasoning, usually garbed in a specialist jargon, in which most of the terms are borrowed from other sciences ranging from geology to ethnology, but often with altered meanings. Most archaeologists tend to take their modes of interpretation for granted but the recent studies of Willey (1953), Phillips and Willey (1953), and Hawkes (1954) undertake a critical reexamination of archaeological methods and theory, which is a healthy symptom of scientific maturity. In this study I propose to examine further some of the problems raised by Willey, Phillips, and Hawkes in regard to the archaeology of predocumentary periods, reviewing both European and American methods of interpretation. The hope is that we shall eventually find exact research tools of universal application, which the pressure of specialization tends to obscure, and point to certain methodological weak points and potential sources of error in archaeological theory which must be corrected before archaeology can claim to be founded on an unimpeachably solid scientific base.

II. LEVELS OF ARCHAEOLOGICAL INTERPRETATION

To illustrate the processes of archaeological reasoning I have constructed Table 1 showing the more frequent archaeological problems treated in the published work of the last century in a graded series of levels indicating the plane of interpretation involved. In constructing this table I have followed Hawkes (1954:161–62) in taking the complexity of the logical processes involved as the basic criterion, and I have incorporated his illustrative sequence. I have also been influenced by the scheme put forward by Willey (1953:363). The distinction between IIA, "Chronological," and IIIB, etc., "Historical," is essentially the distinction between "chronicle" and "historiography" emphasized by Taylor (1948)[2] As in Taylor's work the general concept of culture used is Sorokin's, and the distinction between the terms "sociological" and "historical" in levels III to VI is roughly parallel to his differentiation between structural and dynamic sociology (Sorokin 1947:16).

For the most part Table 1 is self-explanatory, and only a few words of supplementary explanation are required here. Level I includes under "specific forms or types" not only types of museum articles such as flints, pots, bronzes, etc., but also tomb types, forms of habitation sites, ritual monuments, or any surviving structure or other human impingement on nature which can be described, surveyed, or excavated. The field or nonmuseum form of archaeological evidence is usually more complex and frequently of greater importance than museum objects, but in many areas it cannot be used to full advantage because of the relative scarcity of such evidence as compared to museum articles (even if many of these in turn came from habitation sites or other excavations).

In some cases the differentiation among levels, as, for instance, levels I, IV(3) and VII, is only a matter of degree. Thus the deduction that site X is a ritual monument, probably a temple, is level I; the inference that X was a sanctuary of a fertility cult and as such served as center for a wide area would be IV(3), and the further inference that X was also the scene of the inauguration of local chieftains together with an attempt to integrate the role of the fertility cult into the totality of the religious beliefs of the people who built X brings us up to level VII. Or the conclusion that Y is a burial monument of an important person, perhaps a chief, is likely to be an easy deduction and is level I; a comparative study of tombs of the same region and period, which show similarities to Y, might lead to the conclusion that Y is the tomb of a warrior chief who ruled over a stratified society of warriors, priests, smiths, peasants, and slaves, which would be level IV(3). A deeper analysis with ethnological comparisons leading to the conclusion that the society over which the chief buried at Y ruled was divided into moieties, practiced exogamy, and notwithstanding this and the importance of the warrior class had a strong tendency toward matriarchy raises us again to the ethereal heights of level VII.

[2] This dichotomy, which also appears in Willey's (1953) use of the terms "historical" and "processual," is an old one which can be seen in Kant's usage of the words *Geschichte* and *Historie* and in Hegel's distinction between *res gestae* and *historia rerum gestarum*. Cf. Marrou 1954:38–39.

TABLE 1. LEVELS OF ARCHAEOLOGICAL
INTERPRETATION FOR PREDOCUMENTARY PERIODS

I.	Taxonomic and Mechanical	Identification of specific forms or types, use interpretation, technique of production.
IIA.	Chronological	1. Establishing contemporaneity of groups of types through stratigraphy, association, typology, etc. 2. Determination of local period sequences. 3. Determination of absolute chronology by methods of natural science or through historical links to documentarily dated cultures.
IIB.	Ecological	Establishing physical environment and other natural determinants affecting individual sites, series of related sites or local periods.
IIIA.	Economic	1. Functional study of material equipment in relation to IIB. 2. Determination of subsistence and trade economics applied to individual sites, series of related sites or local periods.
IIIB.	Historical (Simple)	1. Tracing development and diffusion of types and their interrelations in time and space. 2. Tracing developments in IIIA(2) in time and space.
IV.	Sociological Stage I	1. Identification of meaningful group patterns within local periods. 2. Establishing graded series of group patterns covering different degrees of cultural differentiation. 3. Simple inferences from material to behavioral and ideological culture: e.g., determination of social and political institutions, simple inferences regarding religious beliefs within group patterns.
V.	Historical (Complex) Stage I	1. Tracing origins, development, and spread of group patterns in time and space. 2a. Tracing cultural continuity and change within group patterns. 2b. Tracing interrelations of group patterns and influences of one upon another. 3a. Tracing origin and diffusion of elements of behavioral and ideological culture as identified in IV(3).

Table 1 (Continued)

		3b. Reorientation of IIIB caused by viewing group pattern as logical unit.
VIA.	Sociological Stage II	1. Determining significance of IV(1) and (2) in sociological terms. 2. Determining sociological conditions in which the events outlined in V(1)–(3) took place.
VIB.	Historical (Complex) Stage II	1. Interpretation of V(1)–(3) in historical terms. 2. Linking VIA and VIB(1) to documentary or other linguistic evidence which can be projected back to proto- or parahistoric times.
VII.	Psychological	Complex inferences from material culture to the behavioral and ideological culture of a social group or of an individual person.

In practice the efficacy of archaeological interpretation is governed by factors of cognition which are more frequently accidental than incidental to the problems under study. In extreme cases these factors can reverse part of our gradation of interpretative levels and make a problem of even level VII simpler than one of IV or V when the range of the pertinent material vehicles used to express and socialize the immaterial aspects of culture is exceptionally rich, well preserved, and well studied. In analyzing what we might call the epistemology of archaeological theory we must therefore bear in mind the varying patterns of cognitional factors involved in addition to the levels of interpretation. These patterns vary according to period,[3] geographical and climatic conditions, and modern circumstances of discovery, as well as according to factors inherent in the culture under examination, such as presence or absence of writing, coinage, or a realistic art which may throw light on the daily life of the people.

Our table distinguishes seven levels, and it must be observed that in the lower three levels the reasoning used is mainly of a deductive nature and the results obtained are probably as secure and certain as any *post factum* reconstruction can be. Here the margin of error is due more to the incompleteness of the physical evidence than to errors of interpretation. On the higher levels the modes of reasoning become more reductive, to use the

[3] In the term "period" I include both the subdivisions of Hawkes's congnitional sequence and classic sequence of Lower and Upper Paleolithic, Mesolithic, etc. It is axiomatic that the ravages of time increase with the passage of time, and the classic sequence is in itself a good graded indicator of different destruction and preservation factors while its economic implications furnish a certain index of the material limitations inherent in the cultures of each period.

terminology of modern logicians (Bochenski 1954:103–4), and less deductive, and also become increasingly hypothetical as we ascend the scale. On the highest or psychological plane it must be admitted that intuition (in the popular sense of the word) often replaced the more logical processes of deduction and reduction, which includes induction.

III. THE PROBLEM OF
THE ARCHAEOLOGICAL CULTURE CONCEPT

The shift from deductive to reductive thinking is not the only significant difference between levels I–III and IV–VII, which are partly parallel to the "lower" and "higher criticism" of Biblical scholars. The infusion of what are described in Table 1 as "group patterns" changes the whole fabric of archaeological interpretation. These group patterns are generally described by archaeologists as "cultures," but in our table we have purposely avoided the term because it not only takes too much for granted but it also may cover a number of quite distinct sociocultural entities. But despite the imperfections of the present concept, which has become an almost unquestioned postulate of archaelogical thinking, the application of this fundamentally ethnological concept to the historical study of predocumentary periods represents the most important heuristic advance in modern archaeology.

Although the idea of an archaeological culture was already inherent in some of the theories of turn-of-the-century scholars such as Sophus Müller and Lord Abercomby and in practice its roots go back to De Mortillet's classifications, the current European application of the concept is largely the result of the personal teachings and publications of Kossinna. This scholar's exposition of his method (Kossinna 1911) bears the misleading title of *Siedlungsarchäologie* despite the fact that most of the distinctions made by him were based on burials rather than on habitations. Since 1911 his equation *Kultur = Volk* has won wide, if not general, acceptance in archaeological teaching and practice.

It is almost fashionable to be derogatory about Kossinna's theories, but his methods were perhaps not as bad as the way in which he himself misused them. It is remarkable how few archaeologists have ever expressly committed themselves on the basic problems of method behind the culture concept and how extremely rare are those who have tried to define the concept. This can readily be seen from Kroeber and Kluckhohn's (1952) survey, which, however, is rather incomplete on European definitions (MacWhite 1954). Of course, the archaeological culture is a specialized concept dealing with only fragments of the totality of culture, a point which is sometimes forgotten. Of the few who have expressed their ideas on this subject we may perhaps take the opinions of Childe as representing a consensus of opinion which (less some of the Marxist overtones in his application of the concept) is generally accepted. Childe's view of culture (for representative examples see Childe 1930:41–45; 1951:15–16) has not changed greatly since his first definition (1929:v–vi) except for a certain shift away from the rigidity of the Kossinna equation. Childe's general approach, which is very different from that of Kossinna, lays heavy emphasis on culture as a social adaptation to physical environment, an emphasis which impresses itself on the archaeologist more readily than on students of nonmaterial aspects of culture. For Childe (1950:2) an archaeological culture is,

> an assemblage of artifacts that recur repeatedly associated together in dwellings of the same kind and with burials by the same rite. The arbitrary peculiarities of the implements, weapons, ornaments, houses, burial rites and ritual objects are assumed to be the concrete expressions of the common social traditions that bind together a people.

In the heading of the chapter in which Childe gives this definition, he uses the word "society" instead of "people." Childe (1935:3) has emphasized that such a culture,

> is not an *a priori* category elaborated in the studies of philosophers and then imposed from the outside upon working archaeologists. Cultures are observed facts. . . . The interpretation of the observed phenomenon is supplied by ethnology. The traits of a culture are thus presented together to the archaeologist because they are the creations of a single people, adjustments to its environment, approved by its collective experience; they thus express the individuality of a human group united by common social traditions.

As an example of an extreme point of view we may cite the recent theories of Pittioni (1950, 1952) who, in elaborating the Kossinna theory, has pushed it well beyond its logical conclusions. He presents us with a complicated scheme wrapped up in somewhat unorthodox terminology, which we have summarized in Table 2. I regret that it is not possible without a long explanation to translate most of the terms from German into English, but the general meaning will be grasped easily enough. Pittioni begins with a reclassification of the Three Period System into *Lithikum* (Paleo- and Mesolithic), *Keramikum*[4] (Neolithic and Aeneolithic) and *Metallikum* (Bronze and Iron Ages). We are then given an ascending graded sequence of archaeological groupings from *Lokalfacies* through *Typus*, *Gruppe*, and *Kultur* to *Welt* which represents a series of related

[4] Compare the "ceramolithic" of Albright (1946:88–318).

TABLE 2. SOCIOLOGICAL AND LINGUISTIC
CORRELATIONS OF ARCHAEOLOGICAL
CULTURE GROUPS ACCORDING TO PITTIONI

I. Sociological Correlations

Archaeological Group	Lithikum	Keramikum	Metallikum
Welt	Allgemeinheit des Kulturwillens	Einheit des Kultur-willens	Volk
Kultur	Einheit des Kultur-willens	Stammhafte Ein-heit	Stamm
Gruppe Typus	Sippenverbands-gruppe Gebunde-ner Sippenverband	Sippenverbands-gruppe Gebunde-ner Sippenverband	Sippenverbands-gruppe Gebunde-ner Sippenverband
Lokalfacies	Sippe	Sippe	Sippe
Unknown	Family	Family	Family

II. Linguistic Correlations

Archaeological Group	Lithikum	Keramikum	Metallikum
Welt	Linguistic stock of the first type	Linguistic stock of the second type	Linguistic family: Sometimes linguistic stock as a survival
Kultur	Linguistic family	Linguistic family	Individual language
Gruppe	Individual language	Individual language	Special modification of individual language
Typus	Possibly special modification of a single language	Beginning of a dialectically orientated modification of a single language	Dialectical specializations
Lokalfacies	—	—	—

Kulturen. It will be observed that the sociological and linguistic connotations of some of these groupings differ in each of Pittioni's three periods.

The approach of American archaeologists to the concept of culture in their own field owes more to the ideas of Wissler and Kroeber than to Kossinna or Graebner. This independent line of research has been intensified in a number of American universities during the last two decades, yielding important contributions to our knowledge of the archaeological aspects of culture. Many of the differences between the results of American and European research are naturally due to differing raw material, but much is due also to the different approaches. While, owing to the scarcity of certain forms of evidence, a good deal of American work on problems of level IIA has in most regions yielded results of limited value compared to the detailed results obtained by intensive research on European chronology, some of the American approaches to cultural analysis on level IV are, if not always spectacular, far more firmly based and more mature in conception than European thinking on the problem. The time is now ripe for a conjoined attack on the problems of archaeological culture and its significance in terms of social and intellectual culture. Here we shall discuss briefly two important streams of American thought which have been crystallizing over the last twenty years, one associated with the Human Relations Area Files (HRAF) and the other with the Midwestern Taxonomic System (MWTS).

As an example of the HRAF school, which grew out of the Yale Cross-Cultural Survey, we may cite the scheme of correlations put forward by Murdock (1953:478) and reproduced in Table 3. The series of equations of archaeological groups with sociological groups reminds us of Pittioni's theories, but biological classifications have been substituted for linguistic correlations.

The MWTS, which is allied in conception to the University of California Culture Element Distribution Survey, does not use any abstraction of culture or of culture elements but archaeological habitation sites. It can, indeed, be truly described as a *Siedlungsarchäologie*. In the MWTS as originally constructed by McKern (1939) the term "component" is applied to the evidence from individual sites and habitation units and the term "focus" to the forms of culture presented by a series of related components. The foci are, in turn, grouped into an ascending series of larger units, "aspects," "phases," and "patterns."

Phillips and Willey (1953:620) have recently put forward some modifications of the MWTS in which they substitute for the McKern term "focus" the word "phase," which they define as "a space time unit possessing traits sufficiently characteristic to distinguish it from all other units similarly conceived, whether of the same or other cultural traditions, geographically limited to a *locality* or *region* and chronologically limited to

TABLE 3. SOCIOLOGICAL CORRELATIONS OF
CULTURE (AFTER MURDOCK)

Culture-bearing Social Unit	Corresponding Cultural Unit	Analogous Biological Unit
Community	Local culture variant	Subvariety
Subtribe	Subculture	Variety
Tribe	Culture	Species
Nation	Culture cluster	Genus
Region	Culture area	Family

a relatively brief span of time." It can, they hold (1953:621), be anything from "a thin level in a site reflecting no more than a brief encampment to a protracted occupation represented in a large number of sites over a region of very elastic proportions. . . ." The sociological equivalent of the component is the community, as defined by Murdock (1949:79) — "the maximal group of persons who normally reside together in a face to face association." In practice they consider that component and phase are sometimes identical since "on the lower levels of cultural development society likewise frequently consists of one community." Phillips and Willey (1953:622) adopt a flexible attitude toward equating their phase with society; they consider the present chances to be against phase's having a definite sociological connotation but are not prepared to deny that in the future phase may be analyzed in sociological terms.

The Kossinna theory, which Zambotti (1946:158) described as a dangerous *petitio principii*, has not passed without raising solid opposition. Tallgren (1937:156) warned against the tendency to see a uniform population group behind forms of material culture and gave ethnographic examples demonstrating the weakness of this hypothesis; so did Wahle (1941)[5] who used a strict historical approach, with special reference to the old problem of identifying Germans, Illyrians, and Celts in northern and central Europe. The often overlooked but obvious fact that behind what archaeologists call "Hallstatt" lie not only Celts but also Illyrians shows clearly that ethnic groups with distinct, even if related, linguistic affinities may possess the same culture. To attach a definite ethnic signification to archaeological cultures as delineated by Kossinna and his imitators without reference to documentary sources is therefore imprudent, and Wahle like Tallgren pleads for a reorientation of archaeological aims and methods to avoid the errors and narrowness of approach which Kossinna's methods inevitably force upon us. In considering the slant which Kossinna gave to the application of his concept of culture we must remember, as Wahle's study clearly shows, that Kossinna's ideas were influenced more by modern concepts of European nationalities than by ethnological views of modern cultures.

Turning to Childe's definition of an archaeological culture, Phillips and Willey (1953:617) express views similar to those of Tallgren and Wahle. They consider that,

> an archaeological culture is an arbitrary division of the space-time continuum defined by reference to its imperishable content. . . . An archaeological culture conceived of as a sliced out section of the space-time continuum corresponds to the observed facts of culture

[5] For comments on Wahle's paper, see Eggers (1950), Kirchner (1950), and Bursch (1953).

continuity but, as with the empirical "designed" artifact types it may or may not parallel the reality of the past social unit *as this might have been conceived by the peoples who composed it.* [Italics mine.]

However, Phillips and Willey hold out the hope that eventually archaeological-sociological correlations may be possible.

As implied in Childe's definition, an archaeological culture is based on *types* — types of pots, weapons, tools, ornaments, houses, and tombs. While modern methods of inferring sociological and economic data from archaeological evidence play some part, and undoubtedly will play a still greater part in the future, in defining cultural patterns, the archaeological culture, like MWTS foci and phases, is fundamentally based on the typological method, which, from De Mortillet (1881)[6] to Montelius (1903), was primarily a time-measuring instrument but in recent times, as indicated by the increased use of the distribution map, is now equally important on the spatial plane. Typological theory is founded on two basic assumptions: (1) that types exist and are significant,[7] and (2) that the changes which they undergo on the time scale and on the spatial plane indicate cultural change.

Phillips and Willey (1953:617) point out that there are two ways of looking at the problem, one envisaging "culture change as a continuous stream to be segmented into types as this best suits the archaeologist's purpose," the other tending "to conceive of types as once existent realities." In the first case the definition of types is "a purely arbitrary procedure, entirely imposed on the prehistoric phenomena by the classifier," while in the second view the task of typology is the recognition of something which once existed. Phillips and Willey do not regard these two opinions as mutually exclusive. From the point of view of a generalizing law of human behavior the two views would appear to be mutually antagonistic, but it must be agreed that both concepts are needed to face the situations presented to us by archaeological evidence.

[6] The works quoted here are designed to give good examples of the basic methods used. De Mortillet proposed his famous classification for the first time in 1869 and presented it to the International Congress of Anthropology at Brussels in 1872. Montelius had worked out the essentials of his method by 1884.

[7] Prof. I. M. Bochenski, O.P. of the University of Fribourg, who kindly read a draft of this paper, gave me some useful observations on the concept of a type from the logical point of view. He views a type as "an *ordered* class of properties" which give rise to a complex relation. Neither the complex relation nor the properties are quite arbitrary; for the relation is defined by the properties which are observable on the object under study. In practice a given object x with a definite set of properties may yield several complex relations and thus we can be faced with a choice of relations and hence of types. But our freedom is limited, firstly by the properties of x and secondly there is a pragmatical limitation according to the heuristic utility of the relation on which the type is based. Prof. Bochenski considers that the logical procedure in the establishment of laws and types is practically the same.

Most lithic types are probably functional types, but the greater number of the subclassifications of the functional types such as Acheulian hand-axes, Levallois flakes, Upper Paleolithic and Mesolithic blade forms, to mention a few flint forms, may represent a developing series where each object differs but slightly from the next, the classifications based on the differences between them being founded on dividing lines drawn by modern observers. Thus Movius (1953:37) acutely pointed out in connection with Irish Mesolithic material that,

> as long as it can be understood that such groupings of the fieldworker . . . are *not* rigid, but rather consist of a series of completely subjective categories for which no very precise definition can be given, and which are intended to help clarify and interpret the present data, progress can and will be made.

The same can be said of the style sequences presented by most art-forms in archaeological material on which so many regional and chronological distinctions have been elaborated. On the other hand, we can cite Nordic flint daggers, Cypriote bronze daggers, Hallstatt swords, or Irish bronze trumpets in which we find consistent repetitions of forms and even of subforms, which must represent deliberate and conscious efforts to satisfy the social and traditional requirements, stronger often than mere fashion, of their users. Between these two extremes many archaeological classifications are probably a mixture of observer-imposed and real types; in this mixed category we can place some of the more elaborate typologies of both European and American prehistoric pottery, and, in Europe, megalithic tombs and Bronze and Early Iron Age fibulae have been the subjects of complicated typologies in which it is difficult to distinguish between differentiations which are observer-imposed and those which are real or inherent in the material itself.

In the last analysis, the definition of types, beyond functional distinctions, is essentially the same as the definition of certain categories in linguistics, both ultimately being bound up in the *Gestalt* framework of the human brain. The problem of real and observer-imposed distinctions exists also in linguistics, especially in phonetics, and in the realm of material culture reaches its highest refinement in the study of fine-art products. The resemblances to archaeological reasoning are patent in the researches of a Strygowski (1923), but the techniques of a Berenson (1947) or of a Venturi (1951–52) in identifying the works of Renaissance painters are not essentially different but only more delicately, and perhaps more intuitively, applied.

As Kroeber (1948:543) shows, the type concept is applicable also to institutions and aspects of behavioral or social culture. Whether we are dealing with material or nonmaterial culture we can discern a significant patterning in the arrangement of types; sometimes this patterning is clear and simple but in other cases the rules we describe as governing the patterns are perhaps mnemonic rather than truly analytical. In either case it is not so much the actual data, whether an Acheulian hand-ax, a La Tène fibula, a Picasso painting, a word or a grammatical form, which really forms the basis of cultural delineations but the "patterns of significance" (Rouse 1939:16) which they show.[8] It must, however, be emphasized that we cannot begin to interpret the patterns of significance presented by archaeological material in either historical or sociological terms unless we first distinguish carefully among patterns, especially group patterns such as archaeological cultures, which are based on observer-imposed, real, or mixed types. In the last case we must decide, whenever possible, whether the mixed types are weighted more heavily in the direction of real types or of observer-imposed types.

The contention of Phillips and Willey that an archaeological culture could not "be said to have existed as an entity until the archaeologist named and defined it" is probably an overstatement, even if valid in some cases. But their warning that these units may not have been felt as in-groups is of more general validity.[9] Some of the entities which archaeologists call cultures very probably were discrete units. But in Europe, especially, the much abused word "culture," leaving aside semantic confusions (Bursch 1950), frequently covers a number of quite different group patterns representing very different sociological situations. Indeed, we can ask how many assemblages so named in any recent textbook of European archaeology or in contemporary monographic studies can live up to the twenty-two simple words of Childe's definition quoted above. A large number are based on a small sector of the "imperishable content" of culture.[10] In many cases the interrelations of these distinctions based on quite different sectors of material culture are far from clear. For instance, in a number of areas and periods in Europe, like the Early Bronze Age in Ireland or the Late Bronze Age in the Iberian Peninsula, the link between the burial material and the habitation material is very weak. In a number of groupings at present labeled "cultures," it is quite difficult to integrate the sequence of metallic types with ceramic forms, a difficulty which is frequently a reflection of the problem of linking burials with habitations.

Due possibly to the influence of Kroeber's (1927) skepticism on the cultural significance of burial rites and funerary customs, the MWTS and

[8] Rouse's pattern of significance may be compared to Bochenski's complex relation.

[9] Thus Tallgren (1937:157) points out that language and, above all, religion are the more important factors in defining the in-group from the point of view of a member of a primitive culture.

[10] Goodwin (1953:154–55) lays down five useful criteria as preconditions for "the acceptance of a new culture" in regard to lithic sites. With modification they could be usefully applied to later periods, as indeed can many of Goodwin's acute observations on problems raised in South African archaeology.

its cognates are inclined to play down the importance of burials. In European archaeology our knowledge of habitation material frequently lags behind our knowledge of burial monuments and their contents. Although in some cases the burial material may reflect a reasonably accurate picture of daily life, it often consists of cult objects including its own pottery forms which have relatively few parallels in habitation material. Even when burial material gives a fairly clear picture of daily life, as, for instance, in the Iberic Iron Age, we may, as Prof. Julian San Valero pointed out to me, have a certain archaistic tendency which can upset our preconceived synchronisms. This may be due partly to the conservative tendencies of cult practices, the presence of heirlooms, or the fact that a person is buried with objects of personal significance which were manufactured during his youth but quite out of fashion at the time of his death.

The European tendency to concentrate on burial material is in part due to cognitional factors such as the fact that burial monuments are often more easy to recognize on the surface than are habitation sites, and, unless the ritual is architecturally complicated, they are easier to excavate. More than a century of collecting, both private and institutional, has resulted in the accumulation of a large mass of material consisting of single finds, now mainly preserved in museums, and these single objects, when we are fortunate enough to know the find-place, together with sporadic associated material, such as hoards, form a body of evidence almost equal in importance, when the quantity permits, to strictly excavation material, whether habitation or burial. We are thus faced with a more uneven pattern of discovery than that which underlies the MWTS. It is always necessary to ask if the basic material is a valid sampling of the "imperishable content" of culture or a distortion caused by accidental features of discovery, e.g., preservation of some types of monuments in nonagricultural areas, the ease of conservation of some types of habitations such as cave sites as distinct from "open" habitations, or peculiar factors of preservation arising from something inherent in the past culture, e.g., the use of an easily decomposable material for much of the material equipment, like bamboo in the Far East, or settlement habits such as in the case of nomads who dwelt in temporary tents but buried in more permanent structures versus a settled village folk who practiced water burial or tree exposure, etc. Many of the cognitional factors which distort our present picture of predocumentary archaeological groupings will eventually disappear with future research and improved techniques of excavation or be recognized as a distortion due to some peculiarity of the culture under study. When our knowledge of habitations in Europe catches up to our knowledge of the burial record, we may be presented with a very different picture on levels V and VI from that presented in contemporary interpretations, even if the broad outlines of present thinking on level IV remain.

Pittioni's complex scheme contains more wishful thinking than scientific analysis and has had a skeptical reception in archaeological circles (Childe 1953; Kirchner 1954). However, it does contain some features which merit serious consideration. The sequence of *Lithikum, Keramikum, and Metallikum* is a useful didactic reminder that in these periods cultural distinctions are generally based on stone, pottery, and metal types, respectively, although it should be remembered that in the last period in Europe a large number of cultures are distinguished on the basis of pottery rather than metal types. Like the series of Murdock and McKern, Pittioni's sequence from *Lokalfacies* to *Welt* is at least an attempt to come to grips with the too often ignored problem of differentiating between varying degrees of cultural groups. While Daniel (1943:31) suggested a fourfold sequence of site, industry, culture, and civilization, it is perhaps significant that McKern, Murdock, and Pittioni have independently arrived at a fivefold sequence, although the center of gravity of each of the series is quite distinct.

Pittioni's insistence that the sociological equivalents of the archaeological group classifications were often different in each of his three periods is fundamentally sound even if his equations are not. Patterson (1945:3) has acutely observed that,

> the further back in time the fewer are the cultural elements found, and so the fewer the implied logical complexes, therefore the less justification for the use of the word "culture" in the anthropological sense. It is exceedingly doubtful if the word can be applied to any archaeological group of complexes prior to historical times. To these earlier groups of complexes the word "industries" has been given, in order, presumably, to get over this difficulty, though it does not seem that the real crux of the matter has been appreciated since, generally, it is to the Palaeolithic groups that the word is usually applied, and "culture" is used for every assemblage of Post-Pleistocene age.

But the relative scarcity of culture elements is not the only feature which differentiates the cultural patterns of groups in the Pleistocene and postglacial periods; the most striking feature, which can be noted to a lesser degree in later periods, is in the tempo of culture change.

While Sorokin (1947:690ff.) decries the theory of the "law of acceleration" in sociocultural processes, as put forward by Novicov (1896), Hart (1931), Ogburn (1922), Ogburn and Nimkoff (1947:524ff.), etc., it cannot be denied that, when we apply the perspective afforded to us by archaeology, there has been a definite and consistent increase in the rate of change of material culture forms from the Paleolithic to the present day. Viewed comprehensively we have a rising graph, although when we examine various periods more closely we can discern some ups and downs, which, however, do not change the general pattern of the upward trend. The time-span of the shortest recognizable cultural space-time unit can serve as a rough index of the tempo of culture change. Thus Abbevillian and Clactonian I appear to have had a span of ca. 114,000 years on Zeuner's (1946) figures based on the Milankovič chronology, and the three first phases of Acheulian cover ca. 200,000 years. Even if current calculations for the Upper Paleolithic are reduced, we cannot think in smaller time units than of 10,000 to 5,000 years. Our time measurement units shrink further during the postglacial Mesolithic, and by the parahistoric Neolithic we can begin to think in units of 500 years and less. The time unit can in certain restricted spheres of culture, like art, come down to a generation in the Iron Age. Indeed it is noteworthy that in Attic figured vases of the middle of the sixth century B.C. the individual can be recognized by stylistic methods even when he does not sign his work, as has been shown by Beazley (1942) and other classical archaeologists. This is probably the earliest point in Europe where we can apprehend individual personal expression through material culture.[11]

Sorokin is, however, probably right in denying the existence of a law of acceleration. To explain the increasing tempo of culture change we must have recourse to a number of factors, of which progressive accumulation is only one. While it is outside the scope of this study to examine the causes of the increasing tempo of culture change, two factors, generally ignored, may be mentioned. The first is physical and the second psychological. These are the means of communication which condition the speed, frequency, and duration of culture contacts through which change may be effected and the resistance/receptivity factor, which may be religious, social, or economic, that results in a new culture element's being adopted or rejected.

But whatever the factors underlying the tempo of change in material culture, it is reasonable to suppose that both culture change and the resultant new configurations will have quite different social significations to the individuals concerned, according to the varying rates. We have two extremes: one in which change is not perceptible to the individual and the other in which the individual is keenly aware of the change. In the former case which certainly holds good at least for the Paleolithic, we must ask whether it is valid to assume that change in material culture reflects change in nonmaterial culture. If, for example the contention of the glottochronologists that in a fixed sector of vocabulary considered to be relatively stable there is a constant retention rate of ca. 81 percent per millennium "for all languages, at all times" (Lees 1953:119) is correct, then in a given theoretical genetically descended group in Paleolithic times, language would have changed basically a number of times within the same

[11] Neither the Three Period System nor the classic sequence of archaeological periods is a good indicator of the changing tempo. For this purpose Albright's (1946:82–83) series of undifferentiated, differentiated, and integrated culture is more suitable.

culture. Thus for the earliest periods linguistic-archaeological indentifications may never be verifiable, and, likewise, it is not possible to ascertain whether or not the rate of linguistic drift was actually constant or whether it, too, increased in tempo together with technological change.

Since the contrasts through the time scale are not so violent as in the Old World, it is not surprising that American archaeology has not faced the problem of the possible variation of sociological correlations of archaeological culture according to period. On a modified scale an increasing rate of change can be noted from Folsom to the Amerind groups of the early colonial period which roughly parallels the rates of the European groups from the Upper Paleolithic and Mesolithic to the Chalcolithic. In the Andes we have a rate comparable to that of the full European Bronze Age in what Willey (1948) calls the "Florescent" and "Expansionist" periods.

The Murdock sequence of equations is almost as arbitrary as Pittioni's, although as unconnected series the elements are better thought out sociologically. The equations show a serious lack of a consistent *fundamentum divisionis* in that the first four members of his cultural series are genetically conceived while the fifth is a geographical concept which can in no way be made analogous to the biological concept of family.

Although the MWTS was specifically devised to meet problems of the North American Midwest, it contains a number of concepts of universal application even though the choice of words to describe them leaves much to be desired. It can, in fact, be applied to any relatively unexplored region as a basis on which the results of a survey combined with a series of strategic excavations could be integrated quite quickly into a solid structure. Since Europe has a different pattern of find material which has already been intensively worked on, it would be uneconomical to try to apply the whole scheme, but in some areas its application could serve as a useful check on the results obtained by the conventional European approach. Furthermore, the use of some term like "component" for the culture of an individual site or a period of a site would avoid some of the abuse which the word "culture" too often receives from archaeologists.

The Phillips and Willey phase is a basic concept, and, modified to allow of the full integration of single finds, hoards, and burials, could be made into the basis of a more precise definition of an archaeological culture, which might now be described as a significant group of space-time units consisting of possibly one but generally a number of phases, whose basic traits belong to the same tradition.

IV. INVASIONS AND ACCULTURATION

Parallel to the problem of the definition and demarcation of culture groups on a static plane there is the dynamic aspect of culture change. Over the last half-century archaeologists in both Europe and

America have succeeded in reducing the chaos of the old battle cries of diffusion versus independent invention, and the debate of *ex oriente lux* versus *mirage orientale* has been reduced to a reasonable semblance of ordered history. While the major problems up to level III and at least the outlines of level IV are now fairly clear, the processes involved in the spread of various types and forms, inventions, and ornaments from one group to another are but hazily perceived.

Faced with certain forms of culture change we frequently have varying historical explanations ranging from a full-scale invasion to "culture-contacts" of a rather tenuous and undefined nature. Thus the Kossinna-style archaeologists see cultural movements mainly as tribal migrations, but their excesses have brought about a reaction in practice as well as in theory which we may exemplify by Raftery's (1947) arguments against postlithic invasions of Ireland. In all cases the fact of diffusion is admitted but the form which it took is debated. Hawkes (1954:165) divides diffusion into two processes: (1) primary diffusion, which comprises "actual folk movements or migrations of peoples, or human groups of whatever size or character," and (2) secondary diffusion, in which culture elements are "transmitted from one group to another without group migration." It may be said in criticism that any form of diffusion entails a migration of some sort, whether it be a visiting trader or a hunter returned after a chance encounter with a neighboring people or a foreign wife captured as part of the booty in a raid on another tribe. If we have a group of traders, a party of hunters, or a number of captured women, we would, following Hawkes's scheme closely, have to class it as primary diffusion, which I doubt was Hawkes's intention. Hawkes's primary and secondary diffusion represent two extreme poles, but as in the case of most extremes in human affairs the majority of cases fall in between. Hawkes makes a timely plea that archaeologists make an effort to avoid such vague terms as "culture-contact," "transmission of elements," etc. Possibly the best basis for a closer definition and analysis of diffusion processes lies in the recent studies of acculturation beginning with the American Social Science Research Council Memorandum (Redfield, Linton, and Herskovits 1936; Herskovits 1938, 1951:523ff.; Beals 1953). Although the idea of acculturation without any significant movement of population is inherent in so many discussions in European archaeology of "influences" and "contacts," it has not, except for Fox's (1932) "absorption," been scientifically applied.

Ultimately the question of invasion or acculturation has to be reduced to demographic terms. In Table 4 we summarize the main demographic situations which underlie most examples of diffusion, whether primary or secondary. In this table "invasion" means an immigration of organized groups and can be peaceful or otherwise: "immigrations" differ wherein the immigrant groups do not enter as part of an organized group. In the second half of the table we have made a distinction between "insular" and "contiguous" situations: these are, of course, again two extremes, but the intermediary situations are too varied to allow of inclusion.[12] Where we have two cultures occupying neighboring territory, assuming peaceful conditions and a reasonable degree of receptivity, the processes of acculturation listed for insular situations (which can be applied to culture groups isolated by desert, mountain, jungle, or any other difficult geographical barrier as well as by sea) become highly intensified, and at present the results are very difficult to analyze through archaeological evidence. Thus visitors can merge imperceptibly into immigrants. If these immigrants then gain the leadership and control of the group which they have joined, and if the immigration is continued, the original language might eventually be displaced by that of the newcomers. As so frequently happens in the archaeology of the Highland Zone of Britain (Fox 1932) we may be faced with a situation in which culture B is absorbed by the more indigenous culture A which modifies the B types in its own way, but we are at a loss to know how far this situation extended to behavioral and social culture and, if so, to determine whether or not A kept its own language.

V. ARCHAEOLOGY AND LINGUISTIC PROBLEMS

Some theorists like Menghin (1952:255), who conceives of a special "linguistic archaeology," lay much importance on the interpretation of archaeological evidence in what are, strictly speaking, philological terms. This, as Tovar (1954) shows in his survey of archaeology and linguistics, is due to the historical problem of identifying in the archaeological record the peoples and tribes mentioned in classical texts and the need to corroborate some of the cultural data obtained about Indo-European groups through linguistic methods, together with the interest in the problem of the Indo-European *Urheimat*. Tovar (1954:334, n. 6) notes a certain negative attitude on the part of a number of philologists regarding archaeology. Indeed, in Europe this attitude is stronger than Tovar's study would lead us to believe, since so many philologists content themselves with disparaging remarks in the classroom and in the lecture hall but do not commit themselves to cold print. Apart from Trubetskoi (1939; see criticisms in Koppers 1944) and his school, this negative attitude is largely the monopoly of philologists of a rigid neogrammarian outlook, and it perhaps reaches a peak of invective in connection with Celtic problems (e.g., O'Rahilly 1946:430ff.) where the failure of archaeologists and linguists to appreciate

[12] One important omission from Table IV is the emporium, or intertribal market. To varying degrees this involves the same relationship as IIIA(1), IIIB(1), and IVA(1), IVB(1).

TABLE 4. PROCESSES OF PRIMARY AND SECONDARY DIFFUSION IN DEMOGRAPHIC TERMS

I. Invasions	1. Migration of whole sociopolitical (ethnic) group.
	2. Migration of a large section of an ethnic group.
	3. Migration of organized groups of family units of an ethnic group.
	4. Migration of organized groups of males of an ethnic group.
II. Immigrations	1. Sporadic settling of family units of same ethnic group.
	2. Entry on permanent basis of specialist groups, usually predominantly male, e.g., traders, smiths, craftsmen, missionaries, etc.
	3. Importation of foreign wives.
	4. Importation of foreign slaves.
III. Foreign agents of acculturation	
A. Insular situations	1. Visits of specialist groups, as II(2), of greater or less duration but who do not settle permanently.
	2. Foreign raiders.
B. Contiguous situations	1. Visits of specialist groups.
	2. Visits from all levels of population of neighboring group (the result can be the same as II 1).
	3. Hostile incursions.
IV. Native agents of acculturation	
A. Insular situations	1. Specialist groups, e.g., fishermen, hunters, traders, smiths, etc., returned after visits to foreign lands.
	2. Warriors returned after raids in foreign lands.
B. Contiguous situations	1. Specialist groups, who usually become bilingual, who have specially close contacts with neighboring group.
	2. Whole of population which has contact with neighboring group.

each other's problems and methods has frustrated the development of a Celtic *archäologie* (MacWhite 1955). On the whole, the American approach to these matters is quite free of such prejudices which result from a total divorce of language from culture, as can be seen from the linguistic section in Kroeber and Kluckhohn (1952) and in the papers of scholars such as Hoijer (1948, 1953, and discussions in Tax and others 1953), due, as

Tovar points out rightly, to the fact that American linguistics are closely bound up with ethnology.

From the point of view of method and theory, linguistic-archaeological correlations pose two important questions. (1) Can an archaeological culture or any other group pattern be interpreted in linguistic terms? And (2) can we establish some basis on which the value of linguistic and archaeological evidence may be assessed?

Without reliable indications from documentary evidence we cannot, at present, answer the first question with an unqualified affirmative. The controversies which rage over the applications of equations of archaeological cultures with language groups are ultimately reflections of the incompleteness of our understanding of the delicate interrelations of language and culture, combined, it must be admitted, with an overeager desire on the part of archaeologists to invest their cultures with more significance than is warranted by the evidence. In some cases, however, as with archaeologists who have tried to make their material comply with Schleicher's *Stammbaum* theory in tracing Indo-European movements, the fault lies in the error of the philologists, who have produced so much deadwood instead of a valid linguistic thesis (Bonfante 1947:350).

The archaeological problem of setting limits to culture forms is paralleled in linguistics by the problem of defining such entities as language (in the sense of De Saussure's *langue*) and dialect. While, as Lounsbury (1953:413) emphasizes, mutual intelligibility, despite the subjective nature of this criterion, must ultimately be the basis on which we mark off linguistic frontiers, the problem of defining a language is rarely easy. Bloch (1948:7) avoids the linguistic problem, which has led to such definitions as "a system of isoglosses" (Pisani 1939:10), by defining language by its speakers, and he introduces the useful concept of the speech community. Before equating an archaeological subgroup with a dialect, we should at least determine which, if any, of the "sociolinguistic patterns" that word used to describe, as outlined by Martinet (1952).

While many aspects of the language-culture relationship are far from clear, a few points are reasonably certain. Thus, as Kroeber (1948:225) states, "so far as the process of their transmission is concerned and the mechanism of their development, it is clear that language and culture are one." It must also be agreed that "a decisive change of speech without some change of culture seems impossible" (Kroeber 1948:226; cf. Graebner 1911:162). Language, which Sorokin (1947:53–56) and others have called the vehicle of culture, must obviously play an important role in any acculturation situation, and this must be better studied before we can interpret in linguistic terms archaeological material produced by an acculturation situation.

Our reply to the second question must vary according to the nature of the problem which is to be solved and according to the nature of the evidence presented by archaeology and linguistic science for the solution of the problem. If a problem is posed in linguistic terms, its solution in those terms must be based primarily on linguistic methods and evidence, which then take precedence over archaeological evidence. Thus Koppers (1944) limits the role of archaeology in the Indo-European problem to taking one position or another based on its own evidence vis-à-vis the philological theories on the problem. This relationship holds good while we have problems which are framed in linguistic terms and on which there is a sufficiently large body of positive linguistic evidence. When a disagreement between archaeology and philology is occasioned by the dependence of the linguistic theory on negative evidence or an *argumentum ex silentio*, the validity of the linguistic argument decreases according as we depart from a fully documented context into Hawkes's proto- or parahistoric periods. The validity of an archaeological *argumentum ex silentio* depends on (1) the degree of exploration of the area concerned and (2) the absence of cognitional factors which might produce an *apparent* absence in the phenomenon in question.

Recently glottochronology (Lees 1953) has begun to receive attention from archaeologists, and, indeed, if the method underlying it proves sound, it will provide us with a framework on which archaeological theories can be more securely attached than anything we have at present. But the theory of vocabulary retention on which it is based must stand or fall on linguistic grounds and not on the presence or absence of corroborative archaeological evidence. Instead of looking to European archaeology to support Indo-European time-depths, as Swadesh (1953) does, it is European archaeology that must look to the results of glottochronological research on time-depths between all Indo-European languages for a time frame to guide their researches. At present glottochronology is based on word counts in thirteen languages and the results are remarkably consistent, but before we can establish it as a sort of linguistic C14 the system must be checked on all languages which give us sufficient records of 500 years or more.

VI. DIAGNOSIS AND PROGNOSIS

While archaeological reasoning on levels I–III may be considered sound and scientific, most of the theorizing carried out on levels IV–VI depends on the archaeological culture concept or is inevitably influenced by it. There is a pressing need to clarify this concept further, to establish a consistent series to cover varying degrees of cultural relationship on spatial and temporal planes, and to determine how far the basic unit, whether a culture in Childe's sense or the more precise phase of Phillips and Willey, is based on observer-imposed as distinct from real typological distinctions, and to what extent it may suffer from distortion due to cognitional features. Eventually more research on economic, religious, and social factors may enable us to make more significant cultural distinctions, but at present most of our delineations are based on typology. When the basic types are real and not observer-imposed, we are probably dealing with once existent realities, and the distinctions based on them can be interpreted in sociological terms.

But the blind application of the traditional methods of European archaeology, even of approaches more refined than Kossinna's (e.g., Menghin 1936), are in need of a critical reexamination before we can generalize on sociological interpretations of archaeological group patterns and their history. The linguists have their problems in regard to language frontiers, which must be solved before linguistic archaeological correlations can really be put on a sound basis. For the solution of these problems we must look not to the neogrammarians but rather to the neolinguists (Bonfante 1947) or to American linguistics. European archaeology tends, perhaps, to look to documentary history as a goal, and American archaeology is more closely bound up with cultural anthropology. The time is ripe for a fusion of methods and a critical examination of theory in order to arrive at concepts of universal application. In many cases both share the same problems but have arrived at different answers.

If our approach in this study has been rather negative, it is because our purpose has been to suggest questions rather than to supply ready-made answers. As an eminent philosopher, who took up archaeological research as a laboratory in which to check his philosophical ideas, the late R. G. Collingwood (1939), never tired of emphasizing, both the meaning of a proposition and its truth are relative to the question it answers. In short the questions must be framed before the answers.

REFERENCES CITED

Albright, W. F.
    1946   *From the Stone Age to Christianity*. 2d ed. Baltimore.
Beals, Ralph
    1953   "Acculturation." In *Anthropology Today* by A. L. Kroeber and others, pp. 621–41. Chicago: University of Chicago Press.
Beazley, J. D.
    1942   *Attic Red-Figured Painters*. Oxford.
Berenson, B.
    1947   *Metodo e Attribuzione*. Florence.
Bloch, B.
    1948   "A Set of Postulates for Phonemic Analysis." *Language* 24:3–46.

Bochénski, I. M.
   1954   "Die Zeitgenössischen Denkmethoden." *Dalp-Handbücher* bd. 304. Bern.
Bonfante, G.
   1947   "The Neolinguistic Position." *Language* 23:344–75.
Bursch, F. C.
   1950   "Vorgeschichte als Kulturgeschichte." *Actes de la IIIe Session du Congrès International des Sciences Préhistoriques*, Zürich 1950 (publ. 1953), pp. 86–91.
   1953   "Ethnologie und Vorgeschichte." *Saeculum* 5:292–303.
Childe, V. G.
   1929   *The Danube in Prehistory*. Oxford.
   1930   *The Bronze Age*. Cambridge.
   1935   "Changing Methods and Aims in Prehistory." *Proceedings of the Prehistoric Society* 1:1–15.
   1950   "Prehistoric Migrations in Europe." *Instituttet for Sammenligende Kulturforskning*, Ser. A: Foresninger 20:5. Oslo.
   1951   *Social Evolution*. London.
   1953   "Review of: 'Vom geistigen Menschenbild der Urzeit,' by R. Pittioni." In *Man*, vol. 53, no. 105.
Collingwood, R. G.
   1939   *An Autobiography*. Oxford.
Daniel, G. E.
   1943   *The Three Ages, an Essay on Archaeological Method*. Cambridge.
Devoto, G.
   1946   "Preistoria e Storia." *Rivista di Scienze Preistoriche* 1:7–18.
Eggers, H. J.
   1950   "Das Problem der ethnischen Deutung in der Frühgeschichte." In *Ur- und Frühgeschichte als historische Wissenschaft (Wahle Festschrift)*, H. Kirchner (ed.), pp. 49–59. Heidelberg.
Fox, C.
   1932   *The Personality of Britain*. (Latest rev. ed., 1943.) Cardiff.
Goodwin, A. J. H.
   1953   *Method in Prehistory*. 2d ed. Cape Town: The South African Archaeological Society, Handbook Series No. 1.
Graebner, F.
   1911   *Methode der Ethnologie*. Heidelberg.
Hart, H.
   1931   *The Technique of Social Progress*. New York.
Hawkes, C. F. C.
   1948   *Archaeology and the History of Europe*. Oxford.

1951 "British Prehistory Halfway through the Century." *Proceedings of the Prehistoric Society* 17:1–15.

1954 "Archaeological Theory and Method: Some Suggestions from the Old World." *American Anthropologist* 56:155–68.

Herskovits, M. J.
1938 *Acculturation, the Study of Culture Contact.* New York.

1951 *Man and His Works.* New York.

Hoijer, H.
1948 "Linguistic and Cultural Change." *Language* 24:335–45.

1953 "The Relation of Language to Culture." In *Anthropology Today* by A. L. Kroeber and others, pp. 554–73. Chicago: University of Chicago Press.

Kirchner, H.
1950 "Frühgeschichtsforschung und historische Kombination." In *Ur- und Frühgeschichte als historische Wissenschaft (Wahle Festschrift)*, H. Kirchner (ed.), pp. 26–42. Heidelberg.

1954 "Review of: 'Vom geistigen Menschenbild der Urzeit,' by R. Pittioni." In *Anthropos* 49:727–28.

Koppers, W.
1944 "La Question racial et Indo-Européenne dans la lumière de l'histoire universelle." *Nova et Vetera*, pp. 167–94.

Kossinna, G.
1911 "Die Herkunft der Germanen." *Zur Methode der Siedlungsarchäologie.* Mannusbibliothek nr. 6. Berlin.

Kroeber, A. L.
1927 "Disposal of the Dead." *American Anthropologist* 29:308–15.

1948 *Anthropology.* Rev. ed. New York.

————, and C. Kluckhohn
1952 "Culture, a Critical Review of Concepts and Definitions." *Papers of the Peabody Museum of American Archaeology and Ethnology*, Harvard University, vol. 47, no. 1.

Lees, R. B.
1953 "The Basis of Glottochronology." *Language* 29:113–27.

Lounsbury, F. G.
1953 "Field Methods and Techniques in Linguistics." In *Anthropology Today* by A. L. Kroeber and others, pp. 401–16. Chicago: University of Chicago Press.

McKern, W. C.
     1939   "The Midwestern Taxonomic Method as an Aid to Archaeological Study." *American Antiquity* 4, no. 4:301–13.

MacWhite, E.
     1954   "Review of: 'Culture, a Critical Review of Concepts and Definitions,' by A. L. Kroeber and C. Kluckhohn." In *Anthropos* 49:718–20.
     1955   "Problems of Irish Archaeology and Celtic Philology." *Zeitschrift für celtische Philologie* 25.

Marrou, H. I.
     1954   *De la Connaissance historique*. Paris.

Martinet, A.
     1952   "Review of: 'La Dialectologie,' by S. Pop." In *Word* 8:260–62.

Menghin, O.
     1936   "Grundlinien einer Methodik der urgeschichtlichen Stammeskunde." *Hirt Festschrift* I. Heidelberg.
     1952   "Urgeschichtliche Grundfragen." In *Historia Mundi, Ein Handbuch der Weltgeschichte* by Kern, bd. I, pp. 229–58. Bern.

Montelius, O.
     1903   *Die Älteren Kulturperioden, I Die Methode*. Stockholm.

Mortillet, G. de
     1881   *Musée préhistorique*. Paris.

Movius, H. L.
     1953   "Curran Point, Larne, County Antrim: The Type Site of the Irish Mesolithic." *Proceedings of the Royal Irish Academy* 56, C, no. 1.

Murdock, G. P.
     1949   *Social Structure*. New York.
     1953   "The Processing of Anthropological Materials." In *Anthropology Today* by A. L. Kroeber and others, pp. 476–87. Chicago: University of Chicago Press.

Novicov, J.
     1896   *Les Luttes entre sociétés humaines*. Paris.

Ogburn, W.
     1922   *Social Change*. New York.
———, and M. F. Nimkoff
     1947   *A Handbook of Sociology*. London.

O'Rahilly, T. F.
     1946   *Early Irish History and Mythology*. Dublin.

Patterson, T. T.
     1945   "Core, Culture and Complex in the Old Stone Age." *Proceedings of the Prehistoric Society* 11:1–19.

Phillips, P., and G. R. Willey
   1953   "Method and Theory in American Archeology: An Operational Basis for Culture-Historical Integration." *American Anthropologist* 55:615–33.
Pisani, V.
   1939   "La Lingua e la sua Storia." *Archivio Glottologico Italiano* 31:1–16.
Pittioni, R.
   1950   "Historische Ablauf und urgeschichtliche Terminologie." *Anzeiger Osterreichische Akademie der Wissenschaften, Phil-Hist.* kl. 87, pp. 57–70.
   1952   *Vom geistigen Menschenbild der Urzeit.* Vienna.
Raftery, J.
   1947   "Some Archaeological Aspects of the Goidelic Problem." In *Féilscríbhinn Tórna*, pp. 101–7. Cork.
Redfield, R., R. Linton, and M. J. Herskovits
   1936   "Memorandum on the Study of Acculturation." *American Anthropologist* 38:149–52.
Rouse, I.
   1939   "Prehistory in Haiti." *Yale Publications in Anthropology*, no. 21.
Sorokin, P. A.
   1947   *Society, Culture and Personality: Their Structure and Dynamics.* New York.
Strygowski, J.
   1923   *The Origin of Christian Church Art.* London.
Swadesh, M.
   1953   "Archaeological and Linguistic Chronology of Indo-European Groups." *American Anthropologist* 55:349–52.
Tallgren, A. M.
   1937   "The Method of Prehistoric Archaeology." *Antiquity* 11:152–61.
Taylor, W. W.
   1948   "A Study of Archaeology." *American Anthropological Association Memoir*, no. 69.
Tax, Sol, and others, eds.
   1953   *An Appraisal of Anthropology Today.* Chicago: University of Chicago Press.
Tovar, A.
   1954   "Linguistics and Prehistory." *Word* 10:333–50.
Trubetskoi, N. S.
   1939   "Gedanken über das Indogermanenproblem." *Acta Linguistica* 1:81–89.
Venturi, L.
   1951–52   *La Peinture Italienne.* 3 vols. Geneva.

Wahle, E.

1941   "Zur ethnischen Deutung frühgeschichtlicher Kultur-
provinzen. Grenzen der frügeschichtlichen Erkenntnis
I." *Sitzungsberichte der Heidelberger Akademie der
Wissenschaften, Phil-Hist.* kl. 1940–41, 2 Abhand-
lung.

Willey, G. R.

1948   "Functional Analysis of 'Horizon Styles' in Peruvian
Archaeology." *Memoirs of the Society for American
Archaeology,* no. 4, pp. 8–15.

1953   "Archaeological Theories and Interpretation: New
World." In *Anthropology Today* by A. L. Kroeber and
others, pp. 361–85. Chicago: University of Chicago
Press.

Zambotti, P. L.

1946   "I compiti attuali della Paleetnologia nel risolvere i
problemi sulla genesi della cultura." *Rivista di Scienze
Preistoriche* 1:156–67.

Zeuner, F.

1946   *Dating the Past, an Introduction to Geochronology.*
London.

IV
ARCHAEOLOGICAL
INFERENCE

LEWIS R. BINFORD

In this classic of the new approach to archaeology as part of anthropology, Lewis Binford applies his methods and theories to a case, the Old Copper Culture of prehistoric North America. Binford rethinks the problems inherent in assigning function to the artifact. He describes three major functions: technomic, socio-technic, and ideo-technic, and employs these distinctions to the changing use of copper in eastern North America. The fact that function serves on three levels, often concurrently, is a sobering thought and merits further investigation, particularly since function is a loaded term within the general field of archaeology.

15   Archaeology as Anthropology

It has been aptly stated that "American archaeology is anthropology or it is nothing" (Willey and Phillips 1958:2). The purpose of this discussion is to evaluate the role which the archaeological discipline is playing in furthering the aims of anthropology and to offer certain suggestions as to how we, as archaeologists, may profitably shoulder more responsibility for furthering the aims of our field.

Initially, it must be asked, "What are the aims of anthropology?" Most will agree that the integrated field is striving to *explicate* and *explain* the total range of physical and cultural similarities and differences characteristic of the entire spatial-temporal span of man's existence (for discussion, see Kroeber 1953). Archaeology has certainly made major contributions as far as *explication* is concerned. Our current knowledge of the diversity which characterizes the range of extinct cultural systems is far superior to the limited knowledge available fifty years ago. Although this contribution is "admirable" and necessary, it has been noted that archaeology has made

Reprinted, with the editorial changes noted, from "Archaeology as Anthropology" by Lewis R. Binford, *American Antiquity* 28 (1962): 217–225, by permission of the author and the publisher.

248

essentially no contribution in the realm of explanation: "So little work has been done in American archaeology on the explanatory level that it is difficult to find a name for it" (Willey and Phillips 1958:5).

Before carrying this criticism further, some statement about what is meant by explanation must be offered. The meaning which explanation has within a scientific frame of reference is simply the *demonstration* of a constant articulation of variables within a system and the measurement of the concomitant variability among the variables within the system. Processual change in one variable can then be shown to relate in a predictable and quantifiable way to changes in other variables, the latter changing in turn relative to changes in the structure of the system as a whole. This approach to explanation presupposes concern with process, or the operation and structural modification of systems. It is suggested that archaeologists have not made major explanatory contributions to the field of anthropology because they do not conceive of archaeological data in a systemic frame of reference. Archaeological data are viewed particularistically and "explanation" is offered in terms of specific events rather than in terms of process (see Buettner-Janusch 1957 for discussion of particularism).

Archaeologists tacitly assume that artifacts, regardless of their functional context, can be treated as equal and comparable "traits." Once differences and similarities are "defined" in terms of these equal and comparable "traits," interpretation proceeds within something of a theoretical vacuum that conceives of differences and similarities as the result of "blending," "directional influences," and "stimulation" between and among "historical traditions" defined largely on the basis of postulated local or regional continuity in the human populations.

I suggest that this undifferentiated and unstructured view is inadequate, that artifacts having their primary functional context in different operational subsystems of the total cultural system will exhibit differences and similarities differentially, in terms of the structure of the cultural system of which they were a part. Further, that the temporal and spatial spans within and between broad functional categories will vary with the structure of the systematic relationships between sociocultural systems. Study of these differential distributions can potentially yield valuable information concerning the nature of social organization within, and changing relationships between, sociocultural systems. In short, the explanation of differences and similarities between archaeological complexes must be offered in terms of our current knowledge of the structural and functional characteristics of cultural systems.

Specific "historical" explanations, if they can be demonstrated, simply explicate mechanisms of cultural process. They add nothing to the explanation of the processes of cultural change and evolution. If migrations can be shown to have taken place, then this explication presents an explanatory problem; what adaptive circumstances, evolutionary processes, induced the migration (Thompson 1958:1)? We must seek explanation in systemic terms for classes of historical events such as migrations, establishment of "contact" between areas previously isolated, etc. Only then will we make major contributions in the area of explanation and provide a basis for the further advancement of anthropological theory.

As an exercise in explication of the methodological questions raised here, I will present a general discussion of a particular systemic approach in the evaluation of archaeological assemblages and utilize these distinctions in an attempted *explanation* of a particular set of archaeological observations.

Culture is viewed as the extra-somatic means of adaptation for the human organism (White 1959:8). I am concerned with all those subsystems within the broader cultural system which are: (a) extra-somatic or not, dependent upon biological process for modification or structural definition (this is not to say that the form and process cannot be viewed as rooted in biological process, only that diversity and processes of diversification are not explicable in terms of biological process), and which (b) function to adapt the human organism, conceived generically, to its total environment both physical and social.

Within this framework it is consistent to view technology, those tools and social relationships which articulate the organism with the physical environment, as closely related to the nature of the environment. For example, we would not expect to find large quantities of fishhooks among the recent archaeological remains from the Kalahari desert! However, this view must not be thought of as "environmental determinism" for we assume a systematic relationship between the human organism and his environment in which culture is the intervening variable. In short, we are speaking of the ecological system (Steward 1955:36). We can observe certain constant adaptive requirements on the part of the organism and similarly certain adaptive limitations, given specific kinds of environment. However, limitations as well as the potential of the environment must be viewed always in terms of the intervening variable in the human ecological system, that is, culture.

With such an approach we should not be surprised to note similarities in technology among groups of similar levels of social complexity inhabiting the boreal forest (Spaulding 1946) or any other broad environmental zone. The comparative study of cultural systems with variable technologies in a similar environmental range or similar technologies in differing environments is a major methodology of what Steward (1955:36–42) has called "cultural ecology," and certainly is a valuable means of increasing our understanding of cultural processes. Such a methodology is also useful in elucidating the structural relationships between major cultural subsystems such as the social and ideological subsystems. Prior to the initiation of such studies by archaeologists we must be able to distinguish those relevant artifactual elements within the total artifact assemblage which have the primary functional context in the social, technological, and ideological subsystems of the total cultural system. We should not equate "material culture" with technology. Similarly we should not seek explanations for observed differences and similarities in "material culture" within a single interpretative frame of reference. It has often been suggested that we cannot dig up a social system or ideology. Granted we cannot excavate a kinship terminology or a philosophy, but we can and do excavate the material items which functioned together with these more behavioral elements within the appropriate cultural subsystems. The formal structure of artifact assemblages together with the between element contextual relationships should and do present a systematic and understandable picture of *the total extinct* cultural system. It is no more justifiable for archaeologists to attempt explanation of certain formal, temporal, and spatial similarities and differences within a single frame of reference than it would be for an ethnographer to attempt explanation of differences in cousin terminology, levels of sociocultural integration, styles of dress, and modes of transportation all with the same variables or within the same frame of reference. These classes or items are articulated differently within an integrated cultural system, hence the pertinent variables with which each is articulated, and exhibits concomitant variation are different. This fact obviates the single explanatory frame of reference. The processes of change pertinent to each are different because of the different ways in which they function in contributing to the total adaptive system.

Consistent with this line of reasoning is the assertion that we as archaeologists must face the problem of identifying *technomic* artifacts from other artifactual forms. Technomic signifies those artifacts having their primary functional context in coping directly with the physical environment. Variability in the technomic components of archaeological assemblages is seen as primarily explicable in the ecological frame of reference. Here, we must concern ourselves with such phenomena as extractive efficiency, efficiency in performing bio-compensatory tasks such as heat retention, the nature of available resources, their distribution, density, and loci of availability, etc. In this area of research and explanation, the archaeologist is in a position to make a direct contribution to the field of anthropology. We can directly correlate technomic items with environmental variables since we can know the distribution of fossil flora and fauna from independent data — giving us the nature of extinct environments.

Another major class of artifacts which the archaeologists recover can be termed *socio-technic.* These artifacts were the material elements having their primary functional context in the social subsystems of the total cultural system. This subsystem functions as the extra-somatic means of articulating individuals one with another into cohesive groups capable of efficiently maintaining themselves and of manipulating the technology. Artifacts such as a king's crown, a warrior's coup stick, a copper from the Northwest coast, etc., fall into this category. Changes in the relative complexity of the socio-technic component of an archaeological assemblage can be related to changes in the structure of the social system which they represent. Certainly the evolutionary processes, while correlated and related, are not the same for explaining structural changes in technological and social phenomena. Factors such as demography, presence or absence of between-group competition, etc., as well as the basic factors which affect technological change, must be considered when attempting to explain social change. Not only are the relevant variables different, there is a further difference when speaking of socio-technic artifacts. The explanation of the basic form and structure of the socio-technic component of an artifactual assemblage lies in the nature and structure of the social system which it represents. Observable differences and changes in the socio-technic components of archaeological assemblages must be explained with reference to structural changes in the social system and in terms of processes of social change and evolution.

Thus, archaeologists can initially only indirectly contribute to the investigation of social evolution. I would consider the study and establishment of correlations between types of social structure classified on the basis of behavioral attributes and structural types of material elements as one of the major areas of anthropological research yet to be developed. Once such correlations are established, archaeologists can attack the problems of evolutionary change in social systems. It is my opinion that only when we have the entire temporal span of cultural evolution as our "laboratory" can we make substantial gains in the critical area of social anthropological research.

The third major class of items which archaeologists frequently recover can be termed *ideo-technic artifacts.* Items of this class have their primary functional context in the ideological component of the social system. These are the items which signify and symbolize the ideological rationalizations for the social system and further provide the symbolic milieu in which individuals are enculturated, a necessity if they are to take their place as functional participants in the social system. Such items as figures of deities, clan symbols, symbols of natural agencies, etc., fall into this general category. Formal diversity in the structural complexity and in functional classes of this category of items must generally be related to changes in the structure of the society, hence explanations must be sought in the local adaptive situation rather than in the area of "historical explanations." As was the case with socio-technic items, we must seek to establish correlations between generic classes of the ideological system and the structure of the material symbolism. Only after such correlations have been established can archaeologists study in a systematic way this component of the social subsystem.

Cross-cutting all of these general classes of artifacts are formal characteristics which can be termed stylistic, formal qualities that are not directly explicable in terms of the nature of the raw materials, technology of production, or variability in the structure of the technological and social subsystems of the total cultural system. These formal qualities are believed to have their primary functional context in providing a symbolically diverse yet pervasive artifactual environment promoting group solidarity and serving as a basis for group awareness and identity. This pan-systemic set of symbols is the milieu of enculturation and a basis for the recognition of social distinctiveness. "One of the main functions of the arts as communication is to reinforce belief, custom, and values" (Beals and Hoijer 1955:548). The distribution of style types and traditions is believed to be largely correlated with areas of commonality in level of cultural complexity and in mode of adaptation. Changes in the temporal-spatial distribution of style types are believed to be related to changes in the structure of sociocultural systems either brought about through processes of in situ evolution, or by changes in the cultural environment to which local sociocultural systems are adapted, thereby initiating evolutionary change. It is believed that stylistic attributes are most fruitfully studied when questions of ethnic origin, migration, and interaction between groups is the subject of explication. However, when explanations are sought, the total adaptive context of the sociocultural system in question must be investigated. In this field of research archaeologists are in an excellent position to make major contributions to the general field of anthropology, for we can work directly in terms of correlations of the structure of artifact assemblages with rates of style change, directions of style-spread, and stability of style-continuity.

Having recognized three general functional classes of artifacts: technomic, socio-technic, and ideo-technic, as well as a category of formal stylistic attributes, each characterized by differing functions within the total cultural system and correspondingly different processes of change, it is suggested that our current theoretical orientation is insufficient and inadequate for attempting explanation. It is argued that explanations of differences and similarities between archaeological assemblages as a whole must first consider the nature of differences in each of these major categories and only after such evaluation can adequate explanatory hypotheses be offered.

Given this brief and oversimplified introduction, I will turn to a specific case, the Old Copper complex (Wittry and Ritzenthaler 1956). It has long been observed and frequently cited as a case of technological "devolution" that during the Archaic period fine and superior copper utilitarian tools were manufactured, whereas, during Early and Middle Woodland times copper was used primarily for the production of nonutilitarian items (Griffin 1952:356). I will explore this interesting situation in terms of: (1) the frame of reference presented here, (2) generalizations which have previously been made concerning the nature of culture change, and (3) a set of hypotheses concerning the relationships between certain forms of socio-technic artifacts and the structure of the social systems that they represent.

The normal assumption when thinking about the copper artifacts typical of the Old Copper complex is that they are primarily technomic (manufactured for use in directly coping with the physical environment). It is generally assumed that these tools were superior to their functional equivalents in both stone and bone because of their durability and presumed superiority in accomplishing cutting and piercing tasks. It is a common generalization that within the realm of technology more efficient forms tend to replace less efficient forms. The Old Copper case seems to be an exception.

Absolute efficiency in performance is only one side of the coin when viewed in an adaptive context. Adaptive efficiency must also be viewed in terms of *economy*, that is, energy expenditure versus energy conservation (White 1959:54). For one tool to be adaptively more efficient than another there must be either a lowering of energy expenditure per unit of energy of conservation in task performance, or an increase in energy conservation per unit of performance over a constant energy expenditure in tool production. Viewed this way, we may question the position that copper tools were technologically more efficient. The production of copper tools utilizing the techniques employed in the manufacture of Old Copper specimens certainly required tremendous expenditures of both time and labor. The sources of copper are not in the areas of most dense Old Copper implements (Wittry 1951), hence travel to the sources, or at least the establishment of logistics networks based on kin ties extending over large areas, was a prerequisite for the procurement of the raw material. Extraction of the copper, using the primitive mining techniques exemplified by the aboriginal mining pits on Isle Royale and the Keewenaw Peninsula (Holmes 1901), required further expenditure of time and labor. Raw materials for the production of the functional equivalents of the copper tools was normally available locally or at least available at some point within the bounds of the normal exploitative cycle. Extraction was essentially a gathering process requiring no specialized techniques, and could be accomplished incidental to the performance of other tasks. Certainly in terms of expenditures of time and energy, as regards the distribution of sources of raw materials and techniques of extraction, copper required a tremendous expenditure as opposed to raw materials of stone and bone.

The processing phase of tool production appears to present an equally puzzling ratio with regard to expenditure of energy. The processing of copper into a finished artifact normally requires the separation of crystalline impurities from the copper. Following this processing phase, normal procedure seems to have been to pound and partially flatten small bits of copper which were then pounded together to "build" an artifact (Cushing 1894). Once the essential shape had been achieved, further hammering, grinding, and polishing were required. I suggest that this process is more time consuming than shaping and finishing an artifact by chipping flint, or even the pecking and grinding technique employed in the production of ground stone tools. It follows that there was a much greater expenditure of time and energy in the production of copper tools than in the production of their functional equivalents in either bone or stone.

Turning now to the problem of energy conservation in task performance, we may ask what differentials existed. It seems fairly certain that copper was probably more durable and could have been utilized for a longer period of time. As far as what differentials existed between copper and stone, as regards cutting and piercing functions, only experiments can determine. Considering all of the evidence, the quality of durability appears to have been the only possible realm which could compensate for the differentials in expenditure of energy between stone and bone as opposed to copper in the area of procurement and processing of the raw material. What evidence exists that would suggest that durability was in fact the compensatory quality which made copper tools technologically more efficient?

All the available evidence suggests the contrary interpretation. First, we do not have evidence that the raw material was reused to any great extent once an artifact was broken or "worn out." If this had been the case, we would expect to have a general lack of battered and "worn out" pieces and some examples of reworked pieces, whereas evidence of use is a common characteristic of recovered specimens, and to my knowledge reworked pieces are uncommon if not unknown.

Second, when found in a primary archaeological context, copper tools are almost invariably part of burial goods. If durability was the compensatory factor in the efficiency equation, certainly some social mechanism for retaining the copper tools as functioning parts of the technology would have been established. This does not appear to have been the case. Since durability can be ruled out as the compensatory factor, we must conclude that copper tools were not technologically more efficient than their functional equivalents in both stone and bone. Having reached this "conclusion," it remains to explore the problem of the initial appearance of copper tools and to examine the observation that there was a shift from the use of copper for the production of utilitarian tools to nonutilitarian items.

It is proposed that the observed shift and the initial appearance of copper tools can best be explained under the hypothesis that they did not function primarily as *technomic items*. I suggest that in both the Old Copper and later cultural systems to the south, copper was utilized primarily for the production of *socio-technic items*.

Fried (1960) discusses certain pertinent distinctions between societies with regard to systems of status grading. Societies on a low general level of cultural complexity, measured in terms of functional specialization and structural differentiation, normally have an "egalitarian" system of status grading. The term "egalitarian" signifies that status positions are open to all persons within the limits of certain sex and age classes, who through their individual physical and mental characteristics are capable of great achievement in coping with the environment. Among societies of greater complexity, status grading may be less egalitarian. Where ranking is the primary mechanism of status grading, status positions are closed. There are qualifications for attainment that are not simply a function of one's personal physical and mental capabilities.

A classic example of ranking is found among societies with a ramage form of social organization (Sahlins 1958:139–80). In such societies status is determined by one's proximity in descent from a common ancestor. High status is accorded those in the direct line of descent, calculated in terms of primogeniture, while cadet lines of descent occupy positions of lower status depending on their proximity to the direct line.

Another form of internally ranked system is one in which attainment of a particular status position is closed to all except those members of a particular kin group who may occupy a differentiated status position, but open to all members of that kin group on an egalitarian basis.

Other forms of status grading are recognized, but for the purposes of this discussion the major distinction between egalitarian and ranked systems is sufficient. I propose that there is a direct relationship between the nature of the system of status grading within a society and the quantity, form, and structure of socio-technic components of its archaeological assemblage.

It is proposed that among egalitarian societies status symbols are symbolic of the technological activities for which outstanding performance is rewarded by increased status. In many cases they will be formally technomic items manufactured of "exotic" material or elaborately decorated and/or painstakingly manufactured. I do not imply that the items could not or were not used technomically, simply that their presence in the assemblage is explicable only in reference to the social system.

Within such a system the structure of the socio-technic component as regards "contextual" relationships should be simple. Various status symbols will be possessed by nearly all individuals within the limits of age and sex classes, differentiation within such a class being largely quantitative and qualitative rather than by formal exclusion of particular forms to particular status grades. The degree to which socio-technic symbols of status will be utilized within an egalitarian group should largely be a function of group size and the intensity and constancy of personal acquaintance among all individuals composing the society. Where small group size and general lack of interaction with nearby groups is the normal pattern, then the abundance of status symbols should be low. Where group size is large and/or where between-group interactions are widespread, lowering the intimacy and familiarity between interacting individuals, then there should be a greater and more general use of material means of status communication.

Another characteristic of the manipulation of status symbols among societies with essentially egalitarian systems of status grading would be the destruction at death of an individual's symbols of status. Status attainment being egalitarian, status symbols would be personalities and could not be inherited as such. Inclusion as grave accompaniments or outright destruction would be the suggested mode of disposal for status items among such groups.

Among societies where status grading tends to be of a nonegalitarian type, the status symbols should be more esoteric in form. Their form would normally be dictated by the ideological symbolism which rationalizes and emphasizes the particular internal ranking system or the means of partitioning the society. The structure of the socio-technic component of the assemblage should be more complex, with the complexity increasing directly as the complexity of the internal ranking system. Possession of certain forms may become exclusively restricted to certain status positions. As the degree of complexity in ranking increases there should be a similar increase in the differentiation of contextual associations in the form of differential treatment at death, differential access to goods and services evidenced in the formal and spatial differentiation in habitations and storage areas, etc. We would also expect to observe differentiation among the class of status symbols themselves as regards those which were utilized on a custodial basis as opposed to those that were personalities. Similarly, we would expect to see status symbols more frequently inherited at death as inheritance increases as the mechanism of status ascription.

Certainly these are suggestions which must be phrased as hypotheses and tested against ethnographic data. Nevertheless it is hoped that this discussion is sufficient to serve as a background against which an explanatory hypothesis concerning the Old Copper materials can be offered as an example of the potential utility of this type of *systemic* approach to archaeological data.

I suggest that the Old Copper copper tools had their primary functional context as symbols of achieved status in cultural systems with an egalitarian system of status grading. The settlement patterns and general level of cultural development suggested by the archaeological remains is commensurate with a band level of sociocultural integration (Martin, Quimby, and Collier 1947:299), that level within which egalitarian systems of status grading are dominant (Fried 1960). The technomic form, apparent lack of technomic efficiency, relative scarcity, and frequent occurrence in burials of copper artifacts all suggest that their primary function was as socio-technic items. Having reached this "conclusion," we are then in a position to ask, in systemic terms, questions concerning their period of appearance, disappearance, and the shift to nonutilitarian forms of copper items among later prehistoric sociocultural systems of eastern North America.

I propose that the initial appearance of formally "utilitarian" copper tools in the Great Lakes region is explicable in terms of a major population expansion in the region following the Nipissing stage of the ancestral Great Lakes. The increase in population density was the result of increases in gross productivity following an exploitative shift to aquatic resources during the Nipissing stage. The increased populations are generally demonstrable in terms of the increased number of archaeological sites ascribable to the post-Nipissing period. The shift to aquatic resources is demonstrable in the initial appearance of quantities of fish remains in the sites of this period and in the sites of election for occupation, adjacent to prominent loci of availability for exploiting aquatic resources. It is proposed that with the increasing population density, the selective pressures fostering the symbolic communication of status, as opposed to the dependence on personal recognition as the bases for differential role behavior, were sufficient to result in the initial appearance of a new class of socio-technic items, formally technomic status symbols.

The failure to perpetuate the practice of the manufacture of copper tools on any extensive basis in the Great Lakes region should be explicable in terms of the changing structure of the social systems in that area during Woodland times. The exact type of social structure characteristic of Early Woodland period is at present poorly understood. I would suggest that there was a major structural change between the Late Archaic and Early Woodland periods, probably in the direction of a simple clan and moiety basis for social integration with a corresponding shift in the systems of status grading and the obsolescence of the older material means of status communication.

The presence of copper tools of essentially nonutilitarian form within such complexes as Adena, Hopewell, and Mississippian are most certainly explicable in terms of their socio-technic functions within much more complex social systems. Within the latter societies status grading was not purely on an egalitarian basis, and the nonutilitarian copper forms of status symbols would be formally commensurate with the ideological rationalizations for the various ascriptive status systems.

This explanatory "theory" has the advantage of "explaining": (1) the period of appearance of copper and probably other "exotic" materials in the Late Archaic period; (2) the form of the copper items; (3) their frequently noted contextual relations, for example, placement in burials; (4) their disappearance, which would be an "enigma" if they functioned primarily as technomic items; and (5) the use of copper for the almost exclusive production of "nonutilitarian" items in later and certainly more complex cultures of the eastern United States. This explanatory theory is advanced on the basis of currently available information, and regardless of whether or not it can stand as the correct explanation of the "Old Copper Problem" when more data are available, I suggest that only within a systemic frame of reference could such an inclusive explanation be offered. Here lies the advantage of the systemic approach.

Archaeology must accept a greater responsibility in the furtherance of the aims of anthropology. Until the tremendous quantities of data which the archaeologist controls are used in the solution of problems dealing with cultural evolution or systemic change, we are not only failing to contribute to the furtherance of the aims of anthropology but retarding the accomplishment of these aims. We as archaeologists have available a wide range of variability and a large sample of cultural systems. Ethnographers are restricted to the small and formally limited extant cultural systems.

Archaeologists should be among the best qualified to study and directly test hypotheses concerning the process of evolutionary change, particularly processes of change that are relatively slow, or hypotheses that postulate temporal-processual priorities as regards total cultural systems. The lack of theoretical concern and rather naive attempts at explanation which archaeologists currently advance must be modified.

I have suggested certain ways that could be a beginning in this necessary transition to a systemic view of culture, and have set forth a specific argument which hopefully demonstrates the utility of such an approach. The explanatory potential which even this limited and highly specific interpretative approach holds should be clear when problems such as "the spread of an Early Woodland burial cult in the Northeast" (Ritchie 1955), the appearance of the "Buzzard cult" (Waring and Holder 1945) in the Southeast, or the "Hopewell decline" (Griffin 1960) are recalled. It is my opinion that until we as archaeologists begin thinking of our data in terms of total cultural systems, many such prehistoric "enigmas" will remain unexplained. As archaeologists, with the entire span of culture history as our "laboratory," we cannot afford to keep our theoretical heads buried in the sand. We must shoulder our full share of responsibility within anthropology. Such a change could go far in advancing the field of

260   Lewis R. Binford

archaeology specifically, and would certainly advance the general field of anthropology.

BIBLIOGRAPHY

Beals, Ralph L., and Harry Hoijer
  1953   *An Introduction to Anthropology.* New York: The Macmillan Co.
Buettner-Janusch, John
  1957   "Boas and Mason: Particularism versus Generalization." *American Anthropologist* 59, no. 2:318–24.
Cushing, F. H.
  1894   "Primitive Copper Working: An Experimental Study." *American Anthropologist* 7, no 1:93–117.
Fried, Morton H.
  1960   "On the Evolution of Social Stratification and the State." In *Culture in History: Essays in Honor of Paul Radin,* Stanley Diamond (ed.), pp. 713–731. New York: Columbia University Press.
Griffin, James B.
  1952   "Culture Periods in Eastern United States Archaeology." In *Archaeology of Eastern United States,* James B. Griffin (ed.), pp. 352–364. Chicago: University of Chicago Press.
  1960   "Climatic Change: A Contributory Cause of the Growth and Decline of Northern Hopewellian Culture." *Wisconsin Archaeologist* 41, no. 2:21–33.
Holmes, William H.
  1901   "Aboriginal Copper Mines of Isle Royale, Lake Superior." *American Anthropologist* 3, no. 4:684–96.
Kroeber, A. L.
  1953   Introduction. In *Anthropology Today,* A. L. Kroeber (ed.), pp. xiii–xv. Chicago: University of Chicago Press.
Martin, Paul S., George I. Quimby, and Donald Collier
  1947   *Indians before Columbus.* Chicago: University of Chicago Press.
Ritchie, William A.
  1955   "Recent Suggestions Suggesting an Early Woodland Burial Cult in the Northeast." *New York State Museum and Science Service, Circular,* no. 40.
Sahlins, Marshall D.
  1958   *Social Stratification in Polynesia.* Seattle: University of Washington Press.
Spaulding, Albert C.
  1946   Northeastern Archaeology and General Trends in the Northern Forest Zone. In "Man in Northeastern

North America," Frederick Johnson (ed.). *Papers of the Robert S. Peabody Foundation for Archaeology* 3:143–67. Andover: Phillips Academy.

Steward, Julian H.
    1955   *Theory of Culture Change.* Urbana: University of Illinois Press.

Thompson, Raymond H.
    1958   Preface. In "Migrations in New World Culture History," Raymond H. Thompson (ed.), *University of Arizona, Social Science Bulletin,* no. 27, pp. v–vii.

Waring, Antonio J., and Preston Holder
    1945   "A Prehistoric Ceremonial Complex in the Southeastern United States." *American Anthropologist* 47, no. 1:1–34.

White, Leslie A.
    1959   *The Evolution of Culture.* New York: McGraw-Hill.

Willey, Gordon R., and Philip Phillips
    1958   *Method and Theory in Archaeology.* Chicago: University of Chicago Press.

Wittry, Warren L.
    1951   "A Preliminary Study of the Old Copper Complex." *Wisconsin Archaeologist* 32, no. 1:1–18.

————, and Robert E. Ritzenthaler
    1956   "The Old Copper Complex: An Archaic Manifestation in Wisconsin." *American Antiquity* 21, no. 3:244–54.

ROBERT ASCHER

All archaeological inferences and explanations have an element of analogy in them. Were it not for the fact that artifacts were made by people and that we know in most general terms how people behave, it would be impossible to explain any archaeological information through analogy. Yet this kind of analogy is so general as to be virtually useless in archaeological explanation. Robert Ascher traces analogy in archaeology, and shows the lack of agreement on the new analogy that places boundaries on the choice of suitable analogs. Ascher, whose article predates the next one by Lewis Binford on the same subject, suggests a number of ways to put the use of analogy on a firmer basis.

16   Analogy in Archaeological Interpretation

The work of the archaeologist can be divided into four tasks. First there is the formulation and refinement of concepts; second, data gathering and processing; third, the interpretation of the data, and finally, synthesis. The four tasks are obviously related in an hierarchical scheme: concepts enable meaningful synthesis, synthesis depends on interpretation, and interpretation is ultimately founded on archaeological data.

Substantial progress has been made in approaches to the first, second, and fourth tasks in recent years. Productive work on concepts is illustrated by the successful *Seminars in Archaeology* of the Society for American Archaeology. The appearance of the new journal *Archaeometry* under the auspices of The Research Laboratory at Oxford, with its concentration on the application to archaeology of instruments developed in other disciplines, indicates how vigorous the attack on the second task has been. The

Reprinted, with the editorial changes noted, from "Analogy in Archaeological Interpretation" by Robert Ascher, *Southwestern Journal of Anthropology* 17 (1961): 317–325, by permission of the publisher.

ambitious work *World Prehistory* by Grahame Clark, if not wholly successful, demonstrates that a synthesis of human prehistory on a global scale is now feasible. What can be demonstrated for concept formulation, data gathering, and synthesis, cannot be easily shown for archaeological interpretation. If it is granted that acceptance of synthesis must vary with confidence in interpretation, it becomes apparent that interpretation warrants attention.

The most widely used of the tools of archaeological interpretation is analogy. In its most general sense interpreting by analogy is assaying any belief about nonobserved behavior by referral to observed behavior which is thought to be relevant. The purpose of this paper is to examine this single interpretative tool. Concentration is on analogies where no historical records are available as aids. Evidence which suggests that there is cause for concern with the present status of analogy as an interpretive tool is presented and some suggestions are sketched.

The introduction of analogy into archaeology can be traced to the era of the classical evolutionary ideology. Analogy in this period was elementary: if it were true that certain living peoples represented early phases of human history, then the interpretation of the remains of extinct peoples could be accomplished by direct reference to their living counterparts. A monument to this logic is Sollas's *Ancient Hunters*. In this work the Tasmanians, Australian Aborigines, Bushmen, and Eskimos were enlisted as modern representatives of four successive paleolithic complexes. The question of the use of any class of paleolithic tools could be satisfied by direct referral to one of the four groups. For example:

> Anthropologists are generally agreed that the Palaeolithic "coup de poing" was not provided with a haft, but was held directly in the hand; and that it was not used simply as a "chopper": it is extremely gratifying therefore to find that the Tasmanians had no notion of hafting their homologue, or rather analogue, of the "coup de poing," and that it served a variety of purposes, among others as an aid in climbing trees.[1]

Interpretation in this mode, however, was not without its anachronisms. It was noted that living representatives of early periods occasionally enjoyed the use of classes of objects which were thought to be distinctive of later periods. In discussing the Australian Aborigines, for example, Sollas noted that polished stone axes "are supposed to be the exclusive characteristic of the Neolithic period; but as the Australians are still in a Palaeolithic stage of culture, they present us in this case with an exception, for which various explanations may be found." In resolving this problem Sollas calculated that they might have invented it themselves or borrowed it from neighbors, but

[1] Sollas 1911:74.

he eventually concluded with the suggestion that the Australian Aborigines learned to polish stone via an extensive network which at one time stretched from Australia to Europe.[2]

The critical reaction to the evolutionary assumptions, coupled with both the unexplained residues resulting from this early approach and the recovery of new data, forced reconsideration. As a result analogy was partitioned, and now at least two broad categories of analogy are recognized.[3]

The first category encompasses the classical evolutionary usage with appropriate shrinkages in the length and breadth of the time and space dimensions. In those areas of the world where history grades into archaeology, or where, in the absence of written documents, analysis of current or recent practices and archaeological data indicate continuity, archaeological data is interpreted by analogy to historical or living groups. In parts of the Near East, for example, archaeological evidence for the process of beer brewing can be interpreted by referral to both ancient texts and contemporary practices. The folk-cultures of Europe exhibit farming tools and practices, structures such as houses and granaries, and devices for transportation, which can be linked directly with the prehistoric past.

What is called the "folk-culture approach" by students of Old World archaeology is paralleled in the New World by the "direct historical approach." Both approaches admit the initiation of study from either end of the time scale. It is legitimate, presumably, to study the historically known prior to close examination of the archaeological unknown, or, reversing the order, to proceed from the archaeologically known to the historically unknown. If there is any subtle difference between the Old and New World approaches it is only that the longer time span in the Old World encourages the conception of smooth continuous passage from archaeology into history whereas in the New World the line between the two is more severely drawn.[4]

The withdrawal of the application of analogy from archaeological data where living representatives were assumed, to data where living or documented representatives could be demonstrated, left uncovered a vast temporal and spatial tract for which archaeological data existed. In order to cover this tract, consisting of over 95 percent of human history and a large proportion of the globe, a second category of analogy came into use. This

[2] *Idem*, pp. 179, 207–209.

[3] A third category has sometimes been distinguished. This third category includes analogies to properties common to all men such as the need for capturing energy and the possession of a language. For purposes of interpretation this third category is meaningless. One does not need to undertake archaeological investigation to know that the individuals in a particular culture engaged in these activities. The question which the archaeologist seeks to answer is what were the particular patterns of a prehistoric people in carrying out these and similar activities.

[4] Compare Steward 1942 with Hawkes 1954.

second category is here called the new analogy to distinguish it from analogy where historical continuity was assumed, as in the past, or is demonstrated, as in the present.

Anxious to avoid the mistakes of the early evolutionary school, and in the absence of any universal and unique model to guide in the recasting of interpretative tools, the new analogy has been set in a restrained format. In effect, the new analogy consists of boundary conditions for the choice of suitable analogs. A consideration of the canon for the selection of analogs, the qualifications placed on the power of the tool, and an example may characterize the theoretical posture of the new analogy.

According to Clark the archaeologist should "restrict the field of analogy to societies at a common level of subsistence," and should "attach greater significance to analogies drawn from societies existing under ecological conditions which approximate those reconstructed for the prehistoric culture under investigation than those adapted to markedly different environments."[5] Willey would select cultures on "the same general level of technological development, perhaps existing under similar environmental situations."[6] V. Gordon Childe advised that an analog "drawn from the same region of ecological province is likely to give the most reliable hints."[7] In summary, then, the canon is: seek analogies in cultures which manipulate similar environments in similar ways.

The qualifications on the new analogy are weighty. The mass of archaeological data yields subsistence or subsistence-connected information; hence, relevant analogies are to be initially restricted to this domain. The archaeologist is cautioned that the new analogy can provide only "useful clues to general conditions, it can be a dangerous guide to the particular manifestations of culture"[8] or may "in fact afford only clues in what direction to look for an explanation in the archaeological record itself."[9] The connection between the living culture or cultures and the archaeological culture in question is purely formal; there is no implication of direct generic relationship nor are any dimensions of space and time implied.

The following citation, from the interpretation of the mesolithic site of Star Carr, is an excellent example of the new analogy:

> The character of the finds suggests that we have to deal at Star Carr with a community rather than with the activities of a specialized group. The masculine element is sufficiently emphasized by the importance of hunting and by the evidence of great

[5] Clark 1953:355.
[6] Tax, *et al.* 1953:229.
[7] Childe 1956:51.
[8] Clark 1953:355.
[9] Childe 1956:49. See also Clarke 1951.

activity in the manufacture of tools and weapons. On the other hand, to judge from analogy with the hunting peoples of North America and Greenland, the importance of skin-working at Star Carr argues for the presence of women. Among the Eskimos generally women are mainly responsible for flaying the kill and preparing the skins for use. Men certainly play their part, especially in the hard task of thin-scraping caribou skins or when for some magical reason, as in preparing drum-skins among the Caribou Eskimos, it is considered wrong for women to undertake some particular task. Generally, though, it is agreed that the task is predominantly feminine and in fact constitutes the main part of women's labor.[10]

It would be misleading to imply that the restraint advocated in some quarters is practiced wherever archaeological data is interpreted by analogy. In fact, it would not be difficult to cite numerous cases in which less caution in the choice and use of analogs is clear. Consider, for example, the following attempt to interpret the *absence* of the caudal vertebrae of the otherwise well represented bovids in the important Australopithicine sites in the Makapansgat valley.

> To "tail" anything still signifies to "track it down." The leaders of Bushmen hunting parties, when tracking down their prey, signal to one another silently with the bushes or tails of the Cape fox. Tails spontaneously form flexible whips or flagella for beating thickets and grass-lands after game. The flagellum was one of the badges of the Pharaoh! The brush of a fox is the trophy of the chase. The warriors of Predynastic Egypt all wore bushy tails, that look suspiciously like fox-tails, and Pharaohs are delineated on Egyptian monuments retreating from the presence of gods looking back and trailing the bushy tails of an animal behind them. Horse-tails used to be emblems of rank formerly in Turkey, the rank depending on the number of tails (e.g., a pasha of three tails). Every South African witch-doctor carries an animal's brush preferably that of a wildebeest as every European witch carried a broom. It seems likely from the significance attached to tails universally by mankind in myth and history that their disappearance from the Makapansgat breccia is significant; they were all probably in great demand as signals and whips in organized group-hunting outside the cavern.[11]

In the engaging, less extreme example below an attempt is made to interpret the persistence of certain ceramic motifs in northern Georgia, U.S.A. Unlike the previous example, an awareness of boundaries is shown, if not rigorously adhered to.

[10] Clark 1954:10.
[11] Dart 1957:167–68.

> I am not quite sure to what extent we can measure general ethnic continuity in terms of ceramic continuity. Modern women of our civilization seem much bolder than men in quickly adopting new fashions which seem to display no continuing evolutionary or gradual developmental stages, although these fashions definitely run in cycles. Modern women's status and functions, however, are of course quite different from those of the average southern squaw. Perhaps in the aboriginal Southeast, important new cultural traits that appeared suddenly and are the criteria for many of our major archaeological period designations were exclusively male interests: new weapons, pyramidal mounds, cult paraphernalia, things adopted by conquered or converted men; while the ladies stayed at home and made pottery that changed only gradually as the generations passed. Or perhaps we might better look at our own china dishware to see an expression of conservatism in spite of almost annual changes in foreign policy, Kinsey attitudes, hemlines, and hairdos. Even the atomic age will probably not change our chinaware, except maybe to break more of it.[12]

If the caution of the new analogy did not curb many, it did inhibit others to the point of not undertaking interpretation at all. In 1948 Taylor's *A Study of Archaeology* confronted New World archaeologists with their hesitancy to venture contextual interpretations. What Taylor did not realize was that to some conscientious archaeologists the strictures on interpretation, at least interpretation by analogy, may have in practice appeared formidable. More importantly, one student has argued that the new analogy is ineffectual in important areas, a second that interpretation by analogy is untenable; a third has abandoned hope of making any impartial judgment of the reasonableness of an archaeological interpretation. It will be instructive to consider these three points of view.

Hawkes perceives several kinds of cognition in archaeology. The distinction between them is marked by the degree to which history can be used in the interpretation of archaeological data. The kind of cognition for which the new analogy must be employed is "a world wholly anterior to textual-historical evidence." In this world, Hawkes contends, interpretation cannot penetrate much beyond technology and subsistence. It is in these very aspects that man, according to Hawkes, is most similar to other animals. Where man is most unlike other animals, for example, in the possession of social, political, and in particular, religious institutions and systems, interpretative tools are near powerless.[13] An extreme position is taken by Smith: "It used to be thought," Smith writes, "that studies of surviving primitive peoples would provide the necessary analogies for

[12] Wauchope 1949:23.
[13] Hawkes 1954:161–62.

interpreting prehistoric societies; but in the event the extension of ethnological studies has only served to show what an incredible variety of codes of behavior in fact actuate human conduct." Given this diversity, to ask for interpretation which utilizes living groups, is to demand "logical alchemy." Statements resulting from interpretations by analogy are assertions, not arguments, according to Smith. Imagine a situation in which at a given site one house structure is larger than all other house structures. If the larger structure is called an X, and not a Y or a Z, where X, Y, and Z refer to uses of a single large structure in living groups, then "You can't really say that you *know* that it is [an X], and if someone criticizes your assertion, it is impossible to produce sufficient evidence to convince him you are necessarily right." Smith finds interpretation by analogy indefensible and argues for its abandonment.[14] A third position is taken by Thompson. He grants primacy to the role of analogy in interpretation but contends that an evaluation of its use in any particular instance can be made only by assessing the competence of the user. Thompson dismally maintains that there is no way to improve this situation other than hoping for "improvements in the methods of measuring the amount of faith we place in an individual's work."[15]

From the foregoing discussion it is apparent that there is no general agreement on the new analogy, either in theory or practice. Certainly a call to abandonment is sufficient cause for discomfort. If it were not for the fact that analogy in archaeological interpretation has suffered chronic ambiguity since the nadir of classical evolutionary simplicity, an impasse could be said to exist. The following suggestions are sketched to aid in placing analogy on a firmer foundation.

1. For any given archaeological situation there usually exists more than a single analogy which can be used in the interpretation of the data. The real problem is to select from this finite range of possible analogs the one which offers the *best solution*. Selection of the best solution is most efficient when the least satisfying solutions are eliminated in a systematic way. Thus, a first elimination may be made on the basis of the economies, a second on the basis of the distances from the archaeological situation to the possible analogs as measured in terms of space, time, and form, and a third elimination may be based on the closeness of fit of the relationships between forms in the archaeological situation with relationships between forms in the hypothesized analogous situations. It may be that archaeologists in seeking analogs work in a systematic manner; but if they do it is seldom evident in the final solutions offered. Consider the following example:

[14] Smith 1955:4–6.
[15] R. H. Thompson 1956:331–32.

In this new soil, which was sticky and grey compared to the loose brown material in which the painted pottery had been deposited, we found polished-stone axes, polished-stone chisels, and flint sickle blades shiny from grain gloss. There was a brief alert when we thought we had come upon a burial, but it was a false alarm. Lying side by side in the soil were two large human thighbones, brown and shiny, polished from much handling. As they were completely alone, they were not part of a burial at all. All I could think of to explain their presence was that the ancient inhabitants of the Canary Islands, who were Neolithic people, had consecrated their kings by holding just such a pair of bones over their heads, and that pairs of thighbones were also used in the rituals of some of the Nilotic tribes of the Sudan. Perhaps the kings of Hotu had been similarly initiated into office. Who knows?[16]

If a systematic approach were used (it is not clear whether or not it was used in the above example), and the alternative solutions for a particular situation stated instead of the usual statement of a single solution (as above), there would be no need to examine credentials (which, in the above case, are extraordinary), but only the argument and the result. There is no touch of alchemy in the procedure outlined. Solutions to any problem are at best approximations arrived at by the elimination of those least likely. Simply, what is being suggested is the introduction of a clear systematic approach and considered statements of results in terms of degrees of likelihood.

2. It has been argued that the existing ethnological literature is inadequate for the purpose of archaeological interpretation because it contains either ideal descriptions of technologies, detailed descriptions without behavioral correlates, or no descriptions of technologies. On this basis it has been proposed that the archaeologist turn to the living community to compile his own inventories.[17] There is no question as to the merit of this suggestion.[18] If the argument which leads to the suggestion is valid, however, then the procedure outlined in section 1 above might be acceptable in theory but not possible in practice. Is the argument valid?

There does exist, as has been emphasized by Kidder and Forde, a rich and suitable literature which is neglected by the archaeologist.[19] The store of information on pottery manufacture and its associated behavior, for example, is copious. A codification of this literature and other similar

---

[16] Coon 1957:186.
[17] Kleindienst and Watson 1956:76–77.
[18] This idea is of course not novel. For an excellent example see D. F. Thompson 1939. Unfortunately most of the studies of this type have been directed at demonstrating that many aspects of a culture are not preserved in archaeological data.
[19] Tax, *et al.* 1953:231–32.

information banks would be useful. There are, further, at least some quantitative models based on ethnographic data which are available and qualitative models can be designed to fit the needs of the archaeologist.[20] Behavioral interpretation, in terms of degrees of likelihood, beyond subsistence-connected activity, is only apparently remote.

3. The past and the present, it is often claimed, serve each other: archaeology depends on ethnographic data for interpretation; ethnology can make use of temporal depth that studies of the past may provide. This dogma, useful as it may be for certain purposes, has contributed to drawing a fast distinction between the ongoing and the extinct, the living and the dead. It is my contention that no clear distinction exists with regard to the material evidence of culture. The point is not trivial, for the generally assumed polarity between the ongoing and the extinct has resulted in the total neglect of striking relevant data.

Every living community is in the process of continuous change with respect to the materials which it utilizes. At any point in its existence some proportion of materials are falling into disuse and decomposing, while new materials are being added as replacement. In a certain sense a part of every community is becoming, but is not yet, archaeological data. The community becomes archaeological data when replacement ceases. What the archaeologist disturbs is not the remains of a once living community, stopped as it were, at a point in time;[21] what he does interrupt is the process of decomposition. The observational fields of ethnology and archaeology overlap on that proportion of a living community which is in the process of transformation. It is the study of this very special corpus of data within the living community which holds the most fruitful promise for analogy in archaeological interpretation.

BIBLIOGRAPHY

Ascher, Robert
1959   "A Prehistoric Population Estimate Using Midden Analysis and Two Population Models." *Southwestern Journal of Anthropology* 15:168–78.
1961   "Function and Prehistoric Art." *Man* 61:73–75.
Childe, V. Gordon
1956   *Piecing Together the Past*. New York.
Clark, J. G. D.
1951   "Folk-Culture and the Study of European Prehistory." In *Aspects of Archæology in Great Britain and Beyond: Essays Presented to O. G. S. Crawford*, W. F. Grimes (ed.), pp. 49–65. London.

[20] For examples of the use of both types of models see Ascher 1959 and 1961.

[21] This erroneous notion, often implicit in archaeological literature, might be called the Pompeii Premise.

1953 "Archaeological Theories and Interpretations: Old World." In *Anthropology Today*, A. L. Kroeber (ed.), pp. 343–60. Chicago.

1954 *Excavations at Star Carr*. Cambridge.

Coon, Carleton S.

1957 *The Seven Caves*. New York.

Dart, Raymond A.

1957 "The Makapansgat Australopithecine Osteodentokeratic Culture." In *Third Pan-African Congress on Prehistory*, J. Desmond Clark and Sonia Cole (eds.), pp. 161–71. London.

Hawkes, Christopher

1954 "Archaeological Theory and Method: Some Suggestions from the Old World." *American Anthropologist* 56:155–68.

Kleindienst, Maxine R., and Patty Jo Watson

1956 " 'Action Archaeology': The Archaeological Inventory of a Living Community." *Anthropology Tomorrow* 5:75–78.

Smith, M. A.

1955 "The Limitations of Inference in Archaeology." *The Archaeological Newsletter* 6:1–7.

Sollas, W. J.

1911 *Ancient Hunters*. London.

Steward, Julian H.

1942 "The Direct Historical Approach to Archaeology." *American Antiquity* 7:337–43.

Tax, Sol, L. C. Eiseley, I. Rouse, C. F. Voegelin, eds.

1953 *An Appraisal of Anthropology Today*. Chicago.

Thompson, Donald F.

1939 "The Seasonal Factor in Human Culture." *Proceedings of the Prehistoric Society* 5:209–21.

Thompson, Raymond H.

1956 "The Subjective Element in Archaeological Inference." *Southwestern Journal of Anthropology* 12:327–32.

Wauchope, Robert

1949 "The Evolution and Persistence of Ceramic Motifs in Northern Georgia." *American Antiquity* 15:16–22.

LEWIS R. BINFORD

*In this companion piece to the preceding article by Ascher,
Lewis Binford discusses how analogy can and should be
used. His article also demonstrates the application of analogy
in a case study situation — smudge pits and their use in
smoking hides. However, Binford extends the limits of
analogy when he writes, "Analogy serves to provide certain
types of questions which can, on investigation, lead to the
recognition of more comprehensive ranges of order in the
archaeological data."*

17   Smudge Pits and Hide Smoking:
The Use of Analogy in
Archaeological Reasoning

The purpose of this paper is twofold: (1) to present a
discussion of analogy and provide an example of the use of analogy in
archaeological reasoning, and (2) to present a functional argument regarding a particular formal class of archaeological feature. The justification
for this type of presentation is a conviction that (a) archaeologists have
generally employed analogy to ethnographic data as a means of
"interpreting" archaeologically observed phenomena, rather than as a means
for provoking new types of investigation into the order observable in
archaeological data. It is the latter role for analogy which is hopefully
exemplified; (b) archaeologists have neglected the formal analysis and
investigation of relationships between classes of archaeological features.
That this situation should be corrected can best be defended by the
demonstration of provocative results obtained through the analysis of
features.

Analogy is the term used to designate a particular type of inferential

Reprinted, with the editorial changes noted, from "Smudge Pits and Hide Smoking: The
Use of Analogy in Archaeological Reasoning" by Lewis R. Binford, *American Antiquity*
32 (1967):1–12, by permission of the author and the publisher.

argument. Thus, in discussing analogy we may profitably consider the criteria employed in judging the relative strength of such an argument regardless of subject matter. Having explored the general characteristics of such arguments, we may turn to a consideration of *anthropological* arguments from analogy, attempting to isolate more general characteristics. Finally, using the conclusions from these two kinds of discussions, we shall offer certain programmatic suggestions which we believe could be profitably followed.

The term *analogy* is defined in Webster's Unabridged Dictionary with the following discussion:

> A relation of likeness, between two things or of one thing to or with another, consisting in the resemblance not of the things themselves, but of two or more attributes, circumstances or effects ...
> Analogy is frequently used to denote similarity or essential resemblance but its specific meaning is a similarity of relations and in this consists the difference between the argument from example and that from analogy. In the former we argue from the mere similarity of two things, in the latter we argue from the similarity of their relations ...
> Biology — correspondence in function between organs of parts of different structures with different origins — distinguishing from homology ...
> Logic — form of inference in which it is reasoned that if two or more things agree with one another in one or more respects they will probably agree in yet other respects. The degree of probability will depend upon the number and importance of their known agreements (Neilson 1956:94).

The crucial or distinctive characteristic common to all the definitions is that an analogy is not strictly a demonstration of formal similarities between entities; rather it is an inferential argument based on implied relationships between demonstrably similar entities. All those arguments which exhibit this form can be studied, and we can ask what characteristics are shared by those arguments which on investigation were verified. [Two] such characteristics have often been found to characterize successful arguments by analogy (these are paraphrased from Stebbing 1961:243–56):

1. *If the initial resemblances are such that the inferred property would account for the resemblances, then the conclusion is more likely to be true.* A good example might be the following argument: (1) A distinctive pattern of wear is observable on the unmodified end of an end scraper recovered from a Magdalenian site in western Europe. (2) The same pattern of wear is observable on the unmodified end of an end scraper hafted in a wooden haft collected from the Plains Indians of North

America. (3) One infers the presence of a functionally similar haft during the period when the archaeologically recovered (Magdalenian) end scraper was in use. The inferred property, the haft, would account for the resemblances in wear observed on both end scrapers. In this case, where it can be said that the inferred relationship or property accounts for the known positive analogy, the positive analogy is said to consist of "important" properties. The term "important" refers to properties which, on the basis of other knowledge or conviction (in this case knowledge regarding the properties resulting from mechanical friction under certain conditions), the posited relationship is said to be justified.

The obvious corollary of the above generalization is that *if the initial resemblances are not such that the inferred property would account for the resemblances, then the conclusion is more likely to be false.* For example, almost any case of attempting to infer specific meaning from an abstract design on an artifact by analogy to a design of known context when there is no demonstrable continuity between the symbolic contexts of the two designs in question would be more likely to be false.

2. *The more comprehensive the positive analogy and the less comprehensive the inferred properties, the more likely the conclusion is true.*

This criterion simply recognizes a major distinction between an argument from example and one from simple enumeration, where a large number of cases sharing limited numbers of attributes are cited, as opposed to an argument from analogy in which a large number of common attributes are cited and the number of cases may be quite small. The more numerous the similarities between analogs, the greater the probability that inferred properties are similar. The corollary of this is: *the more comprehensive the inferred properties, the less likely is the conclusion to be true.* This guide to judging the strength of an argument from analogy rests with the commonsense notion that the more detailed the inference, the more specific must be one's ability to cite the determinants of the positive analogy.

These criteria are derived as arguments from example, since they can be viewed as generalizations from a large sample of arguments by analogy. The incidences of confirmation, as opposed to the incidences of disproof, are tabulated and studied for common properties. In short, these "criteria" are simply a statement of probable outcome generalized from a large sample of cases of reasoning by analogy. They are believed to be independent of the content of particular arguments.

In the examination of anthropological arguments from analogy, we are not concerned with the criteria which will allow us to judge the *form* of a particular argument from analogy as in the previous discussion. Instead, we are concerned with the *content* of the argument. The only guide which I can discover for aiding in this evaluation rests with our previous mention of the citation in an argument of "important" properties. We mean by this properties which, on the basis of other knowledge or conviction, are posited as relevant to the relationship argued. A common situation in which argument from analogy is offered by archaeologists is that in which similarities in form of artifacts are cited between archaeologically and ethnographically observed data, with the proposition that behavior observed in the ethnographic situation (unobserved in the archaeological situation) was also present in the past when the artifacts were in use.

Several persons have addressed themselves to a consideration of the problem of citing "important" properties in argument from analogy and have offered the following suggestions for establishing the conditions of relevance for archaeological arguments from analogy.

1. Relevance can be established by demonstrating, or accepting as demonstrated, that there is a historical continuity between the archaeologically observed unit and the ethnographically cited society or social unit.

2. In the absence of the above demonstrated justification, relevance could be justified by seeking analogies in cultures which manipulate similar environments in similar ways (Ascher 1961).

While certainly not subject to question as such, one wonders at the utility of attempting to specify in the form of suggestions for the "new analogy" all those conditions under which one would expect to find functional linkages between cultural elements. For only with such an exhaustive listing of contemporary anthropological theory and knowledge could one hope to enumerate all of the conditions of relevance which might arise in various anthropological arguments from analogy. Stating this point another way, the only means open to anthropologists attempting to evaluate by inspection any given argument by analogy is in terms of the degree to which the inferred property could be expected to vary concomitantly with the cited features in the positive analogy. Such an evaluation must therefore be made on the basis of our current understanding of the form, structure, and functioning of cultural systems. It is my hope that contemporary understanding goes far beyond the "canon for the selection of analogs" recently advanced (Ascher 1961).

We now turn to the crucial question of the function of arguments from analogy in the broader field of archaeological reasoning. I have chosen to offer one example of such an argument and to attempt an analysis of its form and structural position in a broader logical system of analytical method. Hopefully by such a procedure the formal, functional, and structural characteristics of arguments from analogy in archaeological analytical method will be made explicit.

Previous archaeological reports have occasionally cited the occurrence of small "caches" of carbonized corncobs (Cole 1951:34, 40); yet the specific functions of these small pits have not been previously considered analytically nor has there been any formal analysis of the characteristics common to a number of samples of these "corncob caches." Recent archaeological investigations in the Carlyle Reservoir of south-central Illinois resulted in the excavation of a number of these caches (Binford, Schoenwetter, and Fowler 1964). The recognized formal homogeneity of these features prompted their analysis and systematic description and justification as a distinctive class of feature which, in all probability, had a single function in the activities of the extinct societies represented.

Our procedure here will be: (1) provide a summary of the formal characteristics of this class of cultural feature; (2) document and evaluate the analogy which is demonstrable between this class of feature and certain facilities described ethnographically; (3) offer a postulate as to the function of the archaeological features; (4) develop certain deductively drawn hypotheses that could be investigated to test the probability of the postulates; and (5) cite the procedure employed as an example of a role for analogy in archaeological reasoning which is not believed to be commonly employed among practicing archaeologists.

FORM OF THE FEATURES

The particular cultural features under discussion are best known from the Toothsome site, Clinton County, Illinois, where a total of fifteen such features were excavated and detailed observations were made (Binford, Schoenwetter, and Fowler 1964). Since this sample constitutes the best available data, I will duplicate here the original description of this sample of fifteen features.

The features exhibited so little internal formal variability that there is little doubt that they represent a single type of feature and a single activity. The contents of the pit are always primary and are unaltered by subsequent cultural activity. In addition, the size, shape, and contents of each feature are almost identical to all others included in this category.

Size. These pits are slightly oval, having a mean length of 30.27 cm. and a mean width of 27.40 cm. They extend below the present surface to a mean depth of 33.53 cm.

Shape. All are slightly oval and are generally straight-sided, with essentially flat bottoms.

ELEMENTS OF THE FEATURE

a. Grayish loam soil.
b. Charred and carbonized corncobs.
c. Charred and carbonized twigs (possibly corn stalks).
d. Charred and carbonized bark of an as yet unidentified tree.

e. Charred vegetable material, possibly from other as yet unidentified plants.

f. Occasionally a minor oxidation of soil near the mouth of the pit.

DISTRIBUTION OF THE ELEMENTS

The very bottom of the pit is filled with the charred material for a variable depth of from 7 cm. to within 8 cm. of the mouth of the feature. The charred twigs are generally curled around in the bottom of the pit with the cobs nested in the center. The upper part may be partially filled with the grayish loam soil which was the characteristic soil on the surface of the site. The latter would have *no* included charred material.

GENERAL OBSERVATIONS

The invariable presence of the grayish loam soil in the upper fill demonstrates intentional covering of the pit contents, rather than an accumulative filling with midden and surface debris.

Distribution of These Features on the Site. The pits are distributed peripherally around a small Mississippian farmstead composed of two house structures and one storage structure. In addition to these buildings, the site is internally differentiated into several activity areas, which include outdoor cooking areas and a dump. There is no obvious tendency for these features to cluster; they appear rather well dispersed in a peripheral fashion around the boundary of the site.

Discussion. In the original report on these features it was suggested that they were probably small "smudge pits," since the conditions of combustion which would have resulted in the carbonization of the recovered plant materials would certainly have produced vast quantities of smoke. It was further speculated whether these obvious sources of smoke might have been employed in the control of mosquitoes, which in the experience of the excavators, had constituted a real pest during the summer months.

Possible Occurrence at Other Locations. In addition to the occurrence of these features at the Toothsome site, pits of identical form were observed at a slightly earlier Mississippian farmstead site at the Sandy Tip site in the Carlyle Reservoir (Binford 1964). Later investigations at the Texas #1 site, also in the Carlyle Reservoir, exposed nine additional features of this type (Morrell 1965). The small size of the feature led the investigator to interpret eight of them as postmolds.

> Features 22, 23, 26, and 27; small pits or postmolds filled with charred corncobs. Average diameter .21 meters. A total of nine cob concentrations were located within Unit No. 3, 8 of

which appear to have been postmolds. The cobs are arranged generally in a crescent on the outer edges of the molds, possibly indicating the use of cobs for post tamping and support (Morrell 1965:24–27).

Cutler (1963) suggests that the cobs were broken before they were deposited and probably before they were carbonized. Cutler further suggests that the cobs do not represent a cache of cobs discarded after shelling. Radiocarbon dates were obtained from Features 22 and 23; these are A.D. 1030 ± 85 (GX-0364) and A.D. 1090 ± 100 (GX-0365) respectively (Morrell 1965:24–27).

Small features characterized by the clustering of carbonized corncobs were recently reported from the Lloyd Village site in the American Bottoms near East Saint Louis, Illinois (Hall and Vogel 1963:25–26), and similar features were noted on the nearby Cahokia site (Cutler 1963:16).

The Kincaid site on the Ohio River in southern Illinois, extensively investigated during the 1930s, yielded features which appear to be identical to those described from the Toothsome site. It is interesting that, although they were observed at three different locations on the site (Mx^{v}1D Section I and East Section; Mx^{v}1c), all were in the village area, while none was reported from the mounds so intensively investigated on the site (Cole and others 1951:34, 40, 53, Fig. 3).

Quimby (1957:105) noted the occurrence of "a deposit of fragmentary corncobs that had been burned" in the village deposits under Mounds 1 and 2 at the Bayou Goula site, which is interpreted by Quimby as the remains of a historically known group, closely related to the Natchez, occupying the location between 1700 and 1739.

The archaeological feature of this type believed to be the earliest thus far known is reported from the Williams site, Gordon County, Georgia. This find is described as follows:

> The most important find ... was Feature 7. This was a group of 30 to 40 burnt corn cobs in an area about eight inches in diameter and four inches in depth. . . . Also included mixed in with the cobs was ash, wood, cane and one half of a shelled acorn. No pit was discernible since the group was in the dark brown sand. The cobs were oriented in every conceivable direction and it appears as if the whole unit was thrown into a pit. . . . At 9-Wd-L . . . a group of cobs were found which exhibited evidence of being deposited during a corn planting ceremony. These differed from the Williams Site specimens in being placed in four orderly rows in a specially prepared pit. . . . The Williams Site cache does not give evidence for or against a corn ceremony. However, the cobs were not badly

broken up and some sort of a ceremony would be expected, whether at planting, harvesting, or in between, in a culture concerned with the success of a corn crop. There are many instances of corn ceremonialism in the eastern United States, but they are mainly found in a Mississippian or historical context (Morse and Morse 1960:88).

The Williams site find has been radiocarbon dated at A.D. 470 ± 75 (M-1107, Crane and Griffin 1963:239).

Carbonized corncobs were recovered in two general contexts at the George C. Davis site, Cherokee County, Texas (Newell and Krieger 1949:248–49). Five cases of recovered corncobs are reported from "post-molds" of Structures 31, 8, and 6 respectively, all of which are buildings not constructed on mounds. Three finds were of "caches" of quantities of carbonized cobs similar to those features described from the Toothsome site. Recent radiocarbon dating suggests that these features date at A.D. 1307 ± 150 (M-1186), a period somewhat later than originally proposed (Griffin and Yarnell 1963).

Summarizing our findings, one point is strikingly clear: the geographical distribution of these features is spotty. On sites from the same general geographical provinces, where they are documented, and where one would expect them to have been reported had they been present, there is no suggestion that they were observed. For example, they are absent from sites in the Chickamauga Lake section of the Tennessee River (Lewis and Kneberg 1946); similarly they are unreported from the Norris Basin and the Pickwick Basins of the Tennessee drainage (Webb and DeJarnette 1942; Webb 1938). Moreover, they are not present at the Bessemer site in north-central Alabama (DeJarnette and Wimberly 1941), nor at the Rood's Landing site in Stewart County, Georgia (Caldwell 1955), nor at the Macon Group (Kelly 1938) at Macon, Georgia. The Gordon site also appears to lack these features (Myre 1928). This list of eastern sites apparently lacking the "corncob" features could be greatly expanded. On the other hand, a search of the literature for the Upper Illinois valley and prairie fringe areas as well as for the Great Plains, the Eastern coastal region, the Upper Ohio valley, and the Great Lakes regions failed to yield a single incidence of the "corncob pit." This latter finding is based on my investigation of the context of all the reported incidences of corn which were recently inventoried by Yarnell (1964). In all cases where the context of finds of corn could be determined, it was generally as charred kernels, and, when cobs were reported, they were generally single or in small numbers occurring in the midden fill of recognizable cooking or storage pits.

These investigations suggest that the smudge pits are a feature characteristic of the societies of the Middle and Lower Mississippi River area, with extensions into the Georgia-Creek area to the east and the Texas-Caddo area to the west. The spotty distribution and the lack of data from numbers of sites in this area, however, further suggest that this feature is probably restricted in use to certain limited kinds of activities. This inference is further supported by the documented cases being limited to associations with village house-remains and never with public buildings. Although the functional specificity of the feature may be a major contributor to the spotty distribution of documented examples, my search of the literature made it painfully obvious that archaeologists have neglected the analysis and system-atic description of cultural features, which makes it impossible to assess the degree to which the spotty distribution is a function of events in the past or of the data-collecting techniques and analytical methods employed by archaeologists.

The earliest documented example is from the Williams site in northwest Georgia, A.D. 470 ± 75 (M-1107) where such an early date stands as a unique case. All of the other known examples (if one accepts the revised dating of the George C. Davis site corn) are relatively late, post-dating A.D. 1000. These data suggest that we could reasonably expect the activity in the context of which these features were used to have been practiced by the historically documented groups in the "agricultural east."

There is a variety of functional interpretation offered by investigators who observed these features. At Kincaid they were interpreted as "caches" (Cole and others 1951:156) in spite of the fact that none of the corncobs had kernels attached. Morse and Morse (1960:88) entertain the probability of a "ceremonial" function for the feature. At both the George C. Davis site (Newall and Krieger 1949:248–49) and the Texas site (Morrell 1965) they were interpreted as postmolds, presumably because of their small size. The author (Binford, Schoenwetter, and Fowler 1964) offered the interpretation of a smudge pit, but at that time he could only suggest that the smudge was produced as a means of controlling mosquitoes!

In summary, smudge pits are a class of archaeological features sharing (a) small size, (b) contents composed diagnostically of carbonized corncobs, lacking kernels, and (c) contents exhibiting a primary depositional context. These features are documented from a number of Mississippian sites in the southern Illinois area as well as from sites in the lower reaches of the Mississippi Valley, northern Georgia, and eastern Texas. The context in which the features occur at these sites is invariably that of house areas, as opposed to areas of public buildings, and, in the case of the known farmstead, they are distributed peripherally around the centers of activity within the site. These features are dated as early as A.D. 470; however, the majority are referable to a post-A.D. 1000 time period.

Previous attempts at "interpretation" have shown considerable originality, but all must be considered as conjecture.

RELEVANT ETHNOGRAPHIC OBSERVATIONS

The distinctive form of these features, together with their necessarily limited possible range of uses (all of which must have involved the production of quantities of smoke), made an optimistic search for relevant ethnographic descriptions and references realistic and potentially profitable. The following descriptions from ethnographic accounts were located.

I. Descriptions of the Process of Smoking Hides as Observed among the Southeastern Indians

A. *The Natchez 1700–1750*
According to Swanton (1911:64), Dumont in 1753 said:

> They first dig a hole in the earth about 2 feet deep, with a diameter of six inches at the top and a little less toward the bottom. They fill this hole with cow dung, rotted wood, and maize ears and place it over two rods in the shape of a cross, the four ends of which are slanted in the earth so as to form a kind of cradle on which they stretch the skin they wish to tan. They then set fire to the combustible substance in the hole and fasten the skin down all around by means of many little pegs driven into the ground. Then they cover it with earth over and along the edges, so as to keep in the smoke. The materials in the hole becoming consumed without throwing out the flame, the thick smoke that comes out of it, especially owing to the lack of any exit . . . fastens itself to the skin which it smoke-dries and dyes a yellow color.

B. *The Creek, 1900–1950*

> . . . next, they scooped a hole in the ground, built a fire in it, and put corncobs upon this so that a thick smoke was produced with little flame. The hide was fastened down over this pit with the other surface down and left until it was smoked yellow (Swanton 1946:445).

C. *The Choctaw, 1900–1950*

> If the skins are to be smoked, a process that renders them more durable, a hole a foot or more in depth is dug in which a fire is kept until a bed of hot ashes accumulates. On this are put pieces of rotten oak, no other wood being used for this purpose, these are not permitted to blaze, as the more smoke that arises the better is it for the skins. These already tanned soft and white and perfectly dry, are stretched over the hole and allowed to remain in the smoke an hour or more (Bushnell 1909:11–12).

D. *The Seminole, 1900–1950*

Usually, however, the leather is finished by smoking. The skin is sewed up in a bag-like form and suspended, bottom up from an inclined stick. The edges are pegged down about a small hole in which a smouldering fire burns. The smoke and fumes are allowed to impregnate the hide thoroughly, and then the tanning is completed. . . . (Skinner 1913:72–73).

II. Description of the Process of Smoking Hides as Observed among the Plains Tribes

A. *The Omaha, 1850–1900*

Skins to be used in making moccasins were browned by smoke (Fletcher and La Flesche 1911:345).

B. *The Dacotah (Sioux), 1800–1850*

If after all this working, the skin is hairy or stiff, it is drawn over a cord as large as a finger, for some time, as hard as they can pull, which softens it much: sometimes this is the last process, except smoking. This is done by digging a hole in the ground about a foot deep, putting in a little fire and some rotten wood, when the skin is sewed into a bag and hung over the smoke: in ten minutes the skin is ready for use (Schoolcraft 1856:61).

C. *The Blackfoot, 1850–1900*

The color and finish were imparted by smoking. The skins were spread over a frame similar to that of a sweat house, a hole was dug underneath and a smouldering fire maintained with sage or rotten wood (Wissler 1910:65).

D. *The Crow, 1800–1850*

The greater part of these skins, however, go through still another operation afterwards, which gives them a greater value and renders them much more serviceable — that is, the process of smoking. For this, a small hole is dug in the ground and a fire is built in it with rotten wood, which will produce a great quantity of smoke without much blaze; and several small poles of the proper length stuck in the ground around it and drawn and fastened together at the top, around which the skin is wrapped in form of a tent, and generally sewed together at the edges to secure the smoke within it, within this the skins to be smoked are placed, and in this condition the tent will stand a day or so, enclosing the heated smoke (Catlin 1880:52).

E. *The Arapaho, 1900–1939*

... After it was as soft as she wanted it she dug a hole, about 20 inches deep and about 15 inches in diameter, and built a smudge in it, using either fine chips of wood or bark of cottonwood. She then sewed up the hide to make a sack of it with one end open. She placed this sack over a tipi-shaped framework made of saplings and set this over the smudge. She watched the smudge carefully so there would be no blaze, but only smoke. At the closed end of the sack she had sewed a strip of buckskin with which she tied the sack to the top of the saplings. This held the hide in place. When one side of the hide was sufficiently smoked, the sack was turned inside out and again smoked, thus giving both sides a tan (Hilger 1952:184).

III. *Description of the Process of Smoking Hides as Observed among the Indians of the Great Lakes Region*

A. *Iroquois — General, 1850–1860*

... a smoke is made, and the skin placed over it in such a manner as to inclose it entirely. Each side is smoked in this manner until the pores are closed, and the skin has become thoroughly toughened with its color changed from white to a kind of brown (Morgan 1901:13).

B. *Iroquois — Specifically the Seneca, 1800–1890*

A hole 18 inches in diameter was then made in the ground and the skin suspended above it on upright sticks and smoked until the desired color is produced, by burning rotten wood beneath. The skin was then ready for use (Mason 1891:573).

C. *Ojibwa, 1930–1940*

After the hide was dry the informant removed it from the stretcher, laid it on the ground folding it on head-to-tail line, turned both edges together, and beginning with head end fastened them together by means of clothespins. This made a nearly airtight compartment. In former days edges were sewed together tightly with basswood fiber. The head end of the hide was next fastened to the branch of a tree; the tail end placed so it encircled the rim of a pail of smudge. Two granddaughters ... prepared the smudge by placing bits of birchbark on burning embers fetched from the kitchen stove and packing the remainder of the pail with white pine and Norway cones. Punk was sometimes used in place of cones since it was less inflammable. Jack pine cones were not used. They give an unsatisfactory color.

The worker swung the pail back and forth several times to enhance the smudge and then placed it under the hide, holding it there carefully as to permit the hide to fill with smoke. . . . When it was sufficiently tanned, she loosened the clothespins, turned and folded the edges and again pinned them, she then tanned the reverse side. Smoking not only gave color to hides but preserved them from moths (Hilger 1951:131–32).

D. Menomini, 1900–1920

A hole about a foot wide and six inches deep is dug in the earth in a locality sheltered from the wind, and a slow glowing, smoky fire is made in the bottom of the pit with dead branches, punk, or even dry corn cobs. Over this the inverted bag is suspended and pegged down about the base (Skinner 1921:228).

It is readily observable that two of the documented incidences of the use of corncobs as fuel for smoking hides fall within the distribution as known archaeologically for corncob-filled smudge pits. The single exception, the Menominee, are described as making use of corncobs in the 1920s. It seems reasonable to suggest this might be a relatively recent practice, related to the reservation period rather than to the period of aboriginal adjustment to the northwestern Great Lakes region. This suggestion is further credited by the fact that in all the cases of ethnographic documentation which fall outside of the area of archaeologically known smudge pit distribution, with a single exception, the Choctaw, fuels other than corncobs are cited as being used. This supports the archaeological observations of the absence of corncob-filled smudge pits in the Plains, Great Lakes, and northern Ohio valley. In short, the ethnographic and archaeological distributions of the use of corncobs as fuel in smudge pits are strikingly similar, in spite of obvious lacks in the coverage from both sources.

The correspondence in *form* of smudge pits as known archaeologically and of hide-smoking smudge pits as described ethnographically is essentially perfect. Table 1 presents in summary the comparative information regarding the form of the facilities as known from archaeological and ethnographic sources.

On the basis of (a) the convincing correspondence between the formal attributes of smudge pits as known archaeologically and smudge pits used in smoking hides as known ethnographically, (b) the strong positive analogy between the distribution of smudge pits in which corncobs were used as fuel and the use of corncobs as fuel for smoking hides as documented ethnographically, and (c) the relatively late archaeological documentation for the use of smudge pits, which would make continuity between the archaeological and ethnographic periods reasonable, we postulate that the archaeologically-known features described were in fact facilities employed in the task of

TABLE 1. SMUDGE PIT ATTRIBUTES

Class of Attributes	Archaeologically Observed Attributes	Ethnographically Described Attributes
1. *Size*	Relatively small, shallow excavations in the ground when the facility is a pit.	

	Mean	Range	
Length	30.27 cm.	23.0–42.0 cm.	The cited sizes range from
Width	27.40 cm.	20.2–31.0 cm.	15.24–30.48 cm. (6″–12″) in
Depth	33.53 cm.	25.0–37.1 cm.	diameter and 15.24–60.96 cm. in depth.

Class of Attributes	Archaeologically Observed Attributes	Ethnographically Described Attributes
2. *Contents*	Soft, porous, poorly combustible organic materials. Corncobs, bark, twigs, and possibly cornstalks.	Corncobs, bark, twigs (dead branches), rotten wood, dung, pine cones, and sage.
3. *Treatment of contents*	Contents burned in a reducing atmosphere resulting in the carbonization of the fuels.	Contents burned in a reducing atmosphere resulting in the production of quantities of smoke.
4. *Final condition of the facility*	The facility was abandoned with no disturbance of the carbonized fuels; nothing was removed from the pit, showing that it did not contain the fuels and the items being processed as in the case of roasting pits, fire pits, etc. The archaeological remains of the pit exhibit a primary fill, and secondary fill if present is superimposed.	All the descriptions cite the suspension of the hides over the smudge pit. The items being processed are not contained in the facility with the fuels. Completion of the smoking process and the removal of the hides for use does not result in a disturbance of the contents of the smudge pit.

smoking hides by the former occupants of the archaeological sites on which they were found.

The procedure which should be followed in refuting or increasing the probability of the validity of the proposition would be as follows:

1. Determine if there are any spatial correlates of the activity of smoking hides; in other words, determine if the activity was regularly conducted in any particular location. If so, determine whether or not the smudge pits exhibit such a distribution.

2. Determine if there are any temporal correlates of the activity of smoking hides; was the activity regularly conducted at any particular period of the annual cycle? If so, determine whether or not the smudge pits exhibit such an association with respect to relevant seasonally variable phenomena.

3. Determine if there are any formal correlates of the activity with

respect to other implements or facilities which were employed as parts of a set which also included hide-smoking pits. Was hide smoking normally conducted at the same place and at approximately the same time as the manufacture of clothing from the hides? If so, then there should be demonstrable concomitant variation between the incidence of smudge pits and implements used in clothing manufacture, such as needles.

4. Determine if there are any other activities which employed facilities which shared the same formal attributes as observed in hide-smoking pits. If so, then the specific postulate could be refuted, but a more general one could be stated which could then be tested along the dimensions of time, space, and form.

The following observations are made in the hope that they are pertinent to the formulation of systematic hypotheses:

a. In all the ethnographic cases cited the smoking of hides was women's work; therefore, we would expect stylistic variation in smudge pits to vary directly with stylistic variation in other female-produced items such as ceramics.

b. In all the ethnographic cases cited, when temporal data were given, hide smoking was a spring and summer activity conducted in the "base camp" after the major hunting season was concluded and before the winter hunts were begun. We therefore offer the following hypothesis: Smudge pits should occur almost exclusively in "base camps" occupied during the period of the year when hunting activity was at a minimum.

c. In many cases there were indications in the ethnographic literature that hide smoking and the related manufacture of clothing from smoked hides were activities which would be more frequently performed by individuals possessing recognized skills in these tasks. Therefore, the incidence of smudge pits might be expected to vary independently of the number of persons occupying the appropriate site for any given unit of time. In short, they would be expected to vary independently of such direct measures of the number and duration of occupants as cooking-fires and sleeping facilities.

Aside from these interesting and potentially informative avenues for future research, I think it is necessary to point out another and as yet unmentioned potential source of additional understanding; namely, that the survey of ethnographic literature demonstrated that the practice of smoking hides, particularly deer hides, for use in the manufacture of moccasins, shirts, and leggings, was a practice common to most, if not all, of North America. The major characteristic which appeared to vary from region to region was the fuel used in the smudge pits, as well as the idiosyncracies of construction for suspension of hides over the smudge pit. Our investigations have been limited to the citation of archaeological remains in which corncobs were the fuel. An acquaintance with the general range of size of the feature and with the depth of it can be extremely beneficial. The size appears to be limited by the circumference of a deer skin when sewn into a "bag"; the depth seems to be limited by two general considerations: (a) deep enough to provide an oxygen-starved environment; (b) shallow enough to contain only a limited amount of fuel. This knowledge, along with an acquaintance with the generic class of fuel, and the probability that the contents would not be disturbed (resulting in the archaeological recovery of fairly complete carbonized fragments of soft spongy fuels), enables the recall of numerous examples of features observed on sites from the east coast, the Great Lakes, and the pre-Mississippian occupations in central Illinois which were almost certainly smudge pits in which fuels other than corncobs had been burned.

Our investigations have resulted in the recognition of a generic class of facility which can be expected to vary regionally with respect to the specifics of its contents. This recognition could aid in the documentation of seasonally variable activities in the areas of less aboriginal sedentism, such as the Great Lakes.

The final consideration to be taken up is the degree to which this study can be cited as an example of the use of analogy in archaeological argument and its pertinence to general statements regarding the role of analogy in archaeological reasoning.

The logical steps followed in this argument were as follows:

A. *The Analogy.* 1. The recognition and demonstration of a positive formal analogy between a class of archaeologically observed phenomena and a class of ethnographically observed phenomena.

2. A consideration of the positive analogy between the spatial distribution of the facility as documented archaeologically and ethnographically, and the observation that, although poorly documented, the known distributions show a strong positive analogy.

3. A consideration of the degree to which it would be reasonable to expect a continuity between the archaeologically and ethnographically known cases; for example, the dating of the archaeologically known materials as reasonably viewed as cases of historical priority to the ethnographic data.

B. *The Postulate.* 1. The behavioral context of the use of the archaeologically known features was the same as that described ethnographically for the analogous facilities.

C. *The Development of Testable Hypotheses in a Deductive Framework Given the Postulate Offered.* 1. An examination of the ethnographic "context" of the activity for correlated formal characteristics which could be directly observed or studied archaeologically.

2. Given the postulate set forth in B (1) above and the knowledge of the formal, spatial, and temporal correlates of the activity designated in the postulate, the specification of a number of hypotheses as to the predicted mode of variation expected between the archaeologically observed analog and other archaeologically observable phenomena as specified by the studies of C (1) above.

3. The testing of the stated hypotheses and the refutation, refinement, or verification in probabilistic terms of the truth of the stated postulate.

D. Finally this particular procedure should lead the investigator into the recognition of previously unrecognized relationships as suggested in C (1): the explanation of previously unexplained variation in archaeological data as the outcome of C and, as in the case of this particular example, the recognition of a generic class of phenomena definable by certain general formal characteristics where previously only a restricted class was recognized, isolated by the common occurrence of specific formal similarities (for example, charred corncobs).

CONCLUSIONS

The procedure discussed here is appropriate in the context of a positivistic philosophy of anthropology and archaeology. It denies categorically the assertion of antipositivists that the final judgment of archaeological reconstruction must be based on an appraisal of the professional competence of the archaeologist (Thompson 1956:331). The final judgment of the archaeological reconstruction presented here must rest with testing through subsidiary hypotheses drawn deductively. Questions were also raised concerning the argument made by Robert Ascher (1961) that by following certain of his suggestions for "placing analogy on a firmer foundation" we could in any way directly increase our knowledge of archaeologically documented societies. The arguments presented by Ascher (1961), if followed, could at best serve to increase our understanding of archaeological observations in terms of ethnographically described situations. The archaeologist would be performing a role analogous to that of a historical critic who attempts to translate data of the past into the context of relatively contemporary or culturally prescribed experience. It is maintained here that as anthropologists we have a task quite different; we seek to explain cultural differences and similarities. We approach our task by developing methods and procedures that will permit us to demonstrate order in our data. It is assumed that the demonstration of order implies a set of systematic relationships among cultural phenomena that existed in the past. The understanding of the operation of systems rests in the measurement of concomitant variation between various classes of ordered phenomena and the eventual statement of general laws of cultural variability.

The role of analogy in this process has hopefully been demonstrated in this particular example. Analogy serves to provoke certain types of questions which can, on investigation, lead to the recognition of more comprehensive ranges of order in the archaeological data. In short, we ask questions about the relationships between types of archaeologically observable phenomena that had possibly not been placed in juxtaposition or viewed as orderly. In doing so we can develop a common "explanation" for observed variability in a number of formally independent classes of archaeological data, and thereby we can approach more closely the isolation of systematic variables which operated in the past. It should be pointed out that these gains may obtain regardless of whether the original analogy led to a correct postulate. In short, I do not view interpretations, or syntheses of interpretations as an end product of our investigations; on the contrary, we should be seeking generalizations regarding the operation of cultural systems and their evolution — something which has not been described ethnographically nor thus far achieved through the observation and analysis of contemporary events.

BIBLIOGRAPHY

Ascher, Robert
    1961   "Analogy in Archaeological Interpretation." *Southwestern Journal of Anthropology* 17:317–25.

Binford, Lewis R.
    1964   The Sandy Tip Site; Carlyle Reservoir. Manuscript at University of California, Los Angeles.
    ———, James Schoenwetter, and M. L. Fowler
    1964   "Archaeological Investigations in the Carlyle Reservoir." *Southern Illinois University Museum, Archaeological Salvage Report*, no. 17, pp. 1–117.

Bushnell, David I., Jr.
    1909   "The Choctaw of Bayou Lacomb, St. Tammany Parish, Louisiana." *Bureau of American Ethnology, Bulletin* 48.

Caldwell, Joseph R.
    1955   "Investigations at Rood's Landing, Stewart Co., Georgia." *Early Georgia* 2, no. 1:22–49.

Catlin, George
    1880   *North American Indians* 1:52. Piccadilly, London: Egyptian Hall.

Cole, Fay-Cooper, and others
    1951   *Kincaid, A Prehistoric Illinois Metropolis*. Chicago: University of Chicago Press.

Crane, H. R., and J. B. Griffin
   1963   "University of Michigan Radiocarbon Dates VIII."
          Radiocarbon 5:228–53.
Cutler, Hugh C.
   1963   "Identification of Plant Remains." In *Second Annual
          Report: American Bottoms Archaeology*, Melvin L.
          Fowler (ed.), pp. 16–18. Urbana: Illinois Archaeologi-
          cal Survey.
DeJarnette, David L., and Steve B. Wimberly
   1941   "The Bessemer Site. Excavation of Three Mounds and
          Surrounding Village Areas near Bessemer, Alabama."
          Geological Survey of Alabama, Museum Paper 17.
          University: University of Alabama.
Fletcher, Alice C., and Francis LaFlesche
   1911   "The Omaha Tribe." *Twenty-seventh Annual Report
          of the Bureau of American Ethnology*, pp. 15–655.
Griffin, James B., and Richard A. Yarnell
   1963   "A New Radiocarbon Date on Corn from the Davis
          Site, Cherokee County, Texas." *American Antiquity*
          28, no. 3:396–97.
Hall, Robert L., and Joseph O. Vogel
   1963   "Illinois State Museum Projects." In *Second Annual
          Report: American Bottoms Archaeology*, Melvin L.
          Fowler (ed.), pp. 24–31. Urbana: Illinois Archaeologi-
          cal Survey.
Hilger, Sister M. Inez
   1951   "Chippewa Child Life and Its Cultural Background."
          Bureau of American Ethnology, Bulletin 146.
   1952   "Arapaho Child Life and Its Cultural Background."
          Bureau of American Ethnology, Bulletin 148.
Kelly, A. R.
   1938   "A Preliminary Report on Archaeological Explorations
          at Macon, Georgia." *Bureau of American Ethnology,
          Bulletin* 119, pp. 1–68.
Lewis, Thomas M. N., and Madeline Kneberg
   1946   *Hiwassee Island, an Archaeological Account of Four
          Tennessee Indian Peoples.* Knoxville: University of
          Tennessee Press.
Mason, Otis T.
   1891   "Aboriginal Skin Dressing; A Study Based on Material
          in the U.S. National Museum." *Report of the
          National Museum*, 1888–1889, pp. 553–89. Washing-
          ton: Smithsonian Institution.
Morgan, Lewis H.
   1901   *League of the Ho-De-No-Sau-Nee or Iroquois* 2:13
          New York: Dodd, Mead & Co.

Morrell, L. Ross
1965 "The Texas Site, Carlyle Reservoir." *Southern Illinois University Museum, Archaeological Salvage Report,* no. 23.
Morse, Dan, and Phyllis Morse
1960 "A Preliminary Report on 9-Go-507: The Williams Site, Gordon County, Georgia." *Florida Anthropologist* 8, no. 4:81–91.
Myre, William Edward
1928 "Two Prehistoric Villages in Middle Tennessee." *Forty-first Annual Report of the Bureau of American Ethnology,* pp. 485–626.
Neilson, W. A., ed.
1956 *Webster's New International Dictionary of the English Language.* 2nd ed., unabridged. Springfield, Mass.: G. & C. Merriam Co.
Newell, H. Perry, and Alex D. Krieger
1949 "The George C. Davis Site, Cherokee County, Texas." *Memoirs of the Society for American Archaeology,* no. 5.
Quimby, George I.
1957 "The Bayou Goula Site, Iberville Parish, Louisiana." *Fieldiana: Anthropology* 47, no. 2:97–170. Chicago: Chicago Natural History Museum.
Schoolcraft, H. R.
1856 *Indian Tribes of the United States,* pt. IV, p. 61. Philadelphia: J. B. Lippincott and Co.
Skinner, Alanson
1913 "Notes on the Florida Seminole." *American Anthropologist,* n.s. 15:63–77.
1921 "Material Culture of the Menomini." *Indian Notes and Monographs, Miscellaneous* no. 20, F. W. Hodge (ed.), p. 228. New York: Museum of the American Indian, Heye Foundation.
Stebbing, L. Susan
1961 *A Modern Introduction to Logic.* New York: Harper Torchbooks Edition, Harper and Brothers.
Swanton, John R.
1911 "Indian Tribes of the Lower Mississippi Valley and Adjacent Coast of the Gulf of Mexico." *Bureau of American Ethnology, Bulletin* 43.
1946 "The Indians of the Southeastern United States." *Bureau of American Ethnology, Bulletin* 137.
Thompson, Raymond H.
1956 "The Subjective Element in Archaeological Inference." *Southwestern Journal of Anthropology* 12, no. 3:327–32.

Webb, William
    1938   "An Archaeological Survey of the Norris Basin in Eastern Tennessee." *Bureau of American Ethnology, Bulletin* 118.

————, and David DeJarnette
    1942   "An Archaeological Survey of Pickwick Basin in the Adjacent Portions of the States of Alabama, Mississippi and Tennessee." *Bureau of American Ethnology, Bulletin* 129.

Wissler, Clark
    1910   "Material Culture of the Blackfoot Indians." *Anthropological Papers of the American Museum of Natural History*, vol. 5, pt. 1.

Yarnell, Richard Asa
    1964   "Aboriginal Relationships between Culture and Plant Life in the Upper Great Lakes Region." *Anthropological Papers, Museum of Anthropology*, no. 23. Ann Arbor: University of Michigan.

KWANG-CHIH CHANG

Settlement archaeology, the study of whole communities and their patterning on the landscape, has received wide attention in the past decade. While the study of artifacts gives many insights concerning the makers of the objects and the small social groups which used them, the physical patterning of communities, where it can be determined archaeologically, reveals something about past societies that artifacts alone cannot. Kwang-Chih Chang's article on social groupings is essentially an example of settlement archaeology because it considers the form of prehistoric settlements, but it also illustrates the use of analogy. In his study of Neolithic social groupings, large samples of data from archaeological and ethnographic contexts are employed. Chang examines material patterning in both contexts and only then seeks possible correlations within the ethnographic context and tries to see if these correlations approximately fit in with the archaeological data. While the problems inherent in such an approach are considerable, Chang shows that it can be a fruitful route to more detailed explanation.

18 Study of the Neolithic Social Grouping: Examples from the New World

INTRODUCTION

The difficult task of reconstructing the social organization of the inhabitants of archaeological sites has often been carelessly done. The reconstructions are sometimes no more than surmises made from an archaeologist's common-sense point of view. To be sure, some operational suggestions have appeared, but they are too general to allow more than

Reproduced by permission of the author and the American Anthropological Association from the *American Anthropologist*: Vol. 60, 1958, pp. 298–334. References and bibliography are omitted, and footnotes are renumbered.

inferences, and much of the work still depends upon the archaeologist's insight.

In recent years, New World archaeologists have made some remarkable progress toward understanding various aspects of archaeologically known societies in population, industrial specialization, and settlement pattern. Perhaps it is time to work out an outline of objective procedure which will allow the archaeological skeleton to regain its ethnological flesh and blood. This is a big order, inasmuch as analogies between prehistoric institutions and a single or a limited number of contemporary societies are dangerous, so that one must engage in a worldwide cross-cultural survey, tackling numerous works on primitive societies.

Nevertheless, the present paper attempts to demonstrate that a work of this kind is both possible and necessary. I will narrow my scope to the Neolithic period/stage, and to the single topic of social grouping. First, I shall make a small-scale survey of the literature, trying to find some correlation between the settlement pattern of a dwelling site and the social grouping of its occupants. To test the validity of the correlation and give examples of the operation, I shall then examine New World Neolithic societies in three regions: Mesoamerica, Peru, and Southwest. The period in question has been variously termed the Formative, the Archaic, the Developmental, the Middle Culture, and so forth, and has been defined as "a time of technological progress ... [when] the village community was the basis of the social and political order." I choose to use the term "Neolithic" because it already has an established meaning in Old World archaeology which refers both to an economic stage (agricultural) and to a time horizon (prior to the urbanization in a given area).

RECONSTRUCTING NEOLITHIC SOCIAL GROUPING

The concept of settlement pattern has aroused keen interest among contemporary American archaeologists and considerable effort has been concentrated upon it, but it should perhaps be clarified. "Settlement" was originally a geographic concept, and the geographers have long been concerned with the type and distribution of settlements in relation to physiographic environs. The type and distribution of human settlements, as well as their social and physical determinants, have also been a topic of archaeological interest, receiving occasional attention since the end of last century. These early interests were not crystallized into a purposeful pursuit, in the New World at least, until 1948 when the Institute of Andean Research began its monumental Settlement Patterns Project in the Virú Valley, Peru. Today, after ten years of work, the settlement pattern study has become one of the major goals of the American archaeologists, and the concept itself has begun to take shape. In his *An Appraisal of "Prehistoric*

Settlement Patterns in the New World," Vogt defines the term in the following manner:

> If the concept of settlement pattern is focused upon the patterned manner in which household and community units are arranged spatially over the landscape, one may raise the question as to whether the concept should or should not include an ecological dimension. There is perhaps a certain logical neatness in restricting the use of the concept to sheer spatial arrangements and then proceeding to make three kinds of analysis: one which explores the relationships of living arrangements to geographical features, such as topography, soils, vegetation types, or rainfall zones; a second which focuses upon the social structural inferences that can be made about sociopolitical and ceremonial organization; and a third which concentrates upon the study of change through time with a view to providing materials for generalizing about cultural processes. However, I would not seriously quarrel with the view that the concept of settlement pattern should include the ecological dimension at the outset and thereby provide the basis for the other two types of analysis.

Vogt's statement, cautious as it seems, nevertheless raises two problems of fundamental importance. First, he seems to have overburdened the term. Because of its derivation from human geography, the term "settlement pattern" is implicitly associated with the physiography-settlement relationship; however, this is the subject of Vogt's first analysis only. It seems advisable to use the term "community pattern" in connection with his second analysis and to reserve settlement pattern exclusively for his first. More specifically, I should like to propose the following definitions: (1) Settlement pattern: the manner in which human settlements are arranged over the landscape in relation to physiographic environment. (2) Community pattern:[1] the manner in which the inhabitants arrange their various structures within the community and their communities within the aggregate.

The second question Vogt's paragraph raises is that of the factors which determine the patterns of settlement and community. Only after we have learned what these factors are can we judge the dimensions of the concept in question and the proper order for studying them.

As the present paper is concerned only with Neolithic society, the approach must include: (1) an assumption (which gives our community pattern-social grouping correlation study a conceptual starting-point) of possible determinants of the community pattern of Neolithic societies, and (2) correlation of community pattern and social grouping in a manner

---

[1] The term "community pattern" here must not be confused with that of Beardsley, *et al.* (1956), which is defined as "an organization of interrelationships."

applicable to archaeological use on a number of selected ethnographically recorded societies at a strictly "Neolithic" level.

The impression given by many students is that the settlement pattern (in the old sense) of agricultural societies is determined primarily by physical factors such as topography, climate, agricultural potentials, and so forth. If my distinction between settlement pattern and community pattern is accepted, this problem should of course be viewed from a different perspective. The studies of the Commission de l'Habitat Rural presented to the Geographical Congresses of 1925 (Cairo), 1928 (Cambridge), 1931 (Paris), 1934 (Warsaw), and 1938 (Amsterdam) established that "within the limits of the physically possible the type and distribution of habitat is mainly dependent on the type of rural economy and the stage of its development." On the strength of these works and others I am led to believe that the economic adjustment of a Neolithic community is the primary determinant of its community patterning, though I would not deny that historical derivation, warfare, and cultural beliefs and values might have played limited roles. It is reasonable to say that the economic condition of a Neolithic community determines its community type through the medium of land ownership, which controls the patterned manner in which the land is divided and plotted with dwelling and other houses.

Land ownership is important in being both the medium of economic condition and community pattern on the one hand, and that of kinship grouping and local grouping on the other. In their study *Local Grouping in Melanesia*, Hogbin and Wedgwood have made the following premise:

> The groups which are politically significant all have their roots in land, and as rights to land are determined by descent, we shall be concerned with the way in which local organization and kinship organization interlock and strengthen each other.

After an exhaustive examination of the local organization-kinship organization interlocking in native Melanesia, the authors observe that:

> It will be clear that a full understanding of the social life of any Melanesian people requires study of the kinship organization, the local organization, and the way in which the two are interlocked. There appear to be certain common patterns of interlocking.

"Common patterns of interlocking" are not limited to Melanesia, but appear to be universal. I have examined contemporary "Neolithic" societies for evidences of this interlocking pattern, and have obtained substantial results. The societies selected for this category must be (1) horticultural or agricultural, (2) unurbanized and relatively untouched by urban societies or great religious centers, and (3) comparatively stabilized within a defined area for a considerable length of time. All other features such as natural setting, kind of crops, and the relativity of cultural achievements are secondary. Thus, there are four areas in the world where our samples might exist: West Africa, Southeast Asia (minus urban centers), Melanesia, and the Tropical Forest of South America. The following fifty-three societies were selected because the sources are easily accessible:

West Africa:

Ashanti	Ibo	Yakö
Dahomean	Tallensi	Yoruba

Southeast Asia:

Alorese	Kachin	Puyuma
Angami	Lamet	Rengma
Ao	Land Dyak	Sema
Atayal	Lhota	Siang Dyak
Bontok Igorot	Lushai Chin	Thao
Chala'abus Paiwan	Naga of Manipur	

Melanesia:

Arapesh	Iatmül	Malekula
Banaro	Kiwai	Ngarawapum
Dobu	Kuanua	Siuai
Eastern Solomon	Kuman	Solomon Islanders
Islanders	Kwoma	in San Cristoval
Solomon Islanders in	Lesu	Trobriand Islanders
Guadalcanal		

South America (mainly Tropical Forest):

Achagua	Cubeo	Tupian of Upper
Boro	Guaraní	Amazon
Canella	Patangoro	Tupi-Cawahib
Carib	Peban	Tupinamba
Cayapa	Tenetehara	Witoto

These societies represent a great percentage of the recorded existing Neolithic-type societies and the results of their comparison are, I believe, sufficient for this preliminary study.

In modifying the existing categorization of local groups, I will classify them into three categories, *household, community,* and *aggregate* of communities,[2] and discuss the community pattern-local group/kinship group correlations under these headings. The following outline is part of the result of the cross-cultural survey, and also a suggested methodological

---

[2] I am indebted to Green for his suggestion of using the term "aggregate."

procedure for an archaeological reconstruction of Neolithic social grouping according to the community patterning.

1. The Household

Spatial Identification. In the overwhelming majority of cases the household is easily recognizable spatially. It is usually represented by a house, spatially separated from other houses, which consists of several functionally distinct rooms — living rooms, workshops, storage rooms or granaries, and a kitchen. The material equipment, once its functions are recognized, points to the structure's role as a shelter for a basic living unit. Among some of the Southeast Asiatic aborigines (e.g., Dyaks), New Guinea Melanesians (e.g., Kiwai), and many South American Tropical Forest dwellers (e.g., Achagua, Boro, Cubeo, Guaraní, Peban, Tupinamba, Witoto), a large communal building shelters dozens or even hundreds of inhabitants. In all cases, the separate rooms inside this large building all intercommunicate. However, the individual household is still the basic unit, and sometimes (e.g., in the Dyaks) each unit has its own living compartment and is responsible for its construction and repair. A household in a communal building can be distinguished by (1) interpreting the use of equipment and furniture; (2) distinguishing the partitions separating neighboring households; and (3) finding a separate kitchen or fireplace for cooking. The kitchen or fireplace is the most obvious index of a household, which is by virtue a commensal unit. Among the Dahomeans in West Africa, a household consists of a cluster of houses centering on a court, enclosed by a wattle fence or a mud wall. At first glance such a house-compound could easily be conceived as a hamlet consisting of several households, but closer examination reveals that it is the compound rather than each house which has storehouses, stalls for animals, a fetish hut, and, above all, a kitchen or cookhouse. The separate living houses, functionally not self-contained, are merely the residences of the co-wives in a polygynous family. However, such deceptive cases are rare.

Functions and Symbolic Aspects. As mentioned above, the household is universally a commensal and cohabiting unit, and sometimes a unit of education, economic cooperation, and ownership. In addition, religious rites are sometimes performed by and/or on behalf of the household members. Most of these household functions are symbolized by certain material equipment, technological or religious paraphernalia, and special structures; such objects and structures, properly interpreted, therefore point unmistakably to the functions of the households.

In our sample, related households often constitute a neighborhood in the community. A household may specialize in certain industrial or religious functions within the neighborhood or among other neighborhoods, and this specialization may also be recognized by functional interpretation of material objects.

Composition. A household is composed of a nuclear family, a polygamous family, or an extended family, sometimes with the addition of adopted children and others. It is possible, with care, to ascertain the composition of a household from the tangible remains of the house. In a strictly Neolithic society, the size of a house usually coincides with the size of the household, except for those of a few privileged persons such as chiefs and priests. Households composed of nuclear families can often be distinguished when (1) the space is appropriately small, (2) the equipment and furniture are sufficient for only a few people, or (3) the household resides in a communal house. Households composed of extended families can often be recognized when (1) the space is appropriately large, (2) the equipment and furniture are sufficient for more than a few people, or (3) the houses in the community vary in size and richness of material content to such an extent that the range of variety goes beyond that allowed for families. In addition, household composition is correlated with the total kinship system in a way which will be discussed latter.

2. The Community

Spatial Identification. The community is "the maximal group of persons who normally reside together in face-to-face association." "Every member is ordinarily acquainted more or less intimately with every other member, and has learned through assocation to adapt his behavior to that of each of his fellows, so that the group is bound together by a complex network of interpersonal relationships." Therefore, a community is "a subjective but self-sufficient group united by a consciousness of kind; it is 'essentially a center of feeling.' "

It is not impossible to detect this "feeling" merely from the physical appearance of a community, because the "consciousness of kind" is substantiated by a "network of interpersonal relationships" in economic cooperation, political organization, and religious specialization, all of them susceptible to functional interpretation using material objects and buildings. Most of our samples show a community with a well defined territory, a certain number of dwelling houses, a chief's lodge (often distinguished by its unusual dimensions and elaboration of structure), a community temple (often distinguished by the special structures inside), a communal locality (a plaza, a dancing ground, a sacred area, a men's house), and other special structures such as the Naga's village drums and the lookouts. All these can show the nature of the inhabitants' face-to-face interrelationships and hence the extent of functional self-sufficiency.

The spatial recognition of a community might be difficult where isolated houses or house-clusters are contiguously distributed over a wide area and show no clearly marked limits, but this has not been the case in any of the societies in our sample. Identification is always possible, due both to the spatial evidences (marked by an enclosure in a few cases) and the functional network. Archaeologically, however, this might be difficult where communities moved frequently and when a wide area is covered by house-remains left over a long period. This might occur in areas where vegetation was thick and slash-and-burn agriculture was practiced. When it does occur, nothing can be achieved until the house-remains are carefully cross-dated.

Functions and Symbolic Aspects. A Neolithic community is often self-contained in performing its economic, political and military, and religious and ceremonial roles. Our samples show that these roles and their interrelationships are usually symbolized by some tangible objects. However, the extent of solidarity and social independence of communities often varies with their kinship relational composition. For example, a monolineage community is never socially independent, and many of the religious and ceremonial functions in a multilineage community center around the separate lineages instead of the community as a whole. This aspect will be better understood after we have dealt with the composition of the community.

Composition: Face-to-Face Relational. The physical aspect of the face-to-face relational composition of a community refers to the spatial arrangement of households and functionally specialized buildings and objects. Theoretically, face-to-face relationships involve individuals, and the interlocking pattern of individual activities often does not (as in cases of age-grade systems, men's clubs, secret societies) coincide with the interlocking pattern of household activities. Operationally, however, we can only start from the latter; I have not been able to find a way to correlate the individuals with either the households or the lineages in a consistently patterned manner.

According to the face-to-face relational composition, communities in our sample societies can be grouped into the following types:

1. *Homesteads.* A community of this type consists of households located at or near the fields which their members till; its territory is wide and the households scattered. In our sample this type of community occurs only among the Cayapa.

2. *Village.* A community of this type consists of households or household clusters so situated that their members have to walk a considerable distance to their fields; provisional farming shelters are not uncommon. The remaining fifty-two societies in our sample have communities of this type. It can be divided into three subtypes: (2a) *Unplanned Village,* within which households are arranged irregularly, that is, do not follow any preconceived plan. Communities of this type are found among the Atayal, Eastern Solomon Islanders, Kachin, Lamet, Naga of Manipur, Patangoro, Siuai, and Thao.

(2b) *Planned Village,* within which households and special buildings are arranged regularly according to a preconceived plan. Only those villages where there is but one such planned unit are assigned to this subtype, and a communal house is considered a planned unit. Planned villages are found among the Banaro, Boro, Carib, Dobu, Kuman, Malekula, Peban, Trobriand Islanders, Tupi-Cawahib, and Witoto. (2c) *Segmented Village,* within which households are arranged in groups which form segments of the community or subdivisions of a segment. Ordinarily there is only one segmentation. When there are more, one is more important than the others. Within the smallest segment, the households may or may not be aranged according to a preconceived plan (or in a communal house). Communities found in the following thirty-four societies belong to this subtype: Achagua, Alorese, Angami, Ao, Arapesh, Ashanti, Bontok Igorot, Canella, Chala'abus Paiwan, Cubeo, Dahomean, Solomon Islanders in Guadalcanal, Guaraní, Iatmül, Ibo, Kiwai, Kuanua, Kwoman, Land Dyak, Lesu, Lhota, Lushai Chin, Ngarawapum, Puyuma, Rengma, Solomon Islanders in San Cristoval, Sema, Siang Dyak, Tallensi, Tenetehara, Tupian of Upper Amazon, Tupinamba, Yakö, Yoruba.

Composition: Kinship Relational. The kinship relational composition of a community also cuts across the face-to-face relational composition and therefore is not revealed by the tangible remains of a community, but there appear to be certain patterned correlations between the two categories. In order to seek the kinship relational composition of a community in its material manifestation, and to take greater advantage of the patterned correlations, I propose the following simplified classification of communities according to their kinship relational composition: (1) *Nonlineage Communities,* where a lineage system does not appear and descent tends to be bilateral. Societies which possess communities of this kind are the Cayapa, Eastern Solomon Islanders, Land Dyak, and Siang Dyak. (2) *Monolineage Communities,* where each community is composed of a single lineage which is either independent for a localized section of a widespread lineage or sib. The following societies have communities of this type: Banaro, Boro, Carib, Dobu, Kuman, Malekula, Peban, Trobriand Islanders, Tupi-Cawahib, and Witoto. (3) *Multilineage Communities,* where each community is composed of two or more lineages. Within such a community, the lineages may be intermingled spatially or each may occupy a separate section. In a few cases, all of the lineages belong to the same sib, but more often they belong to two or more sibs which are either localized in this area or are widespread. Communities of the following societies are included: Achagua, Alorese, Angami, Ao, Arapesh, Ashanti, Atayal, Bontok Igorot, Canella, Chala'abus Paiwan, Cubeo, Dahomean, Solomon Islanders in Guadalcanal, Guaraní, Iatmül, Ibo, Kachin, Kiwai, Kuanua, Kwoma, Lamet, Lesu, Lhota, Lushai

Chin, Naga of Manipur, Ngarawapum, Patangoro, Puyuma, Rengma, Solomon Islanders in San Cristoval, Sema, Siuai, Tallensi, Tenetehara, Thao, Tupian of Upper Amazon, Tupinamba, Yakö, Yoruba.

Patterned Correlations of House Grouping and Kinship Grouping. The overwhelming majority of our "Neolithic" societies have lineage communities arranged in agglomerated villages. The patterned correlations of the various types and subtypes of the local grouping and the kinship grouping are shown in Table 1.

TABLE 1. RELATION BETWEEN COMMUNITY
PATTERNS AND KINSHIP COMPOSITION

	Non-lineage	Mono-lineage	Multi-lineage	Total
Homesteads	1	—	—	1
Unplanned Villages	1	—	7	8
Planned Villages	—	10	—	10
Segmented Villages	2	—	32	34
Total	4	10	39	53

This table needs the following supplementary notes:

a. Homesteads. The homestead pattern, seen frequently in the rural districts of urban societies, seems extremely rare in societies of Neolithic level. Our only sample of this type is the Cayapa of Ecuador, who form an enclave in the Andean civilization and whose strictly "Neolithic" nature is hence questionable. Nevertheless this pattern could occur among more primitive societies outside of our sample (e.g., in Enga of New Guinea), one cannot deny the possibility of its occurrence in the Neolithic society. If it should occur, it is likely to be composed of nonlineage kinship groups or lineages in the process of weakening.

b. Unplanned Village. The unplanned village is arranged at random and often varies greatly in size even within the same tribe, but it is by no means a loosely joined unit. The buildings are often agglomerated; a chief's lodge (Eastern Solomon Islanders), a communal house (Lamet) or the like usually stands in a prominent place, marking the nucleus of the irregularly scattered houses. Seven of our eight samples which show this pattern are composed of members of two or more lineages which belong to separate sibs but are mingled spatially; the remaining one is bilateral in descent. It is therefore reasonable to assume that the unplanned village pattern tends to indicate the existence in a community of more than one lineage; moreover, they are intracommunity non-localized and belong to widespread sibs. When lineage structure does not exist, bilateral structure seems to take its place.

c. Planned Village. A planned village is usually small, consisting of a few independent houses arranged according to a preconceived plan. It is a single planned unit, often composed of houses arranged in a circle around a small plaza which sometimes contains a men's house or the chief's house. When a community consists of a single communal house, we classify it as a planned village because the individual compartments are often situated around the wall, and the center is left free to function as a plaza. The rear of the house is sometimes reserved for the chief.

3. The Aggregate of Communities

By aggregate I mean a gathering of a certain number of communities which are bound by close social, political, military, commercial, or religious ties. Although few Neolithic communities are really isolated from each other, they are relatively self-sufficient and the aggregate is not a regular feature. When it exists, it is usually not rigidly integrated territorially or functionally, and the intercommunity ties are largely political or commercial. A community seldom belongs to more than one aggregate, since aggregates seldom specialize functionally. For our purposes, it is sufficient to note: (1) the territorial dimension and the nature of the aggregate, (2) the political, industrial, and ceremonial roles of the respective communities within the aggregate, and (3) the seat of political authority, the marketplace, and the ceremonial center. All of these may be ascertained by functional interpretation of the material traits.

The foregoing is a condensation of the preliminary cross-cultural survey. The results are of course limited to very simple aspects of the total social structure. Moreover, the societies were admittedly not studied exhaustively in every aspect; there are no doubt errors of detail, and the correlation

---

According to our sample, the planned village pattern positively indicates a monolineage community.

d. Segmented Village. With two exceptions (Land and Siang Dyaks), all the segmented villages contain two or more lineages, each localized in one segment of the community. The segments are in effect small, planned, sometimes fenced villages with dwelling houses arranged in a pattern, centering on a plaza, a men's house, or other special buildings; in many cases, each segment is a communal house. The segments are further arranged either regularly or irregularly into a community, which sometimes has an additional common plaza and some community buildings or, occasionally, a big enclosure. The segmented community pattern seems to indicate the existence of several lineages, each occupying a segment. Variations are numerous: (1) The lineage in each segment is usually part of a widespread sib. In a few cases, however, as in the Ibo of Nigeria, the Tallensi in Gold Coast, and the Kwoma in the Upper Sepik of New Guinea, all the lineages in a community belong to the same sib. The segmentation of the community then reflects the segmentation of the localized sib. (2) There is usually only one segmentation. When there are more than one, as among the Yakö of Nigeria, the subsegments represent the sublineages of a localized lineage or the lineages of a localized sib. In such cases, there may be only two segments, each representing a moiety. (3) Occasionally, a community is divided into two segments, but each is an unplanned unit. Thus, among the Chala'abus Paiwan, each segment is a moiety, but the lineages are not localized within each moiety. It should be noted that planned and segmented village types often occur in the same tribe, as among some of the South American Tropical Forest dwellers. When a clearing is large enough and the agricultural potentials are favorable, two or more planned villages might cluster and form a segmented village.

should not be uncritically applied. However, I would like to suggest that the study of social grouping should be the archaeologist's first task in interpreting his prehistoric communities. Once this is established, it should reveal many concomitant institutions such as matrimonial residence, division of labor, ownership of land and other property, and patterns of social behavior.

I have left many subjects untouched, e.g., the manner in which land ownership and other factors dominate the community patterning, the sodalities, and the social changes. With reference to the latter, a word may be said about the observable developmental trend of Neolithic community patterning. The sequence is: Planned Villages→Segmented Villages→Unplanned Villages→Homesteads. The first step of transition is shown by many of the South American Tropical Forest communities, the second by the Nagas in Assam, and the third by many New Guinea Melanesians. This indicates a constant fission and dispersal of lineages and a fairly steady development from monolineage to localized (intracommunity) and then non-localized (intracommunity) multilineage villages, and finally to nonlineage villages and, perhaps, homesteads. This impression depends for verification on more detailed work.

A TRIAL APPLICATION TO THE NEW WORLD

In this section I shall try to apply the method suggested above to some regions in the New World. It must be born in mind that this is a demonstration of method rather than a summary of the history of New World Neolithic community patterning and social grouping.

1. Mesoamerica

The Formative cultures of Mesoamerica have been little investigated, and their community pattern is seldom discussed by the general treatises. This is in part because the lowland region Formative architectural remains are covered by tropical vegetation and difficult to locate; moreover, the Classic and Post-Classic civil and religious buildings have occupied archaeologists' attention during the past decades. The scarcity of data makes it impossible to draw a complete picture of the development of community patterning and social grouping, and also makes it necessary to speak about Mesoamerica as a whole.

Thus, I shall chart the scattered finds according to their proper order of developmental stages. The most elaborate subdivision of Mesoamerican Formative is Wauchope's fourfold division into Maritime or Cave Formative, Village Formative, Urban Formative (MacNeish's Temple Formative), and ProtoClassic. However, I prefer to use Kidder's and Willey's more simplified and noncharacterizing terminology (Early and Late Formative), since community patterning of each stage is not yet fully understood.

PRE-FORMATIVE:

La Perra Culture of the *Sierra de Tamaulipas* sequence.
Semisedentary; living in camps or caves; subsisting by both
agriculture and food-collecting; preceramic.

EARLY FORMATIVE:

Valley of Mexico: Copilco-Zacatenco stage.
Fully agricultural-sedentary: lived in villages which were permanently settled; no remnants of houses are left to identify the
community patterning; formalized ceremonial architecture
seems to be lacking.
Highland Maya: Las Charcas, Arevalo, and Mafadas phases.
Fully agricultural-sedentary; house-mounds of the latter two
phases are found grouped in villages but more specific
characterization of mound-planning has not been reported (on
the basis of modern communities in the Guatemalan midwestern highlands, de Borhegyi states that early Formative communities were "unplanned autonomous village units" which is
a dangerous assumption); some pyramidal mounds at Kami-
naljuyu, probably dated to this stage, seem to function as
ceremonial centers of aggregates, though Willey seeks to
explain this temporal discrepancy with Mexican and Lowland
Maya conditions in terms of cross-dating deficiency.
Lowland Maya: Early Formative stage in Yucatan.
No data concerning community patterning are reported, though
it has been assumed that no ceremonial centers appeared in
this stage.

LATE FORMATIVE:

Valley of Mexico: Cuicuilco-Ticoman stage.
The village pattern continued with two additional features: (1)
the village site was chosen for the security of its position (e.g.,
Ticoman) as well as for the arable land near it; (2) platform
mounds appeared and probably served as ceremonial centers
(e.g., Cuicuilco).
Sierra de Tamaulipas: The Pueblito Culture.
The majority of houses were built upon the summits of steep
hills for defense purposes. The settlement pattern was
obviously governed by the geographical features, but evidence
of community planning is seen: somewhere in every ruin is
found a level portion which was used as a plaza; surrounding
it are small pyramids or large circular masonry house platforms. Usually a large pyramid is located medially on one side
of the plaza (a planned village). Other structures were
situated along the tops of ridges, and occasionally there are
other series of house platforms on the sides of the hill, just
below the top (Segmented villages).

Highland Maya: The Miraflores, Arenal, and Santa Clara phases.
The village patterning of communities continued and large and
elaborate burial and temple mounds were built. No planning
of civil settlements is known.

Lowland Maya: The Middle and Late Formative stages of
Yucatan.

Ceremonial centers appear in the Peten Chicanel and at A-I and
E-VII Sub at Uaxactun. A few sites of civil nature have been
investigated and recorded at Uaxactun and at the Melhado
and Barton Ramie sites in the Belize valley. The Uaxactun
data give the impression of small villages or hamlets. The
Barton Ramie site consists of contiguously located hamlets,
each of which has unplanned house mounds either in or not
in association with the local ceremonial buildings. The
Melhado site is also a hamlet of unplanned layout with two
mounds of unusual appearance. This site was probably one of
the residential satellites of the ceremonial center at Cahal
Pech one mile to the north. Brainerd's statement that "the
necessity for a dispersed habitation pattern among slash and
burn cultivators has long been known" is not supported by
our cross-cultural survey, and his assertions that the Formative
Maya communities were "dispersed," of "nuclear family size,"
and that the hamlet sites at Barton Ramie are "atypical,"
seem to be groundless.

A reconstruction of Mesoamerican Neolithic social grouping according to
the procedure suggested earlier is almost impossible; not only are there
many missing links, but also most reports of Formative sites are preliminary
or publish conclusions instead of details. Therefore, I shall only review
briefly the kinship-relational and aggregate formation aspects of Mesoamerican Neolithic community history.

Generally speaking, over most of contemporary Mesoamerica the community pattern is that of an urban/rural society which is characterized by the
interdependence of city, village, and rural homestead. The community is
highly solidary and tends to be endogamous but not isolated. Communities
in an aggregate always form a rigidly or loosely hierarchical structure with
common markets and political and religious centers. Within the community, the household is the basic unit of social activity; it articulates directly
with the local community, usually without the intermediacy of consanguineal kin groups. There are two general tendencies of descent: bilateral,
which is predominating and tends to induce the formation of demes; and
patrilineal, which is now rare and found mostly in Chiapas. These are
associated with corresponding behavioral patterns and exogamous rules, e.g.,
marriage with first cousins on either line is prohibited in the bilateral
groups.

The contemporary Mesoamerican situation is evidently the result of a long process of urbanization (Classic–Post-Classic) and acculturation (Post-Conquest). Students of modern ethnography have shown us that survivals of many Pre-Colonial and Colonial institutions are still visible in modern communities. With regard to community patterning, the ancient households were probably composed of extended families rather than nuclear families; the institution of the "skeleton town" was probably pre-Columbian; and the ancient villages were divided into barrios. As for kinship grouping, as revealed by modern kinship terminology and ancient chronicles, the contemporary bilateral tendency seems to have been developed through urbanization and European stimuli from the original condition of localized and exogamous lineage societies. In part at least, the patrilineality is also derived from an original matrilineality through an intermediate double descent stage. Archaeologically, the modern situation is readily understandable when we consider the Formative Mesoamerican communities as composed of localized lineages.

During the Late Formative period, the aggregates of communities functioned ceremonially and perhaps politically. Each aggregate was symbolized by a ceremonial center; the resident priests may also have had some jural and political control over the residential satellites. The aggregate seems essentially different from the modern urban domain in that each community was presumably more self-sufficient in subsistence and, to some extent, in political and religious affairs as symbolized by the community plaza and big mounds. As shown by their pattern (both planned or segmented as in Sierra de Tamaulipas and unplanned as in Lowland Maya), the communities were probably composed of either a single lineage (in the peripheral regions) or multiple lineages which were beginning to delocalize (in the seats of higher civilizations). There may also have been local specialization of industries, the beginning of social stratification, and a warlike tendency.

Of Early Formative, we have little to say. In Tamaulipas the Pueblito culture began from the Early Formative, and hence the localized mono- and multilineage societies (as indicated by the planned and segmented community patterning) may have existed in the Early Formative as well. However, intercommunity ceremonialism is not in evidence, with the possible exception of the southern Maya. The local community was probably more rigidly integrated and functionally more self-contained than in the Late Formative.

2. Peru

The history of community patterning in Formative Peru is better known than in Mesoamerica. Thanks to Willey's painstaking effort, the development of community pattern in the Virú Valley of the North Coast has been traced from the Post-Classic back to the Pre-Formative agricultural beginning. However, the community histories of other coastal and highland areas are little investigated.

The Virú Valley is located in the northern part of the Pacific coastal desert and is oriented NE–SW. It consists of a coastal plain and a beach belt surrounded by scattered, isolated small hills and hill spurs branching off from the Andean Massif. Eight units of the Virú Valley Project, under the sponsorship of the Institute of Andean Research, were active in the field during the years 1946–48. The Pre-Formative and Formative cultures uncovered in the Virú Valley are divided into the Cerro Prieto, Guanape, Puerto Moorin, and Gallinazo Periods. Unless otherwise noted, the following chart of the development of community patterning is based on Willey's 1953 report.

CERRO PRIETO PERIOD

Horticultural, fishing, and preceramic. Three large (200 m. in diameter), deep, and compact middens clustered together, were discovered. Dwelling houses have been excavated from one of these middens (V-71). Overlying and thus subsequent to the subterranean house remains, there have been found three small conjoined adobe ground rooms, averaging 3×4 m. in size. This three-room cluster might be a unit, or it may have been part of an agglutination of a number of rooms, most of which were made of perishable material.

Supposing each of the middens to represent a room cluster or a small hamlet, the community pattern would seem to be segmented. These three segments are encompassed within a radius of 500 m. and their separation may be entirely a result of the terrain. Nevertheless, because no symbolic structures were recovered, we do not know whether each of the three hamlets formed an independent planned village or all three formed one segmented village.

GUANAPE PERIOD

Early Guanape is represented by one large midden at Guanape, V-71, 200–300 m. in diameter. This is a continuation of the occupation begun at the largest of the three Cerro Prieto beach-dune middens.

In Middle Guanape, the big V-71 occupation area was still inhabited. Situated in the midst of the midden area is a special building, with a crudely made rectangular stone foundation 19 by 15.75 m. An interior platform of rock is built along the north side. Another small midden of the same phase, V-100, is situated about 1.5 km. inland from V-71. It has no special building.

In Late Guanape, besides some scattered finds of lesser significance, two sets of sites are especially noteworthy: V-83–85/V-84, and V-127/V-128. V-83–85 seem to be planned segments of a single segmented village. They are situated on and around the edges of the hill spurs which project into the valley from the Cerros Compositan. A total of twenty-five to thirty houses and some seventy rooms were tabulated on the two sites. The individual house foundations are small. Each house unit is composed of from one to six rooms, with the average of about two. Individual rooms vary in size from about 4 by 5 m. to 2 m. square. Most of them are large enough to have served as living or sleeping quarters, although a few would have been fit only for storage. On top of the ridge around which the houses of V-83 are clustered, and near the center of the dwelling-house circle, there are two rock-walled platforms. Their location suggests that they may have been shrines or temple sites. Not more than half a kilometer from V-83–85, at the foot of the Cerros Compositan, is V-84, an apron platform site in two levels. Considering its unusual location, the prepared flattened hilltop, and the artificial platforms, Willey regards V-84 as a public building having some relation to V-83–85.

V-128, in the other set of Late Guanape sites, is a midden situated on a ridge top. No building foundations have been found here. On the top of a spur, adjacent to V-128, is the V-127 site, composed of two sections. The principal structure is a large rock-walled quadrangle on a sloping spur; it has an interior division separating it into two unequal parts. Directly behind this part of the site is a detached high knoll upon which there is a similar but smaller rock-walled quadrangle. V-127 was either a compound dwelling site or a temple precinct.

Willey seems to suggest that in the Guanape period there existed functioning aggregates which had a dwelling-politico-religious center and a number of satellites, such as V-71/V-100 in Middle Guanape and V-83–85/V-84 and V-128/V-127 in Late Guanape. However, since V-71 in Middle Guanape and V-83–85 in Late Guanape were well integrated and obviously self-sufficient, with V-100 and V-84 being incomplete sites, and since the nature of V-127 seems more residential (as in the next period) than ceremonial, I am inclined not to accept this view but to regard the aggregates as having little function in comparison to the center-satellites units in the Late Formative Mesoamerica.

Puerto Moorin Period

The Puerto Moorin hamlets are scattered over the valley floor, at the hill bases, or atop the spurs. Each hamlet is composed of a dozen or so houses, which are isolated and roughly planned or irregularly conjoined. The unplanned conjoined house-blocks are sometimes segmented. The isolated house units are composed of one or two small rooms. The conjoined house-blocks are made of small rectangular rooms, and are formed by accretion. In each hamlet there is often a special structure distinguishable from other buildings, but no structure of apparently ceremonial nature is included. This can probably be accounted for by the fact that here and there in the valley are pyramidal mounds which presumably served as ceremonial centers for a number of residential hamlets.

Besides the residential hamlets and the pyramidal mounds, there are fortified sites on the tops of a few spurs. Two of them, called "hill-top redoubts" by Willey, are characterized by a great encircling wall. Within the enclosure are several centers of construction. These include foundations of conjoined and regularly arranged houses, and small, rectangular, flat-topped pyramidal mounds. Willey considers them to be places of refuge. The other fortified sites are "hilltop platforms," and probably served as lookouts and shrines.

Relations among the residential hamlets, the pyramidal mounds, and the fortified sites are somewhat puzzling. On the basis of site distribution, Willey has tentatively grouped them into several assemblages, each consisting of a hilltop redoubt or a big flat-topped pyramid-mound and a small number of hamlets. Moreover, in this period there appear works that suggest intercommunity labor cooperation, such as roads, canals, or extensive walls. However, the evidence is not conclusive.

GALLINAZO PERIOD

Four categories of Gallinazo sites are distinguishable: village sites with pyramidal mounds, those without pyramidal mounds, isolated pyramids, and castillos. There are fourteen village sites with pyramidal mounds, all of Late Gallinazo phase. Their pattern is that of a flat-topped pyramidal mound near the center, with domiciliary houses attached or clustering around, in a somewhat planned or segmented manner. The majority of village sites, however, are devoid of a pyramidal mound. Most of them are isolated hamlets with a planned or unplanned layout, each consisting of several (a dozen or so) conjoined rooms (Willey's agglutinated type or Bennett's beehive pattern). The size of the individual rooms is small on the average, but sometimes one or two larger rooms are incorporated in the cluster. At least two village sites of this type (V-39–40–43, V-63) show some kind of segmentation.

There are six isolated pyramidal mounds and seven castillos in the Gallinazo Period. The castillo is a large enclosure, built around a pyramid mound, some house-platforms, and a plaza; Willey considers it a stronghold for defensive purposes.

To judge from the distribution and function of sites in Gallinazo period, the role played by the aggregates had been considerably enhanced. There are a few villages which are more self-contained than others; there are those which seem dependent in at least the ceremonial aspect and are in the orbit of a pyramidal center; there are also villages so elaborately equipped that they look like residences of the aggregate authorities. Large-scale irrigation and extensive wall construction are also evident in this period.

Virú is the only place in Peru for which a complete sequence of Formative community patterning is known. The sequence in the Moche-Chicama valleys is less complete; there, in the preceramic and premaize Huaca Prieta stage, the communities were clusters of simple underground houses on the seashore. Isolated ceremonial centers of Chavín horizon have been unearthed in the Formative Cupisnique and Salinar stages, but no data have been reported for the pattern of residential communities. In the North Highlands only one site, Chavín de Huántar, has been found where community patterning data are known. The ruins, Early Formative in horizon, cover a large area and are regarded as a purely ceremonial center. Presumably, there was a precedent culture from which the Chavín complex was derived. Archaeologists are also seeking a more advanced succeeding culture which probably gave rise to the Gallinazo of Virú. These, together with the residential villages of Chavín horizon, remain to be investigated. In the Central Coastal area, villages in the Early Ancón-Supe period of Early Formative level are of middling size, but the community patterning is little known. No intercommunity ceremonialism is in evidence, though there are traces of village temples. To the south of the Ancón-Supe area, extensive archaeological works have been undertaken, but no community patterning data comparable to those from the North Coast have been reported. A series of preceramic sites have recently been located and partially excavated on the Central and Southern Coast, but few settlement data are recorded in the preliminary report. In the South Highland area, there is a Late Formative village at Chiripa, Bolivia. There Bennett found fourteen rectangular houses grouped in a circle around a central court, forming a typical planned village, but no specialized structures are noted.

On the basis of the data summarized above, a tentative reconstruction of Peruvian Neolithic social grouping can be outlined.

The Household. As reflected by the size of the house and number of rooms, households were fairly large in the earlier periods of the Virú sequence. In Late Guanape, for example, each house is composed of from one to six rooms; this variety of sizes indicates that households were probably composed of extended families. Since the Puerto Moorin period, the house seems to have become smaller and there has been a tendency toward house accretion; this implies a decrease in size of the household and the gradual prevalence of nuclear families. However, this is not certain; the data on household equipment have not been published together with those on structures, so household limits cannot be identified according to hearths and other functionally significant remains.

It is possible that except in the very beginning (Pre-Formative) of the Virú Formative, the household was an integrated and highly subordinated part of the community. We are assuming that economic cooperation, political authority, and ceremonialism functioned mainly on the community or aggregate level rather than on the household level, although the household was presumably a commensal and cohabiting unit.

The Community. As early as the Pre-Formative, the community was of the planned (if we consider each midden in the Cerro Prieto Virú an independent community) or segmented (if we consider it a segment of a trisegmented village) pattern. In this the Peruvian Pre-Formative differs greatly from the preceramic cultures of Mesoamerica (La Perra in Tamaulipas) and the Southwest (Basketmaker II). The reason is probably that the early Peruvian horticulturists were parttime fishermen instead of hunters and gatherers. Their population was possibly small but their communities had been sedentary for centuries. The community apparently consisted of a localized lineage or a few localized lineages. No symbolic objects or buildings have been discovered, and the community was probably no more than a loose cluster of households.

In the Early Formative (Guanape in Virú, Cupisnique in the North Coast, Chavín in the North Highlands, Early Ancón-Supe in the Central Coast) the community had been fully integrated and was assuming most, if not all, of the residential, economic, political, and religious functions. In both Virú and Supe, well-defined community shrines mark the solidarity of the community as a whole. Many Peruvianists seem to believe that at this early level the ceremonial centers were already the foci of pilgrimages from the satellite residential villages, as in Late Formative Mesoamerica. This may be true to some extent, as indicated by the Chavín and Cupisnique evidence. However, this evidence has been overemphasized and too hastily generalized for all of Peru. One can merely say that in Ancón-Supe, and probably in Virú, the Early Formative community was self-contained not only in material culture but also in religious activities. In the North Highlands and coastal area there might have been ceremonial centers which had taken over at least part of the ceremonial functions of the community. However, this can only be verified by finding residential villages and ceremonial mounds in association. According to available evidence, there are two possible explanations: (1) that the Chavín horizon represents a long time interval, so that changes in community patterning might have taken place gradually during its duration; and (2) that in the northern and central coastal region of Peru there was a Pre-Chavín ceramic horizon as indicated by the undecorated pottery from the Late Huaca Prieta in the Chicama valley, the Early Guanape in Virú, and the lower level of Early Ancón-Supe middens. Further exploration of this horizon might disclose the prerequisite stage prior to the ceremonial-center/residential-satellites patterning of Chavín and Cupisnique. At any rate, the Chavín and Cupisnique patterning cannot be generalized too broadly, nor can it be taken as evidence of Late Formative Mesoamerican borrowing.

In Virú, the Early Formative community pattern shows both planned and segmented villages. This seems to indicate that communities based on lineage continued to exist and had become more highly integrated. Population tended to increase since the Middle Guanape, which chronologically is coincident with the beginning of maize cultivation in the Chicama Valley.

The Late Formative Virú (Puerto Moorin and Gallinazo) communities were still recognizable residential units, but both the economic cooperative and politico-ceremonial activities seem increasingly to have been taken over by aggregates. The following series of events in these two periods is significant: the appearance of unplanned villages beside the planned and segmented types, which seems to indicate the fluctuation of lineage membership; the appearance and increase of politico-religious centers within the orbit of several residential units; the increase of fortified sites; the appearance and increase of public works such as irrigation canals and extensive walls; the extensive exploration of the valley floor, and the increase of population; the casting of metal and, finally, the use of metal tools. These events, I believe, made the community progressively less self-contained and the aggregate more strongly integrated. As for the lineages, they were splitting and moving about. Finally, urbanization (characterized by the interdependence of large politico-ceremonial, commercial, and industrial centers and the relatively small and scattered rural districts) took place with the bilateralization of kinship, which, by the Inca period, had become bilateral with patrilineal tendency, as it is still.

In Central and South Peru, developments in Late Formative community patterning and social grouping are not clear. We know only that in Bolivia, the Chiripa community maintained a clearly planned pattern which indicates the maintenance of lineage integrity. Urbanization did not necessarily occur simultaneously throughout the Andes, so it seems unnecessary to regard the Chiripa village as a satellite of an undiscovered ceremonial center.

The Aggregate. The aggregate grouping of communities did not appear in Pre-Formative Peru, and there was merely a doubtful emergence in the Early Formative. As mentioned earlier, in Ancón-Supe and probably in Virú, the Early Formative communities were still well-integrated and largely self-contained. In Virú, either aggregates which united a number of communities, or one great aggregate uniting the whole valley seem to have appeared and developed during the Late Formative. Intravalley or interval-ley war is in evidence.

One of the most striking features of the Virú aggregates is that the central community seems to be a political as well as ceremonial center. Clusters of residential houses accompany many pyramid mounds and are found in most of the enclosures. Moreover, there are ceremonial structures in some of the residential communities. These facts seem to indicate that the central community of an aggregate was more political than ceremonial. Very possibly a supreme chief and priests dwelt in these communities; the chief himself may also have been the high priest. Large-scale irrigation canals, roads, extensive walls, and large pyramid mounds were constructed, implying a centralized authority more secular than sacred. On the other hand, one reason why Early Formative Peruvian ceremonial centers are difficult to explain is that they are hardly secular centers. For the moment, I am inclined to take the Virú sequence as representative, and refrain from commenting on other areas until more controlled and complete investigations have been made.

3. San Juan Anasazi in the Southwest

Compared with Peru and Mesoamerica, community pattern-ing in the Southwestern Neolithic is much better investigated, and it is easier to reconstruct social grouping according to the method applied above. Moreover, the ethnological and mythological studies of the modern Pueblos are of much help.

There are three broad physiographic provinces in the Southwest: the northern plateau, the central mountains, and the southern desert. The Anasazi[3] domain lay on the northern plateau between elevations of 900 and 2100 meters; it comprised all of Arizona north of the Mogollon Rim, most of Utah, the southwestern corner of Colorado, and northwestern New Mexico. The main drainage systems are those of the San Juan, Little Colorado, and upper Rio Grande Rivers. An archaeological synthesis was first made in the San Juan drainage, and the sequence of community patterning is most complete there. A summary of San Juan Anasazi community patterning is charted below. The period prior to the Pueblo III period is more crucial and fluctuating than the periods following it, insofar as community patterning is concerned, so the data since the formation of Pueblo towns are greatly simplified.

Basketmaker II

(No dates are given to each of the periods because they are
regarded as cultural stages. . . .)

---

[3] Because we are dealing here with a relatively small area, we shall use the term "Anasazi" in a generalized instead of a restricted sense. Likewise, we shall follow the Pecos instead of Roberts or Gila Pueblo phase classification.

Pit-houses in the open and under rock-shelters were used for dwelling, working, storage, and religious purposes. Each house consists of a single room, ranging from 2.5 m. to 9 m. in diameter. At or near the center of the floor is a basin-like excavation which served as a heating device. Metates are a normal feature of each living area. For storage purposes, slab-cists were employed; they were either built in the ground within the house or prepared in shallow caves.

The Basketmakers cultivated both corn and squash, but hunting and collecting were still essential and their way of life was semisedentary. Their community consisted of separate and independent houses (pit-houses), gathered irregularly to form a small hamlet. (The pattern is not ticketed by our terminology because it is not "Neolithic.") No special buildings of ceremonial nature can be singled out.

Basketmaker III

Pit-houses were used for dwelling, working, storage, and religious purposes. Near the center of the room was a fire pit and a short distance away was a small circular hole in the floor which is thought to be analogous to the sipapu of later-day kivas. One of the pit-houses was specialized into a ceremonial chamber. Slab-lined granaries, developed from the slab-cists of the preceding stage, were connected to the dwelling houses.

The excavated communities are of the planned village pattern. The houses are oriented northeast-southwest in a semicircle, around a ceremonial chamber to the northwest.

Pueblo I

Pit-houses were less frequently used for dwelling, working, and storage, and began to specialize into religious structures. Granaries had been converted into domiciles, and assumed most of the domiciliary functions. They were largely one-roomed quadrangular structures of pole and adobe mud — the so-called jacal-type construction. Most of them were erected over a shallow pit, so that the floor level is somewhat below the general ground level. The depth of the pit had been getting shallower with the increase of time. There were sometimes fire pits in the floor near the center of the room, though most of the cooking fire pits were built in the open. Ordinarily, each house consisted of only one room. While many houses seem to have two or three rooms, there is but one main living room; the others are either subsequent additions or storage units.

The community is of both planned and segmented village pattern. Three to fifteen houses (converted granaries) were grouped in small clusters to form a unit; they were built quite close together, but rarely touched. Each unit tends to form a crescent along a SW–NE, an E–W, or a NW–SE axis, because the structures were erected around the borders of a circular kiva or a depression. Such a house-cluster may stand alone as a planned village or several may form a segmented village, which at times is equipped with an additional large kiva.

PUEBLO II

The pit-houses were sunk deeper into the ground and were converted into kivas. The houses converted from granaries became completely above-ground and assumed most of the domiciliary functions. Jacal and slab construction gradually yielded to stone and adobe construction. Houses were conjoined into the so-called "unit-houses" which consisted of a single or double row of rooms forming a rectangular block, with a kiva situated a short distance in front (which is generally to the south). When there were two rows of rooms, the front row usually contained fire pits, storage cists, and pottery, and were presumably used as living quarters, while the rear row contained much charred corn and many metates, and might have served as storage places. The number of rooms in each unit-house seems to have been greatly reduced in comparison with the number in each house-cluster in the preceding period. Sometimes a unit-house consisted of only one or two main living rooms, together with a workshop, a few storage rooms, and a few granaries. However, it may have a greater number of rooms, and sometimes two kivas.

Usually a unit-house stands as a community and thus constitutes a planned village. Rare instances were observed where two or more units are grouped to form a segmented village, as in Pueblo I.

PUEBLO III AND AFTER

The function of the various houses and the community pattern remained much the same as in Pueblo II, while in several regions large towns had been constructed. Most of the towns were gatherings of unit-houses and were therefore of the segmented village pattern. Each segment was distinguished by its possession of a separate kiva. However, this pattern did not last long. Later in the period, while the kivas became incorporated in the town, the town itself became unplanned.

Pueblo III is also the first period in the San Juan which shows a dual division of the community, either in the town-planning or in the appearance of two Great Kivas. Farmhouses without associated ceremonial chambers now appear.

This development of house-concentration lasted throughout the whole Pueblo III period in the San Juan drainage. With the close of this period, most of the area was abandoned forever.

The following outline is a tentative reconstruction of San Juan Anasazi Neolithic social grouping according to the method suggested.

The Household. As a Basic Social Unit. On the whole, the household is the basic social unit throughout, and is domestically self-sufficient and independent. This is evident in the Basketmaker and Pueblo I periods when each house was separate and had its own living quarters, workshop, fire pit, and storage bins or granaries. This isolation disappeared superficially with the conjunction of houses, which began in Pueblo II. Nevertheless, domestic self-sufficiency is still indicated by the partitions between neighboring houses, the functional self-sufficiency of each house as shown by its material content, and the arrangement of doors. In modern Pueblo towns, each household is partitioned from the others and usually consists of three or four rooms which provide a self-sufficient domestic sphere.

Composition. The households of the Western Pueblos are usually composed of extended families based on matrilocal residence and matrilineal descent. The Eastern Pueblos tend to have households composed of nuclear families, but they are not the overwhelming majority; according to Parsons and White, they seem to represent a recent developmental tendency. If we accept Parsons's view that the Eastern nuclear family is the product of male house ownership, and Wittfogel's and Goldfrank's contention that men's superior position (including house ownership) in the East resulted from their control over irrigation and other water-works, it seems reasonable to assume that ancient Pueblo households were generally composed of extended families based on matrilineal descent and matrilocal residence (see the section on the lineage). Archaeologically, this assumption seems to be confirmed by the fact that since the beginning of the Pueblo settlement in the San Juan, a considerable diversity in the size of the houses in one community was the rule rather than the exception. In the Pueblo I and II periods, there seems to be a common practice of constructing additional rooms in the house, which is another feature of the extended family household. It should be noted here that in the Late Formative of the Virú Valley of Peru, as we have seen earlier, there was a tendency toward contiguous addition of new small houses, which seems to indicate the prevalence of nuclear family households.

Functions and Symbolic Aspects. The San Juan Anasazi household was evidently the basic unit of cohabitation, probably of economic cooperation, and, to some extent, of education. It can also be inferred that the household title was held by its female head, and that the household owned the agricultural products obtained by the cooperative labor of its members, if it did not actually own the field.

In general, land ownership is often considered as the best measure of the degree of group solidarity, but additional clues are yielded by the relationship of the household to the community ceremonial nucleus. In the Basketmaker periods the household seems to be self-contained ceremonially as well as domestically, as indicated by the sipapu-like floor hole in the house. However, the appearance of the community ceremonial chamber since Basketmaker II indicates the gradual assumption by the community of most ceremonial functions. This indicates that the community had gradually deprived the household units of some of their symbolic representations, including ceremonials and possibly titles to the land.

The Community. Functions and the Face-to-Face Relational Composition. Throughout the San Juan Anasazi, prior to Pueblo III, the community was composed of a relatively small number of households and, with a single exception, the spatial relationships between them was constant. The exception is the segmented villages in Pueblo I–II, where intrasegment and intersegment relationships of households were presumably of different orders.

Each community was evidently a self-sufficient economic, political, and ceremonial unit, with its solidarity increasing as time went on. This increase of community solidarity and integrity is seen in the general layout, the decrease of the number of kivas relative to the houses, and presumably was reflected in land ownership. Of these, the relationship of the kiva to the living house deserves more attention. In Basketmaker II, ceremonialism seems to be a household affair. In Basketmaker III the spatial arrangement of houses seems to indicate that the community began to be ceremonially configurated, and that at least some of the religious observances were performed in the ceremonial chamber on behalf of the community as a whole. The function of the kiva as a symbolic mechanism for the whole community or the segment was greatly strengthened during Pueblo I and II, when many nonreligious uses of the pit-house began to be absorbed by surface houses, and the kiva thus became the principal, though not the only, place of ceremonial and social activity. (At that time the kiva belonged to the community and hence to the lineage, in the sense that the lineage was localized in the community. However, in the sense of membership, the kiva was essentially cross-lineage because it was presumably linked with the local men's society. In modern Pueblos, probably as the result of lineage fission and dispersal, the kiva-lineage connection has been very much slackened and in many towns has disappeared, while the sodality-kiva connection has been maintained and even strengthened.) Since the beginning of Pueblo III, the kiva-house relationship has gradually changed. The kiva is not related to a particular house cluster or set of houses, but has been incorporated into the town. Ceremonials and social activities taking place in it are concerned not with certain particular households as units but with the community as a whole, or with individuals belonging [to] the particular fraternities or kinship groups. The development of the kiva-house relationship clearly indicates the weakening of household groups, increased community solidarity, and the growing importance of political and association linkages relating to kinship ties.

The Kinship Relational Composition. The modern Pueblos show a marked diversity in the pattern of the unilineal consanguineal kinship groups. All of them have lineages and clans, but from West to East there is a decrease of both clan corporateness and the degree of matrilineality. Hopi, the westernmost Pueblo today, has actively functioning clans, while Tiwa and Tewa, the easternmost, are respectively clanless and show a patrilineal tendency. The question naturally arises: what was the kinship pattern of the ancient Pueblo? Both ethnologists and mythologists have contributed their suggested answers.

Although Reed and Hawley attribute modern diversities to the different origins of the Western and the Eastern Pueblos, Parsons, Strong, Steward, Wittfogel and Goldfrank, and Eggan assumed that there is a genetic interrelationship among all the Pueblo peoples. The last three authors suggest that all the ancient Pueblos possessed a clan organization which was based on matrilineality and matrilocality, and that due to various factors it either disappeared or was converted into patrilineality among some of the Eastern groups. Furthermore, some of the authors have assumed that localized lineages preceded the Pueblo multilineage clans, and that the "clanization" resulted from the growth of population, the widespread migrations, and the necessity for lineages to scatter. On the other hand, mythologists have brought to light the fact that, though the clans are not localized in the town, they were so in ancient times. The delocalization of clans seems to have resulted from constant and extensive intra- and intercommunity movements. Although some authors have rejected the mythologists' reconstruction as "uncritical," it coincides essentially with archaeological discoveries. Their reconstruction is further strengthened by the fact that Hopi historical legends agree with archaeological data in recording such items as the ancient subterranean habitation, the existence of the rainbow-shaped house-row prior to stone houses, and the coincidence of clan movements and the construction of stone houses. Ethnological and mythological studies of modern Pueblos thus suggest that prior to Pueblo III there were small localized lineages; with the dispersal of lineages and the subsequent concentration of houses into towns, the lineages split and became clans, which at first were localized in multiclan towns but later became nonlocalized. This picture is largely in agreement with, and can be strengthened and amplified by, the archaeological materials in the San Juan region.

During the Basketmaker II period, as suggested by conditions among the Western Shoshoni, the many Paiute tribes in the Plains, the Havasupai, and

Pima in the Southwest, it was ecologically impossible for families to remain in one place for a considerable time, or for more than a few families to remain in permanent association. Consequently, the household was the basis of the Basketmaker life, and each community was probably an association of a very few households. These households were perhaps held together by the need for economic cooperation, by the increasingly sedentary nature of their lives, or by necessity of seeking outside marriage-mates, and thus might have developed into small localized (in the sense of lineality rather than settlement) exogamous lineages. Since female land ownership existed among most early horticulturists, these lineages could be matrilocal and matrilineal.

With the growth of population and increasing productivity, the Basketmaker III lineage-community grew in size and became stabilized in one locality. The Shabik'eschee village in the Chaco is of a typical planned pattern, and was undoubtedly a monolineage community. Its symbolic solidarity and corporateness increased with time, but because it was exogamous it was socially dependent on other communities. In the succeeding Pueblo I period, segmented as well as planned villages appeared; a segmented community might have been composed of lineages belonging to different sibs for matrimonial purposes, as suggested by the Owens Valley Paiute (Steward 1938), instead of belonging to the same sib. In the multilineage communities the cohesion was presumably strong on account of matrimonial bonds.

Pueblo I prosperity did not last long. Arable land was exhausted, the recuperation of the semi-arid soil was slow, arroyo cutting was in process, and techniques of exploiting the land remained unimproved. With the growing centralization of settlements and the constant increase in population, the situation finally became disastrous. In Pueblo II, there was a disorganization of large lineages and multilineage communities, and again they split into small groups and dispersed widely. A period of struggle and intercommunity raids and the development of irrigation led to reunification of some Pueblos, with large compound towns composed of lineages and clans, which were no longer localized. The towns were at first segmented, with diverse lineages and clan-sectors occupying particular segments. Later, the clans were delocalized, perhaps due to the difficulty of maintaining clan members in the same neighborhood in Pueblo-type house-blocks. The final abandonment of the San Juan drainage seems to indicate that these efforts were not very successful.

The Aggregate. Unlike Mesoamerica and Peru, the aggregate has never been important in the Southwest, and intercommunity relationships became more hostile through time. There is abundant record of large-scale intertown warfare in the chronicles and native legends. Intertown hostility still occurs in the form of imputing witchcraft. A large Pueblo town is an unusual development, and it would be a mistake to regard it as an end-product of "urbanization."

4. Growth Trends of
the New World Neolithic Society

As by-products of this methodological study, a number of growth trends in New World Neolithic society are disclosed: (1) In the New World Formative stage, the village seems to be the universal community pattern; only when urbanization had deprived the villages of many of their functions was there a tendency toward village fission. Archaeological data in all three areas suggest that the developmental sequence was probably: planned/segmented village→unplanned village→homesteads. (2) In all three areas the Neolithic villages seem to belong to the lineage type of community, and the lineage developmental trend was probably: monolineage→multilineage (intracommunity localized)→multilineage (intracommunity nonlocalized)→nonlineage societies. The impression obtained from our cross-cultural survey of modern Neolithic societies is confirmed by archaeological data. (3) In Mesoamerica and Peru, the developments in community patterning and kinship grouping seem to be closely interrelated. In the Early Formative stage communities were relatively isolated, independent, and self-contained; the lineages were rigid, integrated, and no doubt strongly gemeinschaft in outlook. During the Late Formative, communities became incorporated into politico-ceremonial centers, and were less self-contained. Aggregates grew more important, and the fluctuation and intermixture of population accelerated. At the same time, lineages became disorganized, disintegrated, and delocalized, and household size diminished. But in the Southwest, no real urbanization had taken place and lineage fission and the formation of clans followed different paths. (4) Sometime in the latter part of the Formative, when village life had been established, a warlike tendency developed. It may have resulted in part from hostility between rigidly established lineage communities, in part from economic wants, and in part from the formation of aggregates. (5) In each of the three areas, the process of community patterning and social grouping is similar in principle and its diffusion seems therefore to be out of the question. The diffusion of cultivated plants, however, seems to have been vitally important, although diffusion of other traits, such as flat-topped pyramidal mounds and metallurgy, was apparently not of critical importance. (6) Though the general process of social growth was similar in all cases, it followed distinctive patterns in different areas. In Mesoamerica, the Late Formative aggregates seem to have been ceremonially integrated and the political power of the aggregate authorities ceremonially vested, but the community seems to have retained much economic and political independence. In Peru, on the other hand, the aggregates acquired highly centralized political and administrative as well as ceremonial functions. The Southwestern Pueblo towns have never been truly urbanized; there is no evidence of aggregate integrity or urban-rural interdependence, though the Eastern Pueblos show a highly centralized governmental organization. In other words, while similar factors dominated social growth in all three areas, different cultures might adopt distinctive patterns.

CONCLUSIONS

The methodological procedure described here, which is applicable only to Neolithic societies, has been shown to identify and characterize the social groups of archaeological cultures. The a priori assumption is that one must look at archaeological sites as local social groups instead of as cultures or phases. Cultures are fluctuant, but social groups are clear-cut. Therefore, I suggest that it should be the archaeologist's first duty to delimit local social groups such as households, communities, and aggregates, rather than to identify archaeological regions and areas by time-spacing material traits, since cultural traits are meaningless unless described in their social context. The procedure suggested here is necessarily incomplete, and can yield only very simple results. Its use is limited in that it is applicable only when settlement remains are available, and when detailed cross-dating of house-remains within a site is possible. The dangers inherent in its application cannot be overemphasized, but the initial attempt must be made, successfully or not. Such is the purpose of the present paper.

The same method can also be applied to the Old World. In Europe, for example, the Classical Tripolye village at Kolomiishchina, the Danubian villages at Brześć Kujawski and Köln Lindenthal, and the lake-dwelling village at Riedschachen, to mention only a few, are fairly complete village sites for which a community patterning study seems possible. The village plan seems in most cases to be of the segmented pattern, and each segment is often a communal house. (This is also the case in the Yangshao village at Panpo, Sian, North China.) The Tripolye village is a typical example of a planned segmented village which presumably consisted of a localized clan, composed of a number of lineages, each of which occupied a separate communal house. The study of Old World Neolithic community patterns is another field which calls for the archaeologist's attention and effort.

JAMES N. HILL

*In recent years the most useful research along the lines
suggested by archaeologists advocating new approaches has
included the work of William Longacre and James Hill in the
American Southwest. Hill's account of a prehistoric pueblo
community demonstrates how new approaches can be
brought to bear to discover both the day-to-day functioning
of a prehistoric community — its sociocultural system — and
the manner in which change has taken place in the
community over time. The article illustrates much of what
has been said in earlier selections, from the application of
computers to considerations of hypothesis formulation and
testing.*

19   A Prehistoric Community
in Eastern Arizona

There have been, in recent years, a number of promising
contributions related to the elucidation of prehistoric sociocultural systems.
Most of these are concerned with settlement patterns, ceremonial structures, mortuary practices, social status, and craft specialization (Sears 1961).
Several other contributions are also notable (Longacre 1963, 1964; Freeman
and Brown 1964; Deetz 1960, 1965).

There is a growing feeling, represented especially by the above kinds of
study, that there is much to be gained by attempting to describe (and
perhaps explain) "complete" or "whole" sociocultural systems — much as
it is done by ethnologists. How complete these descriptions can be is a
matter of justifiable concern, but it is evident that at least some headway is
being made in this direction.

This article presents an outline of a case study which may be of value to

Reprinted, with the editorial changes noted, from "A Prehistoric Community in Eastern Arizona" by James N. Hill, *Southwestern Journal of Anthropology* 22 (1966):9–30,
by permission of the author and the publisher. Footnotes are renumbered.

those interested in the so-called "systems" or "structural" approach to the interpretation of archaeological data. It should provide some fodder usable in evaluating this kind of concern; and, at the very least, it is an example of certain ways in which prehistoric material can be interpreted. The explicit purposes of the study were twofold: (a) to *describe* as much of the internal structure and social organization of a prehistoric society as was possible to discover, and (b) to attempt to develop an hypothesis pertinent to *explaining* adaptive changes in this organization.

The focus of the analysis was on Broken K Pueblo, located eleven miles east of Snowflake, Arizona (excavated by the Chicago Natural History Museum, with National Science Foundation support). This archaeological site is a rectangular, ninety-five room,[1] single-storied, surface masonry pueblo, dating from about A.D. 1150 to 1280 (see plan, Fig. 1). The largest and latest site in the Hay Hollow Valley, it is located in a savanna-woodland vegetation zone. The climate is semiarid today, and the landscape has been heavily dissected by the prevailing pattern of torrential summer thunder-showers.

THEORY AND METHOD

The basic theoretical model employed is simply that human behavior is patterned or structured. To put it in its simplest form, people do certain things in certain places within their communities, and they leave behind them many of the structured remains of these activities (e.g., artifacts). It may be useful to state this as a formal postulate since it is fundamental to succeeding interpretations.

The spatial distributions of cultural materials are patterned or structured (nonrandom), and will be so within an archaeological site.

A. These patterns reflect the loci of *patterned behavior* that existed in prehistoric times.

B. The kind of behavior represented in these loci depends on the nature

[1] The room-count is complicated by the fact that the initial wall-trenching (to discover all of the rooms in the pueblo prior to sampling) failed to locate all of the rooms accurately. Rooms 31 and 33 should be considered a single room, as should rooms 35 and 37 (cf. Fig. 1). Room 44 had to be divided into rooms 44a and 44b. Room 92 is located in the west wing; it is numerically out of place because it was not discovered until the simple random sample had already been chosen, thus "freezing" the room numbers. There are five outliers not included in the room-count, but only two of them (to the south of the pueblo) are clearly rooms. The outliers were not included in the initial population sampled and thus were not numbered; but all of them were excavated. There may be one or two undiscovered rooms in the northeast portion of the east wing. The "kiva" in the southwest corner of the plaza was excavated (contrary to map designation); it was either *not* a kiva, or it was unfinished, since there were no kiva features in this rectangular pit. It had been excavated by the prehistoric inhabitants, partially into the sandstone bedrock.

or "behavioral meaning" of the item or set of items, the distribution of which is being studied.

C. These "behavioral meanings" can be determined with the aid of specific ethnographic evidence or general worldwide comparative evidence. There is a great variety of such "meanings" with which items (or stylistic elements) can be associated:

1. Some items or stylistic elements have *functional* meanings (i.e., they are associated with certain economic, sociological, or religious activities).
2. Some of these functional classes of items may reflect the composition of *social segments* (e.g., specific classes of items may be used by men, women, hunters, priests, etc.).
3. Within any given class of items there may be *stylistic differences* associated with the various social segments (e.g., men, women, hunters, priests, households, lineages, clans, etc.).

As has been suggested by others (Eggan 1952:37. Binford 1962, 1964, 1965; Rootenberg 1964; and others), it should be possible to isolate some of these patterns archaeologically. The problem with respect to Broken K Pueblo was to find as many clusters or patterns in the data as possible, and then attempt to interpret them as reflecting parts of a village activity structure and social organization.

The site was too large to permit complete excavation, considering the time and resources available. Largely for this reason, a system of simple random sampling was employed. Nearly all of the existing walls at the site were discovered and mapped prior to excavation. Forty-six rooms were then excavated in the initial sample. The sample was not considered an end in itself, however; eight additional rooms were excavated, as the necessity for doing so became apparent. All the excavated rooms, both surface and subterranean, are shown in Figure 1 as unshaded rooms, which, including outliers, total fifty-four.

Naturally deposited stratigraphic levels were excavated as separate units; and those levels containing cultural materials were screened, in an effort to ensure comparability of samples. Materials found in direct association with floors were kept separate from those in "fill" levels. All possibly relevant materials were saved, and charcoal and fossil pollen samples were taken from most rooms.

A large portion of the data from the site was quantified and manipulated statistically. Three multivariate analyses (factor analyses) were performed on the I.B.M. 7094 computer at the University of Chicago.[2] These analyses permitted the development of nonrandom clusters of pottery-types and

[2] For a discussion of factor analysis, see Fruchter 1954.

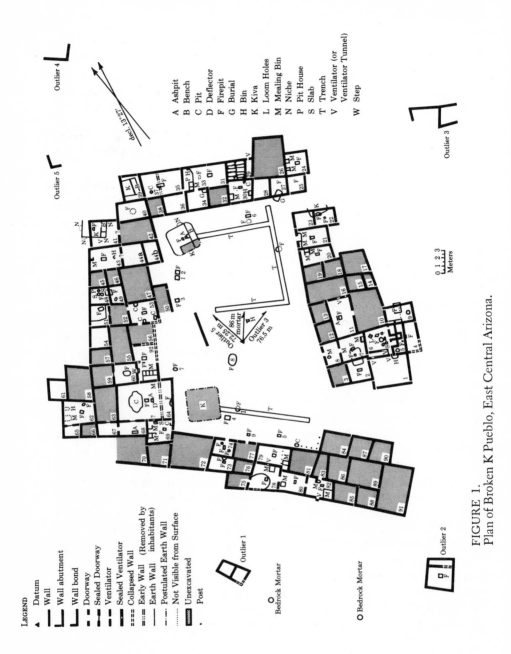

FIGURE 1.
Plan of Broken K Pueblo, East Central Arizona.

ceramic design-elements; and the clusters or "factors" were used in various distribution studies.

THE TEMPORAL VARIABLE

In order profitably to study a community structure, prehistoric or otherwise, it is necessary that the structure be defined at a specific point or points in *time*. The reason it must be studied synchronically is that it may tend to change through time and gradually develop into a different structure. While it is reasonable to compare structures which have existed at different points in time, it would not be very meaningful to consider them all as a single structure.

Since Broken K was not constructed at a specific point in time, it was important that it not be assumed (initially) to represent a synchromic structure. Various lines of evidence, primarily architectural and stratigraphic, were employed in this intra-site dating effort;[3] and it was discovered that, in general, the southern portion of the site was somewhat earlier than the northern portion. This does not imply, however, that the southern portion had been abandoned prior to the northern occupation. There were many rooms in the southern portion that did not contain refuse deposits, and there was much more evidence of remodeling in that area than in the northern portion of the site. It therefore seems likely that people were living in that portion until the end of the occupation of the site. This suggests that we can consider the entire site as a roughly contemporaneous unit, at least near the end of the occupation. But contemporaneity cannot at present be unequivocally demonstrated, however, and the reader should beware of this fact in considering some of the subsequent interpretations. This problem clearly illustrates the importance of accurate intra-site dating when problems such as those dealt with in this paper are considered.

ROOM-TYPES AND FUNCTIONS

Archaeologists have long recognized that there are differences in types of rooms found in prehistoric pueblo sites. Ordinarily, a large room containing a firepit and mealing bin is called a living room or habitation

---

[3] Pollen data were also found useful in intra-site dating. A pollen chronology for the area (Schoenwetter 1962; Hevly 1964) indicated a gradual temporal shift in the relative proportions of pollen types, characterized primarily by decreasing percentages of arboreal pollen (especially *Pinus*) and increasing percentages of non-arboreal pollen during this time period (ca. A.D. 1000–1300). Most of the rooms at the site which, on the basis of other evidence, had been considered "early" contained 20 to 40 percent *Pinus* pollen; while "late" rooms generally contained less than 20 percent, the "late" rooms contained significantly more non-arboreal pollen (especially Compositae, Chenopodiaceae, Amaranthaceae, and Gramineae). It would not be valid to claim that pollen data can be used widely in intra-site dating, but further experimentation seems called for.

room; a small room without such features is called a storage room. A ceremonial room is often recognized as being a subterranean structure (or surface structure) with a roof-entrance, a firepit, a ventilator, some wall niches, and a bench or platform along one or more of the walls — among other distinctive attributes.

This kind of classification is probably adequate with respect to ceremonial rooms, since these rooms often contain many attributes similar to those in present-day Hopi and Zuni ceremonial rooms. It may not be very adequate, however, for isolating habitation and storage rooms. The differences between these room-types are not always obvious, and a classification of them on the basis of one or two attributes may not always be reliable.

Twelve different attributes were used in isolating these room-types at Broken K. One of the attributes was floor-area. I noticed that some of the rooms were much larger than others. Simple statistical manipulations showed that there were in fact two different modes of room-size. Approximately half of the nonceremonial rooms were small, ranging in size from 2.5 to 6.5 square meters in floor area; while other rooms ranged in size from 6.6 to 16.0 square meters.[4]

By means of a series of Chi-square tests of association, it was found that the small class of rooms generally contained few internal structural features (no slab-lined features) and very few artifacts; but they did contain large amounts of the pollen of "economic" plants.[5] The large rooms, on the other hand, were significantly associated with firepits, mealing bins, ventilators, artifacts (including potsherds), lithic waste, animal bone, and seeds; but they contained very little economic pollen. The distributions of the major classes of artifacts, in terms of statistical means, is given in Table 1. Other pertinent distributions appear in Table 2.

The factor analysis of pottery-types was particularly interesting in that it indicated that each type of room was dominated by a different constellation or cluster of pottery-types. Of the thirteen types analyzed, five of them were dominant in habitation rooms; two of them were dominant in storage rooms; and two were largely peculiar to ceremonial rooms. The four remaining types were common to both habitation and ceremonial rooms (cf. Table 3).

The primary goal of this room-type analysis was not the establishment of the types themselves; rather, it was a first step in arriving at some of the *functional* characteristics of the rooms. Many of the functions of these room-types, and the centrally located plaza as well, were determined by

[4] Seven rooms exceeded 16.0 sq. m. in floor area; one was as large as 33.5 sq. m. The distribution did not suggest a definite third mode, however.

[5] Economic plants are defined as those for which there is evidence of their introduction into the site by man rather than by natural agencies. In the present case, they include *Zea, Cucurbita, Cleome, Opuntia*, and several others.

TABLE 1. DISTRIBUTION OF ARTIFACT TYPES

Artifact Type	Mean No. Per Habit. Room	Mean No. Per Storage Room	Mean No. Per Kiva	Total	Dominant Room-Types		
Projectile Points	.92	.08	.50	27	H		K
Arrowshaft Tools	.88	.11	.00	25	H		
Antler Flakers	.08	.08	.25	5			K
Saws	.28	.04	.00	8	H		
Graver-Burins	.20	.20	.00	10	H	S	
Flake Knives	1.70	.23	.00	48	H		
Bifacial Knives	.20	.07	.00	7	H		
Utilized Flakes	2.40	1.00	2.00	96	H	S	K
Blades	.16	.16	.00	8	H	S	
Cores	.92	.23	1.50[a]	35	H		K
Scrapers	3.00	.84	3.00[a]	108	H		K
Choppers	2.60	.44	4.70[a]	96	H		K
Axes	.32	.00	.00	8	H		
Mauls	.28	.11	.00	10	H		
Hammerstones	3.70	.69	2.00[a]	118	H		K
Metates	1.10	.15	.25	32	H		
Manos	6.60	1.00	.25	192	H		
Worked Slabs	.88	.15	.75	29	H		K
Worked Sherds	1.50	.15	.25	42	H		
Bone Awls	1.60	.27	.25	48	H		
Bone Rings and Ring Material	1.00	.11	.25	30	H		
"Ornamental Items"	.96	.19	.50	31	H		K

[a] All from a single kiva (kiva beneath Room 41).

TABLE 2. DISTRIBUTION OF NON-ARTIFACT MATERIALS

Item	Mean No. Per Habit. Room	Mean No. Per Storage Room	Mean No. Per Kiva
Firepits	1.0	0.0	1.0
Mealing Bins	1.0	0.0	0.0
Ventilators	0.5	0.0	1.0
Lithic Waste	98.0	30.0	37.0
Animal Bone	120.0	26.0	29.0
Seeds	9.3	4.2	2.5
Pollen Grains (economic)	22.0	51.0	17.0

examining the differential spatial clustering of both artifact and non-artifact materials, as outlined above. The functional "meanings" of these materials were derived from direct ethnographic evidence or worldwide comparative evidence in most cases. Some of the probable functions of the room-types

TABLE 3. DISTRIBUTION OF POTTERY-TYPES (INDICATES ROOM-TYPES IN WHICH POTTERY-TYPES ARE DOMINANT, AS DETERMINED BY FACTOR ANALYSIS)

Pottery-Type	Habit.	Storage	Kiva
Brown Plain Corrugated, smudged interior	X		
Brown Indented Corrugated, smudged interior	X		
McDonald Indented Corrugated	X		
Tularosa Black-on-White	X		
Snowflake Black-on-White, Hay Hollow variety	X		
Brown Indented Corrugated	X		X
Patterned Corrugated	X		X
Snowflake Black-on-White, Snowflake variety	X		X
Pinto Polychrome	X		X
Brown Plain Corrugated			X
St. Johns Black-on-Red			X
McDonald Corrugated		X	
St. Johns Polychrome		X	

TABLE 4. FUNCTIONS OF THE ROOM-TYPES

Habitation	Storage	Kiva
Food Preparation	Storage of plant foods	Ceremonies
Eating		Weaving
Water storage and use	Storage of non-plant items	Manufacture of hunting tools
Manufacture of hunting tools	"Work"	

are listed in Table 4. In addition to these functions, it seems possible that the habitation rooms also served as centers for the manufacture of pottery, the manufacture of ground and pecked stone implements, and the manufacture of ornamental items. These suggestions are somewhat doubtful, however. In the case of pottery manufacture, for example, the ethnographic evidence suggests occurrence outside of the rooms rather than within them.

In any event, nearly all of the functions given in Table 4 are found to have been carried out in analogous types of rooms among the recent Hopi and Zuni Indians. Thus, this pattern of room usage seems to have changed very little among the western Pueblos during the last seven hundred years.

It is significant that, were it not for the pollen data recovered from nearly all of the rooms at the site, it would have been impossible to state with any certainty that the so-called "storage" rooms actually did serve in a storage capacity. They generally contained so much more *Zea* and *Cucurbita* pollen than did the other rooms that their storage function can hardly be denied (Chi-square, significant at .001 level). The tentative demonstration that pollen data can be used in isolating functionally specific areas within a site may represent a methodological advancement. It may, in the future, be possible to isolate functionally different *sites* by this method. Seasonally occupied sites might be particularly susceptible to differentiation in this manner.

RESIDENCE UNITS

William A. Longacre claims to have demonstrated the existence of two, and possibly three, "localized matrilineages" at a somewhat earlier site in the Hay Hollow Valley (Carter Ranch Site, Longacre 1963, 1964). His demonstration was based on the occurrence of a nonrandom distribution of ceramic design-elements at the site. He was able to show that the north and south halves of the site were different in terms of their constellations or clusters of design-elements; and since modes of design-style are transmitted from mother to daughter within the localized matrilineal framework among the present-day western Pueblos, he was able to interpret the localized clusters of design-elements at Carter Ranch Site as representing the loci of extinct matrilineages. Although there is some question concerning his demonstration of lineality, it is likely that his major conclusions are correct.

The factor analyses of ceramic design-elements and pottery-types, as well as other data from Broken K, have led to somewhat similar conclusions. At this site, however, there seem to have been *five* such localized units; and I have chosen to call them "uxorilocal residence units" instead of "localized matrilineages."[6] These units can be grouped into two larger, more inclusive residence units. The locations of the units may be seen in Figure 2. Their existence, although tentative, was demonstrated as follows:

1. Nonrandom distributions of ceramic design-elements, pottery-types, firepit-types, storage pits, "chopper"-types and animal bone indicated discrete *localizations* within the pueblo (which could not be explained in terms of functionally specific areas). An example of these distributions is presented in Figure 3. The distributions of all of the above categories are given in Table 5.

2. Through the use of ethnographic evidence, it was found that these items and stylistic elements were probably associated with *female* activities (except perhaps choppers and animal bone, for which there is no clear

----

[6] Uxorilocal residence is defined as a residence situation in which husband and wife live in the vicinity of the wife's maternal relatives.

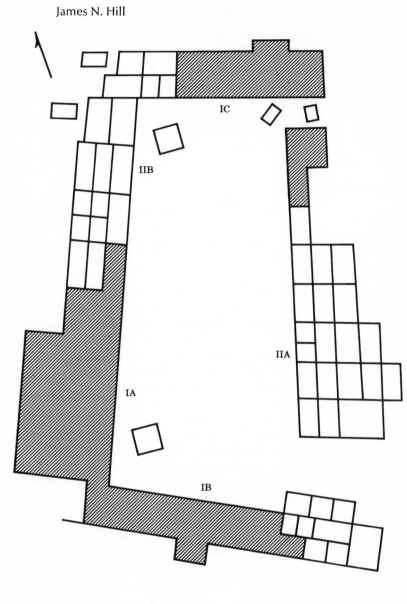

FIGURE 2.
Approximate locations of the inclusive residence units at Broken K Pueblo. Shaded areas indicate Residence Unit no. I and its subunits; the unshaded areas represent Residence Unit no. II and its subunits.

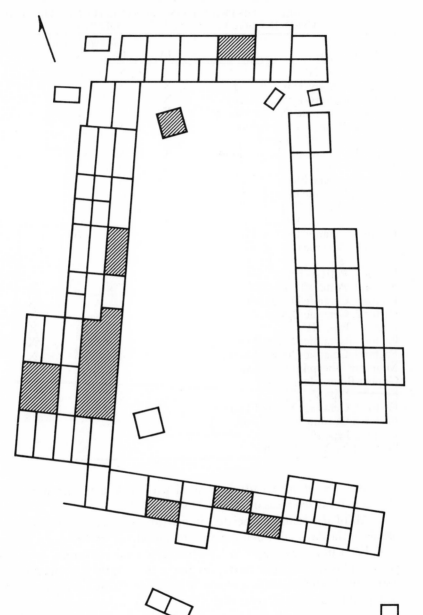

FIGURE 3.
Distribution of Factor 1, analysis of pottery-types found on floors.
The shaded area, indicating the distribution of Factor 1, delineates
the general locus of Residence Unit no. I.

TABLE 5. DISTRIBUTION OF STYLISTIC CATEGORIES
USED IN ISOLATING THE LOCI OF RESIDENCE UNITS

Stylistic Category	Residence Units				
	IA	IB	IC	IIA	IIB
Firepits, Type IV	X	X	X	X	
Factor 2, Pottery-Types, Floors	X	X	X		
Factor 1, Pottery-Types, Floors	X	X	X		
Factor 12, Ceramic Design, Floors	X	X	X		
Factor 2, Ceramic Design, Floors	X	X	X		
Storage Pits, 7–15 Present	X	X	X		
Factor 13, Ceramic Design, Floors	X	X			
Firepits, Type I	X	X			
Flake Choppers, Floors	X	X			
Factor 5, Ceramic Design, Floors	X				
Factor 4, Ceramic Design, Fills	X				
Prairie Dog Bone, Floors	X				
Factor 9, Ceramic Design, Fills	X		X		
Factor 6, Ceramic Design, Floors		X			
Factor 3, Pottery-Types, Floors				X	X
Factor 4, Pottery-Types, Floors				X	X
Factor 1, Ceramic Design, Fills				X	X
Factor 2, Ceramic Design, Fills				X	X
Firepits, Type III				X	X
Factor 3, Ceramic Design, Floors				X	
Factor 9, Ceramic Design, Floors				X	
Mountain Sheep Bone, Floors				X	
Gopher Bone, Floors				X	
Firepits, Type V		X		X	
Factor 4, Ceramic Design, Floors					X
Factor 3, Ceramic Design, Fills					X
Firepits, Type II					X
Storage Pits, None Present					X

evidence). No items clearly associated with male activities were found to cluster in localized areas of the pueblo.

3. All of the female-associated items (above) were found to have been usable in the day-to-day maintenance of a residence unit.

4. Each unit was found to have had temporal continuity — at least 65 years. (This seems conservative, for the entire length of occupation was ca. 130 years; both the north and south halves of the site were thus probably occupied for at least 65 years each.)

It seems likely that this evidence is sufficient for the establishment of uxorilocal residence units, especially when it is considered in the light of the fact that such units are characteristic of the modern Pueblos. Of all residence systems known, only uxorilocal and duolocal[7] systems should be

---

[7] Duolocal residence is defined as a residence situation in which husband and wife live separately, each with his own relatives.

reflected by highly nonrandom distributions of female-associated items or stylistic elements; and in the latter case, one would expect male-associated items to distribute in a non-random manner also (cf. Table 6).

We must assume here, of course, that the entire site was occupied synchronously; as I have already indicated, this cannot be demonstrated with certainty — not, at least, until techniques for intra-site dating are vastly improved. Still, on the basis of the slim evidence presented previously, the assumption of contemporaneity seems reasonably likely. If this was *not* the case, there is no reason to conclude that the exposition to this point is invalid; even when the early and late halves of the site are considered separately, the non-random distributions of female-associated items still emerge. We would simply have indications of *fewer* residence units existing at a given point in time.

The two large residence units at Broken K (I-A,B,C and II-A,B, Fig. 2) can perhaps be considered as representing residence *groups* (rather than simple aggregations of women) because there is some evidence that they were integrated internally. This is suggested by the fact that the subunits within each large unit were much more similar to one another with regard to the above mentioned stylistic elements than any one of them was to the other large unit. This sharing of stylistic elements suggests that there was less "social distance" within each large unit than there was between large units; and it may also be an indirect measure of economic cooperation — but the latter inference is clearly stretching a point. It is also possible, however, that each large unit controlled or used its own kiva. This is suggested because, in general, each ceremonial room had stylistic affinities with only one of the two large units. That ceramic design style can by itself indicate shared control or use of kivas is not completely certain, of course; if such were found to be the case among present-day Pueblo groups, the above inference would be much stronger. As it stands, the possibility is simply a suggestion susceptible to further testing.

To carry this analysis a step further, it is possible that these residence units were "corporate" groups.[8] This is suggested, provided that one can accept the above evidence of style sharing and common participation in kivas. It also seems possible, however, that nonmovable property was inherited within each group (i.e., rooms). Most rooms were apparently inhabited for at least sixty-five years, or roughly three generations, by the same group; and this suggests that they were inherited.

Thus it is likely that Broken K Pueblo contained two major uxorilocal residence units (possibly "groups"), each with at least two subunits — and corporateness might be postulated. It is not possible to infer the existence of matrilineal *descent*, nor would such an inference be desirable, consider-

---

[8] A "corporate" group is defined here as a group of related people who cooperate economically and transmit nonmovable property within the group.

TABLE 6. RESIDENCE PATTERNS AND THEIR
HYPOTHETICAL DISTRIBUTION CORRELATES

Residence Pattern	Definition	Distribution of Female Stylistic Items	Distribution of Male Stylistic Items
Uxorilocal	Husband and wife live in vicinity of wife's maternal relatives	Nonrandom	Random
Matrilocal	Husband and wife live in vicinity of wife's mother	Nonrandom	Random
Matrilocal, with resident male head	Same, but a mother's brother and his family reside within the group	Nonrandom	Random
Virilocal	Husband and wife live in vicinity of husband's relatives — patrilineal or matrilineal	Random	Nonrandom
Patrilocal	Husband and wife live in vicinity of husband's father	Random	Nonrandom
Avunculocal	Husband and wife live in vicinity of husband's maternal uncle	Random	Nonrandom
Neolocal	Husband and wife live separate from either mate's relatives	Random	Random
Bilocal	Husband and wife live either in vicinity of husband's or wife's relatives	Random	Random
Duolocal	Husband and wife live separately, with own relatives	Nonrandom	Nonrandom

ing the present state of social anthropological understanding of descent rules. Furthermore, we clearly cannot excavate social "rules" or norms of any sort.

A comparison of the localization of residence units at this site with the two residence units inferred for Carter Ranch Site is illuminating. In terms of number of rooms, the units at Carter Ranch Site were the same size as the subunits of the two major units at Broken K (ca. twenty rooms per unit); and they may have been equivalent in terms of social organization. This suggests the possibility that Carter Ranch Site as a *whole* was equivalent to only *one* of the major units at Broken K. It may be that as villages increased in size through time, there was an increasing number of large units per village.

The modern Hopi and Zuni also have a hierarchy of social organizational units — lineages, clans, and so forth. It may be that the largest units at Broken K (I and II) were roughly equivalent to clans (or phratries), while the subunits were equivalent to lineages (or clans); but this cannot, of course, be demonstrated. It may, in the future, be possible to compare prehistoric pueblos with *one another* with respect to "equivalent" social units. Eventually it may be feasible to compare other kinds of sites in a similar manner.

ADAPTIVE RESPONSES

A number of sociological changes were evidently occurring between A.D. 1050 and 1300 in the Southwest, changes which may have been promoted by an environmental shift. Although this is merely a hypothesis, there is some rather good evidence for such a shift. It is documented by the nearly simultaneous occurrence of the following events:

1. A shift from a relative abundance of arboreal pollen to a relative abundance of non-arboreal pollen (Schoenwetter 1962; Hevly 1964).
2. A shift from a relative abundance of large sized *Pinus* pollen grains (probably *P. ponderosa*) to a relative abundance of small sized grains (probably *P. edulis*) (Schoenwetter 1962; Hevly 1964).
3. A shift in the widths of tree-rings, from wide to narrow (probably reflecting a shortage of "effective" soil moisture) (Douglas 1929; Schoenwetter and Eddy 1964; Hevly 1964).
4. A widespread "cycle" of erosion (Bryan 1925; Hack 1942; Schoenwetter and Eddy 1964).

There are a number of reasons for thinking that these events may have been related to one another and that they reflect prehistoric conditions inimical to agriculture.

There seem to have been responses to an environmental shift throughout the Southwest. Of major importance was a general decrease in population which was in full force by about A.D. 1250. At about the same time, many villages were abandoned, and people appear to have aggregated into fewer but larger villages along major drainageways. At the same time, it is possible that there was an increase in the scope of inter-village integration, as indicated by the fact that "Great Kivas"[9] became more common between ca. A.D. 1000 and 1200. These kivas may have been associated with inter-village ritual institutions. There is also a suggestion of a broadened scope of intra-village integration, as evidenced by the fact that the ratio of ceremonial rooms to other types of rooms became continuously smaller through time (Steward 1937).

The same trends are noted in the vicinity of Broken K and Carter Ranch Site. Furthermore, in comparing the two sites themselves, it was found that there is a small amount of evidence suggesting a trend toward a broadened scope of intra-village integration. Broken K, the later of the two sites, seems to have reached a more "advanced" stage in this respect, and the evidence is as follows:

1. At Carter Ranch Site, both small residence units apparently owned or controlled their own kivas; while at Broken K, kivas were shared by the small units (subunits) within each *major* residence unit. (This inference is less than sure, however, since we do not really know that shared design-elements in kivas represent shared ownership or control.)

2. The residence units were less strictly localized at Broken K than at Carter Ranch Site, suggesting that internal social division may have been less formal or less important.

3. The architecture and room features at Broken K were much more homogeneous stylistically than was the case at Carter Ranch Site. (This suggests an increased scope of style sharing and communication.)

This evidence cannot be considered conclusive for inferring an increased scope of intra-village integration. One reason for this is that it is difficult to infer aspects of social integration from living arrangements and style distributions alone. There are certainly other hypotheses which could be presented.

The hypothesis offered here is supported to some extent by the fact that the degree of residence localization among present-day Hopi and Zuni Indians seems to be indicative of the degree of intra-village integration in these pueblos. Since the residence units at Broken K appear to have been more localized than are modern western Pueblo residence units, it may be that they were also less integrated (cf. Kroeber, 1917:90–200; Parsons 1925:112; Titiev 1944; Eggan 1950; and others).

In addition to the hypothesized increasing scope of integration and aggregation, however, there is direct evidence that the people of Broken K were responding to an environmental shift. The idea that agriculture was

[9] "Great Kivas" are defined as large ceremonial structures, generally exceeding thirty feet in diameter or length and containing somewhat more elaborate features than do other kivas (cf. Wormington 1959:86; Vivian and Reiter 1960:83–96). A clear definition of Great Kivas has not yet been given, however.

becoming difficult is supported by the fact that there was a significant replacement of domesticates (corn and squash) with wild food crops through time; the quantities of fossil pollen grains representing known domesticates decrease, both within Broken K itself, and between Carter Ranch Site and Broken K.[10] The numbers of charred corn cobs and squash seeds show the same trend.[11] At the same time, the pollen and seeds of "wild" plants increased through time.

An increase in the frequencies of food-grinding implements through time may reflect the fact that more such tools were needed to process the increased amount and variety of wild plants being collected. Furthermore, there was a 20 percent increase in storage space between the early and late portions of the site, suggesting a possible need to store increased quantities of seed for planting in the event of crop failure. We know that among the modern Hopi, the recent assurance of a stable food supply has led to a *decrease* in the amount of food stored for long periods of time (Whiting 1939:11).

There is also evidence that hunting may have become difficult at Broken K. The hunting of deer, mountain sheep, and jackrabbits was replaced through time by the hunting of cottontail;[12] and the relative proportion of "hunting tools" to other kinds of artifacts declined at the same time.

There are, of course, other possible explanations for these responses besides the idea that they were prompted by a shift in the physical environment. The possibilities of flood, fire, "inner cultural tendency," internal dissension, and disease have all been suggested at one time or another; and most archaeologists consider them unlikely. The possibility that "enemy attack" was involved cannot be lightly dismissed; but the fact that people were aggregating along drainageways, and in generally nondefensive locations, suggests that warfare is a somewhat unlikely explanation. There is very little evidence for it in the Southwest at this time period.

It may be, of course, that the trend toward aggregation, and the possible trend toward an increasing scope of integration, were prompted by changes in the physical environment wrought by man himself rather than by strictly natural causes. It is also possible that some of the responses discussed here were not at all related to an environmental shift and a decreasing productivity of agriculture and hunting. Further, one might reasonably suggest that under the environmental conditions hypothesized, the inhabitants of the area would *disperse* rather than aggregate and integrate. Still, once these people were committed to a stable, sedentary agricultural economy, it seems

[10] Early rooms at Broken K contain between 6 and 85 grains of "economic" pollen while the late rooms generally contained 0 to 5 grains (Chi-square, .05 level).

[11] Out of 53 charred corn cobs found at the site, 46 of them were in early rooms. Of 70 squash seeds, 49 of them were found in early rooms.

[12] Tested by Chi-square (0.1 level).

likely that they might have attempted to maintain it in the face of conditions that would probably promote dispersal among less sedentary peoples. The impression is given, in the ethnographic literature, that the Hopi and Zuni would find it difficult or impossible to revert to a strictly hunting and gathering existence.

After Broken K was abandoned, the inferred process of aggregation and integration appears to have continued — both in east-central Arizona and throughout major portions of the Southwest. By 1540, there were only a few remaining large pueblos — at Hopi, Zuni, and along the Rio Grande. An examination of the ethnographic evidence indicates that the Hopi and Zuni have a much wider scope of intra-village integrative mechanisms than are *apparent* at either Carter Ranch Site or Broken K (cf. Kroeber 1917:183; Parsons 1925:112; Bunzel 1932:476; Eggan 1950:116). It is particularly notable that today there is very little descent group localization, and ceremonial society members are recruited from the entire village.

Hopi and Zuni economic integration is extremely important on a village-wide scale (cf. Forde 1931; Beaglehole 1937; Goldman 1937). It is doubtful that individual families or lineages could exist as independent units. It seems at least possible that, beginning about A.D. 1050, an environmental shift made subsistence so difficult for Pueblo adaptive systems that previously separate family or lineage groups were forced to aggregate for mutual support (to maintain an agricultural existence). This aggregation, in turn, may have led to the development of broadened integrative mechanisms which served to bind larger groups together.

CONCLUSIONS

This short paper has presented an example of some of the kinds of inferences which may be made concerning the internal structure and social organization of a prehistoric pueblo site. It has also examined some of the evidence related to an ultimate explanation of changes in site structure through time. Even though the results are tentative, it is hoped that they are suggestive of some of the kinds of problems and inferences with which archaeologists might reasonably deal. This is not to say that the kinds of concerns discussed here should be the primary concerns in archaeology — far from it. I merely suggest that this line of research will not be detrimental, and it should be useful to pursue it further, especially since the techniques for doing so are developing rapidly.

The specific hypotheses developed here do not provide any answers, and they would not be acceptable to many archaeologists as explanations. They are not intended as explanations but, rather, as testable hypotheses. Future research will alter their usefulness, no doubt.

If it is indeed possible to define the outlines of prehistoric activity-structures and residence units in the Pueblo Southwest, it may also be possible to do it elsewhere. Having defined these outlines, it should be possible to compare them in time and space. And further, it should be possible to learn something about the *processes* of change.

One of the crucial concerns for those who are interested in this approach would seem to lie in the further development of research designs and techniques that can be used in recovering and analyzing data that will be useful in making more complete descriptions of prehistoric sociocultural systems and more complete explanations of their change in time and space.

BIBLIOGRAPHY

Beaglehole, Ernest
> 1937 Notes on Hopi Economic Life. *Yale University Publications in Anthropology*, no. 15.

Binford, Lewis R.
> 1962 "Archaeology as Anthropology." *American Antiquity* 28:217–25.
> 1964 "A Consideration of Archaeological Research Design." *American Antiquity* 29:425–41.
> 1965 "Archaeological Systematics and the Study of Culture Process." *American Antiquity* 31:203–10.

Bryan, K.
> 1925 "Date of Channel Trenching (Arroyo Cutting) in the Arid Southwest." *Science* 62:338–44.

Bunzel, Ruth
> 1932 "Introduction to Zuni Ceremonialism." *Forty-seventh Annual Report of the Bureau of American Ethnology.*

Deetz, James
> 1960 "An Archaeological Approach to Kinship Change in Eighteenth Century Arikara Culture." Unpublished Ph.D. dissertation, Harvard University.
> 1965 "The Dynamics of Stylistic Change in Arikara Ceramics." *Illinois Studies in Anthropology*, no. 4. Urbana: University of Illinois Press.

Douglass, A. E.
> 1929 "The Secret of the Southwest Solved by Talkative Tree Rings." *National Geographic Magazine* 56:736–70.

Eggan, Fred
> 1950 *Social Organization of the Western Pueblos.* Chicago: University of Chicago Press.
> 1952 "The Ethnological Cultures and Their Archaeological Backgrounds." In *Archaeology of Eastern United States*, James B. Griffin (ed.). Chicago: University of Chicago Press.

Forde, C. Daryll
   1931   "Hopi Agriculture and Land Ownership." *Journal of the Royal Anthropological Institute of Great Britain and Ireland* 61:357–405.
Freeman, Leslie G., Jr., and James A. Brown
   1964   "Statistical Analysis of Carter Ranch Pottery." In *Chapters in the Prehistory of Eastern Arizona II. Fieldiana: Anthropology,* no. 55. Chicago Natural History Museum.
Fruchter, Benjamin
   1954   *Introduction to Factor Analysis.* Princeton, N.J.: D. Van Nostrand Co.
Goldman, Irving
   1937   "The Zuni Indians of New Mexico." In *Cooperation and Competition among Primitive Peoples,* Margaret Mead (ed.). New York: McGraw-Hill.
Hack, J. T.
   1942   "The Changing Physical Environment of the Hopi Indians of Arizona." *Papers of the Peabody Museum, Harvard University,* vol. 35.
Hevly, Richard Holmes
   1964   "Pollen Analysis of Quaternary Archaeological and Lacustrine Sediments from the Colorado Plateau." Unpublished Ph.D. dissertation, University of Arizona.
Kroeber, A. L.
   1917   "Zuni Kin and Clan." *Anthropological Papers of the American Museum of Natural History,* vol. 18, no. 2.
Longacre, William A.
   1963   "Archaeology as Anthropology: A Case Study." Unpublished Ph.D. dissertation, University of Chicago.
   1964   "Archaeology as Anthropology: A Case Study." *Science* 144:1454–55.
Parsons, E. C.
   1925   "A Pueblo Indian Journal, 1920–1921." *Memoirs of the American Anthropological Association,* no. 32.
Rootenberg, S.
   1964   "Archaeological Field Sampling." *American Antiquity* 30:181–88.
Schoenwetter, James
   1962   "The Pollen Analysis of Eighteen Archaeological Sites in Arizona and New Mexico." In *Chapters in the Prehistory of Eastern Arizona, I. Fieldiana: Anthropology,* no. 53. Chicago Natural History Museum.
   _____, and Frank W. Eddy
   1964   "Alluvial and Palynological Reconstruction of Environments, Navajo Reservoir District." *Museum of New Mexico Papers in Anthropology,* no. 13.

Sears, William H.
  1961   "The Study of Social and Religious Systems in North American Archaeology." *Current Anthropology* 2:223–46.

Steward, Julian Haynes
  1937   "Ecological Aspects of Southwestern Society." *Anthropos* 32:87–104.

Titiev, Mischa
  1944   "Old Oraibi, A Study of the Hopi Indians of Third Mesa." *Papers of the Peabody Museum,* Harvard University, vol. 22.

Vivian, Gordon, and Paul Reiter
  1960   "The Great Kivas of Chaco Canyon." *Monographs of the School of American Research and the Museum of New Mexico,* 22. Santa Fe: Museum of New Mexico Press.

Whiting, Alfred F.
  1939   "Ethnobotany of the Hopi." *Museum of Northern Arizona Bulletin,* no. 15. Flagstaff.

Wormington, H. M.
  1959   "Prehistoric Indians of the Southwest." *Denver Museum of Natural History,* Popular Series, 7.

KENT V. FLANNERY

Like Hill's study of the Broken K Pueblo, this article by
Kent Flannery on early Mesoamerican culture exemplifies the
application of new perspectives to archaeological theory.
Notable in this case is the use of systems theory (also
referred to in other selections, especially Struever's and
Binford's) in viewing the sweep of cultural development over
eight millennia. Systems theory — which considers cultures as
systems within larger ecosystems of which they are a
part — in modern archaeology essentially explains the history
of culture change within an ecological framework.

20 Archaeological Systems Theory and Early Mesoamerica

INTRODUCTION

As work on the early periods of Mesoamerican prehistory
progresses, and we learn more about the food-collectors and early food-pro-
ducers of that region, our mental image of these ancient peoples has been
greatly modified. We no longer think of the preceramic plant-collectors as a
ragged and scruffy band of nomads; instead, they appear as a practiced and
ingenious team of lay botanists who know how to wring the most out of a
superficially bleak environment. Nor do we still picture the Formative
peoples as a happy group of little brown farmers dancing around their
cornfields and thatched huts; we see them, rather, as a very complex series
of competitive ethnic groups with internal social ranking and great preoccupation with status, iconography, water control, and the accumulation of
luxury goods. Hopefully, as careful studies bring these people into sharper

Reprinted, with the editorial changes noted, from "Archeological Systems Theory and
Early Mesoamerica" by Kent V. Flannery in Betty Meggers (ed.), *Anthropological
Archeology in the Americas* (Washington, D.C.: Anthropological Society of Washing-
ton, 1968), pp. 67–87, by permission of the author and the publisher.

focus, they will begin to make more sense in terms of comparable Indian groups surviving in the ethnographic present.

Among other things, the new data from Mesoamerica strain some of the theoretical models we used in the past to view culture and culture change. One of these was the model of a culture adapted to a particular environmental zone: "oak woodland," "mesquite-grassland," "semitropical thorn scrub," "tropical forest," and so on. New data suggest, first, that primitive peoples rarely adapt to whole "environmental zones" (Coe and Flannery 1964:650). Next, as argued in this article, it appears that sometimes a group's basic "adaptation" may not even be to the "micro-environments" within a zone, but rather to a small series of plant and animal genera whose ranges cross-cut several environments.

Another model badly strained by our new data is that of culture change during the transition from food-collecting to sedentary agriculture. Past workers often attributed this to the "discovery" that planted seeds would sprout (MacNeish 1964a:533), or to the results of a long series of "experiments" with plant cultivation. Neither of these explanations is wholly satisfying. We know of no human group on earth so primitive that they are ignorant of the connection between plants and the seeds from which they grow, and this is particularly true of groups dependent (as were the highland Mesoamerican food-collectors) on intensive utilization of seasonal plant resources. Furthermore, I find it hard to believe that "experiments with cultivation" were carried on only with those plants that eventually became cultivars, since during the food-collecting era those plants do not even seem to have been the principal foods used. In fact, they seem to have been less important than many wild plants which never became domesticated. Obviously, something besides "discoveries" and "experiments" is involved.

I believe that this period of transition from food-collecting to sedentary agriculture, which began by 5000 B.C. and ended prior to 1500 B.C., can best be characterized as one of gradual change in a series of procurement systems, regulated by two mechanisms called seasonality and scheduling. I would argue that none of the changes which took place during this period arose de novo, but were the result of expansion or contraction of previously existing systems. I would argue further that the use of an ecosystem model enables us to see aspects of this prehistoric culture change which are not superficially apparent.

In the course of this paper I will attempt to apply, on a prehistoric time level, the kind of ecosystem analysis advocated most recently by Vayda (1964) and Rappaport (1967), with modifications imposed by the nature of the archaeological data. Man and the Southern Highlands of Mexico will be viewed as a single complex system, composed of many subsystems which mutually influenced each other over a period of over seven millennia, between 8000 B.C. and 200 B.C. This systems approach will include the use of both the "first" and "second" cybernetics (Maruyama 1963) as a model for explaining prehistoric culture change.

The first cybernetics involves the study of regulatory mechanisms and "negative feedback" processes which promote equilibrium, and counteract deviation from stable situations over long periods of time. The second cybernetics is the study of "positive feedback" processes which amplify deviations, causing systems to expand and eventually reach stability at higher levels. Because I am as distressed as anyone by the esoteric terminology of systems theory, I have tried to substitute basic English synonyms wherever possible.

PROCUREMENT SYSTEMS IN THE PRECERAMIC (HUNTING AND GATHERING) ERA

Let us begin by considering the subsistence pattern of the food-collectors and "incipient cultivators" who occupied the Southern Highlands of Mexico between 8000 and 2000 B.C.

The sources of our data are plant and animal remains preserved in dry caves in the Valley of Oaxaca (Flannery, Kirkby, Kirkby, and Williams, 1967) and the Valley of Tehuacán (MacNeish 1961, 1962, 1964a). Relevant sites are Guilá Naquitz Cave, Cueva Blanca, and the Martínez Rock Shelter (near Mitla, in the Valley of Oaxaca), and MacNeish's now-famous Coxcatlán, Purrón, Abejas, El Riego, and San Marcos Caves, whose food remains have been partially reported (Callen 1965; Smith 1965a). Tens of thousands of plants and animal bones were recovered from these caves, which vary between 900 and 1900 meters in elevation and occur in environments as diverse as cool-temperate oak woodland, cactus desert, and semi-tropical thorn forest. Because most of the material has not been published in detail as yet, my conclusions must be considered tentative.

Preliminary studies of the food debris from these caves indicate that certain plant and animal genera were always more important than others, regardless of local environment. These plants and animals were the focal points of a series of procurement systems, each of which may be considered one component of the total ecosystem of the food-collecting era. They were heavily utilized — "exploited" is the term usually employed — but such utilization was not a one-way system. Man was not simply extracting energy from his environment, but participating in it; and his use of each genus was part of a system which allowed the latter to survive, even flourish, in spite of heavy utilization. Many of these patterns have survived to the present day, among Indian groups like the Paiute and Shoshone (Steward 1955:Chapter 6) or the Tarahumara of northern Mexico (Pennington 1963), thus allowing us to postulate some of the mechanisms built into the system, which allowed the wild genera to survive.

Each procurement system required a technology involving both implements (projectiles, fiber shredders, collecting tongs, etc.) and facilities (baskets, net carrying bags, storage pits, roasting pits, etc.). In many cases, these implements and facilities were so similar to those used in the ethnographic present by Utoaztecan speakers of western North America that relatively little difficulty is encountered in reconstructing the outlines of the ancient procurement system.

I. Plants

Literally hundreds of plant species were used by the food-collectors of the Southern Mexican Highlands. There were annual grasses like wild maize (*Zea*) and fox tail (*Setaria*), fruits like the avocado (*Persea*) and black zapote (*Diospyros*), wild onions (*Allium*), acorns and pinyon nuts, several varieties of pigweed (*Amaranthus*), and many other plants, varying considerably from region to region because of rainfall and altitude differences (Callen 1965; Smith, 1965b, and personal communication). However, three categories of plants seem to have been especially important wherever we have data, regardless of altitude. They are:

(1) The maguey (*Agave* spp.), a member of the Amaryllis family, which is available year-round; (2) a series of succulent cacti, including organ cactus (*Lemaireocereus* spp.) and prickly pear (*Opuntia* spp.), whose fruits are seasonal, but whose young leaves are available year-round; and (3) a number of related genera of tree legumes, known locally as mesquites (*Prosopis* spp.) and guajes (*Lucaena, Mimosa,* and *Acacia*), which bear edible pods in the rainy season only.

System 1: Maguey Procurement. Maguey, the "century plant," is most famous today as the genus from which pulque is fermented and tequila and mezcal are distilled. In prehistoric times, when distillation was unknown, the maguey appears to have been used more as a source of food. Perhaps no single plant element is more common in the dry caves of southern Mexico than the masticated cud or "quid" of maguey (Smith 1965a:77). It is not always realized, however, that these quids presuppose a kind of technological breakthrough: at some point, far back in preceramic times, the Indians learned how to make the maguey edible.

The maguey, a tough and phylogenetically primitive monocotyledon which thrives on marginal land even on the slopes of high, cold, arid valleys, is unbearably bitter when raw. It cannot be eaten until it has been roasted between twenty-four and seventy-two hours, depending on the youth and tenderness of the plant involved.

The method of maguey roasting described by Pennington (1963:129–30) is not unlike that of the present-day Zapotec of the Valley of Oaxaca. A circular pit, three to four feet in diameter and of equal depth, is lined with stones and fueled with some slow-burning wood, like oak. When the stones are red-hot, the pit is lined with maguey leaves which have been trimmed off the "heart" of the plant. The maguey hearts are placed in the pit, covered with grass and maguey leaves and finally a layer of earth, which seal the roasting pit and holds in the heat. After one to five days, depending on the age and quantity of maguey, the baking is terminated and the hearts are edible: all, that is, except the indigestible fiber, which is expectorated in the form of a "quid" after the nourishment is gone. Evidence of the roasting process can be detected in maguey fragments surviving in dessicated human feces from Coxcatlán Cave (Callen 1965:342).

The Zapotecs of the Valley of Oaxaca, like most Indians of southern Mexico, recognize that the best time to cut and roast the maguey is after it has sent up its inflorescence, or *quiote*. The plant begins to die after this event, which occurs sometime around the sixth or eighth year of growth, and a natural fermentation takes place in the moribund plant which softens it and increases its sugar content. The sending up of this inflorescence is a slow process, which can culminate at any time of the year. The large numbers of quiote fragments in our Oaxaca cave sites indicate that the Indians of the preceramic food-collecting era already knew that this was the best point in the plant's life-cycle for roasting.

The discovery that maguey (if properly processed) can be rendered edible was of major importance, for in some regions there is little else available in the way of plant food during the heart of the dry season. And the discovery that maguey was best for roasting *after* sending up its inflorescence and starting its natural fermentation meant that the plants harvested were mostly those that were dying already, and had long since sent out their pollen. Thus the maguey continued to thrive on the hillsides of the Southern Highlands in spite of the substantial harvests of the preceramic food-collectors: all they did was to weed out the dying plants.

System 2: Cactus Fruit Procurement. Organ cacti of at least four species were eaten at Tehuacán and Oaxaca, and their fruits — which appear late in the dry season — are still very common in Mexican markets. Most are sold under the generic terms *pitahaya* and *tuna*, but the best known "tuna" is really the fruit of the prickly pear (*Opuntia* spp.), the ubiquitous cactus of Mexican plains and rocky slopes. Most cactus fruit appears sometime toward the end of the dry season, depending on altitude, but the tender young leaves may be peeled and cooked during any season of the year.

The collecting of cactus fruit had to take place before the summer rains turned the fruit to mush, and had to be carried on in competition with fruit bats, birds, and small rodents, who also find the fruit appetizing. The fruits are spiny, and some of the Tehuacán caves contained wooden sticks which may have been "tongs" for use in picking them off the stem (MacNeish, personal communication). The spines can be singed off and the fruits transported by net bag or basket, but they cannot be stored for long. By sun-drying, the fruit can be saved for several weeks (Pennington 1963:117–

18), but eventually it begins to rot. It is worth noting, however, that harvest of most of these wild fruits must be done quickly and intensively because of competition from wild animals, rather than spoilage.

The harvesting and eating of cactus fruits, no matter how intensive it may be, does not appear to diminish the available stands of cactus nor reduce subsequent generations of tuna and pitahaya — for the seeds from which the plant is propagated almost inevitably survive the human digestive tract and escape in the feces, to sprout that very year. It is even possible that such harvests are beneficial for the prickly pear and columnar cacti, in affording them maximum seed dispersal. This is only one example of the self-perpetuating nature of some of the procurement systems operating in preceramic Mexico.

System 3: Tree Legume Procurement. Mesquite is a woody legume which prefers the deep alluvial soil of valley floors and river flood plains in the highlands. During the June to August rainy season it bears hundreds of pods which, while still green and tender, can be chewed, or boiled into a kind of syrup (called "miel" in the Oaxaca and Tehuacán Valleys).

Such use of mesquite extended from at least the Southern Mexican Highlands (where we found it in caves near Mitla) north to the Great American Southwest, where it was evident at Gypsum Cave and related sites (Harrington 1933). *Guajes,* whose edible pods mature in roughly the same season, characterize hill slopes and canyons, and were abundant in both the Mitla and Tehuacán caves (C. Earle Smith, personal communication).

The amount of food available when mesquite and guajes are at the peak of their pod-bearing season is truly impressive. Botanist James Schoenwetter, standing outside one of our Mitla caves in 1966 during the optimum mesquite-guaje season, personally communicated to us his suspicion that a family of four Indians could have collected a week's supply of legume pods there "practically without moving their feet."

The pod-bearing pattern of mesquite and guaje demands a seasonal, localized, and fairly intensive period of collecting. The pods can be hand-picked, and probably were transported in the many types of baskets and net carrying bags recovered in the Oaxaca and Tehuacán caves (MacNeish 1964a:533; Flannery, unpublished data). Both pods and seeds can be dried and stored for long periods, but they must be picked at the appropriate time or they will be eaten by animals, like deer, rabbit, and ring-tailed cat.

II. Mammals

Mammals were an important year-round resource in ancient Mesoamerica, where winters are so mild that many animals never hibernate, as they do at more northern latitudes. Deer, peccary, rabbits, raccoons, opossums, skunks, ground squirrels, and large pocket gophers were common in the prehistoric refuse (Flannery, n.d.). However, wherever we have adequate samples of archaeological animal bones from the Southern Highlands of Mexico, it appears that the following generalization is valid: white-tailed deer and cottontail rabbits were far and away the most important game mammals in all periods, and most hunting technology in the preceramic (and Formative) eras was designed to recover these two genera. Our discussion of wild animal exploitation will therefore center on these animals.

System 4: White-Tailed Deer Procurement. The white-tailed deer, a major food resource in ancient times, continues to be Mesoamerica's most important single game species. Part of its success is due to the wide range of plant foods it finds acceptable, and its persistence even in the immediate vicinity of human settlement and under extreme hunting pressure. White-tailed deer occur in every habitat in Mesoamerica, but their highest populations are in the pine-oak woodlands of the Sierra Madre. The tropical rain forests, such as those of the lowland Maya area, are the least suitable habitats for this deer. Within Mesoamerica proper, highest prehistoric populations would have been in areas like the mountain woodlands of the Valley of Mexico, Puebla, Toluca, Oaxaca, and Guerrero.

These deer have relatively small home ranges, and although they often spend part of the daylight hours hiding in thickets, they can be hunted in the morning and evening when they come out to forage. Deer have known trails along which they travel within their home ranges, and where ambush hunters can wait for them. In other words, they are susceptible to daylight hunts, on foot, by men armed with nothing more sophisticated than an atlatl or even a fire-hardened spear, such as used by the Chiapanecs of the Grijalva Depression (Lowe 1959:7). On top of this, they can stand an annual harvest of 30 to 40 percent of the deer population without diminishing in numbers (Leopold 1959:513). Archaeological data (Flannery, n.d.) suggest that the hunters of the Tehuacán and Oaxaca Valleys did not practice any kind of conservation, but killed males, females, fawns, and even pregnant does (as indicated by skeletal remains of late-term foetuses). This does not seem to have depleted local deer populations in any way. In fact, by thinning the herds during times of optimum plant resource availability, it may even have prevented the starvation of deer during the heart of the dry season.

System 5: Cottontail Procurement. I have already discussed the ecology of Mexican cottontails in a previous paper (Flannery 1966) and will only recapitulate briefly here: cottontails are available year round (though most abundant in the rainy season) and can best be taken by means of traps or snares. Throwing sticks are also effective, and the Indians of northern Mexico use a figure-four rock trap or "deadfall" (Pennington 1963:90 and

Plate XII). In the Tehuacán caves there were fragments of whittled sticks and fiber loops or slip knots which may be trap fragments (MacNeish 1964a:533 and personal communication); similar fragments showed up in one of our Oaxaca caves in 1966. The best feature of cottontail trapping is that the only investment of labor is in the manufacture and setting of the trap; it works for you while you go about other tasks. And cottontails are such prolific breeders that no amount of trapping is likely to wipe them out.

REGULATORY MECHANISMS

The ecosystem in which the hunters and collectors of ancient Mexico participated included many regulatory mechanisms, which kept the system successful, yet counteracted deviation from the established pattern. I will discuss only two of these — "seasonality" and "scheduling." "Seasonality" was imposed on man by the nature of the wild resources themselves; "scheduling" was a cultural activity which resolved conflict between procurement systems.

I. Seasonality

The most important divisions of the Mesoamerican year are a winter season (October to May), which is dry, and a summer season (June to September), when most of the annual rain falls. Many edible plants and animals of the area are available only during one season, or part of a season. For example, in the semiarid highlands of Mexico some plants like the *pochote* or kapok tree (*Ceiba parvifolia*), as well as many species of columnar cacti, bear fruit in the late winter just before the rains begin, so that their seeds will sprout that same year. Other trees, like the oak (*Quercus* spp.) and the *chupandilla* (*Cyrtocarpa* sp.) bear fruit after the summer season, so their seeds will lie dormant through the winter and sprout during the following year. These differences, which are of adaptive value to the plant (allowing each species to flower and seed itself during the time of year when it is most advantageous), somewhat predetermined the collecting schedule of the pre-agricultural bands in Mesoamerica: often these Indians had to be able to predict to within a week or two when the maturation of the plant would take place, and then they would have to harvest furiously before the plants were eaten by birds, rodents, or other small mammals.

MacNeish (1964a; 1964b) has shown some of the ways in which human groups reacted to seasonality. During the rainy season, in areas where many wild plant resources were available, they often came together in large groups which MacNeish calls "macrobands," probably consisting of a series of related families (cf. Steward 1955:Chapter 6). During the heart of the dry season, when few edible plants are available, the group fragmented into "microbands," which may have been individual family units. These small units scattered out widely over the landscape, utilizing resources too meager to support a macroband.

The seasonally restricted nature of resources made it impossible for groups to remain large all year, and effectively counteracted any trends toward population increase which might have been fostered by the intensive harvests of the rainy-season macrobands. Thus populations never grew to the point where they could effectively overreach their wild food resources. MacNeish (1964a:Fig. 4) postulates that as late as 3000 B.C. the population of the Tehuacán Valley was no higher than 120–240 persons, in an area of 1400 square miles.

II. Scheduling

So many possibilities for exploitive activity were open to these ancient Mesoamericans that it would have been impossible to engage in all of them, even seasonally. It happens that there are times of the year when a number of resources are available simultaneously, producing a situation in which there is some conflict for the time and labor of the group. Division of labor along the lines of sex, with men hunting and women collecting, is one common solution to these conflicts, but not all conflicts are so easily resolved.

The solution for more complex situations may be called "scheduling," and it involves a decision as to the relative merits of two or more courses of action. Such "scheduling decisions" are made constantly by all human groups on all levels of complexity, often without any awareness that a decision is being made.

It is not necessarily true that the lower the level of social complexity, the fewer the conflict decisions, for hunting and gathering groups of arid America had many scheduling problems to resolve. Food gathering bands of the Great Basin, for example, often depended on "scouting reports" from relatives who had passed through certain areas several weeks in advance. If they noticed an unusually high concentration of antelope or rabbit in a particular valley, or if they saw that a particular stand of wild fruit would come ripe within the next two weeks, they would advise other scattered bands of foragers about this resource (Steward 1955:105–6). Often, while they descended on the area to harvest that particular species, new reports would come in from other areas concerning still another resource. This was not the kind of "hit and miss" pattern of exploitation one might think, for the Great Basin Indians had a rough idea that acorns and pinyon nuts would be available in the autumn, wild legumes and grasses in the rainy season, and so on. The outlines of a schedule, albeit with conflicts, were present; the "scouting reports" helped resolve conflicts and gave precision to the dates of each kind of resource exploitation, depending on individual variations in growing season from year to year.

These individual variations, which are a common feature of arid environments, combined with the scheduling pattern to make it unlikely that specialization in any one resource would develop. This prevented over-utilization of key plants or animals, and maintained a more even balance between varied resources. Because scheduling is an opportunistic mechanism, it promoted survival in spite of annual variation, but at the same time it supported the status quo: unspecialized utilization of a whole range of plants and animals whose availability is erratic over the long run. In this sense, scheduling acted to counteract deviations which might have resulted in either (1) starvation, or (2) a more effective adaptation.

EVIDENCE FOR SCHEDULING IN THE FOOD-COLLECTING AND "INCIPIENT CULTIVATION" ERAS (8000–2000 B.C)

Thanks to the plants and animal bones preserved in the dry caves of Oaxaca and Tehuacán, we can often tell which season a given occupation floor was laid down in. Because of the work of botanists like Earle Smith, Lawrence Kaplan, and James Schoenwetter, we know the season during which each plant is available, and hence when its harvest must have taken place. Even the use of animal resources can often be dated seasonally; for example, in the Tehuacán Valley, we studied the seasonality of deer hunting by the condition of the antlers, which indicates the time of year when the animal was killed.

Assuming that each occupation floor in a given cave represents the debris of a single encampment, usually dating to a single season (an assumption that seems to be borne out by the quantity and nature of the refuse), the combinations of plant and animal remains observed in a given level tell us something about prehistoric scheduling decisions. Analyses of our Oaxaca caves and MacNeish's Tehuacán Caves, by roughly the same group of specialists (MacNeish 1962, 1964a; Flannery, n.d.), suggest the following tentative generalizations:

1. *Dry season camps* (October–March), depending on their elevation above sea level, may have great caches of fall and winter plants — for example, acorns in the Mitla area, or *Ceiba* pods in the Coxcatlán area — but in general they lack the variety seen in rainy-season levels. And perhaps most significantly, they have a high percentage of those plants which, although not particularly tasty, are available year-round: maguey, prickly pear leaf, *Ceiba* root, and so on. These are the so-called "starvation" plants, which can be eaten in the heart of the dry season when little else is

available. These same levels also tend to have high percentages of deer bone. Some, in fact, have little refuse beyond maguey quids and white-tailed deer.

2. *Rainy-season camps* (May–September), as might be expected, show great quantities of the plants available at that time of the year: mesquite, guajes, amaranth, wild avocado, zapotes, and so on. They also tend to be rich in small fauna like cottontail, opposum, skunk, raccoon, gopher, and black iguana. Although deer are often present in these camps, they frequently represent only a small percentage of the minimum individual animals in the debris. Nor are the "starvation" plants particularly plentiful in these rainy-season levels.

3. What these generalizations suggest, for the most part, is that scheduling gave preference to the seasonality of the *plant* species collected; and when conflict situations arose, it was the *animal* exploitation that was curtailed. I would reconstruct the pattern as follows:

A. In the late dry season and early rainy season, there is a period of peak abundance of wild plant foods. These localized resources were intensively harvested, and eaten or cached as they came to maturity; this appears to have been a "macroband" activity. Because "all hands" participated in these harvests, little deer hunting was done; instead the Indians set traps in the vicinity of the plant-collecting camp, an activity which does not conflict with intensive plant harvests the way deer-hunting would.

B. In the late fall and winter, most plants have ceased to bear fruit, but deer hunting is at its best. Since this is the mating season, male deer (who normally forage by themselves) fall in with the does and fawns, making the average herd larger; and since this is also the season when the deciduous vegetation of the highlands sheds its leaves, the deer can be more easily followed by hunters. As the dry season wears on, however, the deer grow warier and range farther and farther back into the mountains. This is the leanest time of the year in terms of plant resources, and it was evidently in this season that man turned most heavily to plants available year round, like the root of the Ceiba (which can be baked like sweet manioc) or the heart of the maguey plant (which can be roasted). These appear to have been "microband" activities.

C. By chewing roots and maguey hearts, the preceramic forager managed to last until the late spring growing season, at which point he could wallow in cactus fruit again. Essentially, his "schedule" was keyed to the seasonal availability of certain wild plants, which climaxed at those times of the year which were best suited for small-game trapping. He scheduled his most intensive deer hunting for the seasons when big plant harvests were not a conflicting factor.

D. Climatic fluctuations, delays in the rainy season, or periodic increases in the deer herds at given localities probably kept the picture more complex than we have painted it, but this cannot be detected in the archaeological record. The constant evolution of new bags, nets, baskets, projectile points, scrapers, carrying loops, and other artifacts from the caves of the Southern Highlands suggests slow but continual innovation. To what extent these innovations increased the productivity of the system is not clear.

Because the major adaptation was to a series of wild genera which cross-cut several environmental boundaries, the geographic extent of the ecosystem described above was very great. This adaptation is clearly reflected in the technological sphere. Implements and facilities of striking similarity can be found in regions which differ significantly in altitude and rainfall, so long as the five basic categories of plants and animals are present. This can be illustrated by an examination of the Coxcatlán Phase (5000–3000 B.C.) as it is represented at Coxcatlán Cave, Puebla (MacNeish 1962) and at Cueva Blanca, Oaxaca (Flannery, Kirkby, Kirkby, and Williams, 1967).

Coxcatlán Cave, type site for the phase, occurs at 975 meters in an arid tropical forest characterized by dense stands of columnar cacti; kapok trees (*Ceiba parvifolia*); chupandilla (*Cyrtocarpa* sp.); cozahuico (*Sideroxylon* sp.); and abundant Leguminosae, Burseraceae, and Anacardiaceae (Smith 1965b:Fig. 31). Cueva Blanca occurs at 1900 meters in a temperate woodland zone with scattered oaks; *Dodonaea*; ocotillo (*Fouquieria*); wild zapote (*Diospyros*); and other trees which (judging by archaeological remains) may originally have included hackberry (*Celtis*) and pinyon pine.

In spite of environmental differences, implements at the two sites are nearly identical; even the seasonal deer hunting pattern and the size of the encamped group are the same. In the past, such identity would have inspired the traditional explanation: "a similar adaptation to a similar arid environment." But as seen above, the two environments are not that similar. The important point is that the basic adaptation was not to a zone or even a biotope within a zone, but to five critical categories — white-tail deer, cottontail, maguey, tree legumes, prickly pear and organ cactus. These genera range through many zones, as did the Indians who hunted them, ate them, propagated their seeds, and weeded out their dying members. This is not to say that biotopes were unimportant; they played a role, but they were also cross-cut by a very important system.

Seasonality and scheduling, as examined here, were part of a "deviation-counteracting" feedback system. They prevented intensification of any one procurement system to the point where the wild genus was threatened; at the same time, they maintained a sufficiently high level of procurement efficiency so there was little pressure for change. Under the ecosystem operating in the Southern Mexican Highlands during the later part of the food-collecting era, there was little likelihood that man would exhaust his own food resources or that his population would grow beyond what the wild vegetation and fauna would support. Maintaining such near-equilibrium conditions is the purpose of deviation-counteracting processes.

POSITIVE FEEDBACK AND CULTURE CHANGE

Under conditions of fully achieved and permanently maintained equilibrium, prehistoric cultures might never have changed. That they did change was due at least in part to the existence of positive feedback or "deviation-amplifying" processes. These Maruyama (1963:164) describes as "all processes of mutual causal relationships that amplify an insignificant or accidental initial kick, build up deviation and diverge from the initial condition."

Such "insignificant or accidental initial kicks" were a series of genetic changes which took place in one or two species of Mesoamerican plants which were of use to man. The exploitation of these plants had been a relatively minor procurement system compared with that of maguey, cactus fruits, deer, or tree legumes, but positive feedback following these initial genetic changes caused one minor system to grow all out of proportion to the others, and eventually to change the whole ecosystem of the Southern Mexican Highlands. Let us now examine that system.

System 6: Wild Grass Procurement. One common activity of the food-collecting era in the Southern Highlands was the harvesting of annual grasses. Perhaps the most useful in pre-agricultural times was fox-tail grass (*Setaria*) (Callen 1965:343), followed by minor grasses like wild maize (*Zea mays*), which may have been adapted to moist barrancas within the arid highland zone (Smith 1965a:95).

We know very little about the nature of the early "experiments" with plant cultivation, but they probably began simply as an effort to increase the area over which useful plants would grow. For example, Smith (1965a:77–78) has suggested that the preceramic food-collectors may have attempted to increase the density of prickly pear and organ cactus stands by planting cuttings of these plants. For the most part, judging by the archaeological record, these efforts led to little increase in food supply and no change in emphasis on one genus or another, until — sometime between 5000 and 2000 B.C. — a series of genetic changes took place in a few key genera. It was these genetic changes, acting as a "kick," which allowed a deviation-amplifying system to begin.

As implied by Maruyama, many of these initial deviations may have been accidental and relatively minor. For example, beans (1) became more permeable in water, making it easier to render them edible; and (2) developed limp pods which do not shatter when ripe, thus enabling the Indians to harvest them more successfully (Kaplan 1965). Equally helpful were the changes in maize, whose genetic plasticity has fascinated botanists for years. While *Setaria* and the other grasses remained unchanged, maize underwent a series of alterations which made it increasingly more profitable to harvest (and plant over wider areas) than any other plant. Its cob increased in size; and, carried around the highlands by Indians intent on increasing its range, it met and crossed with its nearest relative, *Zea tripsacum*, to produce a hybrid named *teocentli*. From here on its back-crosses and subsequent evolution, loss of glumes, increase in cob number and kernel row number, have been well documented by MacNeish, Mangelsdorf, and Galinat (1964).

Another important process, though somewhat less publicized, was the interaction between corn and beans recently emphasized by Kaplan (1965). Maize alone, although a reasonably good starch source, does not in itself constitute a major protein because it lacks an important amino acid — lysine — which must therefore be made up from another source. Beans happen to be rich in lysine. Thus the mere combining of maize and beans in the diet of the Southern Highlands, apart from any favorable genetic changes in either plant, was a significant nutritional breakthrough.

Starting with what may have been (initially) accidental deviations in the system, a positive feedback network was established which eventually made maize cultivation the most profitable single subsistence activity in Mesoamerica. The more widespread maize cultivation, the more opportunities for favorable crosses and back-crosses; the more favorable genetic changes, the greater the yield; the greater the yield, the higher the population, and hence the more intensive cultivation. There can be little doubt that pressures for more intensive cultivation were instrumental in perfecting early water-control systems, like well-irrigation and canal-irrigation (Neely 1967; Flannery, Kirkby, Kirkby, and Williams, 1967). This positive feedback system, therefore, was still increasing at the time of the Spanish Conquest.

What this meant initially was that System 6, Wild Grass Procurement, grew steadily at the expense of, and in competition with, all other procurement systems in the arid highlands. Moreover, the system increased in complexity by necessitating a *planting* period (in the spring) as well as the usual *harvesting* season (early fall). It therefore competed with both the spring-ripening wild plants (prickly pear, organ cactus) and the fall-ripening crops (acorns, fruits, some guajes). It competed with rainy-season hunting of deer and peccary. And it was a nicely self-perpetuating system, for the evolution of cultivated maize indicates that no matter how much the Indians harvested, they saved the best seed for next year's planting; and they saved it under storage conditions which furthered the survival of every seed. Moreover, they greatly increased the area in which maize would grow by removing competing plants.

As mentioned earlier, (1) procurement of "starvation" plants like *Ceiba* and maguey seems to have been undertaken by small, scattered "microbands," while (2) harvests of seasonally-limited plants, abundant only for a short time — like cactus fruits, mesquite and guajes, and so on — seem to have been undertaken by large "macrobands," formed by the coalescence of several related microbands. Because of this functional association between band size and resource, human demography was changed by the positive feedback of early maize-bean cultivation: an amplification of the rainy-season planting and harvesting also meant an amplification of the time of macroband coalescence. MacNeish (1964b:425) anticipated this when he asked:

> Is it not possible as the number of new agricultural plants increased that the length of time that the microbands stayed in a single planting area also increased? In time could not perhaps one or more microbands have been able to stay at such a spot the year around? Then with further agricultural production is it not possible that the total macroband became sedentary? Such would, of course, be a village.

Actually, it may not be strictly accurate to say that sedentary village life was "allowed" or "made possible" by agricultural production; in fact, increased permanence of the macroband may have been *required* by the amplified planting and harvesting pattern.

"RESCHEDULING" IN THE EARLY AND MIDDLE FORMATIVE PERIODS (1500–200 B.C.)

An aspect of early village agriculture in Mexico not usually dealt with in the literature is the extent to which increased concentration on maize production made it necessary to "reschedule" other procurement systems. It is not possible in a paper of this length to discuss all the subtleties of Formative agricultural systems. The basic distinction I would like to make is this: given the technology of the Early Formative as we understand it at present, there were regions where maize could be grown only during the rainy season, and regions where maize could be grown year-round. All differences in scheduling to be considered in this paper ultimately rest on this dichotomy.

Regions where we postulate that agriculture was practiced only during the rainy season include areas with an extremely arid climate like the Tehuacán Valley, or higher valleys where frosts occur in October and continue until April, as is the case in the Valley of Mexico (Sanders 1965:23). Regions where we postulate that agriculture was practiced year-round include very humid areas in the frost-free coastal lowlands (such as the southern Gulf Coast or the Pacific coasts of Chiapas and Guatemala), and areas in the frost-free parts of the interior where one of two techniques was possible: (1) intensive cropping of permanently humid river bottomlands, such as in the Central Depression of Chiapas (Sanders 1961:2) or (2) very primitive water control techniques like "pot-irrigation," such as in the western Valley of Oaxaca (Flannery, Kirkby, Kirkby, and Williams, 1967).

What did this mean, region by region, in terms of "scheduling"? It meant that, in regions of year-round agriculture, certain seasonal activities were curtailed or even abandoned, and emphasis was placed on those year-round resources that did not conflict with farming schedules. In regions where farming was conducted only in the rainy season, the dry season was left open for intensive seasonal collecting activities. Even exploitation of permanent wild resources might be deferred to that time of year. Let me give a few examples:

The Rescheduling of Deer Hunting. Deer hunting in the Formative differed greatly from region to region, depending on whether agriculture could be practiced year-round, or only seasonally. In the Valleys of Mexico and Tehuacán, remains of white-tailed deer are abundant in Formative sites (Vaillant 1930, 1935; Flannery, n.d.), but wherever we have accurate counts on these fragments it is clear that by far the most intensive deer hunting was done in the late fall and winter. Projectile points and obsidian scrapers of many types are plentiful in these sites (MacNeish 1962, Vaillant, *op. cit.*). On the Guatemalan coast, at Pánuco, or in the western Valley of Oaxaca, deer remains are absent or rare, and projectile points nonexistent (Coe and Flannery 1967, MacNeish 1954). It has occasionally been suggested that the lowland areas had such intensive agriculture that hunting was "unnecessary," whereas the highland areas needed deer "as a supplement to their diet." I do not believe this is the case; it is more likely a matter of scheduling. It so happens that the best season for deer hunting in the oak woodlands of highland Mesoamerica is late fall, after the maize crop has been harvested and the frosts are beginning. This made intensive fall and winter deer hunts a logical activity. By contrast, lowland peoples concentrated on those wild resources that were available year-round in the vicinity of the village. Exploitation of these resources could be scheduled so as not to siphon off manpower from agricultural activities. On the Guatemalan Coast, for example, the very rich perennial fish resources of the lagoon and estuary system were relied upon. Some villages, located near mangrove forests, collected land crabs; others, located at some distance from the mangroves, ignored them (Coe 1961, Coe and Flannery 1967). None of these resources conflicted with the farming pattern.

Similar "rescheduling" of wild plant collecting took place in the highlands. The plants that dwindled in importance were the ones that ripened during the seasons when corn would have to be planted or harvested. Plants like maguey, whose exploitation could be deferred until the winter, were still exploited intensively, and in fact eventually came to be cultivated widely in areas where a winter maize crop is impossible. In the arid Mitla region of the Valley of Oaxaca today, maguey is as important a crop as maize, and some years it is the only crop that does not fail (personal communication, Aubrey W. Williams, Jr.).

System 7: Procurement of Wild Water Fowl. Until now, we have not mentioned Mesoamerica's great water fowl resources, since we still have no good archaeological evidence from the food-collecting and "incipient cultivation" periods in any of the lake and marsh areas where those fowl congregate. But beginning with the Formative period, we do have data on wild fowl exploitation from the lakes of highland Mexico and the swamps and lagoons of the coast.

Water fowl in Mesoamerica are as restricted in availability as the seasonal plant resources mentioned above. Only four species breed in Mexico. All the others (perhaps some two dozen species or more of ducks and geese) spend the summer in the prairie marshes of western Canada, principally in Alberta, Saskatchewan, and Manitoba. Before the formation of winter ice in November, these ducks and geese head south down a series of four well defined routes, of which only two will be considered here: the Pacific and Central Flyways. Ducks coming down the Central Flyway, terminating at the lakes of the Central Mexican Plateau (Texcoco, Patzcuaro, Cuitzeo, Chapala), include the pintail (*Anas acuta*), the shoveler (*Spatula clypeata*), and the green-winged teal (*Anas carolinensis*). The coot (*Fulica americana*) is resident year-round in Lake Texcoco, but constitutes only three percent of the water fowl. Ducks coming down the Pacific Flyway reach the extensive lagoon-estuary system of the Chiapas and Guatemala coasts. Among the most numerous ducks taking this route are the pintail (*Anas acuta*), blue-winged teal (*Anas cyanoptera*), and baldplate (*Mareca americana*). There are also a few resident species like the black-bellied tree duck (*Dendrocygna autumnalis*), but they constitute less than 1 percent of the waterfowl. In other words, between 97 and 99 percent of the duck population of Mesoamerica is available only between November and March; by March or April most of these species are either back in Canada or on their way. This necessitated an intense seasonal exploitation pattern similar to that required by perishable seasonal fruits.

It is difficult to compare the relative abundance of waterfowl on the Pacific coast lagoons with Lake Texacoco, because the lake system of the Valley of Mexico was drained by the Spanish, and is now a pale shadow of what it was in the Formative. In 1952, an estimated 33,540 migratory ducks spent the winter in Lake Texcoco (Leopold 1959:Table 4), while the totals for the Chiapas Coast during the same period were over 300,000; some 27,000 of these were in the area between Pijijiapan and the Guatemalan Coast alone, a stretch of only one hundred miles of coastline.

The Early Formative villagers responded quite differently to these popula-tions of winter waterfowl. Every Formative site report from the Lake Texcoco area stresses the abundance of duck bones in the refuse. Vaillant (1930:38) claimed that the animal bones from Zacatenco indicated "con-siderable consumption of the flesh of birds and deer," and his illustrations of bone tools suggest that bones of waterfowl were well represented. Worked bird bone also appears at El Arbolillo (Vaillant 1935:246–47). Piña Chán (1958:17) likewise lists "bones of deer and aquatic birds" from Tlatilco. At Ticomán, bird bones were also common, and the larger ones apparently were ducks (Vaillant 1931). Recently, I have had a chance to examine faunal remains from Tolstoy's new excavations at El Arbolillo, Tlatilco, and Tlapacoya, as well as the Late Formative site of Temesco near Lake Texcoco (Dixon 1966), and ducks of the genera *Anas* and *Spatula* are abundant, confirming Vaillant's impressions.

On the Guatemalan Pacific Coast, as suggested by Coe and Flannery (1967) the extensive duck populations were virtually ignored. Although rich in fish and mollusks, the Formative middens have yielded not a single bone of the ducks that flew over our heads as we traveled upriver to the site each day. Since other birds, like the brown pelican, were sometimes killed and eaten, we assume that ducks must occasionally have been consumed. But the paucity of their remains is in striking contrast to the Lake Texcoco sites.

I suggest that in areas where agriculture was practiced year-round, heavy exploitation of winter duck resources would have conflicted with farming, and hence was not practiced. In areas like the Valley of Mexico, where winter frosts prevent agriculture, ducks arrive during the very time of the year when farming activity was at its lowest ebb, and hence they could be heavily exploited. This may be one further example of the kind of "scheduling" that characterized the Formative.

CONCLUSIONS

The use of a cybernetics model to explain prehistoric cultural change, while terminologically cumbersome, has certain advantages. For one thing, it does not attribute cultural evolution to "discoveries," "inventions," "experiments," or "genius," but instead enables us to treat prehistoric cultures as systems. It stimulates inquiry into the mechanisms that counter-act change or amplify it, which ultimately tells us something about the nature of adaptation. Most importantly, it allows us to view change not as something arising *de novo*, but in terms of quite minor deviations in one small part of a previously existing system, which, once set in motion, can expand greatly because of positive feedback.

The implications of this approach for the prehistorian are clear: it is vain to hope for the discovery of the first domestic corn cob, the first pottery vessel, the first hieroglyphic, or the first site where some other major breakthrough occurred. Such deviations from the preexisting pattern almost certainly took place in such a minor and accidental way that their traces are not recoverable. More worthwhile would be an investigation of the mutual causal processes that amplify these tiny deviations into major changes in prehistoric culture.

REFERENCES CITED

Callen, Eric O.
1965 "Food Habits of Some Pre-Columbian Mexican Indians." *Economic Botany* 19, no. 4:335–43.
Coe, Michael D.
1961 "La Victoria: An Early Site on the Pacific Coast of Guatemala." *Papers of the Peabody Museum*, Harvard University, vol. 53.
———, and Kent V. Flannery
1964 "Microenvironments and Mesoamerican Prehistory." *Science* 143:650–54.
1967 "Early Cultures and Human Ecology in South Coastal Guatemala." *Smithsonian Contributions to Anthropology*, vol. 3. Washington: Smithsonian Institution.
Dixon, Keith A.
1966 "Obsidian Dates From Temesco, Valley of Mexico." *American Antiquity* 31:640–43.
Flannery, Kent V.
1966 "The Postglacial 'Readaptation' as Viewed from Mesoamerica." *American Antiquity* 31:800–805.
[1967] "Vertebrate Fauna and Hunting Patterns." Chapter 8 in *Prehistory of the Tehuacán Valley*, vol. I: *Environment and Resources*. [Austin: University of Texas Press for the] R. S. Peabody Foundation, Andover, Mass.
———, Anne V. Kirkby, Michael J. Kirkby, and Aubrey W. Williams
1967 "Farming Systems and Political Growth in Ancient Oaxaca, Mexico." *Science* 158:445–54.
Harrington, M. R.
1933 "Gypsum Cave, Nevada." *Papers of the Southwest Museum*, no. 8. Los Angeles.
Kaplan, Lawrence
1965 "Archaeology and Domestication in American *Phaseolus* (Beans)." *Economic Botany* 19, no. 4:358–68.
Leopold, A. Starker
1959 "Wild Life of Mexico: The Game Birds and Mammals." Berkeley: University of California Press.

Lowe, Gareth W.
1959   "Archaeological Exploration of the Upper Grijalva River, Chiapas, Mexico." *Papers of the New World Archaeological Foundation*, no. 2 (publication no. 3). Provo, Utah.

MacNeish, Richard S.
1954   "An Early Archaeological Site Near Pánuco, Vera Cruz." *Transactions of the American Philosophical Society*, n.s., vol. 44, pt. V. Philadelphia.
1961   "First Annual Report of the Tehuacán Archaeological-Botanical Project." Andover, Mass.: R. S. Peabody Foundation.
1962   "Second Annual Report of the Tehuacán Archaeological-Botanical Project." R. S. Peabody Foundation.
1964a   "Ancient Mesoamerican Civilization." *Science* 143:531–37.
1964b   "The Food-Gathering and Incipient Agriculture Stage of Prehistoric Middle America." In *Handbook of Middle American Indians*, vol. I: *Natural Environment and Early Cultures*, Robert C. West (ed.), pp. 413–26. Austin: University of Texas Press.
———, Paul C. Mangelsdorf, and Walton Galinat
1964   "Domestication of Corn." *Science* 143:538–45.

Maruyama, Magoroh
1963   "The Second Cybernetics: Deviation-Amplifying Mutual Causal Processes," *American Scientist* 51, no. 2:164–79.

Neely, James A.
1967   "Organización Hidráulica y Sistemas de Irrigación Prehistóricos en el Valle de Oaxaca." Instituto Nacional de Antropología e Historia, *Boletín* no. 27 pp. 15–17. Mexico City.

Pennington, Campbell
1963   *The Tarahumar of Mexico*. Salt Lake City: University of Utah Press.

Piña Chán, Roman
1958   "Tlatilco." Instituto Nacional de Antropología e Historia, *Serie Investignaciones*, no. 1. Mexico City.

Rappaport, Roy A.
1967   "Ritual Regulation of Environmental Relations among a New Guinea People." *Ethnology* 6:17–30.

Sanders, William T.
1961   "Ceramic Stratigraphy at Santa Cruz, Chiapas, Mexico." *Papers of the New World Archaeological Foundation*, no. 13. Provo, Utah.

1965   "The Cultural Ecology of the Teotihuacán Valley."
Pennsylvania State University (multilithed).

Smith, C. Earle, Jr.

1965a   "Agriculture, Tehuacán Valley." *Fieldiana: Botany* 31,
no. 3:55–100. Chicago Natural History Museum.

1965b   "Flora, Tehuacán Valley." *Fieldiana: Botany* 31, no.
4:107–43. Chicago Natural History Museum.

[1967] "Plant Remains from the Tehuacán Project." In
Prehistory of the Tehuacán Valley, vol. I: *Environment and Resources.* [Austin: University of Texas Press
for the] R. S. Peabody Foundation, Andover, Mass.

Steward, Julian

1955   *Theory of Culture Change.* Urbana: University of
Illinois Press.

Vaillant, George C.

1930   "Excavations at Zacatenco." *Anthropological Papers of
the American Museum of Natural History*, vol. 32, pt.
1.

1931   "Excavations at Ticomán." *Anthropological Papers of
the American Museum of Natural History*, vol. 32, pt.
2.

1935   "Excavations at El Arbolillo." *Anthropological Papers
of the American Museum of Natural History*, vol. 32,
pt. 2.

Vayda, Andrew P.

1964   "Anthropologists and Ecological Problems." In *Man,
Culture, and Animals*, Anthony Leeds and Andrew P.
Vayda (eds.), pp. 1–5. Washington: American Association for the Advancement of Science (publication
no. 78).

JEREMY A. SABLOFF
GORDON R. WILLEY

Many civilizations have flourished and collapsed in prehistory, and one of the most brilliant and mysterious was the Maya civilization in Guatemala and Mexico. Several hypotheses have been formulated to account for its demise, but there is no general agreement for this occurrence. Jeremy Sabloff and Gordon Willey take a fresh look at the old evidence supplemented by new data, and offer a hypothesis explaining this historical event. Viewed in the context of other hypotheses, it is weighed and elaborated, but the authors, in their conclusion, still feel their hypothesis has to be proven. Their study demonstrates how archaeological research can be used to explain specific and unique historical events for which no written evidence exists. This method goes hand in hand with the quest to understand man's general patterned process. When both anthropological process and archaeological history have been explored sufficiently, we will discover what life was like in time past, and what specific challenges faced man, and what his solutions were.

21 The Collapse of Maya Civilization in the Southern Lowlands: A Consideration of History and Process

Civilizations grew; civilizations flowered; and civilizations were wiped out, much more often by despots than by diseases, deluges, or droughts. — K. C. Chang, *Rethinking Archaeology.*

Reprinted, with the editorial changes noted, from "The Collapse of Maya Civilization in the Southern Lowlands: A Consideration of History and Process" by Jeremy A. Sabloff and Gordon R. Willey, *Southwestern Journal of Anthropology* 23 (1967):311–336, by permission of the authors and the publisher. References and bibliography are omitted, and footnotes are renumbered.

There "is no such thing as 'historical' explanation, only the explanation of historical events." — L. R. Binford quoting A. C. Spaulding while commenting on "Major Aspects of the Interrelationship of Archaeology and Ethnology," by K. C. Chang.

INTRODUCTION

The problem of the collapse of Maya civilization of the Southern Lowlands, which has long puzzled and intrigued archaeologists and culture historians, has generated numerous hypothetical solutions through the years and has been a topic of much written comment. Moroever, the solutions to the whole question of the fall of Classic Maya civilization have extended beyond the parochial bounds of Maya archaeology to the realm of general anthropological theory. Unfortunately, however, none of the hypotheses brought forward to date has proved to be fully satisfactory.

Recent excavations at the site of Seibal, Department of Peten, Guatemala, by the Peabody Museum, Harvard University, have uncovered new data which, we think, are highly relevant to the problem of the termination of Classic Maya civilization in the Southern Lowlands. Evaluation of this new information, in combination with a reevaluation of other archaeological data from the Maya area, has prompted us to propose a new hypothetical solution. The essence of this hypothesis has occasionally been included as a factor in older solutions but, with a few recent exceptions, has not been given great weight nor outlined in any detail. It is the purpose of this paper to present these new data and to discuss the hypothesis which has been formulated to explain them.

In boldest form, the hypothesis states that the Southern Lowlands (the Guatemalan Peten and bordering portions of Chiapas and Tabasco) were invaded by non-Classic Maya peoples. This invasion began in the ninth century A.D., and it set in motion a train of events that destroyed the Classic Maya within one hundred years. Throughout this paper, the various aspects of this hypothesis are discussed in terms as clear and definite as we could make them. We realize that some details of the hypothesis may be in error, but we hope that our sharp formulation will enable other archaeologists to correct these errors so as to concentrate on the larger picture. Furthermore, it should be noted that the hypothesis brought forward here does not seek to explain all aspects of the Maya collapse but to provide a solid base from which future hypotheses and investigations can be launched.

In other words, the main purpose of this paper is not simply to bring forward a "new solution to the mystery" of the Maya collapse but also to bring about a shifting of methodological priorities. Too often, as will be shown below, workers in the Maya area have attempted to explain the collapse in terms of internal processual events alone, a sort of consideration of Maya culture and its environmental setting *in vacuo*. External forces, such as Mexican incursions, were relegated to a secondary role and were used to fill in gaps in the internally focused hypothesis. What we are saying here, in essence, is that in the Maya area processual factors, such as the ecological suitability of a great civilization in a tropical forest area, the effects of population increases in a "type X environment," or the long term inviability of a "theocratic state," can be understood only after external historical factors are controlled. With a solid historical frame of reference, various hypothetical factors can be treated and tested as independent variables.

Contrary to Toynbee, who has stated: "A civilization which has become the victim of a successful intrusion has already in fact broken down internally," we feel that it was an incursion which set internal processes in motion. The man-nature balance in the Southern Lowlands undoubtedly was precarious; the strains within Maya society were probably equally so; and an invasion was able to precipitate a crisis and bring into play the factors which caused the fall of the Maya. But only by recognizing and understanding the nature of the invasion can we know and appraise these internal processes.

We also feel that the questions discussed in these pages may have some small relevance to what is called in America today the "new archaeology." Recently, in *American Antiquity*, there has been a concerted effort by Binford to redirect his colleagues' attention to the question of the goals of archaeology. This concern, which had been of some theoretical interest in the late 1930s and 1940s, was generally ignored in the 1950s as attention was shifted to implementing theory through the development of new methods and outlooks which were a prerequisite to a historical-functional oriented archaeology. If we understand Binford correctly, he is saying that American archaeologists in general have limited their goals to historical reconstruction and have not sought functional explanation. Moreover, the kind of historical data which this limited type of strategy has produced is not useful for higher level explanations. However, by redirecting their goals and reformulating their research strategies, archaeologists will be able to contribute to the mainstream of anthropological theory.

While agreeing with Binford's goals, and recognizing the stimulus he has provided in the 1960s by emphasizing the need for a new outlook, we do not feel that the path he has outlined is the *only* way to reach the goals he has set. That is to say, we do not think that it is necessary to accept the strictly materialistic evolutionary premises upon which Binford maintains that his arguments must be based in order to arrive at an explanation of historical events.

It is our feeling that, at least at the present state of Maya archaeological knowledge, an understanding of historical events can lead to the placement of processual factors in proper perspective, rather than the reverse. But it should be emphasized that the approach outlined in this paper may not be as useful in other areas and that our methodologies should remain flexible. Furthermore, we do not wish to imply in our statements that by switching the historical-processual priorities we have accepted a theoretical position which is essentially non-evolutionary.[1] In fact, as will be shown below, we believe that after the importance of the invasion of the Southern Lowlands has been recognized and the route and nature of the invasion outlined in detail, the significance of the impact of a "militaristic" society which evolved from a "theocratic" one in the highland sector of Mesoamerica on a "theocratic" society in the lowland sector will become clearer.

To repeat, only after a thorough understanding of the historical events which occurred in the late ninth and tenth centuries A.D. in the Southern Maya Lowlands has been reached can the larger question of process be successfully broached. For if in our eagerness to change our goals from historical to processual ones, we relegate the reconstruction of historical events to a low priority role and ignore the importance of these events, then our efforts will be futile.

VIEWS OF THE COLLAPSE

The Classic Maya "collapse" or "decline" is a concept based upon realities of the historical record — not merely "on a strong professional commitment to prehistory and its material artifacts." Hundreds of major sites were abandoned over at least one-half of the total lowland area, and, in the remaining half, site occupation and construction declined markedly. The "hard" archaeological evidence for the collapse may be summed up as follows. Beginning at about A.D. 810, or 9.19.0.0.0 in the Maya calendar (11.16.0.0.0 correlation), there was a decided drop-off in the carving and erecting of dated Maya monuments and in major building activities throughout the Southern Lowlands. Thereafter, these dated stelae became progressively fewer at each katun (twenty-year) interval, with the last ones — which are extremely rare — dating to A.D. 889 (10.3.0.0.0). In this eighty-year period there was also a general decline in ceramics and other manufactures; many of the ceremonial centers were completely abandoned; and in most of the remainder there was only minor or desultory occupancy. Although data are fewer for the outlying "house mounds" or domestic structures which surrounded the ceremonial centers, it would appear that these, too, were ultimately abandoned by a few decades after A.D. 900. In the north, in the Yucatan Peninsula, the story is less clear, but a similar series of events seems to have taken place. There, most of the great Puuc and

---

[1] If anything, our view would approach that of Steward's "multilinear evolution."

Chenes sites were deserted at about the same time the centers of the south were abandoned; however, one major site, Chichen Itza, became a capital for Mexican, or Mexicanized, invaders and lasted well into the Postclassic Period. Thereafter, the Northern Lowlands continued to be occupied although the archaeological remains reveal a greatly reduced scale in both size and magnificence as compared to the old Classic Period. . . .

As noted above, most of the theories of the past thirty years which have been concerned with explaining the Maya collapse have directed attention to essentially internal processual causes. In brief, as they have it, Maya civilization fell because it contained within itself contradictions in man's relationships to nature or in the relationships between men within the social body.

On the ecological side, neither the Cook-Morley nor the Cooke-Ricketson theory can be supported. The "man-made savanna" hypothesis of the former falls on a number of counts: the absence or near-absence of archaeological sites from savanna areas; the basically different soil type of the savannas; and the lack of any historical evidence that *milpa* cultivation over long periods would have resulted in the development of such grass-lands. The Cooke-Ricketson attempt to extend "intensive cultivation" methods back to Classic Period times fares little better. Not only would such methods have been difficult or impossible, given the soils, climate, vegetation, and lack of fertilizer, but they would have been unnecessary. A substantial population of one hundred to two hundred persons per square mile of farming land could have been maintained in the Peten with milpa methods; and such a population could have easily constructed the Maya ceremonial centers in the seasonal periods when they were not engaged in agricultural activities. Lastly, the *bajos*, which Ricketson believed to have been former lakes, show sediments of very gradual accumulation over very long periods of time, inconsistent with the idea that they could have resulted from man's activities.

Still in the ecological realm, but cast in a more general frame of reference, is Meggers's proposition that the Maya Lowland jungles, by their very nature, placed a limit on cultural advance within the area. This limit was in agricultural potential — whatever the methods of farming — and because of it Maya civilization could only have undergone a decline in that environment. Moreover, such a civilization could not have arisen in this setting but must have been developed elsewhere and brought to the rainforest lowlands, where it eventually and inevitably perished.

Now the proposal that Maya civilization had its hearth elsewhere than in the lowlands has been pretty effectively disproven, although most of the evidence which does this has come in during the past dozen years or so since Meggers published her article. In brief, we can now trace Maya Lowland beginnings to Middle Preclassic village cultures of a rather simple sort.

These relate to other similar cultures of that time (1000–300 B.C.) throughout southern Mesoamerica. Afterwards, in the Late Preclassic, there was a rapid population increase in the Maya Lowlands and the beginnings of a rich ceremonial development, so that by A.D. 300 Maya culture was in Classic Period flower. Although some elements of this growth do appear to have been imported from elsewhere, such as the Olmec region or the Guatemalan highlands, there can be no doubt but that the growth was generated, maintained, and accelerated in the local lowland societies and that a typical Maya imprint or stylistic reworking was placed upon all the imported elements. This burgeoning of Maya civilization from a matrix of simpler beginnings can be seen very well in the cultural sequence at Tikal, for example. Thus, Maya civilization did develop in the jungle lowlands, in spite of whatever natural environmental limitations may have been in its way.

What were these limitations? Since Meggers wrote her article a number of critics have presented strong arguments that the Southern Maya Lowlands offer a greater potential for native agriculture than she was willing to concede and that swidden or *milpa* agriculture, in general, may sustain sufficient population numbers and the degree of centralization needed for the Maya achievements.[2] But does all this mean that we can eliminate, permanently, the factor of natural environment in an examination of causality in the Lowland Maya collapse? We do not think so. In the last analysis, we are dealing with two basic facts which cannot be denied or explained away. The first is that Maya civilization was a substantial achievement which developed in the Peten and surrounding lowlands. And the second fact is that these lowlands, while they must have offered an adequate natural environment for what obviously transpired, are not optimal lands for agricultural production, given the technology the Maya had at hand or, for that matter, given any farming technology known in Precolumbian Mesoamerica. A recent article by Reina, on modern *milperos* in the vicinity of Lake Peten Itza, points up the difficulties of the farmer in such a region. Therefore, it seems highly probable that the balance between agricultural man and nature in the Southern Maya Lowlands was a precarious one, one that the strain of overpopulation — for which there is good evidence in Late Classic Period times — might have seriously disturbed and one that an historical event, such as invasion by an external enemy, might well have upset.

Processual explanations involving internal social forces have been invoked less often in hypotheses about the Maya collapse than those that are grounded in ecology; however, two leading Maya scholars have tended to

---

[2] Still another argument in favor of more than adequate subsistence in the Maya Lowlands is that offered by Bronson in support of root crop staples.

favor them. A. V. Kidder, in rejecting the Cook-Morley and Cooke-Ricketson theories, offered the idea of internal social revolt as more consonant with all the facts than an agronomic explanation; and Thompson has developed this theme at greater length. In the opinion of the latter, the growing demands of the priest-leaders in the ceremonial centers became too burdensome for the sustaining peasantry, and the latter rebelled. As a subsidiary element in this explanation, the introduction of "exotic religious developments," from Mexico, further served to alienate the peasants from their aristocratic leaders; however, Thompson seems to feel that this "introduction" was one of diffusion rather than invasion and conquest.

This internal social revolt hypothesis is extraordinarily difficult to prove or disprove with archaeological evidence. Perhaps if the Maya hieroglyphs are ever translated in their entirety we will know, one way or another, but even this is not certain. As things stand now, the defacing of the countenances of rulers carved on monuments, and other acts of vandalism, are about all the direct evidence we have of possible revolt; and even this could be interpreted as the vandalism of foreign invaders as easily as that of internal rebels.

The question does, though, prompt a closer look at the nature of Maya society — or of what we can reconstruct about ancient Maya society. There are a great many writings on this subject, but four recent essays seem particularly pertinent. Although the lines of argument of these papers are not the same, and they are, at points, in some conflict with each other, they all agree on certain essentials. Thus, Altschuler notes that the Maya class structure of the Classic Period must have been poorly developed politically, that kin-based lineages remained important, and that the aristocracy lacked techniques of coercion which could have been mobilized in case of a peasant revolt. M. D. Coe also sees Maya society as being held together by lineage ties and religious sanctions as opposed to the kind of "organic solidarity" that cemented the more developed Central Mexican states of Precolumbian times.[3] Kaplan feels that Maya society had not yet broken out of a kinship framework and that the Maya "states" had no central monopoly on force. He calls this kind of a social and political organization a "chiefdom" as does Erasmus, who defines the "chiefdom" as lacking the coercive quality of the state, being dependent upon a redistributive economy and retaining the vestiges of a primitive kinship system. All of these opinions, then, converge on the interpretation of Maya sociopolitical structure as relatively feeble and lacking those powers of coercion that would have protected it against revolt from within. But would not this same feebleness have rendered it relatively helpless to attack from without?

[3] Contrary to M. D. Coe's statement that his own position and that of Altschuler are opposed, we feel that their differences are more semantic than real and are related to a slightly different emphasis in the two papers.

Erasmus thinks so: "The most elaborate social and cultural manifestations of the chiefdom type were, by their very nature, the most vulnerable to eclipse through contact with stronger 'state societies.' " And, in the case of the Maya, we are inclined to agree, especially when their potential attackers had been in close contact with peoples who had behind them a long history of "state" development in the Mexican Highlands and were known for their militaristic aggressiveness.

The idea of the Classic Maya of the Southern Lowlands falling before a foreign invasion has not, as we have said, had wide acceptance. A few writers, such as M. D. Coe, have recognized the possibility that Mexican incursions were involved in the collapse of the Maya. But Coe, for example, feels that the foreign invasion could only have happened after Maya civilization had deteriorated to a great extent. As stated above, we do not believe that the Maya were going "downhill" at the time the Southern Lowlands were invaded by non-Classic Maya peoples. All evidence points to the intrusion having occurred just before or by 9.19.0.0.0, a time when Maya civilization was still at its Late Classic peak.

One reason for the general rejection of the factor of foreign invasion lies in the nature of the archaeological evidence and in the way that evidence has been appraised. In the first place, little or no clear occupational evidence of the invaders has been found in the abandoned Maya centers of the south; and, secondly, there is the abandonment itself, the mass depopulation, to be accounted for. The usual "model" of a conquest, as seen archaeologically, has been the "site unit intrusion," followed by a merging of the alien invading society and culture with the resident conquered. Such a "model" seems verified by Chichen Itza, that major site of the Northern Lowlands which represents a fusion of the Mexican-like invader and the old local Classic Maya tradition of the north; but no site in the south quite fills this role.

But, we think, still another reason for the rejection of the invasion hypothesis is that archaeologists have looked upon it as unduly romantic, simplistic, or randomly catastrophic. O. G. Ricketson, for instance, seems to express this view when, in defense of his agronomic explanations of the collapse, he states:

> ... it (the Cooke-Ricketson hypothesis) attributes the gradual abandonment of the region to natural causes alone, without relying upon surmises concerning wars, changes in climate, or catastrophic plagues....

Thus, war is equated with catastrophism, with an "act of God."[4] There is a desire to encapsulate the problem, to view the Classic Maya in a social and

[4] We have not reviewed various "catastrophic" explanations of the collpse, such as disease, insect plagues, earthqukes. They have been dealt with by others and carry little supporting evidence.

cultural vacuum, to reduce the variables in the equation where they may be treated more "scientifically." In a sense, this is understandable, for we would agree that wars or invasions are not "root causes" of behavior. Meggers has expressed this in commenting on the social revolution hypothesis as an explanation for the Maya decline: "(it) is acceptable as far as it goes, but it does not go far enough. It ignores the problem of what precipitated the revolution." We would agree and admit that the question must also be asked, with reference to the invasion idea: what brought about the foreign war? Obviously, we will not arrive at ultimate cause through the descrpition of an historical event, as Spaulding and Binford have emphasized; but causality can be revealed in chains of events and in the manner in which the links of the chain are connected one to another. No link can be ignored. If the Southern Lowland Maya were invaded at that very crucial time in their history — the ninth century A.D. — we cannot ignore it in a search for what appear to be the more ultimate causes of their eventual fate.

At the beginning of this paper, we noted that there have been a few recent exceptions to the general rejection of the invasion hypothesis for the Southern Lowlands. One of the most important, and specific, of these is the idea set forth by R. E. W. Adams as a result of his work at Altar de Sacrificios on the lower Río Pasión. From a point of view different in some respects from that which is taken in this paper, Adams argues for an invasion of the Usumacinta-Pasión system by a group of non-Classic Maya people. Adams's opinions have only been presented so far in preliminary form, but a detailed discussion of his findings and ideas is forthcoming as a part of the Altar de Sacrificios monograph series to be published by the Peabody Museum, Harvard University. In more general terms, another writer, E. Z. Vogt, has advanced the hypothesis that the collapse of Maya culture in the Southern Lowlands resulted from pressures emanating from Central Mexico. More importantly, though, he also takes the general position which we have taken in this paper — namely, that an invasion hypothesis is a better hypothesis than internal processual ones. Finally, there is the survey article by G. L. Cowgill in which, after a general review of the problem, he concludes that Mexican incursions are the most likely possibility for the Maya downfall. Cowgill proposes that such invasions probably lasted over a good many years and that they moved on a broad front which included not only the Guatemalan highlands and Yucatan, where they are generally admitted, but the Southern Lowlands as well. He offers an interesting suggestion to explain the depopulation of the centers of the south. Peoples from these regions might have been moved northward to Yucatan, at the end of the Classic and the beginning of the Postclassic Period, in forced resettlement under the direction of Chichen Itza and its Mexicanized military leaders. That such "mitimae" type operations, reminiscent of Incaic Peru, could have been carried on by the ancient Mesoamericans is a possibility although there is only very slight ethnohistoric evidence in Landa to support it; and the greatest of Mesoamerican imperialists for whom we have ethnographic accounts, the Aztecs, did not seem to practice such resettlement tactics. We think, though, that another statement of Cowgill's is more important to the thesis which we are about to propose. He observes, as an aside: "Perhaps such a movement (resettlement) was assisted by a northward retreat of the Maya from attacks which struck first at the southern and southwestern parts of the lowlands." It will be our contention that this was, indeed, the case. The first invasions, in our opinion, included a movement into the Usumacinta Valley and up that river to the Río Pasión and from there into the southwestern and southern Peten. The invaders were either Mexicans or peoples who had been thoroughly acculturated to their ways. They administered the first shocks which, in less than a century, led to the collapse of the Southern Lowland Maya.

NEW DATA FROM SEIBAL

The site of Seibal is a large Maya ceremonial center which is located on the Río Pasión in south-central Peten, Guatemala (see Fig. 1). Major excavations were begun there in 1965 and have continued through 1966 and 1967. A final season of limited excavation is planned for 1968. The 1965–1967 excavations have revealed a cultural sequence which stretches from early Middle Preclassic times (ca. 800 B.C.) to terminal Late Classic times (ca. A.D. 950). Of particular concern to this paper is the Late Bayal Boca Phase which began at approximately 10.0.0.0.0. (A.D. 830 according to the 11.16.0.0.0 correlation) in the Maya calendar and lasted for about one hundred years.

At the beginning of the Tenth Cycle, a number of non-Classic Maya traits and influences suddenly appeared in abundance at Seibal.... the important ceramic, monumental, and architectural information can be briefly summarized. In ceramics, the major event was the arrival at this time of Fine Paste pottery at Seibal. Heavy concentrations of this ware, including six types in the fine-orange Altar (Y) Group as well as types in the fine-orange Balancan (Z), fine-orange Silho (X), and fine-gray Tres Naciones Groups, have been found in refuse deposits in the small structure units ("house mounds") which surround the ceremonial center. Other deposits have been found on the surface, in architectural fill, and in refuse within the ceremonial center proper. Analyses of the ceramic and architectural associations of the Fine Paste pottery indicate that much of it was probably used for domestic purposes. The whole Fine Paste tradition was alien to Seibal and the Peten and, as will be noted below, probably originated in the Gulf Coast Lowlands.

There also is evidence of much foreign influence on the Seibal stone

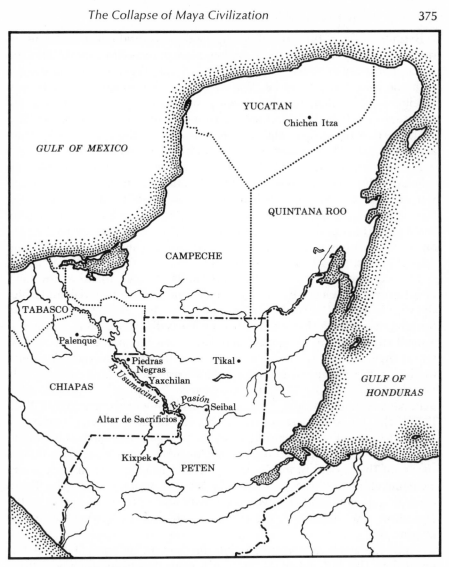

FIGURE 1.
The Maya Lowlands and adjacent areas.

monuments. A whole series of stelae, dating from 10.1.0.0.0. (A.D. 850) to
10.3.0.0.0. (A.D. 890), have numerous non-Classic traits which show resemblances to Yucatan and Central Mexico. A study of the Seibal stelàe by
John A. Graham is now nearing completion and promises to add a greater
perspective to our picture of the foreign takeover of Seibal. Among the
important preliminary results of Graham's study have been the discovery of
several close similarities to the stone sculpture of pre-Toltec Chichen Itza.

Because of the nature, as well as the good preservation, of the designs on the Fine Orange pottery type Pabellon Modeled-carved, we have had the rare opportunity at Seibal to stylistically link the Tenth Cycle monuments with the Fine Paste ceramics. We have been able to isolate over twenty specific stylistic elements and themes which are present on both the sculpture and Pabellon Modeled-carved pots and sherds. Thus, we have evidence that the people who were responsible for the Fine Paste pottery and the Tenth Cycle monuments at Seibal were one and the same.

In addition, the Tenth Cycle architecture and artifacts also reveal alien influences. For example, the only round structure in the Southern Lowlands was recently discovered at Seibal. This building is certainly not in the Classic tradition. The structure dates to the Bayal Boca Phase and can only be compared to the many round structures of Yucatan and Central Mexico. Such architectural features as engaged columns, which are found on the "palace" structure A-14, also have their closest resemblances in Yucatan.

The late figurines at Seibal are quite similar to ones found in the Gulf Coast Lowlands, especially those made of Fine Orange material, and differ stylistically from Classic Maya figurines. Another artifact which shows foreign influence is a thin stone head which was discovered on the surface of a small structure unit. The head may have been tenoned into the wall of one of the buildings. It should be pointed out that the stone head is similar to the *hachas* which form an important part of the Late Classic-Early Postclassic Gulf Coast (Veracruz) yoke-hacha "complex."

Finally, it should be noted that, at the beginning of the Late Bayal Boca Phase, the focus of ceremonial activity apparently switched from the compact Group D (a defensible area) to the open Group A. This would suggest that defensive position was no longer a factor in settlement — a condition that would probably have prevailed if a superior military group were in command of the site. It is in Group A that almost all of the Tenth Cycle monumental and architectural activity was centered. Moreover, at the same time (ca. 10.0.0.0.0), the population at Seibal probably reached its all-time peak.

Thus, the available evidence points to the conclusion that Seibal was invaded in the earlier half of the ninth century A.D. by a foreign group which had links with the Gulf Coast Lowlands (Tabasco-Campeche), Yucatan, and Central Mexico. This group did not merely overrun the site, but it established itself there.

OTHER RELEVANT DATA FROM
THE SOUTHERN MAYA LOWLANDS

New archaeological information from the Usumacinta-Pasión region, as well as a reevaluation of older data, lends weight to and broadens the invasion hypothesis. Recent excavations by the Peabody Museum,

Harvard University, at Altar de Sacrificios, which is located about seventy-five miles downstream from Seibal at the confluence of the Río Salinas and the Río Pasión, have uncovered very large quantities of Fine Paste pottery and figurines. Ceramic and architectural evidence point to a late invasion and occupation. Contrary to the situation just described for Seibal, Adams feels that there was a total population replacement in the Jimba Phase (ca. 10.2.0.0.0.–10.4.0.0.0.) at Altar de Sacrificios.[5] Nevertheless, the Altar and Seibal data are in general agreement that there was a foreign intrusion in the Río Pasión area at the beginning of the Tenth Cycle in the Maya calendar.

At Yaxchilan, which is situated downstream from Altar de Sacrificios, there are also relevant data. Unfortunately, this great site has not been excavated, and so the quantity of available evidence is somewhat meager. A few Fine Paste sherds have been found in the small surface collections made by T. Maler and G. Lowe. In addition, scholars such as Proskouriakoff and Thompson have remarked on the "Puuc" influences which are evident on the Yaxchilan sculpture. Finally, but most importantly, Proskouriakoff has pointed out that Yaxchilan may have been destroyed by an enemy at approximately 9.19.0.0.0. Future work on the historical content of the Yaxchilan hieroglyphs and sculpture along the lines pioneered by Proskouriakoff may add much useful data concerning the identity of the "enemy."

Further down the Río Usumacinta is the important site of Piedras Negras. This has often been used as an example of a Southern Maya site which shows definite physical evidence of some destruction at the time of its downfall. Monuments were defaced and overturned at sometime subsequent to the erection of the latest stela (9.19.0.0.0). We see no reason why these acts of "vandalism" could not have been perpetrated by foreign intruders. Fine Orange and Fine Gray pottery have been discovered at the site.

Excavations at the site of Palenque and in the greater Palenque area are also pertinent to the problem. Rands reports that there was an influx of Fine Paste ceramics in late Tepeu 2 times in the Palenque area. He feels that at least one of the Fine Paste groups may be related to Slateware in Yucatan. He also notes that soon after the introduction of Fine Paste wares at Palenque there was a complete decline. If Palenque was near the homeland of the invaders, a possibility which will be discussed below, then a Tepeu 2 rather than a terminal Late Classic Tepeu 3 date for the introduction of Fine Paste ceramics and political disruption would strengthen the invasion hypothesis. In this connection, it should also be noted that whereas the

[5] Adams would not necessarily agree with the reconstruction presented here. He feels that the Seibal and Altar de Sacrificios invasions my have taken place at different times and may have involved different people. Suffice it to say here that analyses of the Seibal data, especially in relation to the nature of "utilitarian" pottery in terminal Late Classic times and the simultaneous presence of Altar and Balancan Group sherds, have convinced us that the Seibal and Altar de Sacrificios invasions were part of a single phenomenon. . . .

intrusion on the Río Pasión is dated to the beginning of the Tenth Cycle, the decline of the Usumacinta sites is dated slightly earlier at the end of the Ninth Cycle.

It is obvious from the discussion above that we have used the presence of Fine Paste pottery as an important marker of poossible foreign intrusion. "Why couldn't it have been locally made?" or "Why does it represent a non-Classic Maya influence?" one might ask. The answer to these questions and the justification for our reliance on Fine Paste ceramics as markers can be found both in published archaeological works and in very recent laboratory analyses.

Surveys and excavations in the Tabasco Lowlands by Berlin and pioneering syntheses by Brainerd and R. E. Smith have shown that the general center of Fine Paste pottery was in the Gulf Coast Lowlands of Tabasco and Campeche. Following the principle that the area of greatest concentration of an artifact is most likely the source area, it is quite probable that this lowland region was the manufacturing center of Fine Paste pottery. While noting that the Gulf Coast Lowlands were probably the source of Fine Paste ceramics, R. E. Smith pointed out that one Fine Paste group, called the Y Fine Orange or Altar Group, might prove to be an exception. Since this group appeared in large quantities at Seibal and Altar de Sacrificios, its source is obviously of some importance.

Recent studies of Altar de Sacrificios and Seibal Fine Paste types have shown that there are many close similarities between the Altar Group sherds of the Río Pasión and Berlin's Z Fine Orange or Balancan Group material from Tabasco. In addition, preliminary results of a neutron activation analysis of Fine Paste pottery by L. H. Chan of the Brookhaven National Laboratory have also indicated that the source of the fine-orange Altar Group might have been in the Gulf Coast Lowlands.

Dr. Chan has analyzed Fine Orange and Fine Gray sherds from Seibal, Altar de Sacrificios, Piedras Negras, and Kixpek, a site in the Alta Verapaz highlands which is situated near the Río Chixoy (a part of the Usumacinta drainage). The material from Seibal and Altar de Sacrificios included both Balancan (Z) Group and Altar (Y) Group sherds. The preliminary results of the study indicate that all Fine Paste sherds from the four sites are quite similar in chemical composition and that they differ in composition from late Seibal and Altar de Sacrificios non-Fine Paste types. It can be inferred that the Fine Paste sherds from all four sites were manufactured in the same area. As noted above, distributional data would indicate that Balancan Group pottery was manufactured in the Gulf Coast Lowlands and specifically in the general Jonuta area of Tabasco. The compositional identity of the Altar and Balancan Group sherds would indicate that the Altar Group sherds were also made in this area. It is hoped that future neutron activation studies will help to confirm (or disprove) this hypothesis.

Furthermore, stylistic studies show that several Fine Paste types found in the Usumacinta-Pasión area have designs which are definitely non-Classic. Adams has even been able to show stylistic links to several pottery types from Panuco. It has also been noted (see above) that there are close similarities between designs on a Fine Paste type and non-Classic elements on the Seibal stelae. All these data would seemingly justify our belief that Fine Paste pottery was associated with non-Classic Maya peoples.

Turning from the Usumacinta-Pasión drainage to the north-central Peten, it should also be noted that excavations by the University of Pennsylvania at the great site of Tikal have uncovered much evidence of "Postclassic" activities in the general Central Acropolis area. These activities included the moving and resetting of stelae, a curious pattern of tomb looting in the North Acropolis, and the haphazard throwing of living debris all over the Central Acropolis. Interestingly enough, the people who were involved in these activities had Altar Group pottery (e.g., Fine Orange types such as Pabellon Modeled-carved) as part of their ceramic inventory. While W. R. Coe has noted evidence for strong Classic-"Postclassic" continuities at Tikal, there is still a possibility, however, that control of the site in these times may have passed to an alien group of leaders.

THE INVASION HYPOTHESIS

On the basis of the data which have been briefly discussed in the previous section, we advance the hypothesis that the whole Usumacinta-Pasión area was invaded at the very end of the Ninth Cycle by a non-Classic Maya group whose homeland was probably in the Gulf Coast Lowlands. This group reached Seibal by approximately 10.0.0.0.0 and established a base at the site. It should be noted that Seibal is situated on the only high-rise area on the lower Río Pasión and that the site commands a view for miles around. From this advance base, the foreigners probably sent raiding parties throughout the Central Peten. They also kept up their contacts with their homeland.

Furthermore, we feel that the attack on the Peten was part of a general broad front movement which also included the Northern Maya Lowlands, and was probably more or less synchronous with incursions into the Guatemalan Highlands and the Pacific Coast. We have noted, with reference to the latter regions, the presence of a quantity of Fine Orange ceramics in the Alta Verapaz. In addition, some of the well-known monuments of Santa Lucia Cotzumalhuapa show Mexican influences, and resemblances between some of the late Seibal stelae and a few of the Cotzumalhuapan monuments have been recognized. In making these remarks we do not wish to imply that such a broad movement or series of invasions were centrally directed according to plan. Most likely, they were instigated and carried out by politically separate groups but by groups that shared a common or related culture.

We can be no more specific about the identity of the invaders than that they possessed a non-Classic Maya culture which shows Mexican, and especially Central Mexican, elements. They may, indeed, have been displaced peoples from the Central Mexican region who first settled in the Gulf Coast Lowlands. It is quite probable that they began their movements as a result of disruptions in Central Mexico. As is well known, there were social, political, and religious upheavals at Tula in the ninth century A.D.

The invaders were militarily successful against the Classic Maya because they possessed superior weapons, including the dart and the atlatl, and, as was discussed above, were militarily and politically oriented in comparison with the economically and religiously oriented society of the Classic Maya. It should be noted that it may have been difficult for the latter to raise any kind of "standing army" to repel the invaders. It is also possible that the foreigners may have waged war under different "rules" than the Classic Maya. In other words, they may not have "played the game" the same way the Classic Maya did, and so the latter fell easy prey to the invaders. One only has to look at the Spanish Conquest of Mexico to see how it is possible for a small group with superior weapons and different war "rules" to conquer a great civilization with large manpower resources.

Moreover, it is possible that the foreign invaders followed a route and a plan which was not completely new and original. The invasion trail from Central Mexico to the Classic Maya heartland may have first been pioneered by the merchants or armies of Teotihuacan several centuries earlier. At that time, there appears to have been a crisis in Classic Maya civilization in the Southern Lowlands. This is suggested by the hiatus in stelae dates, a cessation which lasted from 9.5.0.0.0 until 9.8.0.0.0 (A.D. 534–593); but this crisis was passed, and one wonders if the Classic Maya were saved from dissolution at this time only by events in the Valley of Mexico which ultimately led to the fall of that first great Mexican power center of Teotihuacan.

Two important questions about the invasion remain to be discussed here. One is: "What happened to the populations in the Southern Lowlands, including the invaders?" This cannot be answered with any degree of certainty at the present time. In a preliminary way, however, we suggest that the invasion from the Gulf Coast may have resulted in many deaths among the Southern Lowland Maya and in disruption and disorganization of agricultural practices. Even a month or two of widespread neglect of the milpas, in a crucial season, could have been enough to tip the balance in the man-nature ecological scales and cause famine among the large Late Classic populations. In other words, the Southern Lowlands could support a society such as the Maya had; but once it became necessary to organize large armies of non-food-producing soldiers for defense, the ecological resources of the tropical forest were overtaxed. The conquerors may have tried to make a go of it in restricted areas — and for a time did manage it in places such as Seibal or Tikal; but the struggle with the jungle may have been too much for a diminished and weakened population, and this would have been especially true if the new leaders were not famiilar with the ground and with local agricultural practices. Faced with a lack of traditional leadership, which had probably been destroyed by the invaders, many of the Maya may have tried to eke out an existence in scattered jungle milpas, and some few centers appear to have sprung up around the shores of the Peten lakes, at such places as Flores and Topoxte where survival may have been easier. It is also likely that many others migrated northward to attach themselves to centers in Yucatan which — for whatever reasons — were more successfully maintained than in the south.

This leads to our second question: "What is the relationship of the ninth-century invasion of the Maya Lowlands to the Toltec take over at Chichen Itza?"[6] It is our hypothesis that the ninth-century invasions of the north brought about the fall of the Puuc sites and paved the way for the eventual establishment of Toltec power at Chichen Itza. Quite probably, the latter event was carried out by a separate militant group, not politically allied to the first invaders but certainly culturally related to them. As Proskouriakoff has stated in relation to Classic and non-Classic styles in Yucatan:

> It seems that some foreign or strongly non-Classic factors were involved probably even before the Toltec Period, and it is possible that the Toltecs entered a country already divided into cultural subgroups dominated by families of foreign extraction.

Proskouriakoff has further pointed out that non-Classic stylistic influences were present in the Northern Lowlands by 9.19.0.0.0. This would tend to support the contention that the intrusions into the Southern and Northern Lowlands were contemporaneous, although stylisic influences alone certainly do not necessarily indicate invasion. But, in addition, Balancan Group pottery has been found in large quantities at Kabah and Uxmal. At the former site there are columns which depict non-Classic warriors with darts and atlatls. Similar figures are found on the Pabellon Modeled-carved type of the Altar Group in the Southern Lowlands, providing another link between the foreign influences in Yucatan and the Peten in addition to those mentioned earlier. Finally, at Chichen Itza, Silho Group ceramics appeared in abundance at perhaps a slightly later date.

In sum, the resemblances between the ninth-century, non-Classic intrud-

---

[6] We follow general archaeological opinion in tracing the flow of influence from Tula to Chichen Itza.

ers in the north and in the south are numerous and close enough to convince us that they were related; however, it is possible that initially there were some differences between the two, because of separation, and that these differences became more marked as the result of stronger and more direct Tula Toltec influences upon the northern contingent.

SUMMARY

Substantive

The hypothesis has been advanced that the Maya were invaded on a broad front, from the west and the north, in the ninth century A.D. This invasion was by peoples from the Gulf Coast Lowlands who were under pressure from and influenced by the Toltec peoples of Central Mexico. The Southern Lowland arm of this invasion swept up the Usumacinta-Pasión drainage at the very end of the Ninth Cycle in the Maya calendar, and the intruders established themselves, principally, at the strategic site of Seibal. Another contingent probably entered the Northern Lowlands at about the same time, and still others may have moved into Highland and Pacific Coastal Guatemala. We have further hypothesized that from the base at Seibal the foreigners raided the rest of the Peten, over a period of sixty years or so (10.0.0.0.0–10.3.0.0.0 or A.D. 830–889) and in so doing broke Maya Classic life and economy. A precarious man-nature balance in agriculture was upset, resulting in widespread starvation and population shiftings and displacement. Much of the old Maya aristocratic leadership was killed off. The invaders attempted to maintain several large Maya ceremonial centers, but this proved unsuccessful. Small bodies of Maya population did cluster around some of the Peten lakes and mountain themselves into the Postclassic Period; other Maya, and probably the military invaders, moved north to settle around those few large centers that remained in Yucatan.

Theoretical

It must be obvious, at this point in the paper, that our hypothesis does not really solve the whole "mystery" of the fall of Maya civilization in the Southern Lowlands, nor does it rigorously attempt to do so. There are many "loose ends," such as the full reasons behind the population shiftings or the continuance of some of the centers of the Northern Lowlands while those of the South perished. Essentially what we have tried to do, rather, is to put the old question of the fall of the Maya on a new footing. A concerted effort is needed to solve the problem of the "collapse," and it is not the aura of "mystery" that makes it an important problem. For surely significant ecological and sociopolitical processes were involved, and the forthcoming answers will have obvious general anthropological interest. To repeat, one of the major purposes of this paper has been to show that the best way to get answers to the processual problems connected with the fall of the Maya is through the building of a proper historical framework.

If research now underway throughout the Maya area strengthens our invasion hypothesis, and we believe it will, although there may be some factual corrections and clarifications, then we will be in a position to formulate new hypotheses which will strike at the heart of the problem of the abandonment of the great Maya centers and the end of Maya civilization in the Southern Lowlands. To give one example, assuming the capture of a site such as Tikal by a small, well-organized, militarily-oriented group, how might we expect a mechanical or unilateral society to respond, and how does this hypothesis accord with the "Postclassic" data from the Central Acropolis area?

To conclude, one of archaeology's unique contributions to general anthropological methodology is the long time perspective it offers for the study of processual problems. Yet it should be remembered that study of anthropological process must go hand in hand with the study of archaeological history. While American archaeology has, on the whole, placed too much emphasis on the latter, we should not let the dialectical reaction to this overemphastis discredit historical reconstrucion. We should take heed of the lesson which past studies of the fall of the Maya offer and realize that by first gaining control of the historical variables we will then be in an excellent position to eventually gain control of the processual ones.

KARL G. HEIDER

The caveat "Don't simplify" concludes Karl Heider's article. This seems a fitting note on which to end a collection of writings on archaeology, because the archaeologist is in constant danger of missing some variable that might significantly modify his explanations. Heider advises caution in the choice of assumptions based on ethnographies, though he advocates their use in making analogies in the reconstruction of past societies. The article serves as a reminder of how much more must be done before archaeologists can place entire confidence in their methods and theories. But all the writings in this volume dramatize an awareness, painful at times, of the immense job of finding absolutely accurate, foolproof methods of making analogies, though at the same time they give assurance that the challenges will be met with imagination. In another decade many of Heider's concerns may well be needless if archaeology continues to develop along the lines indicated in this book.

22 Archaeological Assumptions and Ethnographical Facts: A Cautionary Tale from New Guinea

INTRODUCTION

Archaeologists are accustomed to reconstruct prehistoric cultures from scanty material remains by the use of inferences based on certain assumptions which they make about human behavior. These assumptions

Reprinted, with the editorial changes noted, from "Archaeological Assumptions and Ethnographical Facts: A Cautionary Tale from New Guinea" by Karl G. Heider, *Southwestern Journal of Anthropology* 23 (1967):52–64, by permission of the author and the publisher. Footnotes are renumbered.

are derived from common sense and a passing acquaintance with the ethnographic literature, and they are generally very reasonable. Unfortunately for the archaeological process, cultures are generally quite unreasonable.

In this paper I shall present some ethnographic data from one culture, the Dugum Dani of the West New Guinea (Irian Barat) highlands, data which seriously challenge certain common archaeological assumptions. I have selected only the instances from Dani culture which are the most relevant to my argument; but for a more complete picture of the Dani, the reader is referred elsewhere.[1] In no sense do I propose the Dani or any other single culture as a basis for general archaeological inference. I present these facts simply as a Cautionary Tale.

The Archaeologist as Ethnographer

To some extent the archaeologist works as a historian, piecing together the story of cultural development and change.[2] But most archaeologists spend most of their time excavating the material remains from particular sites and reconstructing the cultures of these sites. In such cases the archaeologist works as an ethnographer. Although its techniques of investigation are highly specialized, archaeology may be considered as a special case of ethnology or ethnography. The archaeologist, no matter how deeply he is immersed in potsherds and broken stones, remains an ethnographer. For a century now, archaeologists have dipped into the ethnographic literature for analogies to bolster their reconstructions.

Most departments of anthropology in American universities are joint departments, where archaeologists and social anthropologists coexist on the basis of a belief that communication between them is possible and fruitful for both parties. But, in fact, communication is rare and seldom useful. The ethnographer writes for ethnographers, and the archaeologist for archaeologists; even the courses in material culture of a generation ago have been dropped from the regular curriculum.

There are really two problems here; what does the archaeologist have to say to the ethnographer, and what can the ethnographer say to the archaeologist? In this paper I shall examine only the latter question and, indeed, shall restrict the discussion to the relatively simple question of material culture: how is the ethnographic knowledge of material culture used in archaeological inference?

---

[1] For further information on the Dugum Dani, see Matthiessen (1962), Gardner (1963), and Heider (1965). Other Grand Valley Dani have been described by Bromley (1960; 1961) and Peters (1965). Closely related Dani groups have recently been studied by Denise O'Brien, Anton Ploeg, and Klaus F. Koch (cf. O'Brien and Ploeg 1964; O'Brien 1967).

[2] Service (1964) deals with the relevance of ethnology to the archaeologist as historian.

Nearly thirty years ago Kluckhohn warned archaeologists that

> If the method and theory are almost wholly beneath the level of consciousness it is axiomatic that they are inadequate. For all aspects of intellectual procedure must be made explicit in order that they may be subject to criticism and empirical testing (1940:45).

The archaeologist is in a particularly unhappy position in respect to his assumptions about human behavior. They can only be tested against the facts of ethnographic cultures. Although for the most part they can never be proven universally valid, only a few counter-examples can throw their usefulness into question.

Curiously, a concern for the validity of archaeological inference antedates archaeology itself. Thucydides, writing at the end of the fifth century B.C., rejected the idea that because in his time the remains of Mycenae were insignificant, the Mycenaean contribution to the Trojan expedition was not, as Homer said, the largest of all Greek states.

> Suppose, for example, that the city of Sparta were to become deserted and that only the temples and foundations of buildings remained, I think that future generations would, as time passed, find it very difficult to believe that the place had really been as powerful as it was represented to be. Yet the Spartans occupy two-fifths of the Peloponnese and stand at the head not only of the whole Peloponnese itself but also of numerous allies beyond its frontiers. Since, however, the city is not regularly planned and contains no temples or monuments of great magnificence, but is simply a collection of villages, in the ancient Hellenic way, its appearance would not come up to expectation. If, on the other hand, the same thing were to happen to Athens, one would conjecture from what met the eye that the city had been twice as powerful as in fact it is (Thucydides 1954:18).

THE DUGUM DANI: AN ETHNOGRAPHIC SUMMARY

There are some 100,000 to 200,000 Dani-speaking people living in the Central Highlands of West New Guinea (Irian Barat). About half of them live in the Grand Valley of the Balim River, and of these Grand Valley Dani, about 350 live in the Dugum Neighborhood. In 1961 the Dugum Dani were not under the influence of government or missionaries. Except that they lacked pottery, they fit the description of a typical neolithic culture: they had ground and polished stone axes and adzes, intensive fallow-cycle sweet potato agriculture, domestic pigs and dogs, and settled villages. Dani society is characterized by nonterritorial patrilineal sibs and moieties, and territorial political confederations of about a thousand people loosely united into alliances of about 5,000 people. Before the recent government pacification programs became effective, warfare, consisting of announced battles alternating with surprise raids, existed between some alliances. In general, Dani social organization conforms to the flexible highland New Guinea pattern outlined by Barnes (1962).

THE DUGUM DANI: AN ARCHAEOLOGICAL PERSPECTIVE

Tools

The basic Dani tools are ground stone axes, adzes, and gouges; bone needles, awls, and spoons; pig tusk scrapers; flint flake scrapers and gravers; rodent tooth gravers; bamboo knives; and wooden digging sticks.

The only source of the ground stone blades is a stream bed quarry some fifty kilometers to the northwest of the Grand Valley, on the further edge of the Western Dani region. The Western Dani quarry and grind the blades, which are then traded into the Grand Valley as finished products. The blades are hafted and re-hafted by the Grand Valley Dani, and there is local variation in both haft and lashing. But in fact the Grand Valley Dani never prepare their own blades.

Axes are hafted with the blade set into a solid wooden handle, the edge of the blade running parallel to the handle; adzes are hafted by lashing the blade to a figure-7-shaped wooden handle, with the edge of the blade at right angles to the handle.

Le Roux (1948:map 3) has shown that stone blades set axe-like in a solid handle are found only in southwestern New Guinea, while axes or adzes hafted to a figure-7 handle are characteristic of the rest of New Guinea. The Grand Valley lies just along the dividing line, and as a consequence it is one of the few areas in New Guinea with both kinds of hafting. In the Grand Valley, adzes outnumber axes by about eight or ten to one. Axes are used only in splitting logs for firewood or planks; adzes may also be utilized for splitting wood, but they are usually employed for felling trees and for finishing planks, digging sticks, and spears.

Typologies

When dealing with a group of related but different traits, be they kinship terms or stone tools, anthropologists customarily subdivide the group on the basis of typologies which are based on functional, lexical, or formal physical criteria. Also, they recognize the difference between their own scientific typology (often called "etic") and the native typology (often called "emic"). The native typology may be explicitly formulated by the natives as words in the lexical typology, or it may be a matter of implicit nonverbal usage, as the functional typology often is.

The ethnographer can easily establish the native functional typology through his observation of behavior in the field, and he can obtain the native lexical typology by questioning the natives in their language. But these systems must then be described in cross-culturally understandable terms by means of a scientific taxonomy which is usually based on the native typology of the ethnographer's own culture.

The archaeologist is at an obvious disadvantage, since he can only infer the behavioral (functional and lexical) typologies of artifacts on the basis of their context, signs of usage, and ethnographical analogies. For some sorts of archaeological reconstruction this does not present major difficulties. An art style such as the "Chavin jaguar" of the Andes, or a unique artifact form such as the *bâton de commandement* of the Upper Palaeolithic period in Europe may be a significant horizon marker even when its exact behavioral significance is unknown. But when the archaeologist attempts to reconstruct the behavior of a particular culture, he pushes beyond his own formal typology of artifacts toward some semblance of the (native) functional typology.[3] Between the formal and functional typologies of Dani tools there are a number of discrepancies which would mislead the archaeologist. Archaeologists usually classify tools according to obvious formal criteria such as general shape, size, cutting edge, and material of the blades. But the Dani tend to make their lexical and functional distinctions on the basis of the entire tool, often ignoring the blade itself.

Archaeologists customarily distinguish axe from adze blades on the basis of the head-on line of the cutting edge: a straight or S-shaped cutting edge indicates an axe, while a symmetric crescent-shaped edge indicates an adze. But the Dani are by no means so logical, and they haft blades indiscriminantly as adzes or axes, depending on what is needed at the time. Thus, crescent-edged "adze" blades are often hafted as axes. Only after considerable use and reshapening does the edge begin to straighten out to "proper" axe form.

The archaeologist would be tempted to subdivide a group of Dani adze/axe blades on the basis of size, cross-section, outline, and stone type. The blades range in length from three centimeters, to forty-five centimeters; in outline from triangular through egg-shaped to oval; in cross-section from oval to rectangular; as for the stone type; there is a softer black stone and a harder stone which comes in a variety of speckled, banded, and solid greys, greens, blues, and blacks. In fact the Dani ignore both outline and cross-section. They do distinguish the soft black stone from the hard stone (and value the latter above the former), but I could get no agreement whatever on the names for the varieties of the hard stone, which seemed strikingly different to me. Also, size is not the basis for any Dani typology

---

[3] In many cases archaeologists prejudice their own attemps at reconstructing particular cultural behavior by building time-hallowed functional terms such as scraper or handaxe into their original typology. In the archaeological process, functional attributes should be end products, not opening assumptions.

except in the case of the very smallest blades, those under about ten centi-meters in length, which are used as adzes for fine finishing work on spears and bows and are called by a different name than that of ordinary adzes.

The gouge is a small ground-stone blade about the size of a person's thumb, with a cutting edge at one end. It is fairly common, and most men have a gouge or two, so it would be logical to assume that it is extensively used in the finer woodworking. But in fact its sole function is to make the hole in an axe handle where the blade is inserted. Like the adze and axe blades, gouge blades are imported from the Western Dani area. However, although in the Western Dani region these stones are common and are an important part of the ceremonial goods of the various lineage groups (Denise O'Brien, personal communication), in the Grand Valley they have no ceremonial significance whatever. This is a striking example of a single object having vastly different meanings in two basically similar cultural areas.

It is axiomatic in archaeology that the replacement of stone tools by metal tools has a revolutionary effect on the culture. The Dugum Dani seem to provide an ideal test case. In April 1961 most of the Dugum Dani men used stone tools most of the time; by December 1963, all men had iron tools and only rarely used stone. But to my great surprise I found no significant changes in Dani culture as a result. This may be explained on the grounds that not enough time had elapsed for iron to work its change. Or it may be that the special circumstances of Dani life allow so much leisure anyway that an increase in tool efficiency by itself has little significance. The basis for the assumption of dramatic change is, of course, that iron tools allow more efficient use of time and energy. I tried to make time studies of many Dani activities, including felling trees with stone adzes, but was constantly frustrated. When a Dani man uses a stone adze to fell a tree he characteristically wastes so much time in stopping to sit down, smoke a cigarette, or talk to nearby friends or shout to distant ones that the actual elapsed time reflects more about Dani work habits than about the actual efficiency of the stone adze.

Settlements

The Dani live in well-constructed houses clustered in large palisaded units which lie a kilometer or less from one another. But the quality of construction, the size of the settlement, and the density of the setlement pattern would all tend to mislead the archaeologist.

In the first place, in the many instances where a compound site is abandoned and later converted into a sweet potato garden, it seems unlikely that there would be much trace of the compound for the archaeologist to find. The posts and walls of the buildings are uprooted and used in new construction elsewhere; the ground is dug up to a depth of about twenty centimeters, obliterating post molds and destroying hearth places. The only remains visible on the ground are those fragments of fire-cracked stone from the steam cooking bundles which were too small to be worth the trouble of carrying to the new site. These stones, together with crude flint flakes which might also have been left behind, would suggest the temporary hunting camp of a people with only crude prehistoric tools.

No midden heaps develop around the Dani compounds. There are no potsherds, of course. There is also no significant organic trash. Foodstuff brought into a village is eaten by people and pigs. Pig bones, after being cooked and cracked for marrow, are burned. However, hearth ashes are strewn on the courtyards and might be noted in an excavation.

But let us suppose that the archaeologist did discover Dani settlement sites with post and wall impressions intact, so that he could faithfully reconstruct settlement plans and patterns. What inferences would he make from these? It is fair to say that the archaeologist would describe organized Dani villages occupied for a decade or so by several hundred people. In fact, although the houses would last about ten years with only minor repairs, the Dani frequently dismantle them and build new compounds elsewhere. The basic Dani living unit is the compound, and usually two to five of these compounds are clustered contiguously. But the compound cluster is a purely geographical phenomenon and is in no sense a social or political unit. In fact, the people of any compound are more likely to have ties with the people of a more distant compound than with those of a contiguous compound.

The Dani habit of moving frequently from one compound to another could not help but confuse the archaeologist. (Indeed, it seriously complicates ethnographic description.) The smallest territorial unit with any population stability is the neighborhood. In the case of the Dugum Neighborhood, about 350 people live in some thirty compounds in fifteen clusters scattered through an area of a couple of square kilometers. These people move as often as every few weeks from one compound to another for a complex variety of reasons, which include access to current gardens and pig rooting grounds, and personal friendships and animosities. Very few people stay in any one compound for as long as a year.

The movement is one of individuals and not so much of family groups. At one moment Compound A may be inhabited by people who the previous month were in Compounds B, C, and D, and who the next month may be found in Compounds C, E, and F. The family itself is particularly ephemeral.

The result is that houses and even entire compounds stand empty for periods of up to a year or two, and there are at least twice as many houses and compounds standing as are being used at any one time. The archaeologist who excavated one complete compound and surveyed all the compounds in a neighborhood would be wrong to infer large village organization, and his estimate of areal population density would be in error by at least one-half.

Along one side of each compound is a rectangular common cook house with a number of cooking hearths, which are shallow depressions in the ground. Again, any archaeological inference based on the assumption of a stable population in the compound would be erroneous. The size of the cookhouse is determined roughly by the number of women planning to live in the compound at the time of construction; ideally each woman has her own hearth to cook meals for herself and whatever members of her family may be around at the time. But after the first few months the population has shifted enough so that some hearths may be unused or some may be serving more than one woman. Like houses, there are perhaps twice as many hearths in a neighborhood as are actually in use at one time.

The situation of pigsties resembles that of hearths. Every compound has one or more pigsties each with up to twenty-five individual stalls. But whole sties often stand empty for months at a time and give no indication of the number of pigs in a compound.

Compounds are enclosed by sturdy wooden fences and often are surrounded by a meter-deep ditch. The logical inference that the compounds were protected from attack by moat and palisade would be false. Although the Dani are constantly at war, compounds are not attacked; the fences serve to keep in pigs, and the ditches serve to drain or irrigate the bananas and other plants of the home gardens. In fact, the weapons of war are wooden spears and arrows which have wooden or bamboo tips and would not be preserved in the ground.

Graphic Art

Graphic art is sometimes found in association with prehistoric sites, and particularly when the art is in relatively inaccessible spots archaeologists assume that it has ceremonial significance. In the Dani case this assumption would only be partly true. The Dani make two sorts of drawings on rock faces. One series of drawings consists of black charcoal outlines of people, ghosts, animals, birds, tree, and gardens; the other series consists of positive and negative hands, crosses, X's, and some creatures, all done in red clay. The black series is found on rock shelters scattered throughout the forests away from the settlements. In each case the charcoal is taken from a nearby hearth. The red series is found only on the nearly inaccessible rock face of an escarpment at the edge of the neighborhood. It happens that the black series has no ceremonial significance at all. The rock shelters are simply refuges for people caught in the woods by rain, where a fire can be built for warmth and for lighting cigarettes. Young men use the charcoal to make the drawings for momentary amusement. Some of these rock shelters also serve as temporary lumber depots, and the youths, by climbing on top of the planks leaning against the rock, are able to make their drawings as high as three meters above the ground. However, the red series of drawings with the positive and negative hands is made during the boys' initiation and does have ceremonial significance.[4]

Inter-area Relations

Archaeological reconstruction of prehistoric trade routes is dependant on those items of trade which are preserved. Goods which are consumed by the receiver or perish in the ground are generally invisible to the archaeologist. On the whole, perhaps, archaeologists are more cautious in their inferences concerning trade than in some of the other areas mentioned above. The Dani give strong support for such caution, since the bulk of Dani trade is of the "invisible" nature.

Ocean shells, particularly cowrie shells, are found throughout the high-lands of New Guinea. There is probably no single group, no matter how isolated, which does not have at least some of these trade shells. The archaeologist would be quite correct to infer an extensive trade network on the basis of the cowrie shell distribution alone.

In central West New Guinea there are two major sources of stone adze blades. Smoothly ground blades with oval cross-sections come from the Western Dani source and are characteristic of the Dani and western groups; roughly ground blades which still show flake scars and have triangular cross-sections are characteristic of the Star Mountain region near the international border and are found as far west as the Eastern Dani of the Jalimo region.

On the basis of shell and stone, consequently, the archaeologist could reconstruct fairly accurately the broad pattern of New Guinea trade. But the specific trade relations of the Dugum Dani would be lost to him. The Dugum Dani use stone blades from the Western Dani region, but they have no direct contact with the Western Dani. They have extensive and frequent trade relations with the Dani groups in the Jalimo, which is the name of a valley system three days' walk to the northeast of the Grand Valley. But this trade consists almost entirely of perishables and consumables. Pigs and salt are the major items moving from the Grand Valley to the Jalimo, in exchange for feathers, furs, fibers, and fine woods. The minor movement of adze blades to the Jalimo and slatey ceremonial stones from the Jalimo would give no hint of the great trading activity between the two areas.

The diffusion of cultural traits from area to area is one of the most obvious phenomena of history and prehistory. Compared to the amount of

---

[4] Unfortunately I have little solid data on these red drawings. I discovered them only in the twenty-fifth month of my field study. I never witnessed an initiation ceremony and was unable to obtain information about the function of the drawings in the ceremonies.

labor devoted to tracing the spread of traits, comparatively little has been done to explain why traits spread as they do. The Dani offer several examples of traits which logically should spread but fail to do so. In each case these are traits which exist among other Dani groups near the Dugum Neighborhood. The traits are known to the Dugum Dani, are within their technological capacity, and would presumably fill the same desirable function in the culture of the Dugum Dani which they fill in the other area; yet they have not been adopted by the Dugum Dani. These traits are: designs on water gourds, tobacco pipes, woven chest armor, and stone boiling.

In the southern part of the Grand Valley, some ten kilometers from the Dugum Dani, the Welesi Dani make elaborate geometric designs on their gourd water flasks. These designs apparently have a purely ornamental function. They are found on no other gourds in the Grand Valley. One can say that there is no reason for other Grand Valley Dani groups to scratch up their gourds; but likewise there is no reason for the Welesi Dani to do it.

All Dani groups smoke cigarettes made of home-grown tobacco wrapped in leaves. In the northern Grand Valley and Western Dani regions, men also smoke tobacco in wooden pipes with bamboo stems coated with pitch. The Dugum Dani know of these pipes but do not themselves use them.

Warfare, fought with bows and arrows and spears, is endemic in the entire Dani region. In the northern Grand Valley and Western Dani regions, men wear a tightly woven fiber chest piece which gives them some protection in battle. Again, the Dugum Dani know of this armor but do not us it.

Finally, Dugum Dani who have been to the Jalimo region bring back large bark dishes and describe how the Jalimo Dani use them to boil sweet potatoes with fire-heated stones. The Dugum Dani heat stones for steaming sweet potatoes, but they do not boil them.

In each of these cases, an item known from a familiar context failed to be adopted by the Dugum Dani. There seems to be no political, supernatural, or technological explanation for these instances.

DISCUSSION

In this paper I have attempted to test some archaeological assumptions against some ethnographic facts from one New Guinea culture. In this one case the assumptions do not fare very well. This challenge may be met or avoided. The Dani can be dismissed as an aberrant case. But I suspect that most cultures, on similarly close inspection, will turn out to be "aberrant" in one way or another. Perhaps archaeologists will refuse to acknowledge responsibility for these assumptions and will reply that I have tailored them to dramatize my point. This would be fruitful if it led archaeologists to examine and explain the assumptions which they use. The non-archaeologist may suspect that such an underlying assumption as "the material remains fairly reflect the culture" is not taken as seriously by archaeologists as I imply. I refer them as a start to the infamous case of Mesolithic Decline: most texts dealing with early European prehistory rhapsodize over the justly famous Upper Palaeolithic cave art and proceed to describe the subsequent Mesolithic period as one of cultural, and particularly artistic, decline on the basis of the poverty of Mesolithic remains. The possibility that the Mesolithic had sculptors who worked in wood, as do most tribal artists today, is simply ignored. Of course, we shall probably never know whether or not this was true, but we cannot reject it as impossible.

I feel strongly that the archaeologist must recognize himself as a prehistoric ethnographer and must take more seriously the implications which ethnographic examples have for his own work. This does not require that he become expert in many of the debates of modern social anthropology which are at best only peripherally relevant to archaeology. It is probably not possible for each archaeologist to study a living contemporary tribal or peasant culture (cf. the suggestions along these lines in Kleindienst and Watson 1956, and the example of Ascher 1962). And, in fact, just as ethnographers are tempted to fall into the curious secondary ethnocentrism of seeing all cultures in terms of whatever culture they first studied, so the archaeologist who had ventured into ethnography would need to guard against basing all his assumptions on one contemporary culture. The point is that these assumptions must be based on a whole range of possibilities, not on any single ethnographic model.

Studies of house-building and pottery-making are all very well, but for the archaeologist the emphasis should be on function and disposal rather than on manufacture: how are houses and pots used, and what happens to them afterwards? There is a useful exercise which might be called Verification by Double Translation. Students are asked to translate documented living culture into archaeological remains and then to develop a reconstructed culture from these remains. The closeness of fit between the original and the reconstructed cultures emphasizes dramatically the strengths and weaknesses of the archaeological assumptions involved.

This paper is not simply a plea for archaeologists to use ethnographical analogies in their reconstructions. It is a plea for archaeologists to do more than indiscriminately raid the ethnographic literature to find convenient hints for ingenious reconstructions. It is a plea for the archaeologist to steep himself in a wide range of ethnographies, and to be explicit, critical, and cautious in his choice of assumptions based on these ethnographies. Reconstruction of prehistoric behavior is not by any means impossible, but it is terribly difficult. I would underline Du Bois's plea that we become more conscious of the uncertainties and ambiguities of our anthropological undertaking (1963:35). If this Cautionary Tale from New Guinea has a moral for the archaeologist, it is, "Don't simplify."

BIBLIOGRAPHY

Ascher, Robert
  1962 "Ethnology for Archeology: A Case from the Seri Indians." *Ethnology* 1:360–69.
Barnes, J. A.
  1962 "African Models in the New Guinea Highlands." *Man* 62:5–9.
Bromley, H. M.
  1960 "A Preliminary Report on Law among the Grand Valley Dani of Netherlands New Guinea." *Nieuw-Guinea Studien* 4:235–59.
  1961 *The Phonology of Lower Grand Valley Dani. A Comparative Structural Study of Skewed Phonemic Patterns.* Verhandelingen van het Koninlijk Instituut voor Taal-, Land-, en Volkenkunde, Deel 34.
Du Bois, Cora
  1963 "The Curriculum in Cultural Anthropology." In *The Teaching of Anthropology*, D. G. Mandelbaum, G. W. Lasker, and E. M. Albert (eds.), pp. 27–38. *American Anthropological Association Memoirs*, no. 94.
Gardner, Robert G.
  1963 *Dead Birds.* A film produced by the Film Study Center, Peabody Museum, Harvard University; distributed by Contemporary Films, Inc., New York. 16mm. 83 min. Color. Sound.
Heider, Karl G.
  1965 "The Dugum Dani: A Papuan Culture in the West New Guinea Highlands." Unpublished Ph.D. dissertation, Harvard University.
Kleindienst, Maxine R., and Patty Jo Watson
  1956 "Action Archeology: The Archeological Inventory of a Living Community." *Anthropology Tomorrow* 5:75–78.
Kluckhohn, Clyde
  1940 "The Conceptual Structure in Middle American Studies." In *The Maya and Their Neighbors*, pp. 41–51. New York: D. Appleton-Century Co.
Le Roux, C. C. F. M.
  1948 *De Bergpapoea's van Nieuw-Guinea en hun Woongebied.* Leiden: E. J. Brill.

Matthiessen, Peter
   1962   *Under the Mountain Wall: A Chronicle of Two Seasons in the Stone Age.* New York: Viking.
O'Brien, Denise
   1967   "The Economics of Dani Marriage." Unpublished Ph.D. dissertation, Yale University.
   _____, and Anton Ploeg
   1964   "Acculturation Movements among the Western Dani." In *New Guinea,* James B. Watson (ed.), pp. 281–92. *American Anthropologist,* Special Publication, vol. 66, no. 4, pt. 2.
Peters, H. L.
   1965   *Enkele Hoofdstukken uit het Sociaal-Religieuze Leven van een Dani-Groep.* Venlo: Dagblad voor Noord-Limburg N.V.
Service, Elman R.
   1964   "Archaeological Theory and Ethnological Fact." In *Process and Pattern in Culture: Essays in Honor of Julian H. Steward,* Robert A. Manners (ed.), pp. 364–75. Chicago: Aldine Publishing Co.
Thucydides
   1954   *History of the Peloponnesian War.* Trans. with an introduction by Rex Warner. Baltimore: Penguin Books.